THE BACKYARD BRAWL®

Elated fans storm the field after West Virginia's 1975 victory over Pitt, which came down to the final play of the game. The celebrations lasted well into the following week in the Sunnyside section of town.

Stories from One of the Weirdest, Wildest, Longest Running, and Most Intense Rivalries in College Football History

BY JOHN ANTONIK

MORGANTOWN · 2012

West Virginia University Press 26506

First edition published 2012 by West Virginia University Press

Printed in the United States of America

20 19 18 17 16 15 14 13 12   9 8 7 6 5 4 3 2 1

Paper:
978-1-935978-82-4

EPUB:
978-1-935978-83-1

PDF:
978-1-935978-84-8

Library of Congress Cataloging-in-Publication Data

Antonik, John.
The backyard brawl : stories from one of the weirdest, wildest, longest running and most intense rivalries in college football history / by John Antonik. -- 1st ed.
p. cm.
Includes bibliographical references and index.
ISBN-13: 978-1-935978-82-4 (pbk. : alk. paper)
ISBN-10: 1-935978-82-9 (pbk. : alk. paper)
ISBN-13: 978-1-935978-83-1 (e-book)
ISBN-10: 1-935978-83-7 (e-book)
[etc.]
1. Football--United States--History--Miscellanea. 2. College sports--United States--History--Miscellanea.. 3. Sports rivalries--United States. I. Title.
GV950.5.A67 2012
796.332--dc23
2012013718

Photo credits: All photos WVU Sports Communications except where noted. Other photos courtesy of All-Pro Photography/Dale Sparks, Bill Amatucci, Dr. Carolyn Peluso Atkins, George Gojkovich, Joedy McKown, Sam Sciullo, Jr., University of Pittsburgh, and WVU Photographic Services.

Dedicated to the

memory of

GEORGE ANTONIK

1935-2011

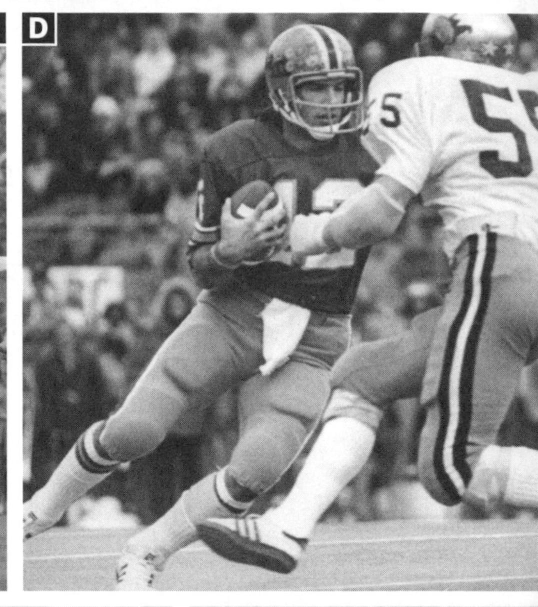

A. Jeff Hostetler scores winning TD against Pitt in 1983.

B. Larry Williams sits on the field in disbelief in 2007. (All-Pro Photography/Dale Sparks photo)

C. Action from the 1975 Pitt game in Morgantown.

D. Matt Cavanaugh runs for yardage against WVU in 1976.

E. Marc Bulger had great games against Pitt during his four-year career.

F. Phil Braxton scores a 79-yard touchdown against Pitt in 2002. (All-Pro Photography/Dale Sparks photo)

G. LeSean McCoy was a one-man show on offense for Pitt in 2007. (All-Pro Photography/Dale Sparks photo)

See color photo sections for detailed captions

CONTENTS

A. No one did more to stoke the emotions of the Backyard Brawl than Jack Fleming.

B. Art Lewis plants a kiss on the forehead of his freshman quarterback Fred Wyant in 1952.

C. Amos Zereoue runs into Pitt's defense in 1997.

D. Bobby Bowden's most embarrassing moment as a coach came at Pitt in 1970.

E. A wide view of WVU's game against Pitt in 1967.

See color photo sections for detailed captions

PROLOGUE

Every Mountaineer fan has a Pitt story. Mine takes place deep within the bowels of Pitt Stadium, at the confluence of dirt and concrete. I have been in my fair share of decrepit football stadiums - old Mountaineer Field being one of them - but Pitt Stadium had a charm and an allure all its own.

From the wooden addition to the press box to the dirt floors leading into the team locker rooms, Pitt Stadium brought new meaning to the phrase "spartan conditions." But in many ways I really liked that place, the way it was nestled in the middle of the campus with all of the university buildings surrounding it, and how it was the center of activity on fall Saturday afternoons. We seem to lose that when stadiums are moved off campus, or when schools share facilities with professional football teams.

If you were fortunate enough to possess a parking pass in the garage next to Pitt Stadium, entry was a breeze. Just drive up to the top of the hill, hang a right and then make a quick left and you were there. I don't recall any traffic jams – even the drive up Forbes Avenue was problem-free, but then again, I don't remember Pitt Stadium ever being entirely full either. Once you parked your car, it was a quick walk across the street, and then you entered the stadium somewhere underneath the press box. Waiting inside were the most depressing accommodations imaginable; Alcatraz seemed more inviting. Looking around, I wondered how in the hell Pitt could have enticed all those great players to go there during the Majors/Sherrill heydays of the late 1970s and early 1980s? But they did.

Subtract several hundred buildings, and the ride leading up to Pittsburgh could very easily have been mistaken for a trip to Morgantown—the topography seemed so similar, remembered WVU running back Artie Owens. "That was an experience in itself, just riding in the bus up there and having all of that time to think about the game," Owens said. "I can remember that trip going up to Pitt with all of the mountains. And the buses had to get up that big hill and I'm thinking, where is this school at? Is this school in West Virginia or what?"

Roughly 75 miles separate the two schools, but culturally, they seem to be in two entirely different hemispheres. Pitt's campus landmark is the 42-story Cathedral of Learning – the second tallest university building in the world – an impressive structure built during the Great Depression and located in the heart of Oakland. West Virginia's campus landmark is the ivy-clad Woodburn Hall, constructed roughly 10 years after the Civil War and sitting regally at the top of a hill above the meandering Monongahela.

Pittsburgh was once a city forged in steel – U.S. Steel, Gulf Oil and other Fortune 500s were headquartered there, but it was the thousands of West Virginians through the years who went underground to dig out the coal that helped fuel the steel industry. And in those mills and in those mines were born some of the toughest football players anywhere. "If you take Pennsylvania and West Virginia and you put them together, there is not a whole lot of difference," explained hall of fame linebacker Sam Huff. "There were the steel mills in Pennsylvania and the coal mines in West Virginia, and we were basically raised the same way – tough guys.

"The Pittsburgh Steelers [are] now, and always have been, one of the toughest teams in the NFL," Huff said. "You're raised tough. If somebody says they are going to whip you then you've got to prove it."

College Hall of Fame linebacker Darryl Talley said the Backyard Brawl was very similar to what he experienced as a kid while growing up in East Cleveland, Ohio, fighting almost every day to keep his lunch money from going to the neighborhood bullies.

"They actually go after a lot of the same kids, and it's just the idea that they've got the same colors you've got on," remarked Talley. "That isn't right. Somebody needs to take those colors off. I was one of those people who believed in turf wars – I'm going to get you out of my area!"

Typically, the city kids gravitated to Pitt and the country kids went to West Virginia, especially in the 1940s, 1950s, 1960s and 1970s, when the region was still well-stocked with outstanding football players. Today, Western Pennsylvania produces a mere fraction of the major college players it once did, and the really good ones usually seem to leave the area altogether. But before the decline, local schools such as West Virginia could make a pretty good living off Western PA leftovers. "We always seemed to get most of our Western PA players from those outside areas," recalled Garrett Ford, a native of Washington, D.C., who played at WVU and later became an assistant coach and school administrator. "We had guys all around the perimeter [of the city]."

Most of West Virginia's successes were with those small-town boys from Burgettstown over to Waynesburg, Masontown, Fredericktown, Carmichaels, Charleroi, Vanderbilt, Brownsville, Uniontown, Connellsville and on into Somerset County. The city kids from Baldwin, Whitehall, Duquesne, Clairton, McKeesport, West Mifflin, Wilkinsburg, Swissvale, Shaler, Monroeville, Penn Hills and Aliquippa usually ended up at Pitt – that is, if Penn State didn't want them first.

"I always thought the best players in Western Pa. always went to Penn State," said Ford. "The ones that Penn State didn't really want went to Pitt. Then the ones that Pitt couldn't get came to Morgantown."

This Penn State-Pitt-West Virginia food chain existed for decades until the Nittany Lions chose to join the Big Ten for the 1993 season. Pitt and Penn State played every year from 1935–1992, briefly revived the series for four more games from 1997–2000, and are scheduled to resume play for two games beginning in 2016.

West Virginia, too, played Penn State annually until 1992, and for the most part, West Virginians harbored a healthy respect for the Nittanys. Not so with Pitt. There were no "Eat (fill in the blank) Penn State" or "Beat the Hell out of Penn State" shirts. Those were reserved for just one school.

"There was never the passion and . . . I'll say hatred . . . that was presented [for Pitt] like when I went to West Virginia," said quarterback Jeff Hostetler, who saw two different sides of the Pitt rivalry while attending both Penn State and West Virginia. "I think a lot of that was the disrespect that West Virginia always felt came from Pitt."

The Panther fans always like to refer to Penn State as their No. 1 target; West Virginia their No. 1 nuisance – their not-so-subtle way of minimizing the West Virginia rivalry. Another was their reluctance to adopt the phrase "Backyard Brawl," which didn't become the game's officially trademarked slogan until just a few years ago (think of all the money the two schools could have made on licensed apparel through the years).

"Whenever I was coaching [Pitt] we had Penn State," recalled the late Foge Fazio, who replaced Jackie Sherrill in 1982. "A lot of people thought, well, we're going to beat West Virginia and there is nothing to worry about there. Let's worry about Notre Dame and Penn State – not so much the players, but the fans and the boosters sometimes buy into what they read."

"When I came to Pittsburgh, it didn't take me long to realize that Penn State was awfully big historically," Johnny Majors said in 2003. "But my friends who loved Pitt told me, 'Oh, man, you're going to hate West Virginia.'"

In the beginning, when Pitt was beating West Virginia like a drum, treating WVU with ambivalence was the best way to handle those nutty hillbillies – or "Hoopies" as

Dan Marino used to call them. Just play the game, beat them, and then ignore them as much as possible and eventually they will go back into the hills – was Pitt's thinking. But eventually, West Virginia started winning some, and later, the Mountaineers began rubbing it in. Soon Pitt's ambivalence and indifference toward West Virginia was replaced by anger, and then hatred. Today, you can probably add a little envy to the list.

"Beating West Virginia is great," former Panther center J.C. Pelusi said during a 2007 Fox Sports Pittsburgh TV special commemorating the 100th anniversary of the football series. "You can't beat them by enough points, as far as I'm concerned. They didn't like us a whole lot and we didn't like them a whole lot, and there wasn't a whole lot of respect."

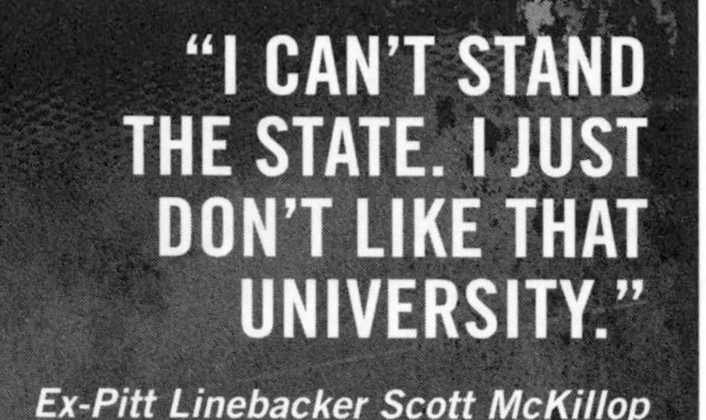
"I CAN'T STAND THE STATE. I JUST DON'T LIKE THAT UNIVERSITY."
Ex-Pitt Linebacker Scott McKillop

"I [expletive] hate West Virginia," ex-Pitt linebacker Scott McKillop told Pittsburgh sports columnist Joe Starkey in 2011. "I can't stand the state. I just don't like that university."

There you have it – so much for ambivalence.

Pitt's single greatest football moment of the last 25 years came in Morgantown on December 1, 2007. The Panthers were 28 1/2-point underdogs facing a Mountaineer team in line to go to the BCS national championship game. All West Virginia had to do was beat a mediocre 4-7 Panther team at home and a trip to New Orleans was guaranteed. In fact, many West Virginians had already booked their flights. But a funny thing happened; Pitt won the game. Afterward, Pitt's coaches were so giddy with delight that they chose to send out Christmas cards to recruits with the final score of 13-9 pasted on the front of them.

So with that stinging loss as a backdrop, I return to my Pitt story. The year was 1994 and I was working as West Virginia's associate sports information director in the days before Twitter, Facebook and the Internet took over our lives. Back then, being able to set up a group dial on the fax machine was considered a valuable technical skill.

In addition to providing team information to the press, it was my job to pull Mountaineer players out of the locker room for postgame interviews. For Pitt games, that task could sometimes be troublesome after a loss, which is exactly how the ending of this one seemed to be turning out.

After leading throughout – at one point by more than 20 points – West Virginia's secondary turned Pitt quarterback John Ryan into John Unitas. With a minute and a half left and Pitt trailing 40-33, Ryan marched the Panthers right down the field and into the end zone. Johnny Majors, then in his second go-around coaching the Panthers, decided to go for the two-point conversion instead of kicking the extra point and settling for the tie. West Virginia's beleaguered defense, which had surrendered large chunks of yardage the entire afternoon, couldn't defend confined spaces either. The Panthers got the two to take a 41-40 lead with just 38 seconds remaining on the clock.

My difficult job had now become impossible. *What player or coach is going to want to come out and talk to reporters after this debacle?* That was what I was thinking as I reentered the depths of Pitt Stadium to use the bathroom and collect my thoughts in a brief moment of monastic solitude. "Monastic solitude" was actually a phrase used by a clever Pittsburgh reporter to describe how open Pitt's Bill Pilconis was when he caught the winning touchdown against West Virginia in 1970, which I guess made him REALLY wide open. That game introduced first-year coach Bobby Bowden to the darker side of Mountaineer Nation – a story you can read about later in this book.

Well, in '94, another monumental Mountaineer collapse was occurring right in front of our eyes. While splashing some fresh water on my face and then adjusting my tie, I heard a commotion out in the hallway. A uniformed policeman had just kicked a garbage can and uttered a few expletives about Pitt's crappy defensive backs. What was he talking about, I wondered?

"Excuse me officer, what just happened?"

"The damned kid from West Virginia scored a touchdown!" he growled.

"What?"

"Yes, the Pitt kid let him run right by him for a touchdown."

I hurriedly walked outside and discovered, lo and behold, that Zach Abraham had somehow gotten past Pitt's Denorse Mosley for a 60-yard touchdown. West Virginia was now leading 47-41, and there were only 23 seconds left in the game – not nearly enough time for Pitt to get through WVU's Swiss cheese D for another score.

How could I have missed this?

For the next 10 minutes, I had to be filled in on one of the most bizarre finishes in Backyard Brawl history. The last three guys out of the locker room were the game's biggest stars – quarterback Chad Johnston, Abraham, and fellow wide receiver Rahsaan Vanterpool; Abraham and Vanterpool accounted for 385 of West Virginia's 396 receiving yards that afternoon.

Reporters swarmed all three, asking them in as many different ways as they could how it happened. When their interviews were finished, the narrow parking lot outside the stadium where the team buses were parked was now empty. Not a single one of them was in sight.

Coach Don Nehlen, in his haste to get out of town, had left without his three best players, and it was up to me to make sure they got back to Morgantown in my beat-up Honda Civic. Johnston caught a ride with his parents, leaving Abraham and Vanterpool under my not-so-adult supervision. Abraham sat in the front seat with a box of game programs between his legs while Vanterpool sank into the backseat with a bag of ice wrapped around one knee and his bare foot dangling inches from my face.

Not a single word was spoken the entire way back to Morgantown.

Today, this annual football game is on the verge of extinction, with Pitt announcing in the fall of 2011 its departure from the Big East for the Atlantic Coast Conference – a month later, West Virginia revealed that it was joining the Big 12. These two longtime adversaries are now charting different courses. Whenever I think of this, I am reminded of something former Pitt coach Dave Wannstedt once said about this series that spans more than a hundred years, thousands of players and dozens of football coaches – some considered among the best in college football history. There is no questioning the fact that Wannstedt has a unique perspective of this game, having played and also coached in it.

"I really think that if you went back, both of these teams are probably closer ability-wise than a lot of people may want to admit," Wannstedt said in 2009. "I think the talent level, for the most part over the years, has been pretty close.

"Their players know our guys. There are a lot of common denominators there – a lot of common threads, that when this game is over, it's not that they get on an airplane and fly three hours away and you don't see and talk about them until next year. This is a game where our players interact with theirs continuously throughout the year."

At least they did. Whether or not that continues on an annual basis is anyone's guess. Fortunately, what we do have are a lot of stories. I hope you enjoy them.

Noel Devine. See page B15

Bill Kern with Jock Sutherland. See page A1

1943-1955
THE RIVALRY RESUMES

The Long Shadow of Sutherland

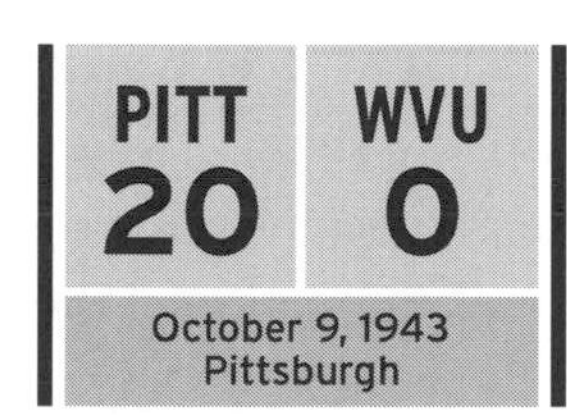

In the spring of 1938, West Virginians watched with great interest the University of Pittsburgh's systematic and almost complete dismantlement of its powerhouse football program. During the period from 1929–38, Pitt had won 79 of 97 games (with seven ties), captured five mythical national championships, played in four Rose Bowls and produced 17 All-Americans.

The man responsible for this phenomenal success was John Bain "Jock" Sutherland, a Scottish immigrant who worked his way through Oberlin Academy by waiting tables and shoveling snow. Sutherland, who played soccer as a young boy, became interested in American football in 1914 when he was accepted into Pitt's dental school. Sutherland turned into an All-American guard while playing for the famous Glenn "Pop" Warner on Pitt's undefeated teams of 1915, 1916 and 1917. After serving in the Army during World War I, he returned to Pittsburgh to open a dental practice. Unsatisfied with dentistry, Sutherland jumped at the opportunity to coach football at Lafayette College in Easton, Pa., and after five successful seasons there (Sutherland's Lafayette teams defeated Pitt twice in 1921 and 1922), he replaced Warner as Pitt's coach in 1924. By 1927, Sutherland had led the Panthers to their first Rose Bowl, where they lost 7-6 to Stanford. By the early 1930s, they were frequently beating the best programs in the country.

Sutherland completely dominated the local college scene during a ten-season period from 1929–38, going 7-0 against Penn State, 8-1-1 against Carnegie Tech, 4-1 against Duquesne and 1-0 with three ties against New York City power Fordham. But no eastern school felt the sheer dominance of Pitt football more than West Virginia: The Mountaineers endured seven shutout defeats during the nine-season stretch from 1930–38 and only managed to score single touchdowns in blowout losses to the Panthers in 1934 and 1935. Pitt's average margin of victory in that span of games was 24.3 points, and during Sutherland's final three seasons in 1936, 1937 and 1938, Pitt outscored West Virginia by a depressing 93-0 margin. "Wait until next year" was not a phrase even worth uttering if you were a Mountaineer football rooter.

In fact, WVU's 1937 performance against Pitt was universally praised as one of its best by alums, despite the fact that the Mountaineers were blanked, 20-0. That's because West Virginia was only trailing 7-0 heading into the fourth quarter, before a pair of late Panther scores put the game away. But despite the staggering success Pitt enjoyed, all was not well in the Steel City. Sutherland was growing unhappy with the support his football program was receiving from the school, and he disputed with athletic director W. Don Harrison over spending money his players failed to receive after Pitt defeated Washington in the 1937 Rose Bowl. Harrison eventually stepped aside, and James Hagan was named his replacement. The new AD eventually became involved in the initiation of a series of athletic reforms, most notably the implementation of the so-called "Bowman Code," which, among other things, dramatically reduced the number of athletic scholarships Sutherland was allowed to award freshmen. Sutherland, whose contract stipulated a two-year notice if he chose to take another job, coached the Panthers for one more season before submitting his formal letter of resignation in the spring of 1939.

Sutherland characterized his situation at Pitt as "intolerable," and despite a last ditch effort by Pitt chancellor John G. Bowman (the man for whom the Bowman Code was named) to reach some accord with his highly successful coach, Sutherland chose to walk away from the college game before the 1939 season. Perhaps the final straw for Sutherland was Pitt's decision in February of that year to place its athletic department under the umbrella of the Big Ten Conference (then known as the Western Conference), with the Panthers pledging to adhere to the rules and regulations of the league in a cooperative agreement that did not, however, include full membership. This occurred following a late-1938 alumni committee study that concluded that the athletic department was in dire need of an "arbitrator between athletes and university representatives." Problems had developed when several freshmen members of the football team threatened to go on strike because of unfulfilled tuition payments and perceived deplorable financial conditions. The committee recommended increasing the power of the athletic director, expanding the faculty committee, and requiring that coaches and athletic department members work together in a more congenial manner. For Sutherland, working in a "more congenial manner" meant looking for another job.

One result of Pitt's internal power struggle was the cessation of the West Virginia football series for a three-year period from 1940–42. According to Eddie Beachler of *The Pittsburgh Press*, the primary reason Pitt discontinued the series was that the Panthers wanted to make room on their schedule for more Big Ten opponents, starting with Ohio State in 1940. In fact, Pitt continued to covet an elusive invitation for full membership in the Big Ten well into the 1950s, when Michigan State was added to the conference. (Ironically, Nebraska, which would eventually join the Big Ten in 2011, was also frequently mentioned as a possible expansion target in those years.) There were also whispers that Pitt was unhappy with guarantee money that West Virginia had failed to pay the Panthers for their 1937 game in Morgantown. According to David W. Jacobs in the winter 1940 issue of *West Virginia University Alumni Magazine*, there was a miscommunication between the two schools regarding West Virginia's financial obligations to the Panthers that led the Mountaineers to believe they owed Pitt less money than they actually did. Pitt, which was accumulating deep debt from lost gate revenue as a result of its athletic reforms, thought otherwise.

Pitt also dropped Duquesne, but the Panthers chose to keep Carnegie Tech, Penn State and Fordham on the grid schedule because games against these teams were both competitive and profitable. By 1941, four Big Ten programs – Purdue, Michigan, Minnesota and Ohio State – were on Pitt's slate, but the Panthers' desire to become a full-fledged member of the Big Ten never gained traction. Further complicating matters was the United States' entry into World War II on December 7, 1941, when the Japanese bombed Pearl Harbor.

After the attack, many college football players and coaches were drafted into military service or enlisted on their own, and the government began issuing restrictions on food consumption, raw materials and travel as the economy shifted to a war production mode. In March of 1942, the Japanese seized plantations in the Dutch East Indies that had produced 90 percent of the United States' raw rubber. Shortly afterward, an elaborate color-coded system of gasoline rationing was devised in the U.S., interestingly enough, to help slow the usage of rubber for automobile tires. These restrictions greatly impacted college athletics, and by 1943, many traditional programs chose to discontinue football until the end of the war. Among notable schools electing to shut down football for the '43 season were Tennessee, Alabama, Auburn, Kentucky, Florida, Arizona, Arizona State, Stanford and Syracuse. A total of 33 programs opted not to play that year, including eight schools from the Southeastern Conference, six from the Pacific Coast Conference, six from the Southern Conference and four schools from the independent ranks.

Discontinuing football at Pitt and West Virginia was not an option because both athletic programs desperately needed the money – even if the games had to be played with 17-year-old freshmen and 4-Fs, who were ineligible for military service. The de-emphasis program Pitt had initiated in 1938 was putting a big financial strain on the athletic department by the early 1940s. There was a sharp decline in attendance for the Panthers during the 1939 campaign – Charles Bowser's first with the Panthers – when attendance dropped to 27,500 from the 39,000 rate during Sutherland's final season, in 1938. Pitt's top gate attraction in 1939 was against Carnegie Tech, with 51,000 showing up to see the Panthers win the cross-city tussle 6-0. In 1940, Pitt's attendance dipped even further, with the top draws being SMU (37,000), Fordham (33,000) and Penn State (29,000).

The Pittsburgh Press estimated that Pitt had lost nearly $200,000 in ticket revenue during the 1940 season, all the while still owing more than $1.5 million on bonds taken out for the construction of Pitt Stadium in 1923. Compounding matters, Carnegie Tech, which rented Pitt Stadium for its games, was also experiencing a decline in attendance; this further impacted Pitt's bottom line because the Panthers were guaranteed 20 percent of the gate receipts for all Tartan home games.

West Virginia, too, was feeling the squeeze from the Depression, with outstanding debt remaining on Mountaineer Field as well as on the Field House, which housed the basketball team and most of the athletic department. "We intend to field a team and play out a schedule because we feel we have everything to gain and nothing to lose by continuing football," remarked athletic director Roy "Legs" Hawley that summer. "The brand of play may not be up to par because our squad naturally will be composed of young, inexperienced boys, but since most of our opponents will be in the same position the competition should be more or less even."

Earlier that spring, Hawley announced the curtailment of baseball and tennis for the remainder of the year, as well as the cancellation of spring football practice. He also made it clear that football would continue in the fall if he could find enough opponents to make up a workable schedule. At the beginning of June, Hawley had only three confirmed games, against Virginia Tech, Kentucky and Michigan State. A fourth foe was added on June 9 when Syracuse agreed to oppose the Mountaineers in New York, but the schedule underwent a series of additions and deletions as teams decided whether or not they were going to play in 1943. Kentucky and Michigan State backed out first, followed by Syracuse and Virginia Tech. Eventually, Hawley was able to piece together a seven-game slate that included Virginia, Maryland, Carnegie Tech, Penn State, Lehigh and Bethany. Pitt also returned to the Mountaineer schedule when the resumption of the series was officially announced on August 3, 1943. The deal was struck during a spring meeting of athletic directors in New York City when the Mountaineers agreed to replace Duke on Pitt's grid slate to give the Panthers a seventh game. Pitt arranged an eighth opponent when Bethany agreed to play the Panthers in Pittsburgh.

In addition to a reconfigured schedule, Hawley also had to contend with the departure of football coach Bill Kern to the Navy. Kern was required to report to Chapel Hill, N.C., on July 1, 1943, and would not be available again until the end of the war. Kern's first three teams at WVU were solid, though not spectacular, winning four, losing four and tying one in 1940, winning just four of 10 in 1941 and posting a 5-4 mark in 1942. Kern's '40 squad upset a decent Kentucky team 9-7 in Morgantown, and he produced a memorable 24-0 victory over Penn State in 1942. West Virginia's football schedule in 1942 was a dramatic upgrade from the preceding years, with difficult games against Boston College, South Carolina, Fordham, Penn State, Kentucky, Michigan State and Miami, Fla. Until the war interrupted things, Hawley thought the football program had been moving in a positive direction, and to maintain some semblance of continuity, he chose to bring back WVU legend Ira Rodgers to coach the team.

Rodgers was the school's first consensus All-American player in 1919 and later coached the Mountaineers for six seasons from 1925–30, with his '25 team posting an 8-1 record and the '28 squad going 8-2 and beating Pitt 9-6 in Pittsburgh. Rodgers later commented that Sutherland's brief words of congratulations after the Mountaineers' victory over Pitt in 1928 was one of the highlights of his life. But Rodgers was unable to duplicate the great success Clarence "Doc" Spears enjoyed on the gridiron before him – he chose to step aside following a .500 campaign in 1930 to devote more of his time to coaching the baseball team and serving as an instructor in the School of Physical Education, though he would continue as the football team's scout.

When Rodgers took over for the second time in 1943, he was inheriting very little in the way of experienced players, as the War Department would not allow air cadets or students enlisted in the military to participate in football. Therefore, in 1942, a squad of 54 players was pared down to approximately 30 when training camp began in late August. Among the handful of veterans remaining were Tony Paulin, Bob Dutton, John

Lucente and Ken Fryer – a standout on the '40 team who was back on campus after being discharged from the Army. Rodgers had less than a month to get his team ready to play a warm-up game against West Virginia Tech. However, a week before the scheduled date, the Golden Bears informed West Virginia that the team did not have enough players to play a competitive game, so the contest was nixed. That meant the opener would come against the University of Virginia on October 2 in Charleston. The Mountaineers lost the opener 6-0.

The Pitt program was in a similar transitional stage with well-known coach Clark Shaughnessy taking over after the unsuccessful four-year tenure of Bowser, who chose the U.S. Navy instead of coaching the Panthers to another losing season in '43. Shaughnessy directed outstanding teams at Tulane in the mid-1920s before moving on to the University of Chicago in the 1930s. His 1940 Stanford squad beat Nebraska in the Rose Bowl 21-13 on the way to an undefeated season and a No. 2 national ranking. Shaughnessy then coached Maryland to a 7-2 record in 1942 before taking the Pitt job in 1943, a decision he later regretted. Shaughnessy, who outfitted Pitt in red and white uniforms, was considered an innovative offensive coach who modernized the T formation with the new wrinkle of adding a man in motion. He later served in an advisory capacity for several professional teams, most notably with the Washington Redskins, where he mentored Dudley DeGroot (later West Virginia's coach for two seasons in 1948–49) in the finer points of the T while DeGroot coached the fabulous "Slinging" Sammy Baugh. Eventually, when Shaughnessy's Panther teams were losing frequently, Pitt wanted him to sever his ties with the Redskins and devote more of his attention to the Panther program – a very reasonable request. Shaughnessy wouldn't do it, and eventually he returned to Maryland. Of course, Shaughnessy had nothing like Baugh to work with at Pitt, the war and the de-emphasis program having completely gutted what Sutherland had built in the 1930s. Pitt had had three straight losing seasons from 1940–42 and was on its way to another one in 1943 following a pair of blowout losses to Notre Dame and Great Lakes to begin the year. Yet despite having a depleted roster, especially by Pitt standards, the Panthers were still superior to West Virginia. The Mountaineers took just 28 players to Pittsburgh for the renewal of the series on October 9. By comparison, Pitt had about 60 civilian players to work with.

Not only were West Virginians excited to be playing Pitt once again, but the game also represented a new opportunity for the Mountaineers to try and end Pitt's long winning streak against them. Trips to Pittsburgh were always a big deal to West Virginians, not only for the entertainment the football games provided, but also for the well-deserved break it gave them from their daily lives. In the years before the highways were paved, the trip from the state's Northern Panhandle to Pittsburgh took the better part of a day. Longtime sportswriter Mickey Furfari remembered breaking his arm as a youngster and his father having to drive him on dirt roads from Morgantown to Pittsburgh to get his arm set. "It took all day to get there," Mickey recalled. When the late Jim Carlen coached West Virginia in the late 1960s, he begged then-governor Arch Moore to improve the state's highway system so he could quit losing Bluefield players to Virginia Tech. In fact, because it took such a long time to drive to Pittsburgh, a good number of West Virginia fans would make an entire weekend of it, trekking up to the Steel City on Thursday afternoon and spending three nights at the William Penn Hotel, which the entire state quickly adopted as the unofficial gathering place for all Pittsburgh events. It was at the William Penn in 1922 that the phrase "West by Gawd Virginia" was conceived.

IT WAS AT THE WILLIAM PENN IN 1922 THAT THE PHRASE "WEST BY GAWD VIRGINIA" WAS CONCEIVED.

As the story goes, and as was often repeated by the late Ned Smith, editor of the *Fairmont Times*, a well-lubricated Mountaineer fan was among those patiently waiting in the hotel lobby to congratulate their conquering heroes after West Virginia's stunning 9-6 upset victory over Pitt. When Coach Clarence Spears finally walked through the door, the fan, overcome with joy, blurted out "it's West . . . by Gawd . . . Virginia!" A loud cheer erupted throughout the lobby and the phrase stuck, forever becoming a part of Mountaineer lore.

But such celebrations were extremely rare. A few years after that great win in '22, an overly festive Mountaineer fan had arranged to have a full band play for guests in the hotel's grand ballroom, which happened to be on the 17th floor. He informed his friends that the only time the band was available was at four o'clock in the morning prior to the big game; he hired them anyway, and waited for his fellow fans to show up. No one did, so he pulled up a chair right in the middle of the floor, and he enjoyed the orchestra all by himself until he dozed off.

On another occasion, following yet another loss, disappointed West Virginia fans returned to the William Penn to commiserate over the day's happenings. To boost everyone's spirits, a few fans started chanting "Beat the Hell out of Pitt!" Soon the entire place chanted in unison: "BEAT THE HELL OUT OF PITT!" Eventually a dueling cheer could be heard from across the street: "GET THE HELL OUT OF PITT!"

In Pittsburgh, what typically began as a weekend filled with great hope for West Virginians always ended up the same way on Sundays – cold, gray and dismal after another loss to the Panthers. The Mountaineers would collect their belongings, plus any new acquisitions they had made that weekend at the city's shops and boutiques, and retreat back into the hills over those bumpy West Virginia roads. It was a pattern repeated year after year from 1929 well into the 1940s.

Those hoping for a West Virginia victory over Pitt in 1943 were once again disappointed. The Mountaineers held the Panthers to just a 6-0 lead at halftime, with Pitt's score coming as a result of a Ken Fryer fumble at the Mountaineer 38. Three Panther runs got the ball to the 2, from where Joseph Kielb eventually got into the end zone.

Early in the third quarter, Fryer broke free for a 29-yard run to the Pitt 34, and then passed to Buddie Pike to the 16 for first down yardage, but the Panther defense held and Pitt took over on downs. Once again, West Virginia got the ball in Pitt territory when Ray Queen recovered a Pitt fumble at the 37, where once more the Panther defense wouldn't budge, forcing Fryer to punt the ball away. The Mountaineers had yet another opportunity to crack the scoreboard when Bill Anderson was interfered with while trying to catch a Fryer pass, placing the ball at the Pitt 32. The very next play, though, Chasey Wilson fumbled, and Pitt recovered at its own 24. Following Wilson's fumble, Thomas Kalmakir eventually took a pitchout and raced 25 yards for a touchdown; Bill Abromitis scored the game's final TD when he went in from the 10. Mountaineer fans were later surprised to read that the very same Bill Abromitis who scored for Pitt in the WVU game had then turned the tables on the Panthers by scoring a touchdown for Penn State – against Pitt. Abromitis could do this because, during the war, players were permitted to switch schools to take special armed services training courses, according to author Jim O'Brien in his outstanding work *Hail to Pitt: A Sports History of the University of Pittsburgh.*

As for the 1943 game, the final score was Pitt 20, West Virginia 0. It was the Panthers' 12th consecutive victory over WVU, and the ninth shutout. Another year, another loss to Pitt, and yet another depressing drive back down to West Virginia for Mountaineer football fans.

Finally!

Roy Hawley knew he was going to need to do something pretty dramatic to keep his job. The year was 1939 and West Virginia's still-wet-behind-the-ears athletic director had heard through the grapevine that some prominent boosters were trying to lure the biggest fish in all of college football to coach the Mountaineers: Jock Sutherland.

Sutherland's impressive tenure at Pittsburgh came to an abrupt end following the 1938 season, when conditions there had become, in his words, "intolerable." Sutherland, tired of battling the administration over the direction of his program, called it quits in the spring of 1939. Meanwhile, in Morgantown, the '39 season was Marshall "Sleepy" Glenn's last as West Virginia's football coach. Glenn, a WVU basketball and football star in the late 1920s and early 1930s, simply had too much on his plate: He doubled as the university's basketball coach – the last person ever to coach those two sports simultaneously at West Virginia – while also pursuing a medical degree at Rush College in Chicago. Because of his divided allegiances, it was impossible for Glenn to devote his full attention to the football program, and by 1939, his record had slipped to 2-6-1 after leading the Mountaineers to an 8-1-1 mark and a 7-6 victory over Texas Tech in the 1937 Sun Bowl. Glenn finally tendered his resignation on December 5, 1939, to open a medical practice in Charles Town.

Sometime in the fall of '39, eager West Virginia boosters, sick of losing to Pitt and wanting a big-time football program, gauged Dr. Sutherland's interest in the Mountaineer job. Aware of Sutherland's struggles at Pitt and willing to sweeten the deal, the group offered him the WVU athletic director's job as well. It is doubtful that Sutherland really had much interest in the West Virginia football-AD position, but it was nonetheless worrisome to Hawley when he caught wind of the scheme, and he immediately realized that he needed to hire a "name" coach in order to keep his own job. Twice before, in 1914 and again in 1930, West Virginia had gone after big-name football coaches, and in both instances the results were less than spectacular.

In 1914, the school's first organized coaching search led West Virginia to entice Sol Metzger into making a return to the sidelines after he had led Penn to an 11-0-1 record in 1908 and then coached Oregon State to a 4-2-1 record in 1909. Metzger's next five years were spent writing a nationally syndicated sports column, "Touchdown Secrets," while also contributing articles to *Colliers* and *The Saturday Evening Post*. Metzger's

WVU tenure lasted for only two years before he took a more lucrative job at Washington & Jefferson; Metzger was most remembered at WVU for notoriously pulling his Mountaineer team off the field over a dispute with the refs in a 1915 game against Washington & Lee in Charleston. The result was West Virginia's first and only football forfeit – and years of ill will in the state's Capital City.

The second "big-name hire" came in December 1930, in the midst of the Great Depression, when athletic director Harry Stansbury convinced West Virginia Wesleyan teammate Earle "Greasy" Neale to become the Mountaineers' third football coach in a span of 10 years. Neale, a Parkersburg native, had played eight years of professional baseball, most notably with the Cincinnati Reds, while also coaching college football during the off-seasons. In 1922, Neale led an 11-man Washington & Jefferson team to a tie against California in the Rose Bowl, and he later coached for six years at the University of Virginia, with mixed success, before taking the West Virginia job in 1931. Neale's brief three-year tenure at WVU included two losing campaigns in 1931 and 1933 before he moved on to much greater success in the professional football ranks, including a memorable stint with the Philadelphia Eagles in the 1940s.

Hawley wasn't interested in hiring another coach who was going to pull the football team off the field when things went against them, or someone looking to use WVU as a stepping stone, but he was after someone with a national pedigree who could grow the program while growing with it. Fortunately, there just happened to be someone who fit the bill up the road in Pittsburgh – and it wasn't Jock Sutherland.

Carnegie Tech's William Franklin Kern was following the happenings going on down in Morgantown, even signaling his interest to the folks in West Virginia should the football job ever come open. Kern learned the game under Sutherland at Pitt, starring at tackle for the Panthers in the mid-1920s before taking an assistant coaching position at Wyoming in 1928. He then played for a year and a half with the Green Bay Packers before returning to Pitt as Sutherland's part-time coach in 1930. In 1934, Kern was elevated to Sutherland's top assistant coach when Andy Gustafson got the Dartmouth job, and Kern was around to see Pitt produce records of 8-1 in 1934, 7-1-2 in 1935 and 8-1-1 in 1936 before he landed the Carnegie Tech post in 1937. The Tartans had become a formidable eastern football program in the 1920s, even finishing the season ranked 11th in the country in 1928. However, it was Kern, with his star players Merlyn "The Magician" Condit and Ray Carnelly, who put Carnegie Tech on the national map in 1938. The team notched a 7-1 regular season record that included big victories over eighth-ranked Pitt and ninth-ranked Holy Cross on the way to capturing the Lambert Trophy as the top team in eastern football. Tech's only loss came in a controversial defeat at Notre Dame, when an official erroneously told Kern's backup quarterback Paul Friedlander that it was third and two when, in fact, it was actually fourth and two, with the ball sitting at the Tech 46-yard line in the fourth quarter of a scoreless game. Tech failed to make the first down and eventually lost the game 7-0.

Near the end of the season, the sixth-ranked Tartans were invited to face top-ranked Texas Christian in the Sugar Bowl, and although TCU defeated Carnegie Tech 15-7 behind the play of Heisman Trophy winner Davey O'Brien, Kern was later named national coach of the year. Kern's third season at Carnegie Tech in 1939 saw his team's record dip to 3-5, with five of his players being ruled academically ineligible in the midst of another very difficult schedule. Then, on January 13, 1940, a month after Sleepy Glenn's resignation, Hawley appointed Kern, 34, as West Virginia's new football coach. Kern was brought down to Charleston, where he attended an alumni gathering at the Daniel Boone Hotel and immediately hit it off with those who wanted big-time football at WVU. Kern's hiring was hailed throughout the state as an important moment in the history of the football program, and it didn't hurt that Kern was getting endorsements from some of his best Carnegie Tech players, including Condit, a Charleston native then playing pro football in Pittsburgh. "Bill Kern is a great coach and really knows his football," said Condit. "With good material, I think West Virginia University will be tough in the east in a few years."

Right away, Hawley upgraded West Virginia's 1940 football schedule with difficult games against Fordham, Penn State, Kentucky and Michigan State. In 1941, the slate included Navy, Fordham, Kentucky, Kansas, Penn State, Army and Michigan State, while Kern's third season at WVU in '42 saw the Mountaineers face Boston College, South Carolina, Fordham, Penn State, Kentucky, Michigan State and Miami (Florida). For the most part, Kern won the games he was supposed to win and lost the games he was supposed to lose. However, he did lead WVU to a memorable 9-7 upset victory over Kentucky in 1940 and a 24-0 whitewash of Penn State in 1942.

In the summer of 1943, Kern enlisted in the Navy and coached service teams for the remainder of the war before returning to the WVU sidelines in 1946. By then, however, he had worn out his welcome with some of the school's most influential boosters – plus, Kern hadn't always seen eye to eye with Hawley. While Kern was coaching the Mountaineers to another so-so season in 1946, first-year university president Irvin Stewart, under pressure from alumni and boosters, initiated an extensive review of the athletic department, looking into the job performances of Hawley and Kern, as well as the process for awarding athletic scholarships – specifically at how voluntary contributions to the football program were being used, according to WVU historians William T. Doherty and Festus P. Summers.

What came out of this review was the creation, in the spring of 1947, of a separate, faculty-dominated athletic council to oversee the athletic department, review athletic budgets and schedules, monitor the awarding of scholarships, and to formulate departmental policies and other administrative practices. Hawley and Kern both kept their jobs, but Hawley was stripped of certain powers and Kern was served notice that his 18-19-1 record heading into the 1947 season wasn't satisfactory.

Kern actually had a pretty good football team coming back in '47, and it could have been even better if Jimmy Walthall's knee was healthy. As a freshman in 1944, Walthall led West Virginia to a 28-27 upset victory over a war-depleted Penn State team, and he was considered one of college football's top freshman players before being called into service. When Walthall returned to campus in 1947, Kern had Walthall penciled in as starting halfback in his newly installed T formation, but Walthall badly injured his knee during spring practice and was lost for the year. Still, Kern had the likes of George "Bud" Freese, who later played major league baseball with the Pittsburgh Pirates, Tom Keane, an Ohio State transfer from Bellaire, Ohio, and Rex Bumgardner, of Clarksburg. Both Keane and Bumgardner would later go on to distinguish themselves in pro football. There were other good players on the Mountaineer roster, too, such as Pete Zinaich of Weirton, Russ Combs and Jim Devonshire, both from Penns Grove, N.J., Huntington native Gene Corum, Ed Kulakowski of Kingston, Pa., Leo Benjamin from New Philadelphia, Ohio, and East Bank's Chet Spelock. Despite the returning talent, Kern gave a cautious preseason prognosis for his team. "We lack strength at the ends, guards, center, and left half," he said. "Freese or Walthall can handle the latter position if their knee trouble doesn't hamper them, but I have my fingers crossed on both of them because of their injuries. No new reserve material is available due to the fact that West Virginia will return to pre-war eligibility standards and freshmen will not be eligible."

KERN ACTUALLY HAD A PRETTY GOOD FOOTBALL TEAM COMING BACK IN '47.

True to form, Kern's 1947 season played out like his prior four – he won the games he was supposed to win and lost the games he was supposed to lose. After rolling to a 4-0 start with victories over outmanned Otterbein, Washington & Lee, Waynesburg and NYU, Kern's Mountaineers dropped their next four to ninth-ranked Penn State, Maryland, Kentucky and 15th-ranked Virginia, with injuries to Keane and Bumgardner playing a big role in the Kentucky and Virginia losses. Following the Virginia defeat, a depressing 6-0 setback in Morgantown on homecoming, the clamor for a new football coach reached a fevered pitch throughout the state. Even a 21-0 victory over Temple the next week couldn't suppress the growing discord, so Kern surprisingly offered his resignation four days before the season finale against Pitt. Perhaps even more surprising – to Kern – was how quickly Stewart accepted it.

Kern sent his resignation letter to Stewart on the morning before his team's Tuesday practice and then read a copy of it to his players in the locker room before they hit the practice field. "Under the circumstances, I think it for the best interest of both the university and myself that I resign as head football coach effective June 30. I want to thank you and everyone else, and the administrative office, for the cooperation and help during the past football season," he said.

The one person Kern didn't thank was Hawley, whom he thought had become too meddlesome with the program. When Kern first arrived in 1940, the staff he formed was made up mostly of Pitt teammates whom he knew and trusted. But, one by one, all of them departed – for one reason or another – and their replacements were chosen for him, not by him. Consequently, Kern began taking on more of the individual coaching responsibilities, and there were complaints that he was becoming too much of a micromanager. Kern also was not overly popular with many of the state's high school coaches, as well as some of the players during his early years at WVU. However, as he mellowed following his return from the war, he became much easier for his players to get along with.

Coaches choosing to resign before their final game had become a sort of trend in 1947. Iowa's Eddie Anderson submitted his resignation letter before the Minnesota game only to see his Hawkeyes upset the favored Gophers. Temple's Ray Morrison tried something similar before the West Virginia game, but in both instances, their resignations were later rescinded. The psychological benefits of quitting before the Pitt game were pointed out to Kern, to which he replied, "By golly, why didn't I think of that first?"

Kern was fully aware of West Virginia's long losing streak to Pitt, and before the game he reminded his players of their years of futility against the Panthers. "I know you can beat Pitt," he said. "I think it would be a great thing for the school and for all you players if you did beat Pitt."

By 1947, though, difficult times had fallen on the once powerful Pitt program; the reforms instituted by Chancellor Bowman had made the Panthers mediocre on the field. After three losing campaigns, Clark Shaughnessy departed in 1945, the coach later referring to his years at Pitt as "a big mistake." Ohio State star player Wes Fesler spent one losing season at Pitt in 1946 before returning to Columbus, where he set the table for Woody Hayes to take over in 1951. So Pitt turned to one of its own, Mike Milligan, to lead the program. Milligan starred at Aliquippa High and later at Pitt before serving as Fesler's top aide in 1946. In 1947, Milligan suffered through a horrendous first season that saw the Panthers lose all but one game heading into the season finale against West Virginia. That lone victory came against Ohio State, when Fesler was unable to make his triumphant return to Oakland. Kern's first meeting against his alma mater as West Virginia's coach came in 1946, a 33-7 Panther beating, yet, despite this outcome, the Mountaineers in 1947 were slight favorites for the first time since 1929, when Pitt had routed West Virginia 27-7. The series had become so lopsided, in fact, that the Mountaineers scored just six touchdowns in 15 games over a 19-year period dating back to 1928.

The team spent that Friday night in Washington, Pa., before busing to Pittsburgh the morning of the game. When the Mountaineers arrived, they were greeted by empty seats and frigid temperatures, but the dismal conditions did little to deter the ones who braved the weather. An estimated 18,000 shivering fans watched West Virginia completely dominate the game. (Incidentally, 18,000 had showed up to listen to General Dwight D. Eisenhower speak at Mountaineer Field earlier that fall, when he received an honorary Doctor of Laws degree from West Virginia University.)

Keane marched West Virginia 43 yards for its first score, the quarterback calling his own number from the 1. The Mountaineers then added 3 more points on a rare 18-yard field goal by Richard Hoffman early in the second quarter. Hoffman's boot was set up by Gene Corum's blocked punt, which he recovered close to the Panther goal line. Corum thought he had scored a touchdown, but when the players were untangled and the snow was swept away from the field, he was sitting on the 5 instead of in the end zone. Keane then capped a memorable first half by throwing a 31-yard touchdown pass to backup end Bernard Huntz with 45 seconds left, giving the Mountaineers a commanding 17-0 lead.

After that, the only thing in doubt was the final score, and it remained that way to a good many spectators even after the game. Some desperate last-minute passing by Pitt moved the Panthers deep into West Virginia territory before the Mountaineer defense stiffened to stop Pitt on downs. WVU couldn't run out the clock to end the game, so

Keane was forced to punt while backed up near his own end zone. Pitt's Carl DePasqua charged through the line to block Keane's kick, and the ball dribbled toward the goal line. Meanwhile, some overenthusiastic Mountaineer rooters had already converged on the goal post to get a piece of history to take back to Morgantown. Someone – possibly one of the West Virginia fans working over the goal post – kicked the ball, as a mass of humanity had begun to converge on that end of the stadium. Meanwhile, high up in the press box, first-year broadcaster Jack Fleming had a difficult time trying to figure out what was going on in the fog down below. Earlier in the game, Fleming had had to keep his wits about him while some intoxicated Pitt fans, unaccustomed to seeing their Panthers getting worked over by those crazy West Virginians, began arguing with the person Fleming was using to help him identify players.

"The fans were getting raucous," Fleming recalled in 1981. "I had an injured football player, a big guy, Vic Peelish from Beckley, working in the booth with me as a spotter, and one of the Pitt fans reached in and punched him, and he picked up a chair and threw it at the fan . . . all of this was happening.

"In the meantime, the goal posts were going down, there were people on the field; and the game ended 17-0 [Fleming thought]. I got downtown, and they used to put out the football extra, and the final score was 17-2. There had been a safety scored down in the middle of that."

No one did more to promote the West Virginia-Pittsburgh football series (and a general hatred of Pitt) than Leo Jack Fleming. Born and raised in Morgantown, Fleming's first vivid memory of the Pittsburgh Panthers was sitting on his mother's lap in his family's First Street apartment, about a block away from the old stadium. It was a beautiful autumn afternoon, and the Mountaineers were playing Pitt in either 1930 or 1932 – one of the few times the Panthers actually came down to Morgantown to play West Virginia during that period – and while watching the Pitt players enter the stadium, Fleming's mother imparted some words of wisdom that he never forgot. "Jackie," she began, "you see that team over there coming into the stadium? Well, that's Pitt and WE HATE PITT!"

Fleming's father frequently encouraged him to go out for the football and basketball teams at Morgantown High, but Fleming was more proficient at describing the games than he was at playing them. He briefly took a stab at becoming a weight man on the track team, but he accidentally hit Coach Art Clyde in the back with a discus during practice. That ended his track career. Fleming had written for the school newspaper and was studying journalism at WVU when World War II broke out. Fleming's career in broadcasting was really born out of an ill-fated mission over France in 1944, when the B-17 bomber he was navigating was shot down by enemy fire. Fleming barely got out in time and parachuted behind friendly lines in the vineyards of Chateau Thierry, where a hard landing drove a stake into his mouth, cutting his lip, breaking his jaw and knocking out his upper front teeth. Fleming was transported to an infirmary in England, and, after later contracting hepatitis, he returned stateside; he continued his recovery at the Greenbrier Resort, which had been converted into a military hospital.

At the Greenbrier there was a public address system that Fleming began to use, first to do quiz shows, and then later to provide news and sportscasts to all of the patients. When he was discharged, Fleming returned to Morgantown, walked into WAJR's offices one afternoon and asked for a job. He eventually began announcing West Virginia University football and basketball games in 1947, and he later added professional football and basketball to his repertoire. His broadcasting immortality was sealed in 1972 when his description of Franco Harris's "Immaculate Reception" was replayed on stations throughout the country, and which today has become one of the most recognizable radio calls of all time. "It sort of went by me like a blur," Fleming recalled of that famous play, in 1987. "That was my big moment in pro football, and I didn't even realize it at the time."

It was while working for the Steelers and living in Pittsburgh that Fleming really drew the ire of Pitt supporters, as he always wore his West Virginia allegiances on his shirtsleeves. "The huge masses of people in Pittsburgh are not interested in the rivalry between West Virginia and Pitt," Fleming stated. "But there are a few fanatics and maybe the support group – contributors and certain people in the athletic department – who do get worked up.

"But I have no quarrel with the city of Pittsburgh. One night while I was filling in for Myron Cope on his talk show, a man called up and complained 'you knock the city of Pittsburgh.' He said I made fun of the Civic Arena. I replied 'Well, Ray Goss and whoever is with him on Duquesne broadcasts make fun of it,' saying how cold it is and dark and so on.

"I have talked about the Civic Arena and I've said Pitt's Fitzgerald Field House, despite renovations, still isn't a great place to play basketball – but I have not knocked the city of Pittsburgh."

Fleming frequently bore the brunt of the ill feelings generated between the two schools as the rivalry grew more heated in the 1970s. He once experienced an unfortunate incident in Morgantown, when a group of Pitt students were encouraged to dump a cup of urine on his head while he was broadcasting a basketball game. From that moment until the end of his broadcasting career in 1996, Fleming was never left unattended whenever he called Pitt-West Virginia games, especially in Pittsburgh. "The thing with [Pitt] gets all stretched out of shape," Fleming said. "I think rivalries are super. I have enjoyed that with Beano Cook over the years. We'd get incensed with him and he'd get incensed with us. And we always came out as friends.

"You can name the great people that have been at Pitt – [basketball coach] Dr. Carlson, for one. But I think it becomes absolutely strange when the supporters of an athletic program become so vehement that they want a man fired or chased out of town because he pulls for a team down the road. This is ridiculous.

"For the people that come around and throw eggs at my house – and that has to be one in a million – or the Pitt fan who poured urine over my head at a basketball tournament, or the people who threatened after one incident to bomb my apartment – this is the fringe. I can't think that the real people at the University of Pittsburgh feel this way."

They didn't.

Following the conclusion of West Virginia's big victory over Pitt, an emissary was dispatched to each locker room to find out what had happened, and that's how everyone learned that, indeed, a safety had been awarded to Pitt. Seventeen to nothing or 17 to 2 . . . it didn't really matter to the delirious West Virginia fans celebrating on the field that afternoon and later that night in the downtown bars and pubs – it was still a great victory to rejoice. In a matter of a few hours, Kern had once again achieved hero status among many WVU fans, and a petition, circulated by a booster group nebulously called "West Virginians, Inc.," was distributed throughout the locker room seeking signatures from players in favor of retaining Kern and removing Hawley. The petition, disclosed by the *Pittsburgh Sun-Telegraph*, read: "We the undersigned, comprising the football squad of West Virginia University, hereby declare that we will not return to West Virginia University and compete in intercollegiate athletics unless the resignation of Roy Hawley is forthcoming and that a review and full consideration be given William Kern's resignation with the purpose of retaining him as head coach."

Kern, in Philadelphia watching the Eagles-Steelers football game the following afternoon, had no knowledge of the petition or the brewing controversy back in Morgantown. A similar petition on behalf of Kern was submitted by the team in 1946 when the Kern-Hawley feud first became public, but some of the players later recanted when they realized that the petition also included the ouster of Hawley – they thought they were merely signing it in support of Kern. In the end, Kern stuck to his resignation. He finished his five seasons at West Virginia with just a 24-23-1 record, but, more significantly, he ended Pitt's 15-game winning streak against the Mountaineers. It remains one of the most memorable WVU athletic achievements of that era. Kern never coached football again, while Hawley remained West Virginia's athletic director for seven more years, until his death from a heart attack in 1954.

Pappy Makes 'em Happy

West Virginia fans driving up to Pittsburgh to watch their Mountaineers play Pitt were doing so with the hope that their favorite team could somehow avoid another embarrassing loss to those "Jungle Cats," as they were often called in the papers.

In the 1940s and early 1950s, children searching for four-leaf clovers were having better luck than West Virginia was against Pitt in this very lopsided series, with the Mountaineers usually returning to Morgantown with their tails between their legs. Just once during a 22-year period between 1929 and 1951 did West Virginia manage to defeat the Panthers – and that 17-2 victory in Pittsburgh in 1947 came with a lame duck coach against a bad Pitt team that won only one game that year. A thoroughly frustrated Bill Kern, a Panther alum no less, announced the week of the Pitt game that he was getting out of the fickle business of coaching to do something – anything – a little easier on the nerves and a lot more beneficial to the wallet.

Ten times during a 15-year span from 1930–45, West Virginia failed to score a single point against the Panthers, including a miserable five-game stretch from 1936–43 when Pitt outscored the Mountaineers 113-0. After a brief interruption in the series from 1940-42, Pitt resumed its annual beatings of West Virginia in 1943, 1944, 1945 and 1946, and then once again in 1948, 1949, 1950 and 1951. By 1952, West Virginia fans were beginning to wonder if another victory over Pitt was even realistic. The coach they had – the burly, bushy-browed, mountain of a man Art Lewis – wasn't exactly setting the world on fire. His first team in 1950 won just two games, beating "powerhouses" Western Reserve and Richmond, while losing to local rivals Pitt, Penn State and Maryland by a combined score of 89-7. In 1951, things got a little better, with West Virginia sporting a .500 record, but the victories that year were against Waynesburg, Furman, Richmond, Geneva and Western Reserve – again, not exactly the cream of the crop in college football. Lewis hadn't been the first choice for the West Virginia job in 1950, nor was he the popular pick, but sheer persistence won out when he stuck his name into the hat on the advice of *The Charleston Gazette* assistant city editor Ed Brannon, who sensed that West Virginia's search committee was stumbling in the fog when Dud DeGroot quit after just two years on the job.

Dudley Sargent DeGroot was one of the most unpopular coaches in WVU history, his two-year stint in Morgantown not one for the scrapbooks. In 1947, DeGroot, a Stanford graduate and somewhat of a Renaissance man, was anxious to get back into the college game after coaching stints in the pros with the Washington Redskins and the Los Angeles Dons had turned sour. DeGroot was also in contention for jobs at Yale, Colorado and Nebraska when the WVU Athletic Council decided to hire him after receiving a glowing recommendation from Merlyn Condit, a Charleston native who played for DeGroot in the pros. Condit had also endorsed DeGroot's predecessor Bill Kern in 1940.

DUDLEY SARGENT DEGROOT WAS ONE OF THE MOST UNPOPULAR COACHES IN WVU HISTORY.

DeGroot possessed a master's degree in oology – the study of birds' eggs – and was actually considered among the nation's foremost ornithologists; his work in the field is still referenced in scientific papers to this day. But DeGroot's bird watching meant very little to West Virginia fans eager to beat those cats up in Pittsburgh and State College. DeGroot inherited a solid team from Kern and had an outstanding first year in 1948, leading the Mountaineers to a 9-3 record and a victory over Texas Western in the Sun Bowl. But his second season in 1949 fell far below expectations, with team dissension eventually finding its way into the newspapers. One assistant coach even quit briefly before changing his mind.

DeGroot was criticized for everything from his tardiness in purchasing a house in Morgantown to his decision to play his son Dudley Jr. Tony Constantine, the popular long-time sports editor of the *Morgantown Post*, began his affiliation with Mountaineer football in the 1920s as the team's unofficial mascot when Clarence Spears was the coach, and he later enjoyed complete access to the program once he got behind a typewriter. That ended with DeGroot. Once, DeGroot gave Constantine permission to watch one of his practices, and Tony made the mile walk from his home across the bridge in Westover only to be turned away by one of DeGroot's assistants when he tried to get in to the stadium. Another sportswriter once complained that his biggest beef with DeGroot was that the coach had a difficult time telling the truth.

DeGroot eventually flew the coop less than two months after West Virginia's season-ending 47-7 loss to Maryland, winding up at the University of New Mexico for less money than he was making at WVU. When *The Charleston Gazette* finally tracked down DeGroot to get an explanation for his rapid departure from West Virginia, he did little to suppress his disdain for the school and its kooky fans. "A person must coach professional football and then come to West Virginia to get a real education," he said. "In all my years of coaching I have never known so many wise guys who know all of the answers as I have met in West Virginia."

Because DeGroot was so unpopular, members of the search committee were led to gravitate to the likeable and outgoing Lewis when they finally met him in Gauley Bridge. Lewis was coaching the line at Mississippi State after his brief and unsuccessful head coaching stint at Washington & Lee during the war years. Lewis, who grew up across the river from West Virginia in Middleport, Ohio, knew well the Mountain State, and he was intrigued by the WVU job because of the large number of top football prospects located within reasonable driving distance of Morgantown. West Virginia coaches had a bad habit of letting the state's best players go elsewhere, and Lewis told the committee that the good West Virginia boys would only leave the state over his dead body. It was music to their ears, and he was literally hired right on the spot, even if some committee members were not entirely sold on his coaching credentials. "I always will feel that they wanted me to take [the head coaching job] for a year or two while they looked around for someone else," Lewis said in 1962, a couple of months before his death of a heart attack in Pittsburgh. Lewis, of course, was referring to famous alumnus Joe Stydahar, who was then coaching the Los Angeles Rams and was a fan favorite for the job. "But I fooled them."

Lewis felt that most of the players he inherited from DeGroot were much like their coach – duds – so he quickly turned over the roster with guys he preferred – big, strong and tough. When Lewis was a player at Ohio University and the Bobcats were playing West Virginia, he grew sick and tired of listening to West Virginia's "Cocky" Tod Goodwin talking during the game, so he hauled off and punched Goodwin right in the mouth, breaking his jaw. "He really shut up Goodwin," recalled Constantine.

In 1960, *The Pittsburgh Press* sports editor Chester Smith recited a story former Ohio State assistant coach Ernie Godfrey used to enjoy telling about the self-confident Lewis. Godfrey had unsuccessfully tried to lure Pappy to Ohio State, and years later at a coaching clinic, the two were reunited in the famed tower room at Ohio Stadium, reminiscing about old times. At some point during their conversation, Godfrey pointed above to a row of pictures and told Lewis that his picture could have been up there with all of the other Buckeye greats dating back to the turn of the century. Lewis asked Godfrey if he had ever been to Ohio University. Godfrey said he hadn't.

"Well go sometime," Lewis said. "And look on the wall. You'll find only one picture, and that's me."

Ohio U. teammate Bob Snyder once recalled Lewis's toughness in a 1954 *Life* profile of the coach. Lewis had fallen so hard during a game that his left arm popped out at the elbow, with the bone protruding. He continued to play until becoming physically ill, called timeout, and then walked calmly off the field into the locker room; Lewis also played without pads or headgear until his junior year, when rules made it mandatory. Pro Football Hall of Fame linebacker Sam Huff remembered once getting the Lewis treatment after the team had performed poorly in a close win at George Washington.

"He was pissed," Huff laughed. "It was a team that we should have just run over because we were much better. Now we're practicing and we're out on the field and he raises hell with me because he doesn't think I played well enough. I was moping around because he moved me down to second string.

"Well, Pappy asks [fullback] Tommy Allman what the hell is wrong with me and Tommy says 'He's pissed off because you've been yelling at him.' I said, 'Since you moved me down to second string and I'm not playing, to hell with it.' Pappy grabbed me by the shoulder pads clear off the ground [Huff easily weighed 230 pounds then] and he said 'Boy, let me tell you something. When I put you down, goddamn it, you better start running!' He put me down and by God I just ran like the wind."

Man-on-man, one-on-one, physical confrontations were how Lewis typically handled playing time. He would line up two players in the nutcracker drill, and it was the toughest guy who wound up with the starting position. Huff recalled getting the best of regular Frank Federovitch in those nutcracker drills to win his starting position. "That was just the way things were handled," Huff said. Lewis also frequently took up for his players, and they loved him for it. Once, a couple of guys (mainly Huff) started complaining that business manager Charley Hockenberry was being too stingy with pencils and writing tablets that the players (mainly Huff) needed for class. "I said, 'Pappy, all we want is what you promised us: Room, books, tuition, and to go to class. Hockenberry will not give us what we need,'" said Huff. "[Lewis] said, 'Come with me.' We go down to [Hockenberry's office] and Pappy just tore his ass up!"

When Huff was a junior and facing Penn State's great tackle Rosey Grier, Lewis said he would buy him a brand new suit if he could do what no one else had managed to do all season – handle big Rosey. Huff played so well against Grier in West Virginia's upset victory that Lewis, mortified that he was actually going to have to buy an expensive oversized suit for one of his players, hemmed and hawed, trying to find a way out of his predicament while still trying to keep his word. Pappy's solution was to pull one of his old suits out of the closet and have his wife wrap it up in a box like it was brand new, and he gave it to Huff in front of the team.

Once, during a game at South Carolina, Lewis instructed his players to come out for warmups wearing just gray t-shirts and acting like they were all worn out in the intense summer heat. When they came back out on the field with their shoulder pads on, the Mountaineers played like tigers, beating the confused Gamecocks, 26-6. Now, if only his Mountaineer teams could do that against Pitt, West Virginia fans imagined . . .

West Virginians were sick and tired of seeing the state's best players starring at other schools. The list was long and depressing – Abe Shires, Dick Huffman and George Cafego at Tennessee; Bob Gain and Bill Leskovar at Kentucky; Gibby Welch, Emil Narick, Biggie Goldberg and Billy Reynolds at Pitt; Piggy Barnes at LSU; Hercules Renda at Michigan; and so on and so forth. A West Virginia sportswriter once estimated that Tennessee had more than 20 West Virginia players on its roster when the Volunteers went to the Orange Bowl in 1946.

When Lewis was an assistant coach at Mississippi State, he was instructed to go up to St. Mary's, W.Va., and do whatever it took to get Reynolds, at the time considered one of the top prep prospects in the country. Reynolds eventually picked Pitt. When Lewis later ran into the speedster after one of their games and asked him how much he had been outbid, Reynolds declined to tell him an exact amount, but he did admit that he had been taken real good care of.

At any rate, Lewis knew he had to start signing some of the state's best prospects if he had any hopes of turning the program around. Not only were there well-known players in West Virginia that everybody wanted, but there were also the hidden gems that Lewis was able to unearth, mainly because other coaches couldn't get to the state to see them play. One of those hidden gems turned out to be one of the greatest football players in school history. Lewis was at a high school basketball game one winter evening down in the southeastern part of the state when he noticed this guy full of muscles playing for Green Bank High. Lewis's jaw dropped when he saw how well the barrel-chested boy moved, and at the size of his arms and his legs. After the game, Lewis slipped down to the Green Bank locker room and asked the coach if his big guy had ever played football. When Pappy found out that he had, he then asked to speak to the boy's father. Lewis had the dad sold on his son going to WVU before he even met the player, who just happened to be Bruce Bosley.

When the North team began training for the annual football all-star game in Charleston, the squad lost a lineman to an injury during practice, and Lewis recommended that the North team pick up Bosley as a replacement, but on the condition that no other college coach there watching practice was allowed to talk to him. He even made Bosley's father, "Big John," promise him that his son would not talk to any other schools. Big John kept his word, and he later became such a fan of Pappy and the Mountaineers that he drove through Hurricane Hazel to see the Mountaineers play Penn State in 1954.

Unlike Bosley, Sam Huff developed himself into a coveted football prospect despite his humble existence growing up in a small coal mining camp near Farmington in the 1940s and the early 1950s. "I was barefoot most of the time," he recalled. "I had a couple pair of blue jeans and some white t-shirts. But I knew there were other things out there." Huff got a glimpse of what it was like beyond Farmington when the famous Frank "Gunner" Gatski of the Cleveland Browns would return to tell stories about playing professional football. It was then that Huff began to realize that football might be his ticket out of the coal mines.

Huff had scholarship offers from Florida, North Carolina, Army and Pitt, but when he visited West Virginia there was no way he was going anywhere else. "I went down to Florida – I flew down there and I had never been on an airplane," he recalled. "I never even met the head coach. They had a student show me around the campus. Morgantown has the worst weather in West Virginia and I went down there and these palm trees were so beautiful. The sun was shining and it was about 85 degrees and I thought this was heaven.

"But I visited West Virginia University and I met Art Lewis," Huff continued. "I still have his picture up in my office. He was the greatest recruiter I've ever known. I met with him and I met with Gene Corum and I remember Art Lewis saying 'Boy, I don't give a damn where you think you're going to go. You better come to West Virginia or else you're going to end up in the coal mines.' I never forgot that."

Up in Warwood, Chuck Howley didn't start playing football until he was a junior in high school because his mother wouldn't let him. He wasn't really allowed to participate in *any* sports until one of his older brothers, while serving as the high school football team's equipment manager, was asked to play when they ran out of substitutes. "He went in and played and my mother found out about it and she said, 'What am I going to do?'" Howley recalled. "From that time on I was able to go on and play football."

Howley not only played football, but also just about every other sport he could, including gymnastics. "It was just something to do," he said of his work on the trampoline. "I enjoyed doing it. When I was in high school I did a lot of gymnastics and I was acquainted with a group of boys that were kind of gymnasts at the YMCA and the PTA shows and high school-type of things. It was kind of a show group at the Y and it was very interesting for me. My agility, I thought, was excellent as a result of that."

Howley was all set to go to Indiana to play for Coach Bernie Crimmins when he changed his mind at the last minute. "Everyone I knew was going to the University, so I changed my mind," he said. "I called Pappy Lewis and asked him 'Coach, do I still have a scholarship because I'd like to come to the University.'" When Lewis regained his senses and picked up the phone after dropping it in excitement, he said he might be able to find a spot for Howley on the roster. Howley was one of the most naturally gifted players to ever play at WVU. In fact, Howley was so big and so fast that Lewis had trouble finding the right spot for him on the field, eventually settling on guard. Later, in the pros, Howley ended up being a great outside linebacker in the 4-3 as a member of the Dallas Cowboys' famed "Doomsday Defense."

HOWLEY WAS ONE OF THE MOST NATURALLY GIFTED PLAYERS TO EVER PLAY AT WVU.

Just across the state line, Joe Marconi was tearing it up at East Bethlehem High in nearby Fredericktown, Pa., and though his high school coach was a WVU fan and managed to hide his star running back from Notre Dame scouts, that didn't keep Maryland's Big Jim Tatum from finding out about him. But after a week in College Park, a homesick and injured Marconi called up Lewis and asked him if he could come to West Virginia. Once again, Lewis was able to conceal his excitement by calmly telling Marconi that he probably could find a place for him on the roster if he showed up at training camp. "This guy shows up at Jackson's Mill on crutches and everyone there is thinking, 'This is the best looking physical specimen we had ever seen,'" said Sports Information Director Eddie Barrett.

But as good as those guys were for West Virginia in the early-to-mid-1950s, the key piece to the puzzle was Fred Wyant, a split-T quarterback on offense and a middle linebacker on defense at lowly Weston High. Wyant was the only good player on his high school team, and his coach would tell the rest of the players that his quarterback was the only person allowed to carry the ball whenever they got inside the 10 yard line. Eventually it moved back to the 25, and then later to midfield. "The people in Weston used to say, 'Well at least when he throws the ball he can't catch it himself,'" Wyant said. "They didn't know the coach was telling me to do this. In the last game of my senior year he said, 'Look, it's your last game and if you don't want anybody else to carry the ball and you want to carry it on every play, go ahead and do it.' So I did."

Lewis wasn't entirely certain what he had in Wyant and didn't start him in the '52 season opener against Furman, going instead with senior Jerry McInerney. The Mountaineers were playing miserably and would eventually lose 22-14. Disgusted with the way his team was performing, Lewis looked down at his bench at his freshman quarterback and told him to go into the game. "I was fourth string and he put me in with nine minutes to go," Wyant recalled.

Wyant went into the huddle and took charge right away. He had played semiprofessional baseball with men twice his age and was comfortable telling much older guys what to do. After three plays got the team close to the first down marker, Wyant looked over to the sideline to see what Lewis wanted to do on fourth down. The coach was motioning for his quarterback to punt the football.

"I turned back into the huddle and I said, 'I don't know about you guys but I don't want to kick the ball,'" Wyant declared, defiantly. "It was like a light bulb went off. They had this look on their face and I got the feeling that 'Well, we'll tell coach that we tried to get him to punt the ball but he wouldn't listen to us because he said he's running the show.' But they all said they didn't want to kick it either." Instead, Wyant chose to go for it, and he threw a long pass to Jack Stone that went for a touchdown. West Virginia scored another late TD and was driving for a third score when time ran out. Lewis had found his quarterback.

The following week, Wyant led West Virginia to its first victory of the season against Waynesburg, 49-12, and then a 35-21 loss to Penn State was followed by a 31-13 triumph over Washington & Lee. The offense had played well, but Waynesburg and Washington & Lee were not in the same league as Pitt, which was sporting a No. 18 national ranking following victories over Iowa, Army and Notre Dame to go with a loss to third-ranked Oklahoma. The Notre Dame win in South Bend is considered one of Coach Red Dawson's finest victories at Pitt. The Panthers were two-touchdown underdogs in that game, but they were able to upset the Irish 22-19, with Notre Dame missing what would have been a game-tying field goal in the fourth quarter.

Dawson was a quarterback at Tulane and later coached the Green Wave to a 36-19-4 record during his six seasons there, including an 8-1-1 mark in 1939 that featured the school's second trip to the Sugar Bowl. He moved on to the pros with the Buffalo Bills and was serving as an assistant coach at Michigan State when he was hired by Pitt to replace Tom Hamilton, who went from the field back to the athletic director's chair full-time. Pitt's best player was Joe Schmidt, who later earned fame as an all-pro linebacker for the Detroit Lions, and it was Schmidt who made the impassioned pre-game speech that fired up his teammates and helped Pitt upset Notre Dame. But Schmidt suffered a concussion against the Irish as a result of a cheap shot by a Notre Dame player, forcing him to miss the Army and West Virginia games. Despite Schmidt's injury, Pitt was still a three-touchdown favorite to beat West Virginia; *Pittsburgh Post-Gazette* columnist Al Abrams predicted a 34-7 Panther victory.

At the game's outset, it looked like Pitt was going to put the first points on the scoreboard when the Panthers marched right down to the West Virginia 12, but on fourth down quarterback Rudy Mattioli's pass fell incomplete, giving the ball back to the Mountaineers. West Virginia eventually got its offense going in the second quarter when Wyant took the Mountaineers 63 yards for the game's first score – the quarterback surprised Pitt with a pass to end Paul Bischoff for a 23-yard TD. On the previous play, Wyant had tried a pass down the sideline to a wide open Dick Nicholson, but Nicholson was unable to hold onto the ball.

In the third quarter, the Mountaineers received more good fortune when Paul Blanda's poor punt hit a Panther teammate at the 47 – WVU recovered the ball to set up Jack Stone's 16-yard field goal, giving the Mountaineers a 10-0 lead. West Virginia tacked on an insurance score late in the game when Gene "Beef" Lamone's recovery of Henry Ford's fumble at the Panther 12 led to Wyant's one-yard touchdown plunge, making it 16-0. West Virginia, playing without its top two ball carriers Eddie Dugan and Tommy Allman because of injury, got a game-best 82 yards on the ground from Carl Norman, while Stone and Danny Williams, playing in place of Allman at fullback, also ran the ball well. Bill Marker and Bischoff each caught four passes, with Bischoff's touchdown grab the biggest reception of the game. Bischoff was on the field for the opening coin toss, and he still possesses that lucky silver coin.

West Virginia's defense manhandled the Panthers, holding Pitt to just 11 first downs and 161 total yards with three different Pitt quarterbacks passing for only 64 combined yards. Lamone was fantastic throughout – one Pittsburgh scribe wrote that Lamone looked like a fifth man in Pitt's backfield that afternoon, and *Morgantown Post* sports editor Tony Constantine estimated that he had 16 tackles for the game, although schools did not keep official tackle statistics back then.

Wyant was able to take advantage of Pitt's defense through the air, completing seven passes for 113 yards – something West Virginia scouts Red Brown and Gene Corum thought was possible after observing the Army game. Afterward, Lewis recalled Brown telling him beforehand that the Panther secondary was susceptible to long passes down the middle, like the one Wyant completed to Bischoff for the game's first score. "You don't beat Notre Dame and Army unless you have a good ballclub," said Lewis afterward. "It certainly wasn't a fluke on Saturday."

As the remaining seconds ticked off the clock, West Virginians began to congregate down on the field to tear down the goal posts. "Before the game we told a West Virginia delegation the goal posts were theirs if they won," remarked a depressed Pitt official after the game. "Well, they took us at our word alright."

According to Eddie Barrett, a confused Pittsburgh police officer got his signals crossed when his supervisor got on the radio and told him to let them have it, meaning to let the West Virginia fans have the goal posts; the cop thought that meant it was OK for him to strike one of them with his billy club. He did, but the well-lubricated West Virginia fan never felt a thing.

Lewis was carried off the field by jubilant players and was taken all the way into the shower, where he was doused with water. Pappy didn't seem to mind, though, slapping players on their backs, hugging others, and even placing a kiss on the forehead of his freshman quarterback. "Our boys were ready to play football," he told a group of reporters who had congregated around him in the locker room. "We've been up for every game, especially Penn State, but we fouled up on that one when we had a touchdown run called back and then were scored on ourselves on an interception. But today we stayed high."

A disappointed Dawson said the better team had won the football game. "We deserved to lose," he said. "They were all of 16 points better than us today. We were flat and you never do much when you're flat. We really had our bad day."

It was West Virginia's first shutout victory over the Panthers since 1898, and the school's first-ever triumph against a nationally ranked team. "This is where it all started," said Wyant of the team's great success in the mid-1950s. "We go into the second year [1953] and we've got 21 of 22 starters back."

Abrams, who predicted a big Pitt victory on Friday, sang a different tune two days later: "As a member in good standing of a fraternity that has witnessed hundreds of odds-on favorites we picked go down to defeat, one would imagine we'd become inured to such happenings. But, you'd be surprised how the unexpected jars still give us a thrill," he wrote.

"Take that 16-0 lathering West Virginia's doughty Mountaineers plastered on Pitt last Saturday. That was something for the records and the memory books.

"There was nothing fluky about this one. Those underrated, underprivileged, poor little boys from Morgantown just up and smacked down the Panthers. They did it with such authority and dispatch to leave no room for the all-seeing experts, this one included, to find an alibi loophole.

"There are some Pitt followers who will argue that if the two teams met on 10 successive Saturdays, the Panthers would claw the Mountaineers the next nine times. They could be right. I wouldn't argue with them about this. All I know is that on the Saturday when the chips were down, the Mountaineers raked them in with both hands in convincing fashion.

"Let us give credit to Art 'Pappy' Lewis and his boys who were up for the game they wanted to win so badly and did."

Bill Evans of the *Fairmont Times* was the one sportswriter in the state capable of capturing the essence of that great victory. It was Evans in 1955 who famously wrote that West Virginians traveling back to Morgantown following the Mountaineers' 26-7 loss to Pitt made up mankind's "longest funeral procession." Evans was also the guy credited with giving West Virginia All-American basketball guard "Hot Rod" Hundley his famous nickname. And Evans would have surely come up with something memorable had he been at the Pitt game, but figuring West Virginia had little chance of pulling off the upset, he instead chose to cover a political speech United Mine Workers of America president John L. Lewis gave that afternoon in Morgantown, stumping for the Democratic Party. "John L. Lewis wasn't very far below the president, particularly around here with so many coal miners," Mickey Furfari recalled. "He was in town making a speech and Bill was always interested in those things. I can remember Bill once coming back from a game at William & Mary after a coal mine explosion in Marion County."

Because the newspaper Furfari worked for in Morgantown didn't have a Sunday edition, Evans asked him if he could cover the game for the *Times*. "Back then they didn't have bylines," said Furfari. "It was a day game and they would have had a Western Union operator next to me to file my story. Of course I didn't tell my employers I was doing this because they were our competitors. Anyway, West Virginia won the game for the first win over a ranked team in school history, and Bill was mad as hell that he wasn't there to cover it."

Many years later, West Virginia assistant coach Gene Corum recalled the team bus being stuck in traffic on the way back to Morgantown; he looked out the window to see waves and waves of cars from West Virginia passing them by, on their way to Pittsburgh to celebrate the Mountaineers' great victory over Pitt.

In the waning moments of the game, another motorist stopped at a gas station to get a fill-up, and when he went inside to pay his bill, he heard the West Virginia-Pitt game on the radio. He asked, "What's the score?" The gas station attendant told him it was 16-0, to which the guy replied, "I thought so – Pitt wins again."

The attendant said no, that it was actually West Virginia who had won the game.

"What?"

Nobody could believe it.

The Power of Positive Thinking

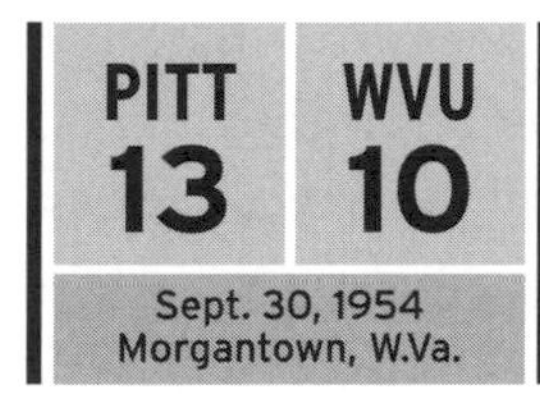

It was an excruciating week for Art Lewis, perhaps one of the most excruciating weeks of his coaching career. His undefeated West Virginia football team was favored to beat Pitt, which was something extremely rare for the Mountaineers in the 1950s. In fact, the last time a West Virginia football team was favored to beat the Panthers was seven years prior, in 1947 – Coach Bill Kern's last hurrah on the WVU sidelines. If it wasn't guard Gene Corum celebrating what he thought was a touchdown after recovering a Pitt fumble near the goal line (he was at the five), then it was radio announcer Jack Fleming's spotter, Vic Peelish, a burly ex-player from Beckley, fighting with some drunk Pitt fans in the radio booth while Fleming was still on the air. Either way, that game was permanently engraved in the memory banks of all West Virginians. Of course, Lewis was oblivious to all of that. Like most successful coaches, he thought history only began when his team began playing. Anything that happened before his tenure was just a meaningless diversion.

And Lewis's immediate history against Pitt was becoming rather impressive. He led the Mountaineers to a stunning 16-0 victory over the 18th-rated Panthers in 1952 for the school's first-ever triumph over a nationally ranked team. Lewis made more history in 1953, when West Virginia defeated Pitt 17-7, becoming only the second coach in school history to produce back-to-back wins against the mighty Panthers (the famous Clarence Spears was the first to do it, in 1922–23). In '54, Lewis had a chance to win three in a row against Pitt, and he was worrying himself sick about it. There was a time when Mountaineer fans had been happy to score a touchdown against the Panthers – *now they were expecting him to beat Pitt on a regular basis!*

After two very ordinary seasons to begin his WVU tenure in 1950–51, Lewis caused a stir in 1952 when his team won seven games, including big road victories at Pitt and South Carolina. Then, in 1953, the Mountaineers broke onto the national scene when they plowed through a soft Southern Conference schedule and recorded memorable victories over rivals Pitt and Penn State, earning an invitation to play Georgia Tech in the 1954 Sugar Bowl.

LEWIS CAUSED A STIR IN 1952 WHEN HIS TEAM WON SEVEN GAMES.

In the early 1950s, three of college football's four major bowl games – the Orange, Sugar and Cotton – frequently had at-large slots available for independents from the East, and there was usually some behind-the-scenes wheeling and dealing by eastern teams that didn't want to be left out. Penn State made an appearance in the 1948 Cotton Bowl, and North Carolina was invited to play in the 1950 game. Maryland made trips to the Sugar Bowl in 1952 and the Orange Bowl in 1954, while Navy was a Sugar Bowl visitor in 1955 and Pitt in 1956. By and large, though, bowl organizers were typically prejudicial against east coast football because of its perceived lack of quality teams.

In 1953, the Sugar Bowl had its eye on Georgia Tech and actually extended an invitation to the Engineers with three games still remaining in the regular season. Coach Bobby Dodd, though, declined the offer because he was uncertain about the outcome of his team's remaining games against Alabama and Duke, and he didn't want to put the Sugar Bowl in a bind. Although Georgia Tech eventually lost to Alabama, they were also being courted by the Cotton Bowl. The team eventually picked warm New Orleans over chilly Dallas.

West Virginia, meanwhile, got into the Sugar Bowl picture after wins over Pitt and Penn State brought them into the national rankings. But a narrow victory over Virginia Tech and a six-point home loss to South Carolina had cast doubt on the worthiness of a team that played in the lowly Southern Conference. The Mountaineers needed to win big over North Carolina State and get some help from the pollsters to tip the balance in their favor. They got the big win, a 61-0 pasting over a completely overmatched Wolfpack team. After the game, Sports Information Director Eddie Barrett and Athletic Director Legs Hawley worked the phones, trying to get as many sportswriters as possible on board before the rankings came out the following week.

"We were told by the Sugar Bowl selection committee that it would be helpful if we could get our ranking as close to the Top 10 as possible to help them in their selection process," Barrett recalled. "We called enough people to get us to 11th in the writers' poll."

The jump from 19th to 11th in the AP poll was likely helpful to West Virginia's cause, but not nearly as helpful as Georgia Tech Coach Bobby Dodd, some in the South believed. In fact, a lot of people were convinced Dodd had conspired to have West Virginia as his hand-picked opponent. Clark Nealon, sports editor of *The Houston Post*, made that accusation when Dodd turned down the Cotton Bowl at the eleventh hour, claiming the Georgia Tech coach chose the Sugar Bowl only because he was able to name his opponent, according to author Marty Mule's account of the 1954 game in *Sugar Bowl Classic: A History*.

Sportswriter Hap Claudi, of *The New Orleans Item*, was so incensed by the Sugar Bowl's choice of West Virginia (he preferred Texas Tech) that he took to calling the game "The Lemon Bowl" and ridiculed the Mountaineers every chance he got. Lewis, conscious of the heavy criticism his team was receiving, wanted to make sure they were thoroughly prepared for Georgia Tech, so he took his team down to Biloxi, Miss. two weeks before to the game. Forty-two players traveled to Mississippi, including eleven of the players' wives.

"We had a tremendous time," recalled quarterback Fred Wyant. "We had a curfew but we were out every night – I'm not talking about drinking – but dancing, going to places and going to the beach. We were allowed to eat whatever we wanted. No one had ever been to one of those before."

Lewis had two-a-day practices with the idea of getting his team accustomed to the heat they were going to face in New Orleans, but as it turned out, the thermometer in Biloxi never reached 50 degrees the entire time the team was there. "The second week we practiced all of the time in the cold and then we go to New Orleans and we stay in an Army barracks," said Wyant. "The guys on the second floor roasted and the guys on the first floor froze to death. Then the next day the temperature went from us working out in 40-degree weather to whatever it was in New Orleans."

Georgia Tech had a football team unlike anything West Virginia had ever seen, Dodd employing a sophisticated Spread T offense that relied on passing, pitchouts, laterals and deception. West Virginia, on the other hand, was a much bigger, more physical squad, averaging nearly 230 pounds per man across its front – one of the biggest teams in college football at the time. Lewis was concerned about Georgia Tech's outstanding speed, so he devised an eight-man defensive alignment to try and eliminate Georgia Tech's wide running plays. That configuration, though, made the Mountaineers susceptible to the pass, particularly because of the way the secondary was playing well off of Tech's receivers. "It was called a Tight Six or a Loose Six," Wyant explained. "Tight Six meant the linebackers were inside between the guard and the tackle and a

Loose Six meant they were outside between the tackle and the end. We weren't using an eight-man front, we were using a six-two, but they were so close that it looked like an eight-man front."

Frank Broyles, then a Georgia Tech assistant, said the coaching staff knew right away that the passing game, behind the arm of quarterback Pepper Rodgers, was going to work against the much bigger – and much slower – Mountaineers. "We looked at five different West Virginia games on film – all we wanted to see – and we sent them out there to pass," Broyles said after the game.

Georgia Tech threw 35 times – 18 times more than it did on average during the regular season – completing 20 for 268 yards and three touchdowns. They jumped out to an early 14-0 lead and led 20-6 at halftime, but Wyant believes a key moment in the game happened midway into the second quarter when the Mountaineers were only trailing by eight, 14-6. On a fourth down play, Wyant had Marconi wide open in the end zone for a certain touchdown, but the fullback was unable to hang on to the football. "If Marconi doesn't miss that pass, we're right back in the game," Wyant said.

Marconi's drop came after Tommy Allman's 60-yard touchdown run on the first play of the game was called back for holding. "I won't say it demoralized them," Lewis said of the holding penalty and Marconi's drop, "but it got them off to a bad start."

West Virginia fumbled four times and threw three interceptions, which ultimately forced the Mountaineers to scrap their running game when they had dug themselves into such a deep hole. "We didn't think we couldn't run against them," Wyant explained. "But when we got behind two or three touchdowns . . . we weren't really a pass-oriented team because we had so many great running backs."

Georgia Tech's 42-19 victory left a lasting scar on the program – Sam Huff later referred to it as his "biggest disappointment" as a WVU player. It also made a negative impression, dragging down the national perception of the West Virginia football program for many years. "After they lost the Sugar Bowl I wrote that the loss set back West Virginia football 10 years," said Mickey Furfari. "Art Lewis gave me hell for that."

Afterward, Lewis was frequently asked to explain the Georgia Tech loss. It came up two years later in an expansive (and highly complimentary) piece in *The Saturday Evening Post* about Lewis's recruiting prowess at WVU. "The thing that irked me the most was talk that West Virginia couldn't win the big ones," explained Lewis when the subject of the defeat eventually came up. "I've got to admit we goofed that time in the Sugar Bowl. These were country boys, and they were tight. Besides, I guess I worked them too hard and they were stale."

When fans called the football office and Lewis answered the phone, they would usually have a question or two about what happened down in New Orleans. Lewis recalled one such instance for *Charleston Daily Mail* reporter Dick Hudson. As the fan began to offer his two cents about the Georgia Tech loss and his opinions on how it could have been avoided, Lewis asked him if he was there to see the game in person.

"No. I couldn't get away," he said.

"Did you hear it on the radio?" Lewis asked.

"No."

"Well, maybe you saw the game on television," Lewis continued, a thought popping into his head.

"Yes, I saw it on TV over at my wife's folks . . ."

". . . Well tell me," Lewis interrupted, "how many other West Virginia coaches or teams have you ever seen on national television?"

The ABC telecast of the 1954 Sugar Bowl was West Virginia's first network appearance, and remained so until 1959. Just days before flipping the calendar to 1957, *The Charleston Gazette's* sports editor, Shorty Hardman, once more revisited the Georgia Tech defeat. Hardman compared the two schools' resources and the sizes of their coaching staffs, something Wyant also believes factored into the outcome of the game. Georgia Tech had a nine-to-three advantage in assistant coaches for that game. "We had great coaches, but three doesn't make up for nine," Wyant said.

Perhaps most damning to West Virginia were the 11,000 empty seats in the 82,000-seat-capacity Sugar Bowl. Future bowl organizers would certainly take that into account the next time West Virginia came under consideration.

Despite the lingering disappointment over the way the team played in New Orleans, excitement quickly returned for the 1954 season. West Virginia opened the year by beating a South Carolina team that had defeated national power Army by 14 points the week before. In fact, WVU completely dominated the Gamecocks 26-6 in the Columbia heat. "Army was supposed to be the best team in the nation and South Carolina beat them," said Wyant. "And then Army went out and beat Michigan, who was number two or number three in the country and number one in the Big Ten, which made South Carolina look really good.

"We were at the team hotel and [South Carolina coach] Rex Enright came over and Pappy brought me, Beef [Lamone] and Chick [Donaldson] downstairs to meet Coach Enright," Wyant recalled. "[Lewis] said to Enright, 'These are the only boys we've got back, and after y'all win this game, we'll go back to West Virginia and call every newspaper person we know in Pittsburgh and West Virginia and we'll make you number one in the county.'" After Enright left the hotel lobby, Lewis looked at Wyant and said, "That sonofabitch won't know what hit him!" The victory over South Carolina got West Virginia back into the national rankings at No. 16, and the Mountaineers' steady climb in the polls continued after wins over George Washington, Penn State and VMI. WVU's triumph in State College was particularly impressive, with Wyant directing the Mountaineers to a pair of fourth-quarter touchdowns to turn a 14-6 deficit in to a 19-14 victory.

Heading into the Pitt game, West Virginia was ranked seventh in the country and was a leading contender for a Cotton Bowl bid with its undefeated record. All eyes, including those of AP writer Gayle Talbot, were on Morgantown to see how West Virginia would perform against the Panthers: "West Virginia was soundly beaten [in the 1954 Sugar Bowl] and that is why the Mountaineers' clash with Pittsburgh this weekend will be watched with great interest by the men who carry around invitations worth a lot of money," Talbot wrote. "While the team from the hill country is undefeated in four starts and holds a victory over Penn State, it still will need to prove itself against the Panthers to become a prime bowl candidate."

Pitt's football program was in the midst of what seemed like an endless series of transitional periods following Jock Sutherland's departure. After Sutherland, Pitt went through seven different football coaches during a 16-year period from 1939-54. In 1952, former Tulane coach Lowell "Red" Dawson was hired away from Michigan State to coach the Panthers. Dawson enjoyed considerable success with the Green Wave from 1936 to 1941, and he never experienced a losing season until he arrived at Pitt, with his '53 Panther team going 3-5-1 against a very difficult slate. Then, in 1954, a "heart irregularity" forced Dawson away from the sidelines after Pitt had dropped its first three games of the season to Southern Cal, Minnesota and Notre Dame.

Athletic Director Tom Hamilton, who had stepped in once before to coach Pitt during the 1951 season, made another substitute appearance when Dawson departed after the team's nine-point loss to the Irish. Hamilton was one of the real power brokers in college athletics in the early 1950s, once famously standing up at the 1951 NCAA convention and imploring his athletic director brethren to resist the seductive temptations of television, which was already well on its way to supplanting radio as the nation's most influential medium. Hamilton believed TV was going to destroy attendance at college football games, the fans choosing instead to watch the games from the comforts of their living rooms.

"Captain Tom," as he was called by those who knew him at Pitt, was a star halfback at Navy who later rose through the ranks at the Naval Academy to become a decorated commanding officer of the aircraft carrier Enterprise during World War II. Hamilton was considered one of Admiral Bull Halsey's most trusted aides and by all accounts was a very impressive man. At Pitt, Hamilton became the guy national sportswriters frequently called upon for his opinion on the prevailing topics of the day, and later, he left Pitt in 1959 to become commissioner of the Pacific 8 Conference. "He had the strongest handshake of anybody I had ever met," recalled Alex Kramer, a longtime Pitt supporter and a student manager for Hamilton in 1951.

When Hamilton returned to the field, he made his presence felt immediately, leading the Panthers to a stunning 21-19 upset victory over ninth-ranked Navy. The new coach made sophomore Corny Salvaterra his starting quarterback, and he ran off the guys who were not fully committed to what he was doing – one of them being starting guard Ed Stowe, who departed after the team's Northwestern win to find work in Daytona Beach, Fla.

"Hamilton is OK, but he carries that Navy stuff all the way on to the football field – too many restrictions," Stowe was quoted by the Associated Press. "Now Dawson was a great guy, he had the respect of everybody.

"Hamilton is getting all of the credit now that we won a couple of games, but Red is the one who set up the offenses and the defenses for the Navy game and made some lineup changes that helped," Stowe added. "It's just that Dawson wasn't a real tough guy who could make you get out there and win."

Pitt had a modest two-game winning streak and growing confidence heading into its late-October meeting with West Virginia. Ticket sales in Morgantown were off the charts as anticipation grew for the big game. To accommodate what had become Mountaineer Field's first ever advance sellout crowd, the decision was made to erect portable wooden bleachers underneath the scoreboard in the open end of the stadium. Exactly how many seats there were in the old stadium was always a point of contention among fans and sportswriters, and there was never a definitive answer to which game represented the largest attendance in school annals. Many say it was the 1949 West Virginia-Pitt contest, when an estimated 31,000 showed up to watch the Panthers defeat the Mountaineers 20-7, while others thought it might have been the 1947 game against Kentucky. No one knew for sure because attendance figures were always estimated in those days. Then, in 1953, after another large home crowd for the South Carolina game, the university finally undertook an official count that showed the actual capacity of Mountaineer Field to be 31,325. The addition of 2,000 bleacher seats under the scoreboard gave the stadium a capacity of 33,325 for the Pitt game. "We could have sold 50,000 tickets for this ballgame," Assistant Athletic Director Lowry Stoops predicted before the game. Fans stuck in traffic trying to get to the South Carolina game had learned their lesson and arrived much earlier for the Pitt contest. Considering what was at stake, many believed it was the most important football game in school history.

An estimated crowd of more than 34,000, about 700 more than capacity, was tightly packed inside Mountaineer Field to watch one of the most unforgettable games in the stadium's 55-year history.

The first half was about to end as a scoreless affair when it appeared that West Virginia had wasted a 43-yard Dick Nicholson run deep into Pitt territory. While Wyant's pass into the end zone fell incomplete with no time left on the clock, Pitt's John Paluck was flagged for a roughing-the-passer penalty, and the ball was marched to the Pitt 8 with one untimed play still remaining in the half. Lewis ran out the field goal team and Chick Donaldson, a married 28-year-old ex-serviceman, booted the 19-yarder through the uprights for the Mountaineers' first field goal of the season and a 3-0 halftime lead. After both sides traded turnovers for most of the third quarter, Pitt eventually became the first team to cross the goal line with less than two minutes remaining in the quarter, with Salvaterra tossing a 9-yard touchdown pass to backup halfback Andy "Bugs" Bagamery. Pitt's score was set up by Wyant's fumble at the Mountaineer 30. Bagamery's PAT gave the Panthers a 7-3 lead with 1:13 showing on the clock.

The Mountaineers responded with a drive deep into Pitt territory, Nicholson once again slipping free of the Panther defense and racing 28 yards to the 20. But as he tried to fight for additional yardage, Pitt's Hal Hunter took the football right out of Nicholson's arms and began running in the other direction before being tackled at the 31. Hunter's alert play ended West Virginia's scoring threat and made an already tight Mountaineer team play even tighter. "He stole the ball – literally," Furfari recalled 57 years later in 2011. "It was right along the sideline, and he took the ball away from Nicholson."

But Pitt couldn't do anything with its big break and was forced to punt, which Gene Lathey got a hand on to deflect the ball out of bounds at the West Virginia 46, just 5 yards past the line of scrimmage. Wyant found senior Bill Hillen for 6 yards, and then Nicholson carried for 8 to the Pitt 32. After an illegal use of hands penalty on Jack Rabbits's run pushed the ball back to the 44, Joe Marconi romped for 14 to the 30. Five yards were tacked on after Pitt was called for delay of game, and two more Wyant runs got the football to the Panther 12. Three plays later, on fourth down, Marconi bounced in from the 4, giving the Mountaineers a 10-3 lead after Donaldson's successful conversion. Then, Pitt returned the ensuing kickoff to the 45, and Salvaterra coolly marched the Panthers toward pay dirt. Salvaterra first ran for 7 and then found end Joe Walton for 7 more to the West Virginia 41.

Another Salvaterra keeper netted 16 yards, taking him to the 25 before he was pushed out of bounds. His second pass completion of the drive, this one to Nick Passodelis for 10 yards, got the ball to the WVU 15. Salvaterra then ran for 13 yards to give the Panthers a first and goal at the West Virginia 2. Here the Mountaineer defense stiffened. Donaldson stopped Henry Ford for no gain, and Bruce Bosley broke free to throw Salvaterra for a 4-yard loss back to the 6. Bobby Grier's short run on third down set up a fourth down play at the 4. It was there that Salvaterra was able to locate Fred Glatz behind the West Virginia defense for the go-ahead score with only 2:22 showing the clock.

Wyant, one of the team's 60-minute players that season, doubled as defensive back and was late getting over to bat down Salvaterra's pass. "I looked over and saw that the [defensive] halfback was not covering the right position and it looked like [the movie] *The Longest Yard*. I ran over and missed knocking it down or intercepting it by about six inches," Wyant recalled.

Bagamery's missed PAT gave West Virginia, now trailing 13-10, a chance to tie the game with a field goal. Wyant marched the Mountaineers to the Pitt 32, where the Panthers' Rich McCabe was able to bat down Wyant's pass with two seconds left. Wyant's desperation heave also fell incomplete, but Pitt was once again whistled for roughing the passer when Louis Palatalla struck Wyant in the face with his forearm. That gave WVU's quarterback one more try to get the ball into the end zone from the 17, but his pass into a mob of players was batted down.

The stadium fell silent, with the exception of a few hundred Pitt fans that had converged on the west end zone to tear down the goal post. West Virginia fans slowly filed out of the stadium, realizing that their team had once again blown an opportunity to reach the big time. In the locker room, players quietly shuffled about, removed their uniforms and kept their conversations to a minimum. Sitting atop a table in the corner of the locker room was a visibly disappointed Lewis, who was talking softly to reporters. "I don't mind for myself," Lewis said of the loss, "but I sure feel sorry for these kids."

Lewis thought West Virginia's four turnovers, three by fumble, were the deciding factor in the game. "You can't fumble that ball around and expect to win," he explained. "Pitt has a big, tough ball club."

Before the game, Hamilton had lined up his players in the lobby of their hotel in Uniontown and read them an excerpt from *The Power of Positive Thinking* by Norman Vincent Peale. The ploy worked. Not only did Pitt benefit from four West Virginia turnovers, but the Panthers also kept the ball away from West Virginia's powerful offense by running 78 plays, compared to the Mountaineers' 58. Salvaterra was magnificent, completing eight passes for 105 yards and adding 97 more on the ground, helping the Panthers accumulate 334 yards of offense. Wyant was not nearly as effective as his Pitt counterpart, completing just five-of-19 passes for 34 yards. West Virginia did manage 226 yards on the ground. "You were always beat up after the Pitt game," Wyant recalled. "Pitt was the physical team and Penn State was more finesse. Penn State you were tired and everything, but they weren't rough like Pitt was."

Despite having four regular season games remaining, the loss to Pitt, combined with the previous year's Sugar Bowl performance, effectively ended West Virginia's chances of earning a bowl bid. Wyant still felt West Virginia had a shot at a bowl game if it played well the rest of the way in games against Fordham, North Carolina State, William & Mary and Virginia. He thought an impressive victory at Virginia to end the season would have done the trick. "If we beat Virginia by two touchdowns, we get in the Cotton Bowl," Wyant said. But it didn't happen. West Virginia only defeated the Cavaliers 14-10, and the Cotton Bowl organizers ended up selecting Arkansas to face Georgia Tech. As for the Sugar Bowl, Navy got the nod to play Ole Miss.

Following the Pitt game, West Virginia athletic director Red Brown unsuccessfully tried to slip out of the press box and avoid the crowd. He ran into *Charleston Daily Mail* reporter Bob Mellace, a former WVU player and member of Bill Kern's Mountaineer coaching staff in the early 1940s. Mellace asked Brown his thoughts on the Cotton Bowl. The athletic director said he hadn't heard from them. Mellace then asked Brown if he had heard anything from the Sugar Bowl. Brown frowned, and then replied, "We couldn't get into the Sugar Bowl with a search warrant!"

Pass the Sugar

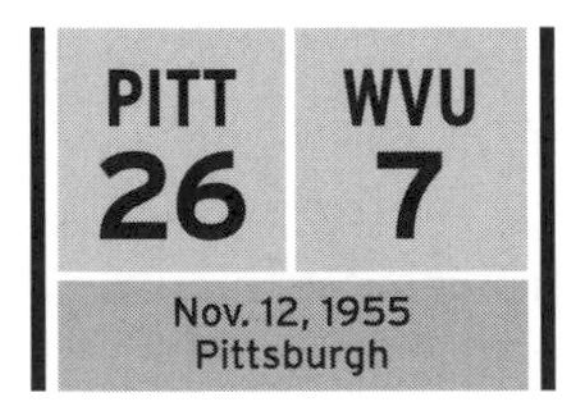

Art Lewis was a very worried man, and the more his football team won, the more worried he seemed to get. West Virginia was undefeated heading into November for just the third time in school history and had risen to near the top of the polls at No. 6 in the country. In the world of big-time college football, the Mountaineers were trekking up Mount Everest.

Just twice before had a WVU team even come close to this: Clarence Spears's 1922 squad rolled through its 11-game schedule with a tie to Washington & Lee as its only blemish in the pre-poll days, while Lewis's 1953 team lost to South Carolina in its next-to-last game of the season on the way to an 8-2 record. In Morgantown in late October 1954, West Virginia suffered its only loss of the season against Pitt, when Corny Salvaterra dashed the homecoming hopes of Mountaineer faithful with a game-winning touchdown pass to Fred Glatz.

Revenge, as it's said, is best served cold, and revenge was certainly on the minds of West Virginians when the Pitt game finally came. And many West Virginia fans couldn't wait for things to be settled on the field. A couple of them broke into Pitt's Ellsworth Center practice field a few days before the big game and placed a sign on a fence that read, "Revenge 54." Next to that sign was another one that read, "Pitt Pushover."

Back in Morgantown, a fraternity "panty raid" emblazoned the newspapers, leaving WVU president Dr. Irvin Stewart and director of student affairs Joe Gluck with a little extra weekend work to tend to. Singing and yelling along WVU's Fraternity Row eventually turned into a run on several sorority houses, with some house mothers having to fend off the perpetrators with hoses. Even Stewart was doused with water. The Friday night raid was the culmination of a week's worth of excitement building up to the WVU-Pitt football game.

BACK IN MORGANTOWN, A FRATERNITY "PANTY RAID" EMBLAZONED THE NEWSPAPERS.

West Virginia supporters were certain redemption was in store for their Mountaineers on Saturday afternoon. Lewis was not. He saw how poorly his offense had performed in a lackluster 13-7 victory over George Washington the week before, a game that was much, much harder than it should have been. The Mountaineers fumbled five times and threw an interception against a so-so GW team that went on to finish the year with a 5-4 record. After the GW game, Lewis closed practices and worked his players even harder.

Away from the practice field, Lewis was forced to defend his team's weak schedule. West Virginia's seven victories that year were not exactly awe inspiring, the Mountaineers having little trouble with Richmond, Wake Forest, VMI, William & Mary and Marquette to go along with the GW win. Only a 21-7 home victory over a .500 Penn State team was really even worth mentioning. Before the Pitt game, Lewis was asked to compare his West Virginia program to the nation's two other unbeaten teams at the time:

Oklahoma and Maryland. "I can't see that West Virginia's schedule is any weaker than that of Maryland and Oklahoma," he said. "Oklahoma played only two tough games – Pitt and Texas – and they loafed through an easy conference card . . . UCLA and Baylor are the only tough teams played by Maryland.

"Like Oklahoma, we are committed to a conference schedule [Southern], and it is unfortunate that all of these teams cannot be put in the big-time class. But I feel that overall our boys are facing just as tough tests as many of the better teams in the country."

By comparison, 17th-ranked Pitt was extremely battle tested and scarred, having played one of the toughest slates in the country. Pitt's five wins were against California, Syracuse, Nebraska, Duke and Virginia, and its three losses were to Oklahoma, Navy and Miami – all three ranked among the Top 10 at one point or another during the season. Lewis was well aware of this, looking like a man about to be condemned to the gallows when his team arrived in Pittsburgh for a light Friday afternoon workout.

Sports Illustrated's James Atwater was assigned to cover the game, and he was there to chronicle Lewis's compulsions. According to Atwater's account, someone asked Lewis about his health and recommended some aspirin. Lewis said he ate them like peanuts. Another asked about the health of his team. He said it was fine and then rushed over to one of the wooden goal posts at Pitt Stadium and tapped it for good luck. Lewis was notoriously superstitious; whenever his team played Pitt, he always wore the same brown suit that he wore when West Virginia had upset the Panthers 16-0 in 1952. During the week, to take his mind off the game, Pappy and assistant coach Ed Shockey might go down to the Warner Theater to take in part of a movie, slipping out before the ending. On Friday mornings, Lewis could usually be seen walking down High Street talking to local store owners on his way to the Hotel Morgan for a cup of coffee. At any time during his morning stroll, he might stop, lick his right thumb and stamp it three times into the palm of his left hand. He would also sometimes make an imaginary X in the air and compulsively spit through it.

For Pitt games, his wife Mary Belle was required to remain in Morgantown, wearing the same dress and listening to the same transistor radio that blared out West Virginia's big win over Penn State in 1953. At the team hotel after practice, Pappy sought out the same friend he talked to before West Virginia beat Pitt 17-7 in 1953, and then later, he took his 12-year-old son Johnny out for a lobster dinner. Of course, it was lobster Lewis dined on before West Virginia's two big wins over the Panthers in '52 and '53. For the 1954 loss to Pitt, it was older son Camden who was allowed to go to the game while Johnny had to stay home. Camden had the misfortune of spoiling Lewis's luck.

Pappy may have been superstitious, but the talent he was assembling at West Virginia was certainly nothing to sneeze at. Sam Huff, Bruce Bosley and Joe Marconi – all seniors in 1955 – as well as sophomore Chuck Howley, each earned all-pro status at some point during their future NFL careers. Sophomore fullback Larry Krutko played in the pros for the Pittsburgh Steelers, as did quarterback Fred Wyant for a brief time. Huntington's Bobby Moss probably could have played professionally as well, but after being picked in the fourth round by the Cleveland Browns, he opted for a military career instead.

Wyant was the quarterback and middle linebacker on a Weston High team that had won only two games his senior year, and Huff was born about an hour southwest of Morgantown in Edna Gas. Lewis discovered Green Bank's Bruce Bosley while watching a high school basketball game. Marconi came from nearby Fredericktown, Pa., and after a brief stay at Maryland, showed up at training camp one fall morning. Moss was the best high school runner Marshall Coach Cam Henderson had ever seen. Joe Nicely was a high school fullback from Rupert whom Lewis turned into a standout lineman at WVU. Bob Guenther came from nearby Clairton, Pa., where he won the Pennsylvania state title in the shot put, beating out future WVU teammate Bill McGinnis, considered at the time to be the best athlete to ever come out of Latrobe, Pa.

Gene Lathey was a 5-foot-10-inch, 205-pound spark plug from Dunbar High whom Lewis sought as a guard. Mickey Trimarki, from Burgettstown, Pa., was considered the best T quarterback to come out of Western Pa. since Connellsville's Johnny Lujack went to Notre Dame. Shifty Ralph Anastasio showed outstanding breakaway speed at Follansbee High and was an effective open field runner at WVU. Likewise was Jack Rabbits, a three-sport star at Jeannette (Pa.) High who was also the starting centerfielder on West Virginia's baseball team. Krutko earned high school All-America honors at Carmichaels, Pa., and was being groomed as Marconi's successor.

Lewis had a Welsh father and an Irish mother, but that didn't stop him from digging up some obscure distant relative of Slavic or Italian descent whenever he felt he needed to. When he recruited Trimarki, Lewis had the family convinced that he was Italian. Once, while recruiting another player from Pennsylvania, Lewis went to the player's high school graduation and the subsequent party afterward; during the party, the player's mother brought out a big jug of moonshine and asked Pappy to drink a toast to her son's graduation. Lewis patiently waited for ice and water to dilute the drink, but it never came, and he had to struggle to keep from choking. "But we got the boy," Lewis said.

Another time, Lewis was recruiting a player whose father was devoutly religious. When Pappy told him his brother was also a preacher, the father led him into another room, where he had scratched out on the chalkboard his complicated version of the *Book of Revelation*. Lewis had no idea what he was looking at and deferred to his assistant coach Gene Corum. Later, Pappy admitted that what he saw on the blackboard looked more like the pairings for a basketball tournament than the diagram for eternal salvation.

A Pitt coach was once tipped off about a good prospect who lived off the beaten path, and after two passes over creeks and a 1/2-mile walk up a hill to the player's house, he knocked on the door and was let in, only to find Lewis holding court in the family rocking chair.

"Coming out of high school, I was recruited by everybody and I could have gone anywhere I wanted," recalled tight end Ken Herock, a Lewis recruit and later a long-time NFL executive with the Oakland Raiders, Atlanta Falcons and Green Bay Packers. "Pitt and Penn State were really heavy on me, and Pappy came up to our house two times. When he came up he ate dinner, drank beer with my dad, and he was like a part of the family. He told my dad, 'Listen, I'll tell you what, if your son comes here he will have his degree.' He didn't talk football much, just about what it was like to go to West Virginia.

"That was it. My dad said, 'Hey you need to go to West Virginia because this guy is interested in you getting your degree.' I was the first one in my family to go to college, so what Pappy said was very important to our family."

Fifty-seven of the 60 players on WVU's 1955 roster came from either West Virginia or Pennsylvania. There were three exceptions: Roger Chancey from Pomeroy, Ohio; Tom Huston from Arlington, Va.; and Bob King from Allegan, Mich. Collectively, the teams of 1952-55 were probably the greatest array of football talent ever assembled at West Virginia University.

FIFTY-SEVEN OF THE 60 PLAYERS ON WVU'S 1955 ROSTER CAME FROM EITHER WEST VIRGINIA OR PENNSYLVANIA.

The buildup for the 1955 West Virginia-Pitt game was beyond anything the Mountaineers had ever experienced. For one thing, Pitt had won most of the games, so that usually put a damper on enthusiasm. But Lewis began changing that in 1952, when he took an underdog West Virginia team up to Pittsburgh and whipped the 18th-ranked Panthers 16-0. A year later, the Mountaineers won again, 17-7. With Pappy Lewis on the sidelines barking out instructions and smoking cigarettes, West Virginians now believed they at least had a fighting chance whenever the Mountaineers took on the Panthers.

On the other side of the football field, Pitt was breaking in another new coach. John Michelosen was a single-wing quarterback at Pitt for Jock Sutherland in the late 1930s who later became the youngest head coach in the modern era of professional football in 1948, when he was appointed at the age of 32 to lead the Pittsburgh Steelers. Seven years later, he chose a more stable situation at the University of Pittsburgh, where he kept three current Pitt assistants, added two others, and introduced the split-T to the Panther offense. Michelosen was a man of few words, and regardless of the outcome of games, he was always the same in practice the next week – pacing back and forth, pigeon-toed, with his eyes pointed toward the ground. In the mid-1960s, when rumors were swirling that Pitt was going to fire him, Michelosen remained silent. And when the ax did finally fall in 1965, he still kept silent, never lashing out, passing blame or casting aspersions, which he very easily could have done.

Pitt enjoyed immediate success under Michelosen, knocking off California 27-7 and Syracuse 22-12 before slugging it out with top-ranked Oklahoma in a 12-point loss. After another setback against Navy, Pitt recovered with two more outstanding wins against Nebraska and Duke, and then added an 18-6 triumph over Virginia that enabled Michelosen to rest some of his best players before the West Virginia game. Lou Cimonelli carried only four times against the Cavaliers while still recovering from an infected leg. Fullback Bob Grier, guard Al Bolkovac and end Joe Walton were also able to heal from ailments. Still, Pitt played up the underdog role before the game, and Panther assistant coach Jack Wiley, responsible for scouting the Mountaineers, did a lot of the sandbagging. "[West Virginia is] the biggest college squad I've ever seen all around," Wiley told reporters. "They're a lot better club than last year. Look at their statistics. They've averaged 437 yards per game and 34 points to their opponents' seven.

"What is their weakness?" Wiley continued. "I might lose a lot of sleep dreaming up a weakness, but I don't know of any."

Lewis was actually the one suffering insomnia – caused by, one, the way his football team was playing and, two, all of the attention his team was getting in the papers. The night before the big game, West Virginia officials spent time in Pittsburgh, wining and dining scouts from the Sugar and Gator bowls. Most of the tickets had been sold weeks in advance, with one of the largest West Virginia-Pitt crowds ever expected to show up for the game. "Any time we play Pittsburgh, it's always a big game," Lewis said.

In fact, the game was so big that a travel advisory was issued to West Virginians making their way to the Steel City. Fans coming to the game on Routes 19 and 51 were urged to drive through the tunnel, and, instead of turning onto the Boulevard of the Allies, they were instructed to get off at Webster Avenue and continue to the top of the hill, where special parking had been established. Mickey Furfari recalled getting stuck in a traffic jam trying to get to the game to cover it for the *Morgantown Dominion-News*. "The streetcars were on strike and it was difficult to get to the game, but they still had about 58,000 at Pitt Stadium," he said.

West Virginia had a lot riding on this one – national prestige, a Sugar Bowl berth and a 17-game road winning streak first and foremost in people's minds. Atwater captured the tense scene in West Virginia's locker room before the game, describing the players quietly sitting on green benches and staring at the floor while listening to the crowd filling up the stadium above them. Lewis, sipping a bottle of Coke, reminded Wyant of the plays he wanted called during the game while fishing in his jacket pocket for something to put in his mouth – either gum, salted nuts or a cigarette. The Mountaineers had every reason to be nervous because the Panthers were ready to play. Pitt, starting with backup quarterback Pete Neft under center, scored the game's first touchdown on its second possession. The Panthers got a 38-yard run from sophomore Dick Bowen to the West Virginia 8, and then two plays later, Neft located Joe Walton alone in the end zone for a 6-yard touchdown. Twice Pitt converted fourth downs on the drive, and Bugs Bagamery's extra point gave the Panthers a 7-0 lead.

West Virginia's best scoring opportunity of the first half came late in the first quarter, when Marconi recovered a Bowen fumble at the 46. The Mountaineers got to the Pitt 14, but a mishandled option keeper on third and 2 gave West Virginia a fourth and 5 at the 17. Lewis opted to go for it instead of trying for a field goal, and Marconi's run up the middle was stopped inches short of the first down marker. Still, West Virginia was able to keep it a one-possession game at halftime, though signs pointed toward trouble in the second half.

Wyant injured his knee early in the second quarter on a quarterback sneak and ran with a noticeable limp afterward. "Their player broke through the line and the safety came across and got a good hit from the side on my knee," Wyant recalled. The quarterback was West Virginia's Iron Man, starting every game since his freshman year in 1952, and not having him at full strength was a big blow to the offense. Then, Howley broke his leg, and shortly after that, Lathey had to be helped to the sidelines with an ankle injury.

When Wyant absorbed another hit to his knee early in the third quarter, the game started to unravel for West Virginia. Two fumbles led to a pair of Panther touchdowns within a span of 85 seconds; one fumble was by Wyant at the Pitt 25, setting up Neft's 7-yard touchdown run, and the second was by Trimarki, on an errant pitch that gave Pitt great field position at the 24. Salvaterra then ran 23 yards to the 1, from where Tom Jenkins took it in on the next play. Pitt missed both extra point tries, but it didn't matter because the margin was still too great for West Virginia to overcome. "You didn't notice [the injuries] until the second half when they were falling like ducks," Furfari recalled.

Pitt added another score late in the fourth quarter, when backup quarterback Darrell Lewis marched the Panthers 66 yards before taking it in from the 6 himself. With 2 1/2 minutes left on the clock and Pitt fans clamoring for a shutout, West Virginia was the beneficiary of two pass interference penalties, the second coming with no time left on the clock near the Panther goal line. As Pitt fans began streaming onto the field to celebrate, Lewis walked over to congratulate Michelosen. Just as he met Michelosen to shake his hand, it was announced on the loudspeaker that the game could not end on a penalty, so West Virginia had to run one more play. That part of the field was cleared off, and Lewis watched from behind the end zone as Marconi smashed over from the 5. With both goal posts already gone, the extra point was awarded to West Virginia. Pitt's Beano Cook said Panther assistant coach Steve Petro was barking from the sidelines, "Don't give them anything!"

The loss was a bitter disappointment for West Virginia. More than 50 years later, Wyant believes his injury, as well as the injuries to Howley and Lathey, were the deciding factors in the outcome of the game. "We're down one touchdown and we're going to score and we would have scored another touchdown," he said. Wyant also recalled a special play West Virginia had planned to spring on the Panthers that they were never able to use. "We practiced that play all week to Larry Krutko, and he said he didn't remember it," Wyant said.

West Virginia had a slight advantage in first downs, 16-15, but Pitt outgained WVU on the ground 275-195. The Mountaineers tried 23 passes, completing only four, for 43 yards. West Virginia's three turnovers were each momentum killers.

It was West Virginia's worst defeat in four years, dating back to a 54-7 loss at Maryland in 1951. Pitt's 275 yards rushing were the most allowed by a Mountaineer defense since the Terrapins netted 523 yards in that 47-point loss in College Park. "That was the most important win for Pitt since the Fordham game in 1938," Cook recalled in 2007. "That put Pitt back into the national picture."

The Sugar Bowl scouts, who had come to see West Virginia play the Panthers, instead ended up inviting Pitt after it knocked off Penn State 20-0 to finish the season with a 7-3 record. The Panthers lost to Georgia Tech, 7-0 in the bowl game West Virginia could have played in.

A week after the Pitt loss, the Mountaineers' slim hopes of earning a Gator Bowl berth were dashed in the snow in Morgantown when Syracuse defeated the Mountaineers 20-13, with Wyant watching from the sidelines. A 27-7 victory over a weak North Carolina State team gave West Virginia a final record of 8-2, but that wasn't nearly enough to remove the sting from the disappointment up in Pittsburgh. *Fairmont Times* sports editor Bill Evans called the cavalcade traveling back to West Virginia "the longest funeral procession in mankind."

The description was fitting.

Pitt fans claim a goal post. See page A8

Fred "Colt 45" Colvard. See page A10

1957-1965
WILD TIMES

West Virginia Survives

The natives were beginning to get restless with Art Lewis. Citing a lack of "big-game" victories and late season swoons, in early November 1957, Beckley sportswriter George Springer decided to take the West Virginia coach to task. Springer noted that Lewis's 48-26-7 (at that point) record included an inordinate number of wins against inferior teams, and he cited Lewis's much more pedestrian 21-23-1 record against top-quality competition as more reflective of the type of coach he really was.

To a degree, Springer had a point. In 1953, West Virginia was rolling along with seven consecutive wins, including triumphs over Pitt and Penn State, only to lose 20-14 to South Carolina in Morgantown and then completely fall apart against Georgia Tech in the 1954 Sugar Bowl – the school's first-ever major bowl appearance. The Mountaineers started 1954 on fire, knocking off South Carolina to open the season, then beating Penn State 19-14 in an unforgettable game at State College before losing 13-10 to Pitt in the first advance sellout in Mountaineer Field history. The Pitt loss ended up costing West Virginia a return trip to a bowl game. In 1955, the Mountaineers began the season by winning seven straight, reaching as high as sixth in the national rankings before getting embarrassed at Pitt in a 26-7 loss. The following week, with starting quarterback Fred Wyant on the shelf, the Mountaineers dropped a 20-13 decision to Syracuse to eliminate themselves from bowl game consideration.

In 1956, losses to Pitt, Syracuse, Penn State and Miami – the four toughest games on the schedule – led to a very ordinary 6-4 record. And then in 1957, after tying Virginia and defeating Virginia Tech, the Mountaineers went on the road to Wisconsin and were bludgeoned by the Badgers, 45-13. A month after that, Penn State had little trouble taking care of WVU, 27-6, to drop the Mountaineers' record to 4-2-1 and once again cast a pall over the entire state. Lewis was never considered a great tactical coach like Woody Hayes, Bear Bryant and some of his other contemporaries, but he did recruit many great players, treated them well and got them to play at a high level most of the time. Wyant once recalled Lewis's hands-off approach to game strategy: "We were driving down the field at the end of the game against South Carolina [in 1954] and I went by the sidelines and I said 'Coach, is there anything you want called?' He said 'Nope, you're doing great,'" Wyant chuckled.

Where the program really struggled was with its association with the Southern Conference – both competitively and also when it came to recruiting beyond the immediate area. The Mountaineers thoroughly dominated Southern Conference play during the five-year period from 1952–57, going 24-1, with its only loss being an embarrassing 22-14 setback to Furman at the beginning of the 1952 season, in a game where Lewis was playing mostly underclassmen. Just once in 1956 did the Mountaineers play as many as five Southern Conference opponents in a single year, with WVU going 5-0 against the Southern Conference and 1-4 outside of league play. In 1954 and 1957, the Mountaineers chose to play just three Southern Conference games. Besides West Virginia, only one other Southern Conference program was invited to play in a bowl game during the mid-1950s, when George Washington defeated Texas Western 13-0 in the 1957 Sun Bowl (the Mountaineers defeated the Colonials that season in Morgantown, 14-0). The two most recognizable non-Mountaineer players in the Southern Conference at that time were The Citadel's Paul Maguire and Virginia Tech's Carroll Dale. Prior to the 1955 Pitt game, when West Virginia was getting national attention for its undefeated record, Lewis was forced to spend most of the week leading up to the game defending his weak conference schedule. In the ensuing years, Lewis tried unsuccessfully to balance a soft Southern Conference slate with much tougher road games at Texas, Miami, Wisconsin, Oklahoma, Indiana and USC, but the Mountaineers managed to win only one of those, at Texas in 1956, the year before Darrell Royal arrived in Austin.

Lewis also frequently blamed the Southern Conference for his inability to sign top out-of-state prospects, particularly good northern black players who were showing up on the rosters at rival schools Penn State, Pitt and Syracuse. Lewis had a decent chance of landing New Jersey prospect Dave Robinson (who wound up starring at Penn State), but his mother would not let him play at a "southern school." "Once they heard the word 'southern,' that was it," recalled former Sports Information Director Eddie Barrett. Lewis also tried to land Weirton's Tom Bloom and Clarksburg's Gene Donaldson but was unsuccessful (both went to Purdue). It took his successor Gene Corum until 1962 before he finally was able to recruit black football players at WVU.

Southern Conference football reached its pinnacle in 1951, when third-ranked Maryland finished the season with a 10-0 record by soundly defeating Tennessee in the Sugar Bowl. It was the fifth time in a span of six years that a Southern Conference team had finished a football campaign ranked in the Top 10. But all was not well in the 17-member league. In the summer of 1951, the Southern Conference joined the Big Seven Conference in prohibiting its members from participating in post-season bowl games, joining an ongoing movement by a number of NCAA institutions to de-emphasize college football. Tulane and Vanderbilt spearheaded a de-emphasis program in the Southeastern Conference (although it did not include the banning of bowl games), and new Big Ten member Michigan State was also opposed to bowl games.

THE SOUTHERN CONFERENCE WAS ROCKED BY AN EMBARRASSING ACADEMIC SCANDAL.

Meanwhile, the Southern Conference was rocked by an embarrassing academic scandal at William & Mary that shook the small Virginia school to its core. During a four-year period from 1947–50, several football and basketball players were given credit for classes they did not attend, while others had their transcripts altered to remain academically eligible. Despite the school's size, the Indians had the goal of becoming a college football power under coach Rube McCray – and it succeeded, to a degree, capturing a pair of Southern Conference titles and earning bowl bids in 1947 and 1949 before the improprieties were discovered. The problems at William & Mary caused many schools in the Southern Conference to reexamine their priorities, and one of the league's solutions to the problem was to no longer accept post-season bowl invitations. The Southern Conference's choice to do so was bitterly disputed by Maryland and Clemson, and both schools decided to play in bowl games anyway. As a result, Clemson and Maryland were ineligible to compete for the Southern Conference title in 1952, thus setting in motion the eventual withdrawal of those schools – plus the Carolina schools – to form the Atlantic Coast Conference in the summer of 1953.

In December 1953, two months after the University of Virginia was invited to become the ACC's eighth member, West Virginia and Virginia Tech were also under consideration for league expansion. From the time of the split, the two schools had supporters who wanted them brought into the league as a package deal. And West Virginia's candidacy became even more appealing when the team won eight of its nine regular season games and was invited to play Georgia Tech in the Sugar Bowl, adding to its already sterling reputation as a college basketball power. (In November 1953, the Southern Conference voted to remove the league's anti-bowl ban, enabling West Virginia to accept a Sugar Bowl invitation. Helping the decision was a split of bowl-game revenue that was heavily weighted toward the conference.) Virginia Tech had some appeal as well: It was a charter member of the Southern Conference, was located near most of the schools in the ACC, boasted a solid academic reputation, and had an athletic program that possessed a lot of potential. The ACC met on Friday, December 4, 1953 in Greensboro, N.C., and University of North Carolina Chancellor Robert House officially moved to admit West Virginia and Virginia Tech as the league's ninth and tenth members, but ACC President James T. Penney of South Carolina ruled the motion out of order since the matter wasn't officially on the agenda. After a short closed session, the eight schools opted to table expansion indefinitely because West Virginia and Virginia Tech couldn't garner the necessary two-thirds votes to gain admittance. United Press's Ken Alyta reported a four-four split, although the schools for and against were not publicly revealed. The reason to table the motion was obvious – support for membership wasn't clear cut, both parties wanted to avoid the embarrassment of a public discussion when the Mountaineers were getting ready to play in the Sugar Bowl, and ACC members believed further expansion would detract from the original goal of having a compact, more closely aligned league instead of the cumbersome, 17-school conference they had just left.

In the same light, ACC vice-president F.W. Clounts of Wake Forest made his school's preferences known on the eve of the meeting. "I believe Virginia Tech would be the most logical choice because the school is close to the other conference members, especially Virginia, and is easy to get to," Clounts told a United Press reporter. "West Virginia is too far away and too hard to reach because of the mountains."

WVU's distance from the other ACC schools and a lack of a suitable airport near Morgantown were certainly factors, as was West Virginia's land-grant philosophy of providing an affordable education to anyone, a philosophy that was frequently scorned by some of the schools in opposition. It was also believed that Maryland Coach Jim Tatum held a grudge against West Virginia for the Mountaineers' support of the league's anti-bowl rule in 1951 – that and a game the Terps played against WVU early in Tatum's tenure, when he claimed that the Mountaineers had used ineligible players. West Virginia's failure to gain admittance into the Atlantic Coast Conference was one of athletic director Legs Hawley's biggest disappointments. Just three months after seeing his alma mater denied admission into the ACC, Hawley died of a heart attack on March 24, 1954, at age 53, in Pittsburgh.

Hawley's replacement, Red Brown, was more forgiving of the watered-down Southern Conference. Brown considered the league a convenient avenue for the basketball team to reach the NCAA tournament, which it did 10 times during a 13-year period ending in 1967. Plus, he had grown close to many of the schools' administrators throughout the league and enjoyed being in their company socially. However, Brown's views eventually began to change when he hired Jim Carlen to take over the football program in 1966. Carlen knew right away that intercollegiate athletics at West Virginia University could only go so far with the school a member of the Southern Conference, and he set out to convince Brown that independence was the proper course, eventually succeeding in 1968. "When I would talk to Mr. Brown, he would say, 'You can't do that.' I said 'Mr. Brown, I know you are a basketball man and everything, but we're in a different world here now,'" Carlen recalled. "These people need something to grab ahold of and Marshall is not going to be it. You've got to help me a little bit here now.

"I wanted to get out of the Southern Conference because we're better than that," Carlen explained. "I wanted to play Kentucky and Tennessee. I wanted to play where our people could drive and see us [play against top competition] and I wanted to get into a bowl game."

When West Virginia left the Southern Conference after the 1967 season, the football program had claimed eight conference titles, posted a 51-7-3 record (minus the departed ACC schools), recorded 11 shutouts and won by an average margin of 13 points per game. Outside of the Southern Conference, the Mountaineers were only 31-55-5 during that same period.

All during its 18-year affiliation with the Southern Conference, West Virginia fans were frequently deceived by the Mountaineers' gridiron success before getting a reality check when the Pitt game arrived on the schedule. Four times in a span of six seasons from 1950-55, West Virginia had the better record going into the Pitt game, and all four times the Panthers came out the victors. There were two losses that stung the most – in 1954, when an undefeated Mountaineer team lost 13-10 to a sub .500 Pitt squad on homecoming, and then in 1955, when the Panthers once again knocked the Mountaineers from the ranks of the unbeaten and in the process ended up stealing West Virginia's bid to the Sugar Bowl. Even well into the 1960s, Pitt's so-so records were usually deceiving. "We played Citadel, Richmond, VMI and those schools, and the Southern Conference was not close to being as competitive as the national teams that Pittsburgh was playing," running back Garrett Ford explained.

In 1957, the circumstances were very similar. The Panthers got off to an excellent start, going 3-1 against Oklahoma, Oregon, USC and Nebraska before suffering consecutive losses to Army, Notre Dame and Syracuse. West Virginia, meanwhile, showed victories over Virginia Tech, Boston University, George Washington and William & Mary heading into the Pitt game. And although West Virginia's slate was considerably weaker than Pitt's, both teams were besieged with injuries. Pitt was without co-captain Charley Brueckman and top ground gainer Joe Scisly, while the Mountaineers were minus their best player, Chuck Howley, who broke his jaw in practice before the Penn State game. "I don't even know if we were in pads, but somehow I stuck my head in there and caught a knee in the jaw," Howley recalled. "I think it was on a Tuesday or a Wednesday, and they decided to send me back to Wheeling to have it operated on and just as soon as it was finished they could take me to Penn State to play in the football game.

"Of course after I got in the hospital and had the surgery the doctor said, 'He's not going anywhere.' I thought that was all it was – just go in there and get it wired shut and then go off and play a game, but that's not the way it was."

Lewis also couldn't settle on a quarterback, intermittently using Mickey Trimarki and Dick Longfellow at various times throughout the year. Naturally, as usually happens when two quarterbacks are used, factions formed, with some preferring the taller Pennsylvania native Trimarki while others opting for the state native Longfellow from Spencer. "Tricky" Mickey seemed to be the guy to replace Fred Wyant in 1956, passing for 419 yards and adding an additional 25 yards on the ground, but his 16-to-1 interception-to-touchdown pass ratio was enough to make Lewis want to pull his hair out. A strong spring gave Trimarki the starting nod at the beginning of 1957, but he was replaced by Longfellow after the team's bad loss at Wisconsin, and then Longfellow saw the majority of the action in the Penn State game. But Trimarki and Longfellow would both play against Pitt.

"TRICKY" MICKEY SEEMED TO BE THE GUY TO REPLACE FRED WYANT.

Mountaineer fans weren't the only ones confused with the team's quarterback play heading into the Pitt game – the oddsmakers were also having a difficult time getting a handle on things. The United Press listed the Mountaineers as six-point favorites, but after further checking, it was discovered that it had gotten the point spread backwards. Pitt was actually the favored team for the 50th meeting between the two schools. Before the line was corrected, Lewis couldn't believe his ears when he heard about his team's favored status, despite losing by three touchdowns to Penn State the week prior and enjoying infrequent success against the Panthers. "They must have not sharpened their pencils when they made up those odds," remarked Lewis.

Frigid 33-degree temperatures, gusting winds, injury-depleted lineups and some erratic play led to a lackluster game that was ultimately decided when Pitt's Ivan Toncic missed an extra point early in the third quarter. The Panthers had finally gotten on the scoreboard when end Art Gob got past Ray Peterson for a 51-yard touchdown reception, but a high snap forced Toncic to rush his extra point attempt, and the football sailed left of the upright.

West Virginia's sole touchdown came as a result of Bill McClure's 45-yard punt return to the Pitt 6 late in the first quarter. McClure hauled in the punt at his own 49, veered right, and followed a wall of blockers down the far sideline. Had McClure not cut back to his left at the 15, he might have gone the distance. Two plays later, fullback Larry Krutko bulled in from the 3, carrying two Pitt defenders with him into the end zone.

Senior Whitey Mikanik (a Pitt transfer) managed to punch through the extra point that turned out to be the difference in the game. Neither team could do much offensively, Pitt gaining just 88 yards on the ground, 202 yards total, and accumulating only 11 first downs. West Virginia, too, found real estate tough to come by, the Mountaineers producing only 12 first downs and 222 total yards. Five West Virginia fumbles and an interception stymied the offense; miscues ended two West Virginia drives deep in Panther territory in the second quarter. The first happened at the Pitt 17, when Dave Rider fumbled, and the second took place in Pitt's end zone when Longfellow's pass from the Panther 18 was picked off by Fred Riddle.

The WVU defense was able to bail out the offense midway through the second quarter, when another turnover, this one by Ray Peterson at the Pitt 38, gave the Panthers great field position. Toncic marched Pitt all the way to the 1, but a tremendous goal-line stand by the Mountaineers turned away the Panthers. Also, twice Trimarki gambled for it on fourth and 1 on West Virginia's side of the 50, and both times he managed to get the first down. A third successful fourth-and-1 try late in the game was wiped out by penalty, forcing the Mountaineers to punt. On Pitt's final possession, when Toncic could only pass, West Virginia's Terry Fairbanks sacked the Panther quarterback three consecutive times to give the ball back to the Mountaineers. When the final seconds began winding down and Pitt could no longer stop the clock, the Mountaineer fired his musket and jubilant West Virginia fans swarmed onto the playing field. The victory snapped a three-game Panther winning streak over WVU that had dated back to 1954.

Embattled seniors Trimarki, Krutko and Ralph Anastasio – the players who were supposed to carry on the winning tradition begun by Wyant, Huff, Bosely, Marconi, Moss and company – had their ups and downs, but they responded with an outstanding effort in their last crack at the Panthers. Trimarki orchestrated West Virginia's ground attack, converting those two key fourth down plays, and giving the ball to Krutko, who bulldozed his way to a game-high 67 yards rushing and scoring WVU's lone touchdown. Anastasio did it all, running and catching the ball on offense, punting five times into a stiff wind to pin Pitt deep in its own territory and making several yard-saving tackles on defense.

The victory propelled the Mountaineers to a strong finish and a 7-2-1 record – the last winning season for Lewis, whose WVU team slipped to 3-7 in 1959 before his resignation in the spring of 1960. The Panthers recovered from the West Virginia loss to upset rival Penn State 14-13 two weeks later, before dropping their last regular season game to Miami 28-13 to finish the year with a disappointing 4-6 record. It was third-year coach John Michelosen's first losing season for the Panthers.

A "Pitt-iful" Performance

WVU	PITT
23	15
Oct. 17, 1959 Morgantown, W.Va.	

At the height of West Virginia's football resurgence in the mid-1950s, the Mountaineers had an opportunity to dramatically upgrade their football schedule. In exchange for Fordham, Marquette, Waynesburg, Washington & Lee and other similar teams the Mountaineers were beating up on a regular basis, Athletic Director Red Brown decided to schedule some of the top football programs in America – all of them on the road. In 1956, West Virginia made a trip out to Austin, Texas, to face the Longhorns, and the team also traveled down to Miami to play the nationally ranked Hurricanes. In 1957, it was out to Madison, Wis., to play the Badgers. In 1958, WVU made trips to Oklahoma and Indiana, and the 1959 schedule showed a late-season cross country trip to face USC in Los Angeles. Brown wanted reassurance from his football coach Art Lewis that scheduling these teams was the right thing to do. "Bring 'em on," Pappy said. "We'll play 'em anywhere, any time." By agreeing to the games, Lewis was actually tying his own noose. The terrific football players he had recruited in the early-to-mid-1950s – perhaps the finest collection of talent ever assembled at West Virginia University at one time – were all gone. By the end of the decade, the well of top-shelf talent had run dry. After three consecutive eight-win seasons in 1953, 1954 and 1955, including an appearance in the 1954 Sugar Bowl, West Virginia slipped to six victories in 1956, recovered to win seven games in 1957, and then posted a 4-5-1 record in 1958 – Lewis's first losing record in eight seasons at WVU.

The prospects for another losing campaign in 1959 were very real, with nearly two-thirds of the lettermen from the previous year having departed. The nucleus of the '59 team was made up of sophomores, primarily because of recruiting difficulties Lewis had encountered in 1955, 1956 and 1957. Of the group he brought to campus in 1955, only four remained in school throughout their careers – Dave Rider, Ray Peterson, Joe Wirth and Ben McComb. The rest left the program, either willingly or unwillingly.

West Virginia started the '59 season with a 27-7 loss at Maryland, and after two lack-luster wins against Richmond and George Washington, fell 7-0 to Boston University in a game marred by mistakes. In one instance, the Mountaineers had Boston backed up deep in its own territory, where the Terriers attempted a quick kick on third and long to try and change field position. But as BU's Henge Bradley went back to punt the ball, Boston was flagged for a penalty, and despite having ample warning of another quick kick, West Virginia let Bradley's second boot sail over its head for 63 yards, giving the Mountaineers poor field position.

Later, with the game still a scoreless tie and Boston facing a third and long situation, backup quarterback Jackie Farland was able to elude pressure and complete a 21-yard pass to Gene Prebola for a first down, setting up the winning touchdown. Lewis, disgusted with his team's play, decided to shake things up before the Pitt game in Morgantown. The coach assembled one unit comprised of 10 sophomores and one junior, and another group consisting of eleven regulars, and he told both squads that he wasn't going to pick a starting unit until after he observed them during pregame warm-ups.

On the other side of the field, 20th-ranked Pitt was coming in supremely confident, having won three of its first four games against one of the toughest schedules in college football. The Panthers were the beneficiary of a near-miraculous rally against UCLA, when quarterback Ivan Toncic threw three touchdown passes in the final six minutes of the game to defeat the Bruins 25-21. Pitt's other victories were against Duke and Marquette, with the lone blemish coming against a very strong Southern California team (a day after Soviet Premier Nikita S. Khrushchev visited Pittsburgh during his tour of the United States, coincidentally). The Panthers were touting three All-America candidates that year: Toncic, tackle Bill Lindner and tight end Mike Ditka, whose 11 catches heading into the West Virginia game included four touchdowns. On paper, the game was a mismatch.

Lewis decided to go on a hunch and play his sophomores at the start of the game, but that led to an early Pitt touchdown when India-born guard Norton Seaman broke through the line and blocked Curt Harmon's punt, enabling teammate Dick Mills to scoop up the football and run it in from the 6. Lewis went back to his regulars, and quarterback Danny Williams led a drive into Pitt territory before pinning the Panthers at their own 1 with a perfectly placed pooch kick. West Virginia's defense forced a Pitt punt, which Peterson returned to the Panther 34. Williams then hit John Marra for 10 yards, threw another pass to Peterson for seven yards, and a Bob Benke run got the ball to the Pitt 12. From there, Williams hooked up with Marra for a touchdown pass, and Johnny Thackston's conversion tied the game at seven. The defense came up with a big play on Pitt's next possession when Glenn Bowman got to Toncic, hitting his arm as he was attempting to throw the ball, and his wobbly pass landed in the arms of West Virginia guard Bill Lopasky.

Lopasky hauled the ball in at the 42 and ran 24 yards to the Pitt 18, where Dick Mills caught him from behind with just 54 seconds left in the half. A short Williams pass got the ball to the 14, where Thackston kicked a 30-yard field goal to give the Mountaineers a 10-7 halftime lead. West Virginia took control of the game on its opening possession of the second half, driving 80 yards in 14 plays. Williams handled the option flawlessly with pitches to Peterson and Marra before finding Peterson out in the flat for a 17-yard pass to midfield. Another Williams pass to Marra for 26 yards got the ball to the Pitt 26, and three plays after that, Williams ran an option keeper for first down yardage to the 12. Williams later sneaked in from the 1, giving the Mountaineers a 10-point lead. Pitt answered early in the fourth quarter when Andy Sepsi scored from the 2 – Pitt's 75-yard drive coming mostly on the ground, with runs by Fred Cox, Curt Plowman and Sepsi. On the conversion, Pitt faked the kick and Toncic rolled out to hit Steve Jastrzembski for two points, reducing West Virginia's lead to 17-15.

The Mountaineers couldn't hold on to the ball and had to kick it away with 2:04

remaining and Pitt taking over at its own 17. It was on Pitt's side of the 50 that Point Pleasant's Dick Herrig made the play of the game, intercepting Toncic's pass at the 30 and running it into the end zone for the clinching score. Another interception, this one by Peterson, put the game on ice. When Peterson got up after his pick, he looked over to Ditka (Toncic's target on the play) and said, "It's all over, big boy."

"Ditka slugged him," laughed Eddie Barrett.

Toncic, who came into the game with seven touchdown passes and was the hero in Pitt's victory over West Virginia in 1958, had a miserable day – he completed just six-of-14 passes for 35 yards, with five interceptions. Williams was much more effective in wet conditions, completing 11 of his 19 aerials for 123 yards and a touchdown. Pitt's Sepsi led all rushers with 75 yards on seven carries, but West Virginia outgained Pitt 260-237. Both teams were stunned by the outcome, and when the coaches met at midfield, briefly interrupting Lewis's victory ride to the locker room, Pitt's John Michelosen shook Lewis's hand and congratulated him on a great win. One of Pitt's assistant coaches later remarked that West Virginia had only one player on its roster (Lopasky) good enough to make Pitt's second string that year. It was the first time the Panthers had lost a football game to West Virginia in Morgantown.

For Danny Williams, it was easily the best performance of his career, earning him a spot on the national "Backfield of the Week." West Virginia's three touchdowns equaled the total number of TDs the team had scored coming into the game, and it gave Lewis a fourth victory against Pitt. It was just the 13th time West Virginia had defeated Pitt in school history. "The boys really gave it all they had," the coach said afterward. "The sophomores are growing up. They really helped us."

Pitt publicist Beano Cook didn't mince words when he analyzed the team's poor performance in his recap the following Monday. "West Virginia did beat the 'H' out of Pitt and there is no reason to start making excuses," he wrote. "The Mountaineers deserved to win. They outcharged, outhustled and outplayed Pitt for nearly the entire game.

"Naturally Pitt fans can replay the game for the next few weeks, but West Virginia had more right to edge the Panthers than Pitt did defeating UCLA.

"But that game is over. Art Lewis did a great job and deserves a lot of credit. He took a squad, which was thin on material, and won. That's football."

"Beano was crazy as hell," recalled Dick Hudson, who covered the Mountaineers for the Charleston *Daily Mail*. "What was funny was back in those days Beano used to write these things that were derogatory toward the Pitt coaches. If he would have worked at West Virginia and done that they would have hung him."

Cook was easily the most outspoken publicist in college sports, which proved helpful when he became the top public relations man at ABC and later found a spot on the air as a college football commentator. Cook once tried to pose Dr. Jonas Salk (inventor of the polio vaccine) with Pitt All-American basketball player Don Hennon for a poster. The title Beano wanted to use? America's Great Shot-Makers. Not only was Cook able to get his stuff published in the far-away daily newspapers and weeklies that were too small to cover the Panthers on a regular basis, but his copy was also being picked up by some of the biggest newspapers in the country. He was successful because he was such an outstanding writer, he wasn't afraid to take on controversial topics or criticize his superiors, and because his work was usually funny. Once, Cook wrote a stinging editorial criticizing Frank Carver's scheduling practices in basketball, maintaining that Pitt's athletic director (and his boss) wasn't giving Panther basketball coach Bob Timmons a fair shake. Carver, once a PR man himself, understood the business and would frequently defend Cook when Pitt's coaches came into his office to complain about him. "Carver told the coaches, 'If you guys wanted to win as bad as Beano does, we wouldn't be in the shape we're in,'" laughed Eddie Barrett.

COOK WAS EASILY THE MOST OUTSPOKEN PUBLICIST IN COLLEGE SPORTS.

Hudson recalled that Cook also ran a pretty good media pool in the press box before games. "Beano used to have some kind of lottery all of the time," Hudson said. "By the time the game started, he was going around collecting dollars from each of us and then having us put on a piece of paper the total score of the game. The NCAA would raise hell now if that happened."

Many years later, Cook achieved cult status with some Mountaineer fans when he picked West Virginia to win the national championship in 1988, mainly on the basis of the weak schedule WVU was facing that season. Cook got a lot of mileage out of his pick when it nearly came true, especially when he later predicted that Notre Dame quarterback Ron Powlus would win two Heisman trophies and he didn't even win one.

Art Lewis was hopeful that the '59 Pitt victory would reinvigorate his football program, but it didn't. Syracuse clobbered the Mountaineers 44-0 the following week, setting in motion a five-game slide that would eventually cost Lewis his job. Following a depressing 20-14 loss to The Citadel in front of fewer than 10,000 fans at Mountaineer Field, the Athletic Council voted unanimously to recommend that University President

Elvis Stahr fire Lewis. *Dominion-News* editor Bill Hart found out about the secret vote at a Christmas party and called his reporter Mickey Furfari, who was out in California covering the basketball team's appearance in the Los Angeles Classic. Stahr was also in California on the trip.

"Bill called me early in the morning and he said, 'Mickey, get ahold of the president and ask him when he's going to act on the council's unanimous recommendation to dismiss Pappy Lewis as head football coach.' I said, 'I'll do that Mr. Hart and I will get back to you.'"

Furfari went down to the hotel lobby and, as his luck would have it, he ran right into Stahr before he could enter the elevator. "I said, 'Dr. Stahr, when are you going to take action on the athletic council's unanimous recommendation to change football coaches?' He said, 'Uh, uh, uh I'm going to do that when I get back,'" Furfari recalled.

Mickey was able to get an exclusive story, beating the rival *Fairmont Times*, whose editor Bill Evans was a member of the Athletic Council and knew of the decision but was unable to report it. When the basketball team returned from California, a horde of reporters was waiting at the Pittsburgh airport to talk to Stahr, but he managed to avoid them. A week later, Stahr went on statewide radio and made a 10-minute address to proclaim that he was rejecting the athletic council's recommendation to fire Lewis and was retaining the embattled coach "by the skin of his teeth."

Lewis, realizing his untenable situation, remained the coach until the start of spring football practice, when he made the announcement that he was stepping down to take a scouting job with the Pittsburgh Steelers. Lewis made this choice to protect his assistants, knowing the school couldn't undertake a protracted coaching search so late in the school year. Longtime assistant coach Gene Corum was hired as Lewis's replacement.

Pitt's classy AD Frank Carver remarked that Lewis had added a lot to college football in the region. "We are genuinely sorry that Art came to the conclusion that he could no longer stay in Morgantown," Carver told *Pittsburgh Press* sports editor Chester L. Smith. "Everybody knows they grew into one of our toughest opponents during the 10 years Lewis coached them, and we're still shivering out here when we remember the shocker they hung on us last fall. It was our biggest upset of the season – many seasons for that matter.

"It's good for football in our section when West Virginia is strong and the same thing can, of course, be said for Penn State," he continued. "There have been periods when we were up and both the Mountaineers and the Lions were down and the game in this district was the loser by that fact. Nowadays, when we beat either one of them we think we've accomplished something to be proud of. I hope the situation never changes, and Art Lewis was one of the men who helped bring it about."

Pappy's 10-year tenure was the most successful in school history up to that point. He led the program out of the Waynesburg-Otterbein era and into the ranks of big-time college football. He was nationally recognized as one of college football's top recruiters, with one national news magazine even following him around for a week on the recruiting trail. In addition to his four victories over Pitt, Lewis also defeated Penn State three times, and he was the first coach in school history to get the Mountaineers into the national rankings. The first sellout in Mountaineer Field history, in 1954, also occurred under Lewis's watch.

Lewis had his faults, to be sure, but he was often able to overcome most of them with his great sense of humor. Such was the case in Los Angeles in 1959, after watching USC completely dismantle his outmanned Mountaineer team. After the game, sportswriters tepidly approached Lewis in the locker room, looking to get a couple quotes from the losing coach. Earlier that year, Ohio State coach Woody Hayes famously got into an altercation with a Los Angeles reporter when the reporter tried to enter the team locker room to talk to Hayes's players. Lewis, recalling the Hayes incident, scanned the room and after a long pause, boomed out in a voice loud enough to be heard down the hall, "Which one of you guys slugged my friend, Woody Hayes?"

The room erupted in laughter, and when Lewis was finished, everyone left with a favorable impression of the West Virginia coach. Most West Virginians felt the same way about him.

Three years later, in 1962, Lewis died in a Pittsburgh hospital following complications from a heart attack. Two months prior to his death, Lewis gave a revealing interview to *Charleston Gazette* sports editor Shorty Hardman. Pappy touched on his 10-year coaching tenure, recalling how he became West Virginia's coach in 1950 while working as an assistant at Mississippi State. He said he met with a WVU group in Gauley Bridge to talk about the job, and they had wound up making him an offer on the spot.

Lewis also reflected on some of the difficult times he had during his final two seasons in 1958 and 1959, when many of the fans turned on him, hanging him in effigy time and again. "They put me up there so much I had to pay a night watchman 50 cents a head to cut me down in the early morning before the students got out of bed," Lewis joked.

As for the athletic council's recommendation to fire him after the 1959 season, Lewis thought the process was mishandled and wondered why Red Brown didn't intervene to defend him. Despite that rough period in his life, Lewis said he held no grudges for the way he was treated at WVU. "I made an awful lot of friends in West Virginia," Lewis said, "and I have always had a feeling I will come back here someday to do something, even if it isn't in athletics."

Sadly, Lewis never got the chance.

The Garbage Game

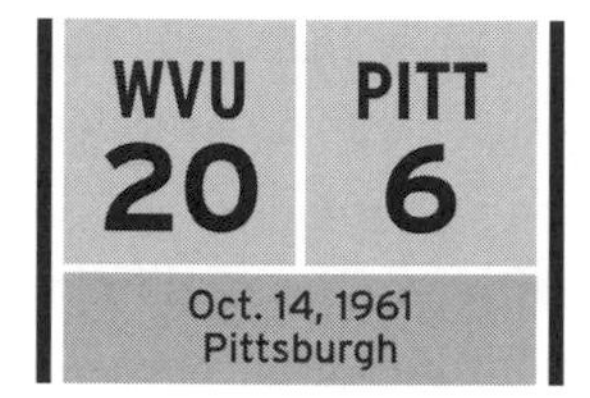

Eddie Barrett, West Virginia's hard-working and well-liked sports information director, was at Frank Gustine's restaurant in the Oakland section of Pittsburgh to make a speech promoting the WVU-Pitt football game. Before he began, one of the sportswriters attending the luncheon walked up to Barrett's table and told him about a story that had appeared in the Pitt student newspaper that morning. The gist of it was that one of the Panther players had made a derogatory remark about the West Virginia team. When Barrett was finished with his talk, he walked over to the Cathedral of Learning, where *The Pitt News* was located. He asked someone at the front desk if they could spare six copies, because his kid brother was in the paper that day (a white lie, of course). When he began scanning the sports page, his eyes grew as big as saucers. *Did he really say that?*

The Pitt player was John Kuprok, a senior end from Duquesne, Pa., who did put down the Mountaineers in a roundabout way. Jim O'Brien, today a popular local sports author, was editor of *The Pitt News* at the time and was traveling with the Panthers to their game down in Miami. On the bus ride back to the airport, O'Brien overheard a conversation among some players who were discussing the scores of that afternoon's other college football games. When someone mentioned the West Virginia-Richmond score, a 35-26 WVU loss, one of the players remarked that the Mountaineers could still surprise some people, because they were rebuilding. That's when Kuprok replied, "Yeah, they're rebuilding with Western Pennsylvania garbage." Kuprok had no idea his comment would end up in the newspaper on Monday morning.

Barrett put the newspapers in his attaché case, keeping them concealed for the rest of the week and not mentioning them to anyone. "I was so excited I couldn't sleep, but I also didn't want to let it out because it could have boomeranged," Barrett recalled. "After the Friday afternoon warm-up practice in Pittsburgh, I called [West Virginia coach] Gene Corum aside and I showed them to him."

Barrett pulled out the newspaper and gave it to Corum, and a smile formed on the coach's face as he began reading. Corum then grabbed assistant coach Russ Crane and told him to have a look. "Whoa, ammo!" was Crane's response, according to Barrett. Corum had the newspaper article plastered throughout the locker room Saturday morning before the game, and then he read Kuprok's "garbage" quote to the team one more time before they took the field.

For the Western Pa guys in the locker room that afternoon – Steve Berzansky (Portage), Pete Goimarac and Keith Melenyzer (Charleroi), Gene Heeter (Windber), Ken Herock (Munhall), Joe Kiselica (Tarentum), Larry Niedzalkoski (Greensburg), Bill Schillings (Isabella) and Jerry Yost (Rogersville) – it was like pouring gas on an open flame.

"They always said we got the leftovers and that was always upsetting to the guys from Western Pa.," said Herock. "I remember when that article came out because [Corum] talked about it, but I was never garbage!"

West Virginia coaches never needed much to get their players excited for Pitt, but in this instance a little boost was in order, because the Mountaineers were in the midst of one of their worst periods in school history. The team lost seven games in 1959, went winless in 1960 and dropped its first three games of the '61 season to Richmond, Vanderbilt and Syracuse. The school's 18-game winless streak was finally snapped on October 7, 1961, when West Virginia blew out Virginia Tech, 28-0. The four touchdowns scored against the Hokies were two fewer than the team had scored for the entire 1960 season. Corum, West Virginia's first-year coach in 1960, made the decision to play mostly sophomores. "I wrote about first downs instead of touchdowns that year," Barrett quipped.

Gene Corum was the clear choice to replace Art Lewis when Lewis abruptly announced his resignation just days before the start of spring practice in 1960. Corum had spent 10 years as Lewis's top assistant coach, working with the ends for the vast majority of that time. After starring at Huntington High, he played two seasons at West Virginia in 1940–41 before his playing career was interrupted by World War II. When he returned from military service at the conclusion of the war, Corum played two more years for the Mountaineers, in 1946-47. During that time, he was involved in one of the school's most memorable victories, a 17-2 trouncing at Pitt in 1947 that ended the Mountaineers' 19-year losing streak to the Panthers. Corum played a key role in that victory when he pounced on a Pitt fumble in the snow near the goal line, both teams believing that he had scored a touchdown. But when the players got up and the snow was cleared, it was discovered that he had landed on the ball at the 5 yard line.

After graduation, Corum coached two seasons at nearby Point Marion (Pa.) High School before joining Lewis's West Virginia staff in 1950, at age 29. In addition to earning two degrees and raising a young family, he also found time to serve two terms as a member of Morgantown's City Council, chairing the committee that supervised the construction of the city's municipal swimming pool. Corum's easygoing demeanor (his nickname was "Gentleman Gene") and his great rapport with West Virginia high school coaches made him a popular member of Pappy's coaching staff. After spending two days as the team's acting coach, Corum was unanimously selected to lead the football program on April 20, 1960, when University president Elvis J. Stahr got enthusiastic approval from the Athletic Council.

After his hiring, Corum immediately attempted to chart a different course from his predecessor – both in his approach and personal manner. Tactically, the biggest criticism of Lewis's WVU teams was their lack of sophistication on offense. For most of Lewis's tenure, West Virginia struggled in both attempting and defending passes. Corum soon addressed both topics. "We need a pass defense, and we need a pass offense," Corum said. "You just don't develop pass defenses in a day. It takes hard work and it takes a lot of know-how."

Corum painted a very pessimistic picture, admitting that it might take a couple of years before his program could really take off because of a lack of experienced players. He also noted a drop off in high school talent in the state. "We've got plenty of good college football players on our squad," Corum said. "But we do not have the truly great ones like we did get here for a while – fellows like Gene Lamone, Sam Huff, Bruce Bosley, Joe Nicely, Joe Marconi, Fred Wyant, Bobby Moss and a few others.

CORUM PAINTED A VERY PESSIMISTIC PICTURE.

"You've got to have two or three sprinkled around to make full use of those who level off at just plain good," he added.

Then again, even the realistic Corum could have hardly imagined what was in store for him in the fall of 1960: His team failed to win a single game. Corum, in 1962, recalled spending some lonely afternoons at Mountaineer Field during WVU's only winless campaign in school history. (West Virginia tied Richmond and Boston University to finish the year 0-8-2.) "A fellow called me from Clarksburg one Friday night and asked me what time our game started the next day," Corum joked. "I said, 'I don't know, what time can you get here?'"

"When you get there obviously you think you are going to have a good team, but I didn't have any idea," said Herock. "We were isolated. We weren't on the varsity [in 1960] and we didn't even know what the varsity was. I didn't expect our team to be that bad when I was a sophomore, but we played mostly all of the young kids, and as a result we weren't that good."

Tom Woodeshick, later an all-pro fullback with the Philadelphia Eagles, was a sophomore on the 1960 team, and he too remembered the talent being very sparse that season. "The only great players we had my first year were on the other side of the line of scrimmage against us in the alumni game [West Virginia played an annual varsity-alumni football game each spring in those days]," recalled Woodeshick. "I'm looking across the line of scrimmage in the spring of my freshman year and I'm saying to myself, 'Wait a minute, I've got Sam Huff in the middle and Chuck Howley on the outside.'

"Even though he was a fullback for the Bears, probably the toughest linebacker of them all was Joe Marconi," Woodeshick continued. "The other two are basically laughing their way through it. Every time I got down in my three-point stance Huff would say, 'Hey Woodeshick, are you coming through here?' I'll tell you what, I had one eye on Sam all of the time. But the guy who really got me was Marconi. Oh man, he was hell."

Things weren't looking much better for the Mountaineers at the start of the 1961 season. Donnie Young, then a 190-pound high school guard from Clendenin, came up to Morgantown to watch the Richmond loss. Young grew up wanting to play for the Mountaineers but wasn't sure if he could. "Richmond kicked the crap out of us," Young laughed. "I said to myself, I can play here."

Pitt wasn't exactly setting the world on fire either. The Panthers had some success in the mid-1950s under John Michelosen, going to the Sugar Bowl in 1955 and playing in the Gator Bowl in 1956, but tough schedules led to average seasons for the Panthers in 1958, 1959 and 1960. In 1958, Pitt started the year with consecutive wins over UCLA, Holy Cross and Minnesota before falling to Michigan State. The Panthers also lost games that season to Syracuse, Nebraska and Penn State. In 1959, Pitt's four losses were to USC, West Virginia, TCU and national champion Syracuse. In 1960, Pitt fell to UCLA, Oklahoma and Penn State. Had the schedule been friendlier, Pitt's records during those seasons would certainly have been much, much better.

At the time of the West Virginia game in 1961, the Panthers were 1-2, with a season-opening victory over Miami that preceded a pair of losses to Baylor and Washington.

The Panthers were alternating quarterbacks, with flashy sophomore Paul Martha sharing time with Jim Traficant and Sam Colella. Michelosen had some issues to deal with on that team, particularly with Traficant, who once notoriously remarked, "I made two mistakes in my life – the first one was coming to Pitt, and the second one was staying." Traficant, from Youngstown, Ohio, later became a U.S. congressman, serving from 1985–2002 before being indicted for accepting bribes, filing false tax returns and racketeering.

West Virginia, meanwhile, was finally having some success throwing the football. Not since Dick Longfellow finished sixth in the country in passing in 1958 did the Mountaineers have a quarterback really capable of airing out the football. Fred "Colt 45" Colvard wasn't the second coming of Y.A. Tittle, but he was a pretty good athlete, voted the state player of the year at Logan High in 1959, and his 133 yards passing in the Virginia Tech win doubled what West Virginia was able to accomplish through the air in its first three games of the season. A double-slot back formation the Mountaineers were using undoubtedly helped with the passing game. West Virginia was also doing a better job of defending the pass (a bugaboo dating all the way back to the Georgia Tech loss in the 1954 Sugar Bowl) by intercepting seven passes, including one returned by Jim "Shorty" Moss for a touchdown against Syracuse.

At the game's outset, West Virginia showed that it meant business against Pitt, marching 74 yards in 17 plays to reach the end zone on its opening possession. West Virginia's score came as a result of Woodeshick's fumble at the 2, which was recovered for a touchdown by end Paul Gray. West Virginia, using a two-platoon system, alternated quarterbacks Colvard and Dale Evans on the drive, with the entire backfield taking turns carrying the football. The big play to set up the score was a 19-yard run by fullback Glenn Holton. The Panthers got to within 1 point with 2:30 remaining in the first half, when Trafficant connected on a pair of passes before taking it in from the 1 himself. But Trafficant's two-point conversion pass failed, giving West Virginia a 7-6 lead that held through halftime.

West Virginia took control of the game in the third quarter. Two Roger Holdinsky scores – one a 30-yard pass from Colvard and the other a 31-yard sweep around the right end – boosted West Virginia's lead to 20-6. Holdinsky was the school record holder in the 220-yard dash and the triple jump – then referred to as the "hop, step and jump" – and the Moundsville native became the first West Virginia player to score multiple touchdowns against the Panthers since Nick Nardacci did it in 1923.

West Virginia could have had a couple more scores if not for some costly mistakes. Moss's 55-yard punt return for a touchdown was called back because of a clipping penalty, and two fourth quarter fumbles killed drives in Pitt territory. Colvard lost the ball to Pitt's Ed Clark at the Pitt 12, and Rick Leeson recovered Eli Kosanovich's fumble at the Pitt 38. During the scrum to retrieve Kosanovich's fumble, Colvard was hit above his left eye, requiring five stitches to shut the gash. He had to be helped off the field. Later, in the locker room, a still-woozy Colvard had to ask a teammate what the final score was. In the second quarter, WVU blew an opportunity to score right before Pitt's only TD, when Glenn Bennett missed a field goal try from the Panther 10. Then, in the third quarter, West Virginia was stopped on fourth and inches at the Panther goal line.

All afternoon, West Virginia chose to run right at Kuprok on sweeps, sometimes sending as many as four or five players at him. Late in the game, when Kuprok was slow to get up after another Mountaineer running play, Kosanovich stood over him and couldn't resist saying something any longer. "Hey, Kuprok, if we're garbage then what are you guys?" Kosanovich asked.

"[Western Pa. players] had a certain arrogance about them with their football prowess, and rightfully so," said Woodeshick. "But you didn't have to wear it on your shirtsleeve."

West Virginia completely dominated the game. The Mountaineers had sizable advantages in first downs (17-9), rushing yards (196-104), total yards (306-148) and total plays (70-55). Afterward, West Virginia players freely joked about Kuprok's garbage quote. Halfback Jim Procopio chanted, "We are the garbage boys – you can't beat the garbage men!" Fairmont guard Bob DeLorenzo said he couldn't wait to get to church on Sunday morning. He had been taking a terrible ribbing about the team's recent struggles, and he wanted to see what they had to say now. "I am going to the seven, eight, nine and 10 o'clock mass so I can see them all," he yelled.

Corum readily admitted that O'Brien's column helped fire his team up. "It's hard to put your finger on the degree to which psychology helps," said Corum after the game, "but there is no question these boys were ready to play."

In the losing locker room, Pittsburgh reporter Myron Cope asked Kuprok if he had really made the garbage remark. "Well, yes I did," Kuprok complained, "but I didn't think the so-and-so would put it in the paper!"

Michelosen, as was customary for the time, was hanged in effigy on the Pitt campus – a dummy of his likeness could be seen dangling from a flagpole, with a sign attached to it that read "Take a hike, Mike." A similar dummy had asked him to take a hike following Pitt's loss to West Virginia in 1959. The Pitt coach was noticeably disappointed with the way his team had performed against the Mountaineers, offering some prophetic words after the game. "I don't know how we'll do the rest of the season," he said. "But we better improve or it will be worse." It did get worse. Pitt lost 20-6 to UCLA and also dropped games to Syracuse, Notre Dame and Penn State to finish the season with a 3-7 record.

West Virginia, too, came back to earth the following week by losing to Boston University 12-6 and then completing the year with a 4-6 record – its fourth straight losing season. However, one of those four wins came at Army, 7-3, when Glenn Holton's 121 yards was more than the entire Army team gained on the ground. Dick Hudson recalled in 2011 the difficult circumstances West Virginia had to overcome to defeat the Black Knights that afternoon. "Army had their student body real close to the field, and some of the coaches called Gene [Corum] and said if they get real close to you and start yelling, call timeout and tell them you're not playing again until those people shut up," said Hudson. "Well, Gene did that. The officials made them shut up because they were really almost out on the field.

"Up in the press box there was a bunch of retired generals, and they thought they were all kings," Hudson continued. "When they made Army shut up, those generals started raising hell and Mickey Furfari turned around and just gave it to them. [Former Army coach Earl Blaik] was sitting there with them, and he said that was the first time those generals had been dressed down like that since they were cadets."

Bolstered by the great Army victory, the pieces were finally in place for a remarkable comeback in 1962. Junior Jerry Yost replaced Colvard at quarterback (Colvard transferred to Florida State to play baseball), and Yost teamed with ends Gene Heeter and Ken Herock to give the Mountaineers a formidable passing attack that led to an outstanding 8-2 record, including a memorable 17-6 victory at Syracuse to end the season. That was the game when Woodeshick signed a professional contract with the Buffalo Bills underneath the goal post at Archbold Stadium. Later, Woodeshick also signed with the Philadelphia Eagles, making him one of the few players to ever sign contracts with two different professional teams at the same time. Woodeshick managed to get his initial contract with the Bills voided because he signed it before Buffalo had drafted him, and they did not own his rights. Woodeshick went on to have an outstanding professional career with the Philadelphia Eagles, becoming one of the NFL's top fullbacks by the late 1960s.

As for O'Brien, he was still going after the "garbage men" on his typewriter in 1962. While trying to make amends for his '61 column, he wrote another story entitled "Dump the Garbage Men" leading into the WVU-Pitt game. Corum put that one up on the bulletin board, too, and West Virginia whipped the Panthers a second time, 15-8. That victory was just the third time in more than 40 years that the Mountaineers were able to win back-to-back games against the Panthers.

And both were undoubtedly aided by an eager young sports reporter.

The Battle of the Brothers

PITT	WVU
13	10
Oct. 19, 1963 Morgantown, W.Va.	

Red Brown did just about everything he could think of to persuade CBS to televise the Mountaineers' 1963 football game against Pitt in Morgantown. West Virginia University's personable athletic director explained to the network that the state was celebrating its Centennial anniversary that fall, that a brand new press box would be completed in time for the start of the season and that the game would have a Hatfield-McCoy flavor, with brothers Paul and Richie Martha playing against each other.

Brown got the Panthers involved, too, by convincing them to take the *Gateway Clipper* riverboat (renamed the *SS Panther Trail* for the trip) to Morgantown, recalling the way the two teams used to travel when the rivalry first began before the turn of the century. Pitt's Frank Carver was a willing collaborator, agreeing to a plan that included a boat trip down the Monongahela River to Brownsville, Pa., where about 100 Panthers supporters would spend the night at the Summit Hotel, near Uniontown. The next day, the fans would resume their journey to Morgantown on a bus while the steamer continued to Star City, where the Panther football team would get off their buses and board the boat to complete their four-mile ride to Mountaineer Field.

When the boat pulled up to the Pleasant Street landing, a cavalcade of dignitaries (including West Virginia Gov. Wally Barron), a full brass band, and Paul's little brother Richie were there waiting to greet them with a CBS film crew capturing it all. The whole charade was concocted, of course, but CBS loved the idea and Red Brown had his TV game.

The Martha brothers, of Wilkinsburg, Pa., were an interesting contrast in ability, style and temperament. The handsome Paul was the family's natural athlete, whose gridiron exploits at Pitt had old-timers recalling the days of Marshall Goldberg and the great "Dream Backfield" of the late 1930s. Paul would achieve fame as a professional player for the Pittsburgh Steelers and then later fortune as a jet-setting attorney and professional sports executive. Richie, meanwhile, was the overlooked scrapper, "a 110-percenter" in the words of his Mountaineer teammate Jerry Yost. He was just the type of football player Gene Corum liked recruiting at West Virginia, the coach reasoning that he didn't have to waste a lot of his time motivating guys like Richie Martha, who always played with a big chip on his shoulder anyway. Richie was no slouch as a football player, though, leading Wilkinsburg High's three major sports teams to a combined 35-6 record during his senior year and being invited to play in the Big 33 football game. Richie just happened to be a few inches shorter than his big brother Paul, who chose to play his high school ball at the more prestigious Shadyside Academy.

A day before the Pitt game, Richie remarked that he had been waiting two years for the opportunity to get a crack at his famous big brother. "A chance to play against Paul was a big reason I came to West Virginia," the sophomore halfback told Mickey Furfari. Richie added that if he got the opportunity he would try and put a big lick on his brother. "I'd tackle him even harder than anyone else if I got the chance," he said. "We have been very close all of our lives, but I like to play football and I like to win."

To show equal support for their two sons, the Martha parents chose to split up during the game, the mother sitting with the West Virginia fans and the father sitting with the Pitt fans. High above them was a beautiful, brand new, three-tiered press box that stretched West Virginia's already thin finances to the limit. "We were broke paying for that press box," former Sports Information Director Eddie Barrett recalled. "It cost $160,000 and at that time that was an awful lot of money, which we didn't have."

Eleanor Lamb, Red Brown's assistant in charge of business affairs, concurred. "I remember sitting on my desk I had two or three stacks of invoices, and I would use priority as to which one I would pull off to send in for payment. It was that bad for a while." Things were so tight that Barrett literally had to beg Brown to buy him a couple of extra chairs to fill out his office when CBS announcers Red Barber, Johnny Lujack and Jim Simpson arrived in Morgantown for the Pitt game. "Because my office only had one chair for visitors, I persuaded Red to spend $100 for four used chairs so Red Barber and his crew could sit down when they arrived," laughed Barrett.

Barrett may have been excited to hob-knob with broadcasting royalty, but he wasn't too thrilled to promote their work. Asked by reporters which stations would be televising the game, Barrett answered evasively. "As you know," he told one West Virginia scribe, "our club isn't going too good these days, and if we are going to beat Pitt we need a lot of backing. We don't want the student body home in their easy chairs before the television." Barrett purposely kept TV information out of his game advances because he was not only concerned about attendance (or a lack thereof), but also about antagonizing Jack Fleming, whose game descriptions had become a fall ritual for Mountain State radio listeners.

Another ritual for Mountaineer football supporters was bracing for big-game disappointments, which at the time happened quite frequently, especially against Pitt. West Virginians have always taken their lumps harder than most, and no thrashing was more painful to watch than Roger Staubach's surgical dissection of West Virginia's secondary in the '63 opener against Navy. The Mountaineers were reasonably confident they could slow down Staubach, with Pete Goimarac, Bernie Carey, Milt Clegg, Glenn Holton, Tom Yeater and a handful of others returning from the 8-2 team of 1962 – as well as a highly regarded freshman class moving up to varsity. A sellout crowd (just the fourth in school history) was packed inside a freshly painted Mountaineer Field to cheer them on. "We left practice on Friday and stayed out at Mont Chateau at Cheat Lake, and then the next day we drove back before the game and, wow, the placed looked beautiful," remarked former athletic director Ed Pastilong, a backup quarterback on that team.

"They were painting the stadium at 11 o'clock. It was a beautiful day – that was what we said about it: A beautiful day, new press box and freshly painted stadium," laughed Barrett. "The only thing bad about it was the game."

By the end of the third quarter, Staubach was standing on the sideline, his afternoon finished after completing 17-of-22 passes for 171 yards on the way to a 51-7 Navy victory. Corum knew his linemen were too slow to catch Staubach, so he widened his ends to keep the quarterback from getting outside, and he brought his linebackers up to the line of scrimmage to help stop Navy's running game. "We contained his running, alright," said Corum, "but that made it impossible to stop his passing." After the game, a couple of fans stopped Red Brown as he walked to his car to ask him why in the world he would ever schedule a team as good as Navy to start the season. "Well, when I scheduled them, [Staubach] was just a freshman in high school," he sighed. Another blowout loss to Mel Renfro-led Oregon two weeks later further soured the mood of West Virginia football rooters.

Meanwhile, Pitt's mood was anything but sour. In 1962, Panther coach John Michelosen had successfully fought off the pitchforks and torches to keep his job when chancellor Edward Litchfield wanted the Panthers to play a more wide-open style. He now boasted of a superior team with 27 returning lettermen, including three fifth-year linemen who turned down pro offers to remain in college: tackles John Maczuzak and Ernie Borghetti, and guard Ed Adamchik. Junior center Marty Schottenheimer would also later make a name for himself in the pros; stocky quarterback Freddie Mazurek was an elusive runner and an accurate passer; and the backfield of Martha, Bill Bodle, Rick Leeson and Eric Crabtree gave Pitt its most explosive group of playmakers since the "Dream Backfield" of Goldberg, Stebbins and Chickerneo in the late 1930s. This Pitt team was also extremely intelligent: There were six players studying pre-med, 10 in dentistry, six in engineering and three in pre-law.

Three consecutive victories over West Coast teams UCLA, Washington and Cal gave the Panthers a No. 3 national ranking when the West Virginia game arrived on its schedule. Pitt had the nation's No. 2-ranked offense, averaging 416 yards per game, and was looking to avenge a pair of defeats to West Virginia in 1961 and 1962. The Panthers were two-touchdown favorites, despite eight of the prior 11 games between these two schools being upsets.

Speaking of upsets, some would consider African Americans Dick Leftridge and Roger Alford playing football games in the Southern Conference quite a shocker in the early 1960s. Southern Conference football was not integrated in 1962, when West Virginia University informed member schools that its football program was planning to start recruiting black athletes. That period was a particularly trying time for race relations in the country. Federal troops were needed to maintain order in Oxford, Miss., in 1962 when James Meredith became the first African American student to enroll at the University of Mississippi, and a year later, in 1963, Bull Connor infamously used fire hoses and dogs to disperse protesters (many of them children) in the streets of Birmingham, Alabama. Nineteen sixty three was also the year that Dr. Martin Luther King gave his famous "I Have a Dream" speech from the steps of the Lincoln Memorial in Washington, D.C.

THAT PERIOD WAS A PARTICULARLY TRYING TIME FOR RACE RELATIONS IN THE COUNTRY.

Morgantown, W.Va., didn't experience the racial tensions many bigger cities did at the time, but the university was a member of a conference comprised of southern schools, and there was some concern about sending an integrated football team to some of those places. "We were prepared for the worst," admitted Barrett. West Virginia was the northernmost school in the Southern Conference and the only one not located in a former confederate state (West Virginia was independent from Virginia and Union-aligned by the end of the Civil War, and George Washington University, in Washington, D.C., was also situated in a free territory). WVU had already primed the Southern Conference for change when sprinter Phil Edwards was added to the track team in 1961 and competed in meets that spring. Barrett recalled telling sportswriters throughout the region that integration was in the plans for the football program as well. "We said to them individually that this was coming and that we were actively recruiting black athletes at the time," he said. "There were no problems with the press in the Southern Conference or in West Virginia."

By the early 1960s – almost 10 years after the 1954 landmark United States Supreme Court case *Brown v. Board of Education* declared that state laws establishing separate public schools was unconstitutional – it was well beyond time for schools throughout the country to integrate their football programs, and West Virginia was desperately trying to do so. For years, Art Lewis and Gene Corum tried to keep the state from hemorrhaging its best black football players. Iowa and Purdue had developed a nice pipeline in West Virginia – the Boilermakers plucking Tom Bloom out of Weirton and Gene Donaldson from nearby Clarksburg – while Iowa was able to sign Weirton's Bob Jeter.

During the late 1950s, West Virginia's three immediate northeastern football rivals – Pitt, Penn State and Syracuse – were all fielding integrated football teams. Penn State had great success with black players Lenny Moore and Roosevelt Grier, and Syracuse coach Ben Schwartzwalder (a WVU graduate) had a string of terrific black running backs, starting with Jim Brown in the mid-1950s and continuing into the 1960s with Ernie Davis, Jim Nance and Floyd Little. Pitt's Bobby Grier made national headlines in 1956 when he became the first African American to play in the Sugar Bowl, although he wasn't the first to integrate Pitt football. That had happened in the late 1940s.

In 1960, Lewis and Corum thought they had their dilemma solved with Moorestown (N.J.) High standout linebacker Dave Robinson, but his mother refused to let her son play football in the South, so Robinson chose instead to play at Penn State. The next opportunity to break the color barrier came in 1961, when Hinton High's Dick Leftridge arrived on the scene as the state's top football prospect. The son of a railroader and one of 10 children, Leftridge had a rare combination of size (6-foot-2, 210 pounds), speed (clocked at 10.6 in the 100-yard dash) and power that enabled him to score 130 points in nine games, mostly on long touchdown runs. But Corum was fighting the losing trend of seeing great southern West Virginia players such as Charlie Cowan and Lionel Taylor migrate to the black colleges in the South – Cowan and Taylor both attended New

Mexico Highlands University. As for Leftridge, he was being hotly pursued by several schools, including Ohio State, which had already integrated.

A key point in Leftridge's recruitment came when two high-ranking emissaries from Gov. Barron's office went down to Hinton to meet with Leftridge and impress upon him the importance of remaining in-state. They reasoned that because he was so well known, his decision to attend West Virginia University could lead to other black athletes and students enrolling at WVU in the future. Simultaneously, Corum was recruiting Wintersville, Ohio, guard Roger Alford after finding out about him from Alford's high school coach Bob Kettlewell, once a teammate of Corum's at WVU. In addition to being a solid football player, Alford was an honor student who was the fourth member of his family to earn a football scholarship. Corum felt that Alford could help provide the support and companionship Leftridge would need at a school that had almost no minority students at the time. In fact, according to Barbara Ann Williams's 2004 account in *West Virginia University Alumni Magazine*, there were only five African American students on the entire campus at the time Leftridge and Alford arrived as freshmen in 1962.

Even six years later, in 1968, not much had really changed socially at WVU for African American students. Black students were unable to join fraternities and sororities, and those wishing to do so, had to go to Pitt to join them. There were no public places in Morgantown for black students to get haircuts, listen to music or enjoy the experiences that they were used to, particularly those who came from the bigger northeastern cities. "There was hardly any social life," recalled John Mallory, a New Jersey native. "In those days there were maybe 100 black students in the university, and out of those 100, there were only about 12 of those students who were athletes. There were no fraternities for us. During rush they used to bang on our door, and when we would come to the door they would say, 'Oh, we have the wrong room.' We knew what that was about. I don't ever recall in my first years there whether there was a black professor on campus [the first known African American faculty member was Victorine Louistall, who joined the faculty in 1966]. And there were not that many black women, maybe one or two at the time."

Mallory recalled his first meeting with Coach Jim Carlen and his immediate concern that all of Carlen's coaches were from the South and had thick southern accents. But they made it clear to him right away that race would have no bearing on their decision-making. Carlen was concerned about their continuing difficulty in recruiting black players to West Virginia, and he asked Mallory what the school could do to improve the situation. "I told him he had to go out and get black women," Mallory said. "When you bring kids on campus, they see the situation. If they can't have dates and be normal, they're going to go other places where they can. They're going to go to the Big Ten; they're going to go to Penn State or Syracuse where they're treated fairly well.

"The way I understand it, Carlen went to the administration and they made a great effort of getting more minority students into college here, particularly females."

Yet in 1962, when Leftridge and Alford first arrived on campus, none of this was on anyone's radar screen. Most of the concern revolved around how WVU alums and other schools in the Southern Conference would react to West Virginia fielding integrated teams. "There were two alums who told us they would never go to another game," Eddie Barrett recalled. "We thought there was going to be this big outcry, and it turned out those were the only two people that felt that way."

Although the Southern Conference was not close to being on par athletically with the ACC, the SEC or other major conferences in the region, the individual schools soon realized that, in addition to being morally right, integration was also necessary to maintain some semblance of competitiveness. Soon, George Washington and other Southern Conference schools began admitting black athletes. According to Martin Pushkin, then Virginia Tech's track coach, coach Jerry Claiborne was looking for a way to introduce black players into the football program, and he thought the best way to do it was by initiating the process in another sport. Claiborne encouraged Pushkin, a WVU graduate, to begin the integration process in track. In 1967, Pushkin was able to recruit sprinter Jerry Gaines from Virginia Beach, and that eventually opened the door for black athletes to participate in other sports at Tech. It wasn't too long afterward that all of the Southern Conference sports programs were fully integrated.

"We're such a small state, and if you look at the evolution of *Brown v. Board of Education* and our transition, it was not as traumatic and controversial as the rest of the country – and that spoke loudly to the people of West Virginia," said Dr. Dana Brooks, professor and Dean of West Virginia's College of Physical Activity and Sports Sciences, and the author of several books on racism in sports. "Have we come a long way? Absolutely. Are we making progress? Absolutely. Do we have work to do? Absolutely."

Leftridge was in the starting lineup at fullback when the Mountaineers squared off against Pitt in 1963, while Alford was a backup right guard playing behind starter Steve Kush. In the early 1960s, NCAA rules prohibited free substituting, which meant players were required to play both ways. Two offensive players were usually released of their defensive duties, typically the quarterback and another offensive back, and when substitutions were made it entailed changing entire units. "The offensive guard flipped around and played defensive guard," recalled Donnie Young, a former Mountaineer coach and a backup guard that year. "The game was much more in the hands of the players back then. The backups would usually play in the second quarter. That's why deep teams like Penn State typically pulled away in the latter stages of the game."

The day was sunny and unusually warm (76 degrees) when West Virginia's Chuck Kinder placed the football on the tee to kick off to the Panthers. Martha fumbled Kinder's kick, but Mazurek was there to pick up the ball at the 7 and return it to the 22. On his second touch, after a Leeson 34-yard run and a pair of keepers by Mazurek got the ball to the West Virginia 17, Martha fumbled it again. This time Holton was there to recover it for West Virginia.

Pitt took the lead on its next possession, though, marching 71 yards in 12 plays, the two biggest plays being Mazurek passes of 19 yards to Bill Bodle and 17 yards to Leeson. The quarterback capped the drive by flipping a three-yard touchdown pass to end Joe Kuzneski, who managed to get between Holton and Leftridge at the goal line. Leeson's kick made it 7-0 Panthers. West Virginia appeared to tie the game midway through the second quarter when Bill Fleming returned a Pitt punt 70 yards for a touchdown, but a clipping penalty was called on sophomore Bob Dunlevy at the 12-yard line while Fleming was entering the end zone. The Mountaineers claimed that the infraction occurred after Fleming crossed the goal line, but to no avail. The ball was placed back at the 27, and West Virginia eventually had to settle for a 31-yard Kinder field goal.

The Mountaineers had a great opportunity to take a 10-7 lead on their opening possession of the second half, driving from their own 31 to the Pitt 2. On a first and goal play, though, Leftridge bobbled Yost's handoff and the ball was recovered by Pitt's Charles Ahlborn in front of the goal line. "I never really got a good grip on the ball, sort of had it up under my arm too far," said Leftridge after the game. Each team possessed the ball twice in the third quarter before West Virginia forced Pitt to punt from its own end zone early in the fourth quarter. The Mountaineers took over at the Panther 40 and used Yost passes of 22 yards to Yeater and 13 to Holton to get to the Pitt 4. Three plays later, Yost found Leftridge open in the end zone for a 5-yard TD. Kinder's kick gave the Mountaineers a 10-7 lead and a big opportunity for them to record a major upset with just 8:20 remaining in the game.

Pitt took over at its own 20 and got to the 27, where on third down it appeared that the Mountaineers had forced a Panther punt, with Homer Criddle stopping Leeson short of the sticks. But Ken Woodeshick was flagged for lining up offside, giving Pitt a first down at the 32 with 7:40 left. Two Mazurek passes to Leeson of 16 and 7 yards set up the biggest play of the game – a reverse to Paul Martha, who was able to outrun West Virginia's defense for a 46-yard touchdown. Pitt assistant coach Steve Petro called the play from the press box. "Steve had been hounding us to call it," recalled longtime Pitt assistant coach Bimbo Cecconi in the book *Tales from the Pitt Panthers*. "It was a play we had used before, but maybe not in that game. The ball went to Bill Bodle, who gave it to Paul Martha, and Martha came back to the right and took it in." Until that carry, Martha had just 12 yards rushing. Leeson's kick for the extra point failed.

After an 11-yard Yost pass to end Bill Sullivan gave the Mountaineers a first down at the 38, Yost's second throw was intercepted by Bob Roeder at the Pitt 42. Had Yost been able to get more loft on it, he had Holton free at the Panther 35. "I could almost feel that ball just when he intercepted it," said Holton.

Taking over at midfield, Pitt was able to run the remaining 4:19 off the clock. "I've said right along that you can't beat experience, and Pitt had nine seniors on the first unit," said Corum. "We had four sophomores and they didn't have any." Leeson led all ball carriers with 82 yards on 11 carries, while Martha added 68 yards on 10 totes to help the Panthers accumulate 193 yards on the ground. Mazurek was seven of nine through the air for 72 yards and a touchdown. Yost, who failed to complete a single pass in the first half, finished the game seven of 14 for 91 yards and a touchdown. Leftridge was WVU's top rusher, with 56 yards on 11 carries, though the Mountaineers managed just 13 first downs and 179 total yards. "We had the game and let it get away," Corum said. "Our boys made a few mistakes, which really hurt, and just when we had such a good chance to win. But they gave great effort and I'm proud for that."

"WE ARE NEVER SURPRISED WHEN WEST VIRGINIA GIVES US SO MUCH TROUBLE."

Ex-Pitt Coach John Michelosen

"We are never surprised when West Virginia gives us so much trouble," Michelosen added. "After that first drive we seemed to sour and they kept getting tougher. West Virginia was by far the toughest team we've played."

As for the Martha family, mom, dad and Paul were all happy with the outcome. Naturally, Richie wasn't. "Richie played a real good game for West Virginia," Mrs. Martha said. "And Paul . . . well, look what he did, and it was a real good, close game. We couldn't ask for anything more."

Pitt's only defeat of the season came the following week at Navy, 24-12. The Panthers ended the year impressively with consecutive victories over Syracuse, Notre Dame,

Army, Miami and Penn State. Pitt was originally scheduled to play Penn State in Pittsburgh on November 23, but the game was postponed for two weeks because of the assassination of President John F. Kennedy. The Panthers could have accepted a bid to a minor bowl (most likely the Sun Bowl), but they chose instead to wait until after playing their game against Penn State, which they won 22-21. By that time, however, all of the bowl slots were taken, with the exception of the Cotton Bowl, which chose Navy instead of Pitt to face Texas on New Year's Day. The 1963 Panthers, ranked third in the country, have to be considered one of the best teams in college football history not to earn a bowl bid. West Virginia, meanwhile, ended its season with a 4-6 record. It was West Virginia's fifth losing campaign in six years.

Points Galore

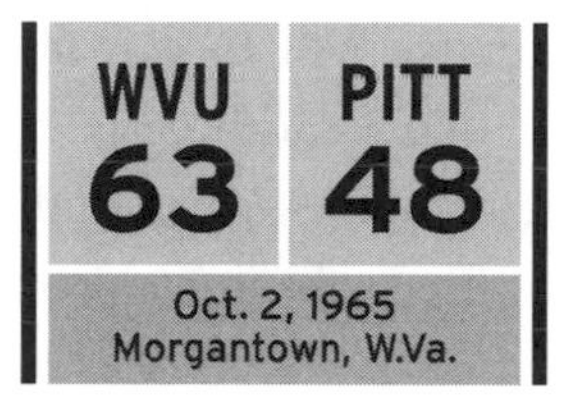

WVU
63
PITT
48
Oct. 2, 1965
Morgantown, W.Va.

Gene Corum rarely used swear words, but he was having a difficult time refraining from letting out an occasional "damn it" or "hell" as he watched his defense give up touchdown after touchdown. The year was 1965 and Corum's cursing was taking place at Mountaineer Field as he witnessed one of the wildest and wackiest West Virginia-Pitt football games ever played. "I can still see Coach Corum coming over to the sideline and him saying, 'John, damn it did you see that? What in the hell is going on out there? I just don't know what the hell is going on out there?'" defensive back John Mallory chuckled. "And Gene wasn't one to use cuss words."

"That's why they called him 'Gentleman Gene.' He was like [Dallas coach] Tom Landry was when I was with the Cowboys," said Mountaineer end Bob Dunlevy. "You didn't swear in front of Tom Landry because everybody respected him so much. If a cuss word came out of someone's mouth they immediately apologized to him. And that was the same way with Coach Corum."

Corum had every reason to let a few cuss words slip out. His defense was falling apart at the seams right in front of his eyes after his offense had built an early 21-0 lead, thanks to a 16-yard touchdown run by the Mountaineers' bulldozer of a fullback Dick Leftridge, and then a pair of touchdown passes from Allen McCune to Dick Rader – the first two TDs of Rader's college career. "I remember we were winning 21-0 and I thought, 'Oh, we're going to blow them out,'" Dunlevy said. "What a mistake that was."

That's because Panther quarterback Kenny Lucas also had a hot hand, throwing a 13-yard touchdown pass to end Michael Rosborough and then taking one in from the

2 himself. After a Garrett Ford 58-yard touchdown run, the Panther QB engineered yet another scoring march when fullback Barry McKnight plowed in from the 2, reducing West Virginia's once-21-point lead to eight, 28-20, by halftime. The intermission did nothing to slow down the scoring – or Corum's cussing. Pitt's speedy Eric Crabtree crossed the goal line on Pitt's opening possession of the second half, the senior hauling in a Lucas pass and out-racing West Virginia's defense for a 43-yard score. Lucas then tacked on the two-point conversion to knot the game at 28. And the scoring continued. McCune bounced in from the 1, only to see Pitt's Crabtree break loose again for a 71-yard TD. The Panthers' two-point conversion attempt – one of six they tried that afternoon – was unsuccessful, giving West Virginia a very shaky 35-34 advantage.

Early in the fourth quarter, West Virginia expanded its lead to eight when McCune made a great run fake and then found Jim Harris open for a pretty 17-yard touchdown pass. Chuck Kinder's conversion – one of nine he made that afternoon – gave Corum what he thought was a little breathing room at 42-34. But Kinder had to kick off to Crabtree. Kinder's first kick rolled out of bounds as he tried to keep the ball away from Pitt's speedster, resulting in a five-yard penalty. Then, the second one went directly to Crabtree, and 92 yards later he was celebrating with his teammates in West Virginia's end zone. Another Lucas two-point pass, this one successful, tied the game at 42 with 13:46 remaining.

Four minutes later, West Virginia scored again, McCune finding Rader in the right corner of the end zone from 15 yards for their third TD hookup of the game. Four minutes after that, Pitt was also back in the end zone. Lucas orchestrated a 70-yard drive that ended with halfback Robert Dyer crossing the goal line from the 1. Considering the way the two teams were scoring, it's difficult to believe that the play of the game actually came from either team's defense. But that's exactly what happened on one of Pitt's two-point tries, when West Virginia end Bill Sullivan stopped Lucas a yard short of the goal line. Lucas rolled out to his right looking for someone to throw the ball to, but West Virginia surprisingly had everyone covered and Sullivan was able to wrestle Lucas to the ground just before he reached the end zone. Sullivan's stop preserved a 49-48 lead. A week later, Corum dryly noted to *Sports Illustrated* writer John Underwood that Sullivan's tackle was one of the few either team made all afternoon.

McCune wasted little time adding to the lead when he found Ford out of the backfield for a beautiful 59-yard touchdown pass down the near sideline. Kinder's kick, with four minutes still showing on the clock, gave the Mountaineers a 56-48 lead. Two interceptions, one thrown by Lucas and the other by McCune, maintained the suspense for a little while longer, until Pitt gave the football back to West Virginia on downs at its own 5 with 1:20 to go. Ford reached pay dirt on the very next play, and Kinder tacked on the conversion to provide the remaining points in West Virginia's 63-48 victory. "I've never seen a game like it in my life," Corum said. "It seems unbelievable that a team scoring 48 points could lose."

A combined 16 touchdowns were scored, and neither team held onto the football for longer than five minutes at one time. A touchdown was produced nearly every four minutes, and the two teams combined for 1,071 yards of offense – 624 coming from West Virginia. There were at least eight school records set by West Virginia in a game *The Charleston Gazette's* Shorty Hardman called "an orgy of scoring" – a somewhat peculiar phrase for the still-conservative mid-1960s. At the time, Pitt's 48 points were the most ever produced in a losing effort at the college level, exceeding Bradley's 47 points scored in an eight-point loss to Drake in 1956. Afterward, both coaches provided their versions of what they had just witnessed. "I'm the oldest 44-year-old coach in the country," Corum joked. "We won and lost the game on at least a dozen different occasions. It's a game you'd have to see to believe. We score, then Pitt scores, and then you just wonder if you can score again and keep up."

"It was a fantastic game for both offenses, but the defenses went to pot," added Pitt's John Michelosen. The coach was asked if he was going to spend more time the following week working on defense, to which he replied, "There are only so many hours in a day."

Decades later, when interviewed in 1991 for West Virginia University's 100th anniversary highlight video, Corum said he had no reason to believe such a high-scoring affair would take place that sunny Saturday afternoon. "We came into the game and we thought it would be a cliffhanger and a reasonably low scoring game," he recalled. "But the first three times we got the ball, we scored, and then Pitt kept working back. It seemed like both teams . . . we would hold for two downs and then something would break loose."

In 1965, expectations were sky high for Gene Corum's WVU football team, winning five out of their last six regular season games of 1964, when McCune was moved from safety to quarterback. Moundsville's Ed Pastilong was expected to be the team's No. 1 signal caller, but Pastilong's bad throwing shoulder forced Corum to put McCune under center against Rice. It was a surprise to just about everyone on the team when McCune made the switch from safety to quarterback. "How would any of us have ever thought somebody coming in from defense would do what he did?" said Dunlevy.

"[McCune] was one of those quarterbacks like Terry Bradshaw [not always pretty]. He just got the job done."

McCune played at East Bank High (Jerry West's alma mater) for Roy Williams, a coach who typically preferred to put his best players on defense. That was how West Virginia found out about McCune, although he did quarterback Williams's single-wing offense. McCune was actually better known in basketball, holding more than 40 scholarship offers in that sport compared to only four in football, but one of those four just happened to be from West Virginia. McCune began his Mountaineer career in the secondary until, in desperation, Corum tried him out at quarterback in the 1964 loss at Rice. The Mountaineers didn't reach the end zone against the Owls, and McCune didn't blow anybody away with his passing, but he did show an ability to move the team. Two weeks later, he got another crack under center against Virginia Tech, and he played much better in leading West Virginia to a 23-10 victory. An early touchdown pass to Homer Criddle gave McCune the confidence he needed to move forward. "To anybody else it was just another touchdown," McCune said. "To me it was more like a turning point. Until then I never really realized I could throw."

Prior to that touchdown, West Virginia had gone 12 straight quarters without scoring. McCune was never a picture-perfect passer, his throws often tumbling like a Phil Niekro knuckleball, but they were soft enough to catch and usually close to their intended target. "He wasn't a great passer, he wasn't a great runner – he wasn't great at anything, he was just a winner and he got the job done," said Dunlevy. McCune accounted for every point in the team's 26-21 victory over Kentucky, and he finished the 1964 campaign completing nearly 60 percent of his passes for 1,034 yards and 11 touchdowns. At the time, he was only the third quarterback in school history to throw for more than 1,000 yards in a season.

In addition to switching quarterbacks, Corum was making other changes as well. He had reorganized his coaching staff after a disappointing 1963 season that saw West Virginia win just four of 10 games against one of the toughest slates in school history. Corum brought in Bob Patton from The Citadel to coach the defensive line, he added Tennessee's Ralph Chauncey to run the defense and he hired young Rip Engle protégé Galen Hall from Penn State to take over the offense. After leading the Nittany Lions to a Gator Bowl victory over Georgia Tech in 1961, Hall played two seasons of pro football with the Washington Redskins and the New York Jets before getting his start in the coaching profession at WVU. In Hall, Dunlevy and the rest of the offensive players could right away detect a very innovative young coach. "He was a real good coach," Dunlevy said. "He ran the whole offense."

And Hall had some weapons to work with. In addition to having a stabilized quarterbacking situation with McCune in 1965, Hall had a nice, tall receiver to take advantage of in Dunlevy – one of the biggest players on the team (6-foot-4 inches and 215 pounds) with speed and hands to match. As a junior in 1964, he caught 18 passes for 279 yards and a pair of touchdowns, one going for 50 yards to beat Syracuse 28-27 in the final game of the regular season. Just prior to kickoff, Syracuse had accepted a bid to play LSU in the Sugar Bowl, and in making the announcement the Sugar Bowl had prematurely included a victory over West Virginia among Syracuse's wins. Later, the bowl folks were noticeably disturbed when Dunlevy scored the go-ahead touchdown, and then indigestion set in when the final seconds ticked off the clock and some of the Syracuse players congratulated the conquering Mountaineers with flying fists. Shorty Hardman, a wise guy when he wanted to be, wrote in *The Charleston Gazette* the next morning that if the Sugar Bowl ever wanted to put on a boxing tournament, they would be well-served to consider some of the Syracuse players, who, according to Hardman, "seemed to be pretty handy with their dukes."

It was after the Syracuse victory that the Liberty Bowl decided to pick West Virginia to face Utah in the first-ever indoor bowl game, to be indoors at the Atlantic City Convention Center – site of the 1964 Democratic National Convention, where Lyndon Johnson received his party's nomination. Villanova athletic director A.F. "Bud" Dudley had created the Liberty Bowl in 1959, and the first five games were played in Philadelphia's 100,000-seat JFK Stadium to sparse crowds. It was the only bowl game played in the Northeast at the time, often in below-freezing conditions, and clever sports columnists began referring to it as the "Deep Freeze Bowl," the "Masochist Bowl" or the "You're-Out-Of-Your-Mind Bowl." Dudley had seen his game absorb losses in excess of $40,000 in 1963, and he was willing to listen to any offer – the best one turning out to be a $25,000 guarantee from Atlantic City for moving the game to the 12,000-seat Convention Center. ABC made a commitment to televise the game and brought in its top announcing crew of Curt Gowdy, Paul Christman and Jim McKay. Dudley's biggest obstacle was coming up with a suitable playing surface to use indoors (this was in the days before Astroturf). A four-inch thick grass surface, with two inches of padding underneath, was trucked in to place over the concrete. Artificial lighting was needed to make sure the grass continued to grow. Phil Pepe of the *New York World-Telegram* cracked, "If the game is dull, you can sit there and watch the grass grow. It's McCune against [Roy] Jefferson and both of them against the grass. The grass is a three-point favorite."

"It was as hard as a rock," recalled West Virginia guard Donnie Young.

The end zones were eight yards in length instead of the standard 10 yards, and the teams' dressing rooms were on a stage above the end zone. "There was no place to even hang your clothes," recalled Dunlevy. The Miss America pageant folks were not exactly thrilled with the idea of having flying footballs knocking out the new lights that had been installed before the political convention, and those covering the game saw it for what it really was – a TV gimmick. "WVU chose to defend the boardwalk while Utah picked the Miss America Pageant stage," wrote *Philadelphia Inquirer* columnist Red Smith.

The game was awful. West Virginia was no match for Utah's speed, the hard surface undoubtedly aiding the Redskins in their 32-6 triumph. Probably the most unforgettable moment of the entire game was PA man Dave Zinkoff's fourth-quarter announcement: "Only two minutes left in the game . . . Thank God!"

"The liveliest thing I saw that weekend," wrote Mickey Furfari, "was the gale-force winds blowing outside."

Still, it was a bowl appearance for the Mountaineers and an opportunity for Corum to build from for the following season. In 1965, West Virginia would have a loaded backfield with senior Dick Leftridge and touted sophomore Garrett Ford, who beat out junior John Piscorik for the starting halfback job, basically from the moment he moved up to varsity. "Coach Corum lined up the starting team when I was a sophomore, and those guys just hated that because I was taking their guy's spot," Ford recalled. "Those guys didn't like me and I would talk back to them, 'I'm running here and try and stop me.' They hated that."

Ford was discovered by former West Virginia player Bob Guenther, then living in Gaithersburg, Md. Guenther told Corum about Ford, a star player at DeMatha High in Washington, D.C., and the West Virginia coach paid Ford a surprise visit one day at school. "I kept getting phone calls from a guy from West Virginia named Gene Corum," Ford recalled. "I never even answered the phone. When I was at DeMatha, I worked in the kitchen washing dishes to pay for my lunch. Well, one day I was washing dishes and putting them through the machine when Coach Corum and [assistant coach] Dick Ware showed up and told me they were from West Virginia University."

Ford finally agreed to take a trip to Morgantown to see the campus. "Guenther called and said he was going to drive me over to Morgantown. I knew about Jerry West, but I didn't know anything about West Virginia and I didn't want to go," Ford said. "They told me I could bring some buddies with me, so I picked about five of my friends that I grew up with and we all got in a car and came to Morgantown. We drove across the old bridge at Cheat Lake that was shaking; we came up that hill, around the bend, and drove into Morgantown."

When he first arrived, Ford was not all that impressed with what West Virginia University had to offer. Then Ford noticed something he had never seen before – white garbage collectors. "I had never been in a place where I had seen poor white people," Ford said. "There were poor white people living with poor black people up in those hills, and they were eating off the same plate. They were in the same situation." At that moment he began to see Morgantown in a different light – a place he could relate to – so he decided to give WVU a try. "You'd meet people here and they'd say 'thank you' and 'come again.' You'd hear, 'How are you doing?' on the street," said Ford. "You didn't get that in a big city."

Ford's teammate and friend John Mallory said he chose West Virginia University because of a personal, hand-written note he had received from Corum. "What it boiled down to was a last-minute thing where Gene Corum saw some film of me, offered me a scholarship on the spot and I showed up," said Mallory. "I think I signed in either May or June and I was one of the last signees. Initially, I decided to go to Maryland and I don't think my parents were happy about that. Maryland had just had their first black player in football, and he took me around and one of the assistant coaches there told me I was the best back on the east coast. The next thing you know, another guy shows up there and [the same assistant] says *he's* the best back on the east coast – so I ended up at West Virginia.

"I figured, well, West Virginia . . . I liked history and I knew the western counties of Virginia had seceded from Virginia, and I knew about Jerry West and Sam Huff. Yeah, this is going to be OK. Well, I got a rude awakening when I got there," Mallory chuckled.

"WELL, I GOT A RUDE AWAKENING WHEN I GOT THERE."

Ex-WVU Safety John Mallory

Dick Leftridge had already established himself as one of the best runners in the Southern Conference by gaining 534 yards and scoring five touchdowns as a junior. The sky was the limit for Leftridge, but a carefree attitude and his reluctance to remain in tip-top shape kept him from enjoying the long and prosperous professional football career that many had envisioned for him when he was drafted in the first round by the Pittsburgh Steelers in 1966. Leftridge also enjoyed testing Corum's patience. Once he asked his coach for permission to go home for the weekend and Corum agreed, provided he returned to campus by 10 a.m. on Monday morning. At 10 o'clock on Monday, Leftridge called his coach to tell him it was snowing and he didn't have a way back to Morgantown. Corum was beside himself. Five minutes after calling Corum, Leftridge walked into his office and said, "When I heard how mad you were, coach, I took a jet."

At the outset of the '65 season, West Virginia was averaging 44.5 points and 481.8 yards per game in victories over Richmond, William & Mary, Pitt and The Citadel, and the Mountaineers were even getting an unheard-of 222 yards per game through the air. A 25-2 win over The Citadel had finally put Corum over the .500 mark after 53 games (a winless first season in 1960 had him digging out of a big hole to begin his coaching career), and it looked like West Virginia was headed for a return to the national rankings, as well as back-to-back bowl game appearances for the first time in school history.

Then the roof caved in against Virginia in the Tobacco Bowl, in Richmond. The Tobacco Bowl was a regular-season game played each year from 1949–1982 at Richmond City Stadium during the National Tobacco Festival. The loss to the Cavaliers was inexplicable, one, because Virginia was not very good that season (the Cavaliers winning just four games), and two, because of how poorly the Mountaineers played in a 41-0 loss. Virginia recovered two fumbled kickoffs for touchdowns, and some West Virginia players openly rebelled when the score started getting out of hand. One even walked off the field and refused to go back into the game. "I had never seen that before – and he got away with it," said Ford.

"We fell apart," said Dunlevy. "We got our butts kicked and the season went to hell after that." The team's fall was swift and dramatic. The following week, Penn State beat West Virginia 44-6, and Kentucky followed with a 28-8 pasting in Lexington. By the end of the season, some players were skipping practice and others were dismissed from the team for disciplinary reasons. In two months, Corum went from having his team profiled in *Sports Illustrated* in October to being out of a job by early December. Dick Hudson, who covered West Virginia football for 36 years, believed the odds were stacked against Corum at the outset of his WVU coaching tenure in 1960. "Pappy had arranged things – he kind of quit at a spur of the moment and they were kind of in a bind and Gene was there, so he automatically got the job," said Hudson. "I think some of them kind of resented the fact that Pappy kind of maneuvered around them into making Gene the coach."

The football program Corum inherited in 1960 had very little money and very little support from the university. The athletic dormitory situation at WVU in the mid-1960s was less than ideal – with the vast majority of the players living off campus – and that contributed to some of the disciplinary problems Corum had encountered. A few years later, the Towers dormitory complex was constructed out in Evansdale. Corum also had an impossible time working around players' class schedules, rarely having a full squad together during the fall semester. But instead of complaining about the problems, Corum opted to take the high road by submitting his letter of resignation. He also chose to keep his teaching position in the School of Physical Education. "He was a wonderful guy," Hudson said. "I never knew a guy I liked better than Gene Corum."

But despite public comments to the contrary, Corum was pressured to resign. University president Paul Miller issued a four paragraph statement that included such phrases as "*esprit de corps* of the football team" and "the cultural life of the university." Naturally, the state's sports writers had fun with that. With the exception of the loss to Virginia in 1965 and a defeat to Richmond in the 1961 season opener, Corum's teams probably won the games they should have won and lost the games they should have lost. He defeated Pitt three times, won twice against Syracuse and claimed four out of five against Virginia Tech. Corum's three triumphs against the Panthers were the second most by any coach in school history at that time, and the 63 points the Mountaineers put up against Pitt in 1965 are still the most a Mountaineer team has ever scored in a single game against the Panthers.

Corum may have had better wins at WVU than the 1965 triumph over Pitt – many old-timers still believe his 1961 victory at Army and his 1964 upset win over ninth-ranked Syracuse were his two best – yet people mostly recall Corum's Pitt victory for the staggering numbers it produced. It was said that when announcer Jack Buck read the game's score on KMOX during a St. Louis Cardinals baseball game in Houston he deadpanned, "Did anybody tackle anybody in that game?"

After Western Union operator Homer Sampson sent out the final score from the press box, the home office suggested that he quit drinking during games. And Corum recalled one of his coaches sitting in the press box of the game he was scouting, listening in disbelief at the scores he kept hearing announced on the press box PA system. "Of course he was interested in getting our Pitt score," Corum said in 1991. "It kept coming in 28-27 in the third quarter or 35-34 at the end of the third quarter or some such score, and he said they kept sending back, 'Please send corrected score.'"

Garrett Ford finished the 1965 game with 198 yards rushing and 76 yards receiving, scoring three touchdowns and accounting for more than 300 all-purpose yards for the game. "Garrett Ford had the best performance I had ever seen of any individual," said Mallory. "Guys were bouncing off him." Ford's 133 yards rushing in the second quarter were a school record that lasted for more than a quarter of a century, and his terrific game overshadowed other great performances on both sides of the field. Pitt's Kenny Lucas completed 16-of-27 passes for 252 yards and two touchdowns, and Eric Crabtree ran four times for 75 yards, caught three passes for 76 yards and had an additional 153 yards in kickoff returns for 304 all-purpose yards. All three of Dick Rader's catches went for touchdowns covering 101 yards, and then there was Allen McCune's passing, which really turned Pitt's defense upside down. He completed 18 of 25 for a school-record 320 yards and five touchdowns.

Before the West Virginia game, Pitt's popular groundskeeper Leo "Horse" Czarnecki placed a picture of McCune passing the football on the team bulletin board, and underneath it in red ink was Czarnecki's inscription, "When you are on your back, the only place you can throw is UP . . . Make him an airplane watcher." It was McCune who had everyone looking toward the sky that afternoon.

Sadly, he died in an automobile accident in 1973. He was just 30.

Fullback Dick Leftridge. See page A13

Artie Owens. See page B1

1967-1979

THE BIRTH OF THE BACKYARD BRAWL

"Jusk" for Kicks

WVU	PITT
15	0
Oct. 7, 1967 Morgantown, W.Va.	

Jim Carlen blew it. It was 1966, and West Virginia's first year coach was trailing Pitt by a field goal and had the football at the Panther 4-yard line when time ran out on his team, ending a 17-14 loss to the Panthers – which turned out to be the only victory for woeful Pitt that season. Carlen eschewed a game-tying field goal, choosing instead to go for the win (a pass that ended up just short of the end zone). And that wasn't the only questionable decision the rookie coach made. A more egregious mistake occurred right before the end of the first half, when Carlen chose to take a Panther punt that had rolled out of bounds at the West Virginia 3 instead of making them re-kick the ball after Pitt was penalized for illegal procedure. Accepting the penalty would have placed the ball back at the 49 and required another punt, but instead, Carlen opted to have his quarterback Tom Digon try a quarterback sneak. Digon fumbled, and Tom Mitrakos's recovery enabled first-year Pitt coach Dave Hart to call for a field goal with nine seconds left, giving the Panthers the game's deciding points.

Carlen's young offensive coordinator Bobby Bowden tried a variety of trick plays that ended up accomplishing very little. One, a halfback pass from Garrett Ford to end Larry Sine, would have easily scored a touchdown, but Ford slipped as he was about to throw the football and was ruled down where his knee touched the ground. The loss on the play left Chuck Kinder with a much more difficult 51-yard field goal try that landed just short of the cross bar. Then, following Pitt's second touchdown, Bowden tried a lateral pass on the ensuing kickoff return. Pete Secret took the ball inside his own 10 and threw the ball directly across the field to the team's fastest player, John Mallory, who caught it and started up the sideline. Mallory got to the Pitt 46, where he was forced out of bounds near the Panther bench.

And on the game's final drive, Bowden tried the halfback pass again – Ford this time got the football airborne toward Allen "Emo" Schupbach in the end zone, but his toss had too much loft on it, giving a Panther defender enough time to recover and bat the ball to the ground. "I thought too much about it," Ford recalled. "I threw the ball, but I kind of lobbed it because I wanted to make sure he would catch it, and I remember the safety coming over and knocking it down."

Trick plays were not really part of Jim Carlen's repertoire; Carlen was a Bobby Dodd disciple who was hired to replace Gene Corum on January 14, 1966 – 29 days after Corum was pressured to resign. Carlen was Georgia Tech's defensive coordinator in 1965 when West Virginia Athletic Director Red Brown telephoned Dodd to get his opinion about a couple coaches he was looking at, one of them being Cornell coach Tom Harp, who wound up taking the Duke job. Dodd said the guy Brown ought to hire was Carlen, who was then just 32 years old but already full of ideas and a willingness to speak his mind.

Carlen really fit the profile Red Brown was looking for in a head coach – young, eager and seemingly compliant. Brown didn't put up a big fight when highly successful basketball coach Fred Schaus decided to leave for the Los Angeles Lakers in 1960, and he didn't come to the defense of Art Lewis when the Athletic Council was ready to drop the hatchet on him after his disastrous 1959 season. After Schaus and Lewis, all of Brown's remaining football and basketball hires were assistant coaches – George King, Bucky Waters and Sonny Moran in basketball, and Gene Corum, Jim Carlen and Bobby Bowden in football. As for Carlen, he knew very little about West Virginia, not seeing the school until after accepting the job, but he was anxious to run his own program.

"Coach Dodd said, 'Are you leavin' me?' I said, 'Well Coach, yeah. I've got to get a head job.' He said, 'Well, you don't think I'm going to retire?' I said, 'Well, I don't know because your age is not that bad,'" Carlen recalled. "I said, 'Coach, let me be honest with you because my whole thing is about telling you what I think.' He said, 'I know, that's what I appreciate the most about you. Sometimes I don't like it because you're so straight-forward.'

"I said, 'Coach, if you give me the job tomorrow, I would only bring two or three of the coaches on this staff.' He said, 'You're kidding!' I said, 'No, I'm not kidding. They don't work, they don't recruit and they second guess.' The ones that I wanted I took with me to West Virginia."

Carlen grew up in Cookeville, Tenn., and was a punter and backup linebacker for Dodd on the 1953 Georgia Tech team that defeated West Virginia in the '54 Sugar Bowl. After spending time in the Air Force, Carlen asked Dodd if he had a place for him on the football staff, because he wanted to get into coaching. "Coach Dodd tried to talk me out of it, but I said, 'No, I just want to see if I can coach,'" Carlen remembered. "He let me coach. He let me hand out the books to the students, and then I worked my way up to defensive coordinator."

As a coach, Carlen had defense, kicking and the running game covered. What he was looking for was an innovative offensive coach to create some fan interest and inject life into the program he was taking over. And Bobby Bowden turned out to be the guy Carlen was looking for. "What I knew about Bobby was I knew he knew the throwin' game, and I knew he was kind of a fool-'em coach; he ran trick plays and stuff," Carlen said. "I was just a very limited-knowledge coach. I believed if you run the ball on offense and you control the ball, you don't have to worry about playing defense because [then] the other team doesn't get the ball."

Carlen inherited a Mountaineer program that had problems that needed to be addressed. There were widespread reports of player misbehavior, others were not attending class regularly, and the team's best player – fullback Dick Leftridge – was allowed to play his senior year despite rarely attending classes during the fall semester. Also, quarterback Bob Uchic decided to get married and had lost interest in football. Carlen cleaned things up right away, issuing strict rules covering everything from class attendance to the way the players dressed, wore their clothes and cut their hair. He also demanded that they go to the church of their choice. "I learned to be fair; I learned that you've got to get along with everybody, but I also learned that you've got to make sure that you keep up with your players," Carlen said.

He ended the tradition of going to Jackson's Mill for preseason training camp, instituted an off-season conditioning program, made his players lose weight, changed the uniforms, demanded that football have its own athletic trainer and team doctor, and fought with the administration over such mundane things as purchasing an ice machine for the locker room. It was an extreme culture shock for most of the returning players.

"They came here and they introduced an off-season program. We didn't know what that was," said Ford. "We didn't do anything before that. We'd maybe run a couple of laps around the track. They came in and they had these little drills where you'd hit your helmets and that kind of stuff.

"Coach Carlen was scary. They would bring water out to you during practice and you drank it through your helmet," Ford said. "You never took your helmet off, and if you drank water you were considered soft."

"He spoke the truth," added wide receiver Oscar Patrick. "Just like he told my mother, he said, 'Look, I'm not going to guarantee your son a down of football. But I am going to guarantee him an education.'" Patrick had played at all-black Excelsior High until his school merged with Big Creek High School, where West Virginia enjoyed success in recruiting other outstanding players. Patrick had been signed by Corum's staff, so Carlen's coaches knew very little about him – other than the obvious fact that he was big and fast.

"They hadn't seen any film at all, and I wanted to stand up with your hands on your hips like Art Powell of the Oakland Raiders, but they had a philosophy of receivers being down in a three-point stance," Patrick recalled. "So the first play of practice I stood up, I ran a curl, caught the ball, and ran it for a touchdown on the first pass they threw me. Coach [Carlen] is up on the tower, and he says, 'Son, can you do that again?' I said, 'Yeah, Coach.' The same thing, went down, did a curl, ran around the guy and went for a touchdown. He asked me if I could do it again and I said, 'I don't know, Coach, I'm pretty tired.'" Patrick would later thrive in Bowden's offense, becoming the first player in school history to catch 50 passes in a season, in 1968, before a serious knee injury derailed his career in 1969.

Another big change Carlen made was to convince WTRF in Wheeling to produce a weekly television show during the season, just like the one Bear Bryant had when Carlen was growing up in the South. "I wanted to have a TV show, and I knew it would be terrible driving to Wheeling, so I got some of my student managers and I put them in state cars, and we only had one wreck the entire time I was there," Carlen said. "After every ballgame we would cut that show.

"There were four TV stations. I think Bluefield was one. Charleston was one, Wheeling and one in Parkersburg. We never had one up in the other part of the state toward D.C.," Carlen said. "We should have and that was a mistake on my part. I never could get anybody interested over there, plus there weren't a lot of good players over there at the time."

Carlen wisely understood that a TV show would help people become more interested in the Mountaineer football program. "What I was trying to do was to sell West Virginia to the fans, but also where players would be seen by the people from their hometowns," he explained. "If you get the right coaches and you bring in the right players, the fans will come. If you don't have good coaches and you bring in good players, then they won't be coached well. If you get those two ingredients and you win, people will come."

Carlen also made sure to ingratiate himself with the well-connected people of the state, recalling a visit he once made to Joe Manchin's grandmother's house. When he stepped inside, sitting at the kitchen table were Senators Robert and Edward Kennedy. "I said to Mr. Manchin, 'What is it about that young kid [Teddy]? He's kind of a screwball,'" remembered Carlen. "He said when he comes up here we put him on the road; we give him some money and we tell him to avoid everything that we do – 'Just don't be around and stay gone.' Then he goes on and does such a great job in the Senate. I will never forget that, though. He was like a loose cannon in the Kennedy family."

When Pitt coach John Michelosen was pushed out the door after a 3-7 record in 1965 (including consecutive blowout losses to Syracuse and Notre Dame to end the season), the first guy Pitt athletic director Frank Carver set his sights on was retired Oklahoma coach Bud Wilkinson, then working for ABC. Wilkinson was content doing television, though, so Carver had to widen his search. After interviewing internal candidates, local high school coaches and college assistants, Carver ended up giving the job to Navy assistant coach Dave Hart. Immediately, Hart came to understand the insurmountable obstacles he had to overcome. On the field, the Panther defense was atrocious in 1965, giving up 69 points to Notre Dame, 63 to West Virginia and 51 to Syracuse, while also playing an impossibly difficult schedule that included Oregon, Oklahoma, Duke, Navy, Miami, USC and Penn State. Off the field, the Panthers were having trouble recruiting players because of the school's high academic standards, which featured tough foreign language requirements. In fact, Pitt's freshman class in 1965 was so small that the Panthers had to cancel their freshman football season. However, Hart's biggest impediment was the school's unwillingness to open up the checkbook. Sam Sciullo, Jr., who has written several books on University of Pittsburgh athletics, recalled just how frugal the Pitt administration was in the mid-1960s. "Years ago they had concrete-floored, spartan dorms erected in the concourse of the stadium, and when Dave Hart got the job he wanted to know if he could get accommodations for his staff coming in," Sciullo said. "Frank Carver said no, they can stay in those makeshift dorms at Pitt Stadium. They had cots they slept on, and they had to pay to rent the cots in the winter-spring of 1966."

Finances also prohibited Hart from bringing in the guys he wanted for his coaching staff. "Hart wanted to hire Homer Rice and Chuck Knox as his coordinators, and he needed something like $1,500 or $2,000 [extra] each to get them, and the administration wouldn't do it," Sciullo said. Hart was a Western Pa. native, growing up in nearby Connellsville and playing first at the University of Georgia for two seasons before finishing his college career at St. Vincent (Pa.) College. His coaching career began in high school before advancing to the college ranks, where he coached two seasons at the University of Kentucky, and then going to Navy for the two years prior to his appointment at Pitt. "Hart was an interesting hire because he wasn't a Pitt guy," Sciullo said. "He was a real enthusiastic, energetic, go-getter type of guy. But he was fighting a losing battle."

Whereas Michelosen was phlegmatic and undemonstrative, Hart could be impish and impulsive. Before each spring game, Hart would excite Panther fans by lining up his recruits and proudly introducing them all to the crowd, reciting their heights and weights. Hart's 1967 freshman team was proclaimed the best freshman class in Pitt history, its three losses that year notwithstanding, but the plebes by then were still performing much better than the varsity. When Hart was eventually forced out, the one improvement he could claim was increasing Pitt's roster size from 40 players when he took over in 1966 to 80 after his final season in 1968.

HART'S 1967 FRESHMAN TEAM WAS PROCLAIMED THE BEST FRESHMAN CLASS IN PITT HISTORY.

Indeed, Hart found out right away in 1966 just how tough things were going to be for him at Pitt, dropping his first game to UCLA, 57-14, and absorbing other beatings against Cal, Navy, Army, Syracuse, Notre Dame, Miami and Penn State. All Hart could hang his hat on was the 3-point victory over West Virginia in a game the Mountaineers had gift-wrapped for him.

In 1967, before West Virginia could even think about a rematch with Pitt, it first had to contend with Syracuse. The Orangemen, as they were known back then, were coming off an 8-3 season in 1966 that included a 6-point loss to Tennessee in the Orange Bowl. Those Syracuse teams of the 1960s were considered among the meanest and toughest in college football, and they were coached by one of the toughest guys around in Ben Schwartzwalder, who happened to have played at West Virginia University before joining the Army and participating in the Normandy invasion during World War II. Bobby Bowden recalled a story Schwartzwalder had once told him about his first few days on the beaches of France. "I'll never forget him telling me about one morning when he was lying out there and rolled over and got his knife out to cut an apple," Bowden told *The*

The 1943 Mountaineer football team was comprised mostly of freshmen and 4-Fs. Because of the ongoing conflicts in Europe and Asia, a roster of 54 players in 1942 was pared down to approximately 30 when West Virginia began training camp in the fall of 1943. Twenty-eight players made the trip to Pittsburgh to face the Panthers on Oct. 9, 1943.

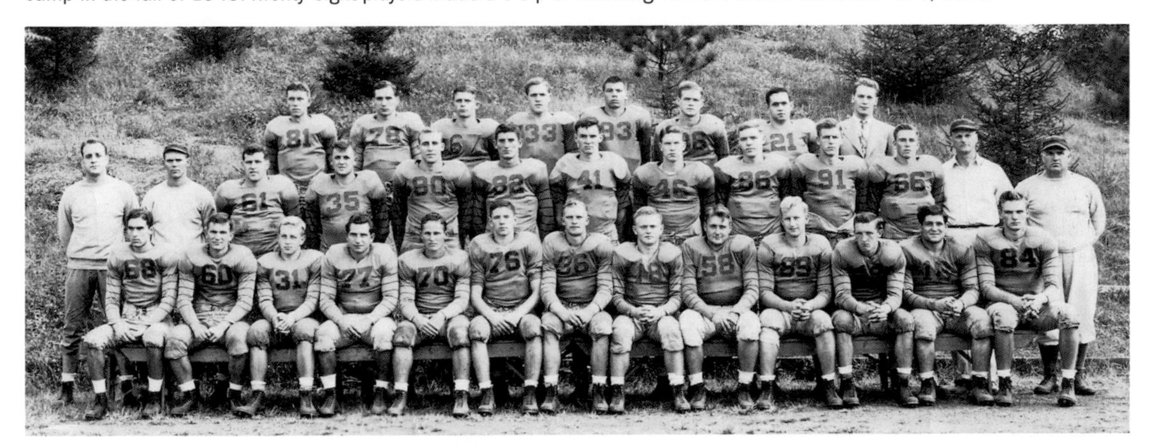

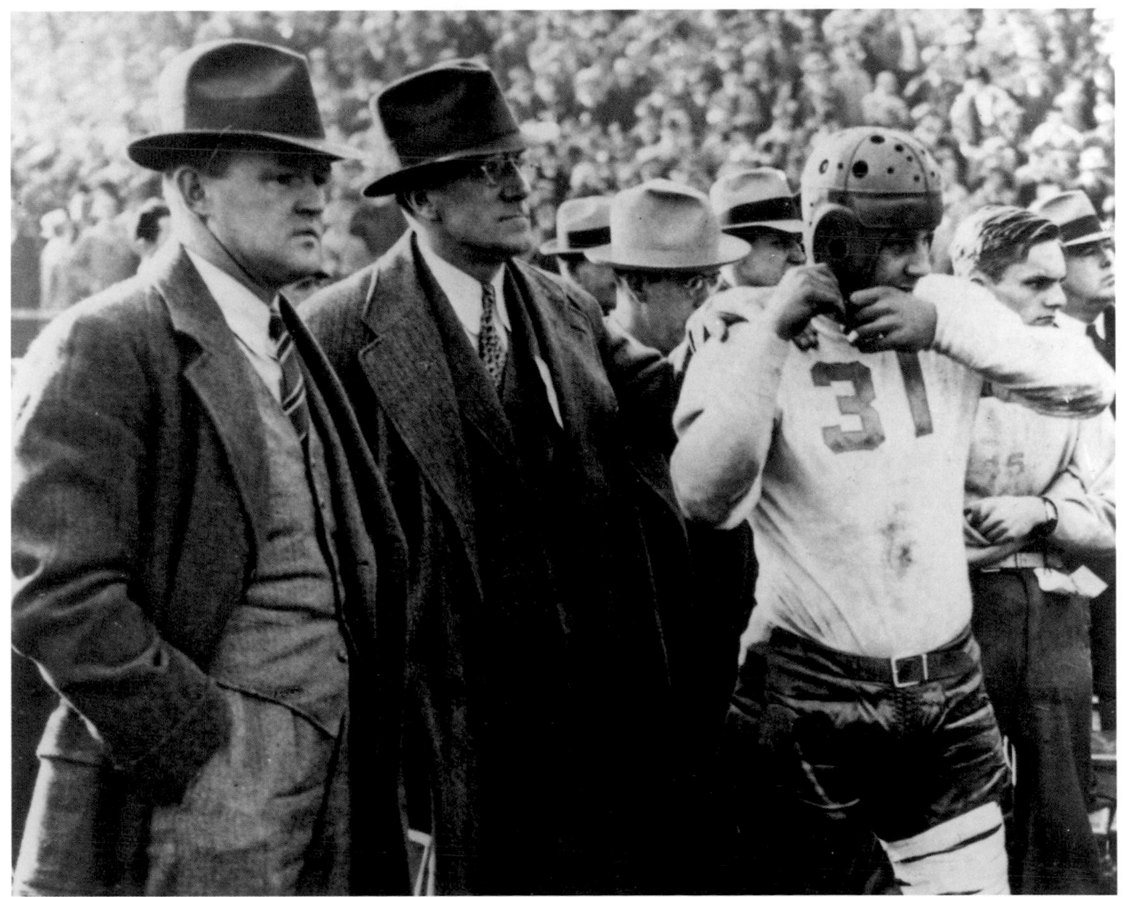

Bill Kern, pictured here with Jock Sutherland, was an All-American tackle for Sutherland at the University of Pittsburgh in 1927 before eventually joining Sutherland's Panther coaching staff in 1930. (Courtesy of University of Pittsburgh)

Roy "Legs" Hawley served as West Virginia's athletic director from 1938 until his death in 1954. It was Hawley who hired Bill Kern in 1940 after discovering that some Mountaineer boosters had gauged Jock Sutherland's interest in the dual role of football coach-athletic director.

Roy Hawley asked Ira Rodgers to coach the Mountaineers for the remainder of the war after Bill Kern reported for military duty on July 1, 1943. Rodgers, named West Virginia's first consensus All-American football player in 1919, also coached the Mountaineers for six seasons, from 1925-30.

Bill Kern coached West Virginia to a 24-23-1 record during his five seasons at West Virginia. After submitting his resignation the week of the Pitt game in 1947, Kern never returned to the sidelines. Here he is pictured in 1940 with West Virginia players Pete Yost and Peter Antolini.

No one did more to stoke passions in the West Virginia-Pitt rivalry than the legendary "Voice of the Mountaineers," Jack Fleming, who also became well known in the Steel City as the regular radio play-by-play man for the Pittsburgh Steelers. Here Fleming shows his allegiances during a Mountaineer basketball game, in 1987.

Quarterback Tom Keane, from Bellaire, Ohio, scored one touchdown and threw another to lead West Virginia to a 17-2 victory at Pitt Stadium in 1947. Keane became an All-Pro defensive back and later was a long-time NFL assistant coach.

It was end Paul Bischoff's 23-yard touchdown reception early in the game that helped propel West Virginia to a 16-0 upset victory over 18th-ranked Pitt at Pitt Stadium in 1952. The win was the Mountaineers' first ever against a nationally ranked football team.

West Virginia coach Art Lewis plants a kiss on the forehead of freshman quarterback Fred Wyant after the Mountaineers upset 18th-ranked Pitt, 16-0, at Pitt Stadium on Oct. 25, 1952. Standing behind Wyant is fullback Tommy Allman.

Quarterback Fred Wyant cracked the starting lineup as a freshman in 1952 before going on to post a 30-4 record as a starter during his four-year career. Wyant led the Mountaineers to three straight victories over Penn State and a pair of wins against Pitt.

Sam Huff, raised in nearby Farmington, was one of 33 West Virginians on the Mountaineer football roster during the 1953 season. Huff was elected to the high school, college and pro football halls of fame.

Bruce Bosley and Gene "Beef" Lamone, both unheralded coming out of high school, went on to become two of the greatest linemen in WVU history. Bosley was later a four-time All-Pro for the San Francisco 49ers in 1961, 1966, 1967 and 1968.

Chuck Howley lettered in five sports at West Virginia (football, wrestling, gymnastics, track and swimming), and despite nagging injuries that plagued his Mountaineer football career, he was the 11th player selected overall in the 1958 NFL draft, by the Chicago Bears.

Coach Art "Pappy" Lewis had a 58-38-2 record during his 10 seasons coaching the Mountaineers, from 1950–59. Lewis led West Virginia to three consecutive eight-win seasons in 1953, 1954 and 1955, including a 1954 trip to face Georgia Tech in the Sugar Bowl.

Pitt fans claim one of the goal posts after the Panthers stunned sixth-ranked West Virginia, 26-7, at Pitt Stadium on Nov. 12, 1955. The loss knocked West Virginia out of contention for a Sugar Bowl berth.

Parsons, W.Va., end Terry Fairbanks sacked Pitt quarterback Ivan Toncic on three consecutive plays late in the game, helping preserve West Virginia's 7-6 victory at Pitt Stadium on Nov. 9, 1957.

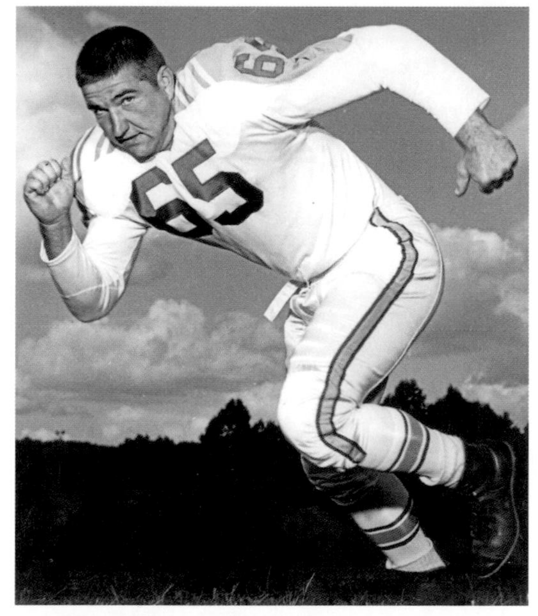

Bill "Hard Coal" Lopasky, from Lehman, Pa., was the only West Virginia player one Panther assistant coach thought would be good enough to make Pitt's second string in 1959. But that didn't keep the Mountaineers from upsetting the 20th-ranked Panthers, 23-15, in Morgantown, for one of their three victories that season.

After producing the only winless season in school history, in 1960, "Gentleman" Gene Corum recovered to win eight games in 1962. He later led the Mountaineers to a Liberty Bowl appearance in 1964, marking a highlight of his six-year coaching tenure at WVU.

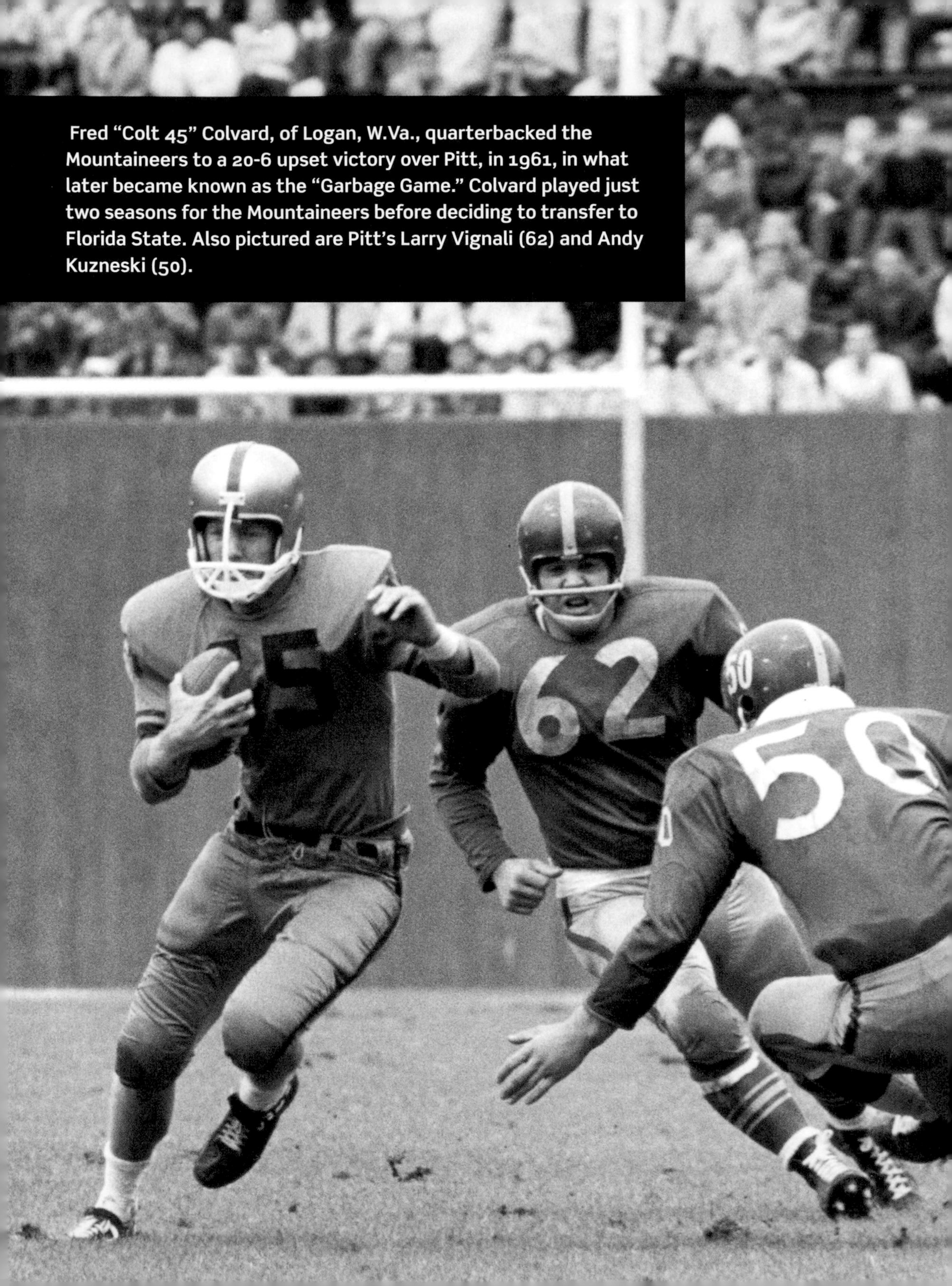

Fred "Colt 45" Colvard, of Logan, W.Va., quarterbacked the Mountaineers to a 20-6 upset victory over Pitt, in 1961, in what later became known as the "Garbage Game." Colvard played just two seasons for the Mountaineers before deciding to transfer to Florida State. Also pictured are Pitt's Larry Vignali (62) and Andy Kuzneski (50).

The 1962 freshman football team, at Jackson's Mill. This team included the first two black players in school history, in Dick Leftridge (44, in second row) and Roger Alford (65, in back row).

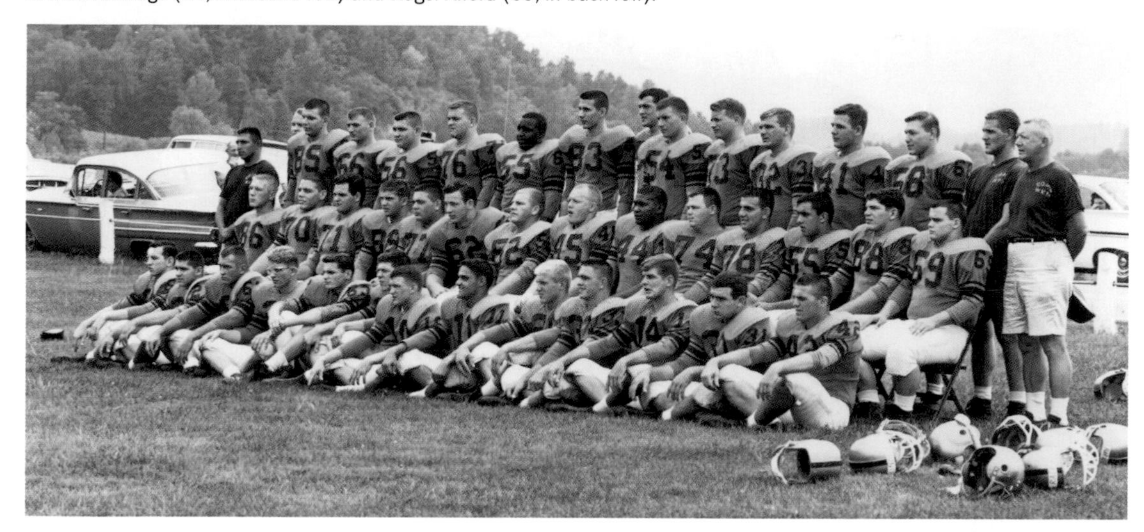

West Virginia athletic director Red Brown persuaded CBS to televise West Virginia's 1963 game against Pitt as part of the state's Centennial celebration. Some of the planned festivities included the West Virginia showboat *Rhododendron*, which transported the Pitt football team from Star City to Pleasant Street, downtown, where local dignitaries were waiting to greet them. (Richard Phillips photo)

The 1963 Backyard Brawl pitted brother against brother: Ritchie and Paul Martha. Paul, a standout player for the Panthers, later became a well-known professional football player and sports executive.

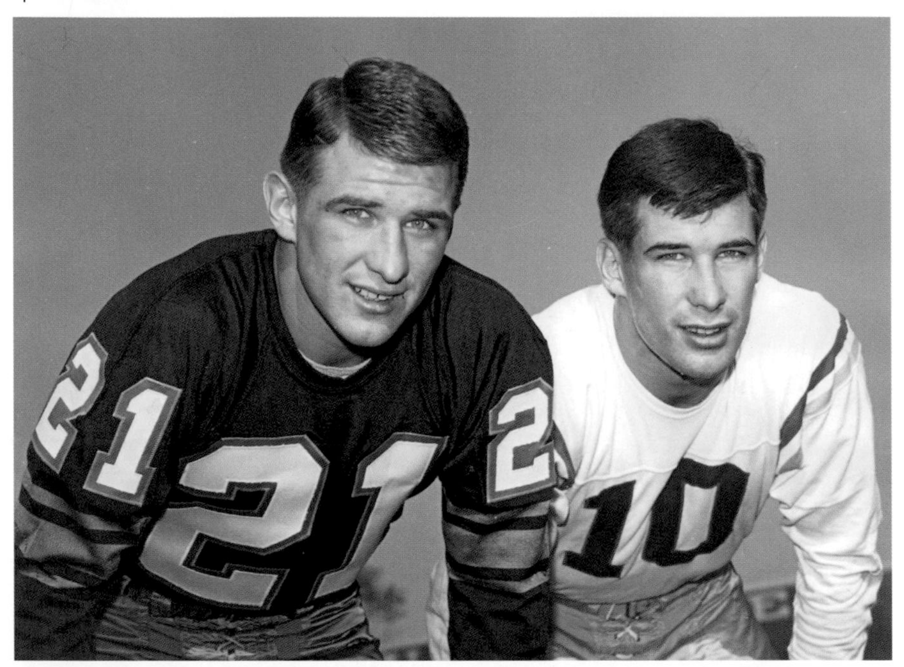

The "Big Four" athletic directors pose for a photograph in 1963: Penn State's Ernie McCoy, Pitt's Frank Carver, Syracuse's Jim Decker and West Virginia's Red Brown. Although not officially recognized as an athletic conference, the Big Four regulated such things as officiating, scheduling and the practice of redshirting between the four schools during the 1960s and early 1970s.

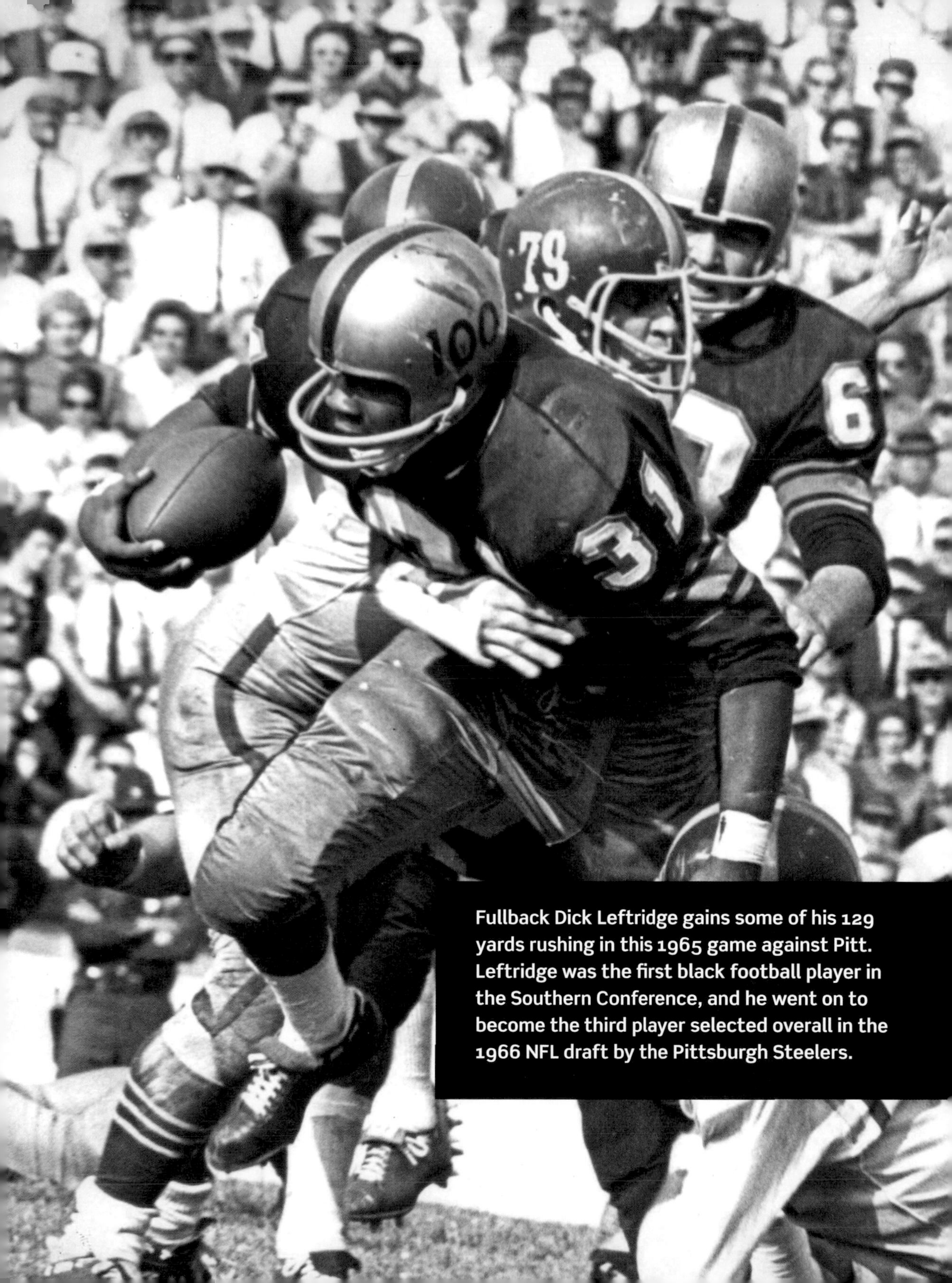

Fullback Dick Leftridge gains some of his 129 yards rushing in this 1965 game against Pitt. Leftridge was the first black football player in the Southern Conference, and he went on to become the third player selected overall in the 1966 NFL draft by the Pittsburgh Steelers.

Some of the offensive stars from West Virginia's 63-point explosion against Pitt in 1965 check out the local headlines. Pictured from left to right are fullback Dick Leftridge, placekicker Chuck Kinder, quarterback Allen McCune and halfback Garrett Ford.

The Jim Carlen Football Show aired throughout most of the state in the mid-1960s. It was the first football television show of its kind in West Virginia, and it was Carlen who convinced Wheeling's WTRF to produce it. The late Jennings Martin served as the show's co-host.

Kicker Ken Juskowich's five field goals accounted for all of the points in West Virginia's 15-0 victory over Pitt in 1967. The Panthers produced only 25 yards of offense and managed to cross the 50 just twice in the game, prompting Pitt coach Dave Hart to call his team's performance "a complete humiliation."

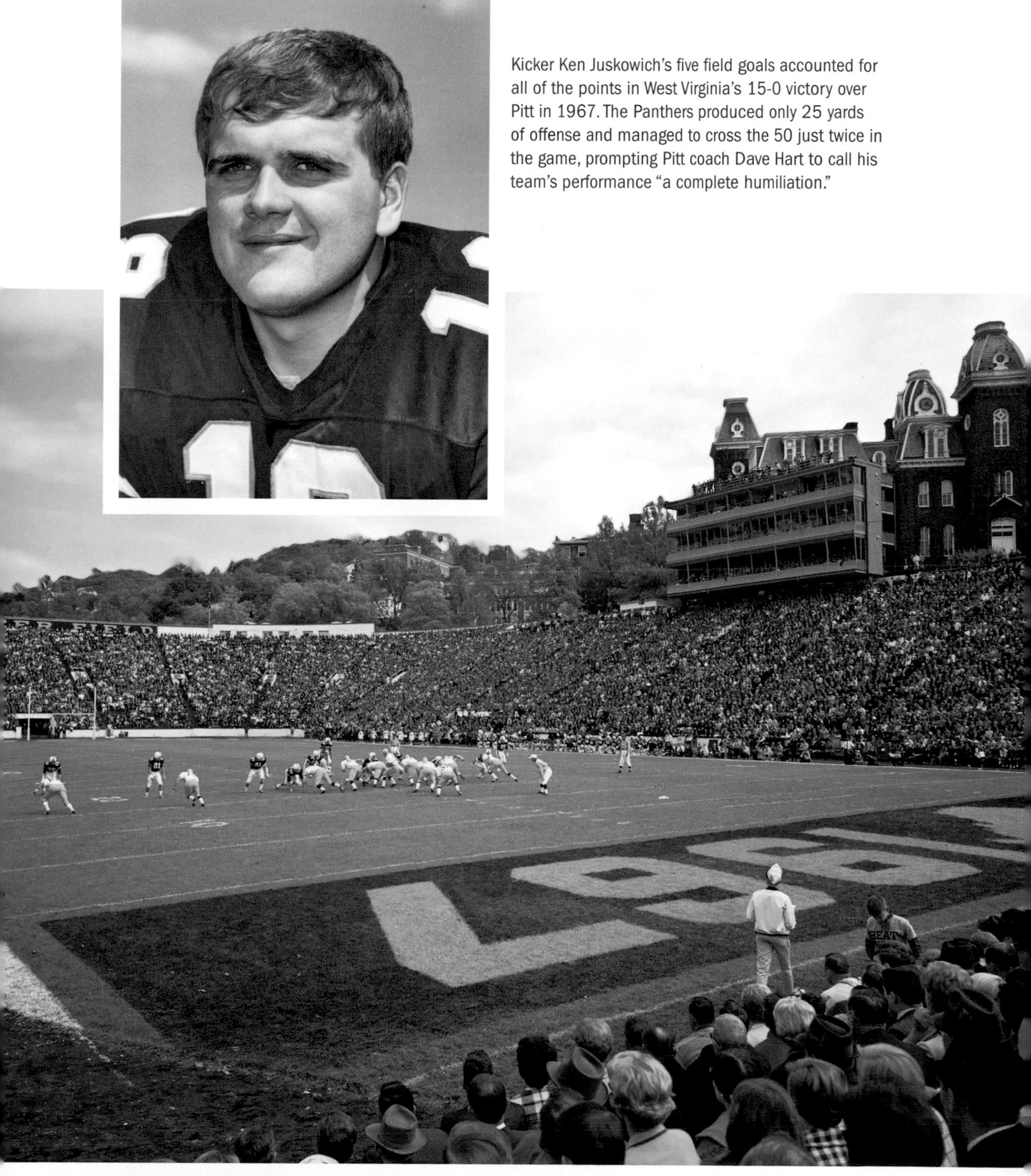

A wide view of jam-packed Mountaineer Field during West Virginia's 1967 game against Pitt.

West Virginia coach Bobby Bowden called his 1970 defeat at Pitt the most embarrassing loss of his coaching career. Bowden chose to sit on a 35-8 halftime lead, and the Mountaineers ended up losing the game, 36-35, to the underdog Panthers. Bowden is pictured here at Pitt Stadium in 1974, with assistant coach Garrett Ford and equipment manager Carl Roberts standing in the background.

Elated fans storm the field after West Virginia's 1975 victory over Pitt, which came down to the final play of the game. The celebrations lasted well into the following week in the Sunnyside section of town.

Post-Standard of Syracuse in 2004. "He said there was blood all over the knife, and he just didn't think anything of it and proceeded to cut that apple."

The Schwartzwalder story the West Virginia old-timers used to love telling was about the time he was coaching at Sistersville High in the 1930s: He took his wrestling team over to Buckhannon to meet an Eastern Panhandle school halfway because the roads in the state were so awful. After the heavyweight match, the score was still tied, and Schwartzwalder was adamant that no one was leaving until a winner was determined, so he challenged the other team's coach to settle the thing on the mat. Schwartzwalder, also a wrestler at WVU, instantly pinned the other guy, and Sistersville drove back home the victors.

By the early 1960s, Schwartzwalder had turned Syracuse into a college football power, and the string of running backs he had then rivals any in college history (including USC), beginning with Jim Brown in the mid-1950s and continuing with Ernie Davis, Jim Nance and Floyd Little well into the 1960s. All of them were fantastic runners, but the one guy who really struck fear into the hearts of opposing teams was Larry Csonka – standing 6-foot-3 and weighing 240 pounds, he was easily the biggest player on the football field. And Csonka pretty much had his way whenever he played against West Virginia, especially in 1967, when he rumbled for more than 100 yards on bulldozer-like blasts up the middle. After one particularly impressive run, WVU kicker Ken Juskowich noticed teammate Charlie Fisher and Csonka having a little conversation when the two got up off the ground. Curious, Juskowich asked Fisher what Csonka had told him. "Charlie told me he said 'Let me help you up, little fella.' Charlie Fisher is our tackle and one of our biggest defensive players, and Csonka is calling him 'little fella!'" laughed Juskowich.

Thad Kucherawy, a backup defensive back who was full of pep and energy, got into the game and immediately tried to pump up his discouraged teammates. . . . *Come on! This guy's not that good! Csonka is not that good. We can get him!* Linebacker Ron Yuss, who had spent the entire afternoon trying to slow Csonka down, stopped Kucherawy before he could say anything else. "Hey," Yuss yelled. "This is the toughest sonofabitch I've ever played against in my entire life. It's easy for you guys because he runs through all of us and we grab on to him, and all you have to do is pile on at the end!"

To this day, the 1967 Syracuse game might be one of the worst physical beatings a Mountaineer team has ever absorbed. The final score was only 23-6, but Syracuse sent several WVU players to the hospital, including two on one play – a punt. "One of our guys [Ben Siegfried] got a concussion, and the other guy was Bob Zambo," said wide receiver Oscar Patrick. "He came over to the sideline and they had like a dugout with no cover over it, and I'm sitting there and I said, 'Hey Zam, what happened to you?' He said, 'Hey Oscar' as he was holding his wrist, so I asked him if I could look at his arm. I pulled his hand up and you could see his bone sticking out of his arm. I said, 'You ought to get the trainer to look at that.' I didn't want to sound too excited because I didn't want him to go into shock."

"They knocked our quarterback out; we had running backs knocked out with broken jaws. That was the meanest bunch of guys we ever saw," said Bowden. "We couldn't leave afterward until they let all our injured guys out of the hospital. We joked about that game for years. . . . we didn't leave town – we were evacuated."

Garrett Ford didn't see much action against the Orangemen because he was nursing a nagging ankle injury that plagued him throughout his senior season, but he was in the game long enough to get a sampling of what his teammates were going through. "They did beat the crap out of us," Ford laughed. "As a matter of fact, it was almost like we didn't want to play them. Syracuse back then was hot. They were rolling and they were just much better than we were back then.

"We lost to Penn State and Syracuse every year," Ford continued. "Deep down inside I don't think we ever really thought we had a shot at beating Penn State and Syracuse. Penn State used to beat the heck out of us. I think they would play their third team and give their regulars a break the week they played us. And then Syracuse was always so physical."

That may have been the case with two of West Virginia's three main football rivals, but not so with Pitt.

The Panthers were licking their wounds after season-opening losses to UCLA and Illinois. Pitt's offense played poorly in both games, so Hart decided to shake things up, moving sophomore split end George "Doc" Medich to tight end, inserting junior Art Alois at one of the starting offensive guard spots and juggling his running back duo of Paul Bergman and Gary Cramer. The Panthers' biggest offensive threats were quarterback Frank Gustine and receiver Bob Longo, although the unit had managed just 14 points in its two blowout losses.

West Virginia, too, was in bad shape despite a 3-1 start. Fans enthused about the Mountaineers' early victories over Villanova, Richmond and VMI were given a heavy dose of reality up at Syracuse. Zambo was lost for the season with a broken right arm, quarterback Tom Digon hurt his neck and Siegfried, playing in place of injured Garrett

Ford, also went down with a concussion in the Syracuse game, although he was able to return to the field and play against the Panthers. Digon's injury, initially believed to be a cracked vertebra, left sophomore Garland Hudson in charge of the offense, and sophomore Eddie Silverio got most of the carries at running back. Consequently, Carlen wanted to play things conservatively against Pitt, relying on his strong defense and utilizing Juskowich, a former Mountaineer soccer player who came out for the football team in 1966 at the urging of soccer coach Greg Myers. Juskowich was a prep All-American soccer player who had scored a goal for the U.S. national team in the 1964 Guatemalan Games, but he suffered a pair of broken ankles and was no longer capable of playing the sport. "I remember going out there at the end of practice," Juskowich said. "It was Chuck Kinder's final year coming up, and they both said, 'let's see what you can do.' I started kicking, and it wasn't 20-25 minutes when Coach Carlen came over to me and he said, 'Son, I want you to get your stuff [from] wherever you are living on campus, because you are going to move into the dormitory and you are going to be on scholarship.' To make a decision like that for somebody who had never played a game or kicked a football in front of people . . . people don't make decisions like that anymore."

Juskowich proved right away that Carlen knew what he was doing, kicking four field goals in the Mountaineers' season-opening 40-0 victory over Villanova. Thinking back to before that first game, Juskowich remembers two very concerned coaches trying to boost the confidence of a young kicker. "I think Carlen and Bowden gave me all kind of pep talks," Juskowich laughed. "I had never kicked in a game before, and to be honest, I had a lot of power, but I was just OK in practice. And then in the game I said, 'Wow, this is fun.' I had a different attitude toward the games, and after the Villanova game I said, 'This wasn't so hard.'" Juskowich kicked two more field goals in succeeding games and came into the Pitt contest as the team's leading scorer, with 28 points. "By the time we came to the Pitt game, I was getting a lot of press, and Coach Carlen and Coach Bowden had a lot more confidence in me," said Juskowich.

It wasn't long into the Pitt game when Carlen went to Juskowich. His offense had fumbled away a great scoring opportunity at the Panther 1 on its opening possession. On its second possession, WVU got to the Pitt 16, where Hudson's third down pass, intended for tight end Jim Smith, fell incomplete. Juskowich came in and booted a 32-yard field goal to give the Mountaineers a 3-0 lead. Juskowich trotting on to kick field goals would be a recurring theme throughout the game – his second one coming with 1:24 remaining in the first half, when West Virginia's drive stalled at the Pitt 17. His third occurred midway through the third quarter, when WVU was stuffed at the Pitt 7.

Then, seven minutes later, field goal number four took place at the Panther 13, when Hudson couldn't hook up with Emo Schupbach on third down. And finally, with just seconds remaining and the outcome of the game already decided, Carlen rushed Juskowich back out onto the field with only four seconds left for a fifth field goal try. This one was his longest – 35 yards.

"I remember the fifth field goal because I kicked four in the first game, and I think that was a record at that point," Juskowich recalled. "The fifth field goal was right near the end of the game, and what Carlen did was let me go back in to kick that fifth field goal to break that record I had from the Villanova game, which they don't do very often. They don't usually care about records."

Hart didn't really care much for the field goal, either, or his putrid offense that finished the game with minus-21 yards rushing, 25 yards of total offense and just two first downs. The Panthers crossed West Virginia's 50 only twice, reaching the 48 in the second quarter and the 40 midway through the fourth quarter.

It got so bad that some of the 35,000 fans jam-packed into Mountaineer Field were distracted by two attractive females playing tennis on the courts down below the field. Unable to come up with anything positive to write about the game, one Pitt reporter described West Virginia's pass rush as being "like bubble dancers at a stag picnic."

Pitt's Hart was less colorful but more succinct: "This was a complete humiliation," he said. "This has got to be the worst football game I have ever been associated with, from my standpoint."

He continued:

"It was a complete disaster, especially offensively for us. It just seemed that my boys did not want to play football – neither their hearts nor bodies were in the game; West Virginia was up and played great defensive football, and I can't take a thing away from them.

"They didn't do a thing we didn't know about, and had worked on – they used their regular plan of attack – but they just executed their plays so much better than we did," Hart said.

Carlen was delighted with the victory – his first over the Panthers – but he wasn't the happiest person in the stadium. The Juskowiches from nearby Bethel Park, Pa., could easily make that claim. "I had uncles and aunts, and they were scattered all over the stadium, and my dad was there," Juskowich said. "My mother said he couldn't talk. He kind of froze up because he was seeing this game and I was scoring all of the points. I remember one of my uncles saying he was never coming to another game because he will never see anything like this again.

"And they didn't come back again."

The headline in the Sunday Morgantown newspaper told the story: Juskowich 15, Pitt 0.

Bobby Blows It

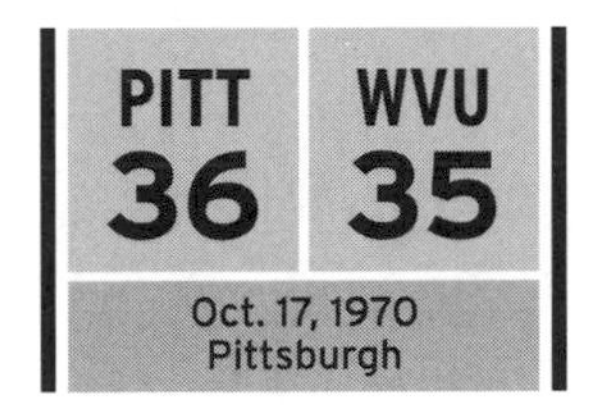

PITT
36
WVU
35
Oct. 17, 1970
Pittsburgh

There are many games Bobby Bowden remembers during his hall of fame coaching career, but there is only one that he will never forget. Bowden has admitted many times throughout the years that West Virginia's 36-35 loss to Pitt on October 17, 1970, was the most embarrassing defeat of his coaching career. On that overcast October afternoon, Bowden saw his Mountaineer team blow a 27-point halftime lead in a game that still defies logic. All West Virginia needed to do was stop Pitt's offense just one time in the second half to win the game – ONCE – and the Mountaineers couldn't do it.

"I embarrassed the whole state of West Virginia, I embarrassed myself; I embarrassed my team," Bowden said in 1991. "We were leading them 35-8 at the half. It was a rout. And then we go out there in the second half and get beat. That was the worst thing that has ever happened to me in football."

By all accounts, Bowden in 1970 inherited an excellent offensive football team from Jim Carlen. The vast majority of the players that helped WVU win 10 games and defeat South Carolina in the 1969 Peach Bowl were back. "The '70 team had a lot of talent there," recalled Bowden assistant coach Frank Cignetti. "It was sort of a carry over and the expectations were very high. In 1970, they were coming off a bowl win and they had [Jim] Braxton, [Bob] Gresham and [Mike] Sherwood coming back."

The boastful Carlen, who was just getting settled in at his new job at Texas Tech, immediately put the pressure on his former offensive coordinator – speaking with a Houston reporter, he made some eye-opening comments that eventually made their way back to West Virginia. "I left Bobby a real good team," Carlen said in the summer before the start of the '70 season. Although Carlen said he "didn't want to put any undue pressure on Bobby," he went on to say that he thought West Virginia had "at least a half-dozen players good enough for All-America consideration." West Virginia fans, many with memories like elephants, would not forget Carlen's remarks.

Bowden and Carlen were polar opposites when it came to football strategy. Carlen preferred to keep things conservative, relying on his defense and kicking game. Bowden liked to throw the football and was enamored with trick plays. When Carlen was Bobby Dodd's defensive coach at Georgia Tech, he saw the success Alabama was having throwing the football with Joe Namath, and he decided to find someone who understood the passing game when he got the West Virginia job in 1966. "When I went to West Virginia, I openly said 'I know defense, I know the kicking game and I know the running game, but I don't have a clue about the throwin' game,'" said Carlen.

But Carlen found somebody who did: Bobby Bowden. Carlen got to know Bowden a little bit when Georgia Tech and Florida State would get together for clinics during the summertime. At the time, Bowden was spinning his wheels as Florida State's wide receivers coach, and he was getting impatient for an offensive coordinator job. When Carlen was hired at West Virginia and he saw what little talent he had to work with, he began to think about Bowden. "I met him at a clinic. I did not really spend a lot of time with him, but I realized right away he was my kind of coach – real strong Christian Baptist; had a good family, and I realized he had the ability to recruit because he was so personable and got along with everybody," said Carlen

Most of the time, Carlen let Bowden do as he pleased with the offense: on the opening play of the 1966 season, he let Bowden call a trick play that ended up going for a long touchdown to John Mallory. Another time, Carlen was supportive when Bowden completely changed the offense to use little Pete Secret at quarterback; Bowden chose to run the option against Kentucky, in a game that ended in a tie. For the most part, though, Bowden preferred to throw the ball and score as many points as possible. Cignetti, who later became Bowden's offensive coordinator, admitted to feeling pressure to score touchdowns when he was calling plays for Bowden. "He was the kind of guy who liked it wide open," Cignetti recalled. "Man, if you didn't have 21 points on the board in the first four or five minutes . . . I'll never forget one day we were out there and we're running the football in a game against Miami, and he gets on the phone and he says, 'Frank, don't you have faith in your quarterback?'"

There were times when Carlen and Bowden didn't always see eye to eye. Once, in a game where West Virginia was comfortably ahead, Bowden wanted to call a halfback pass because he knew the play would be wide open for a touchdown. Carlen had ordered no more passing, but an irritated Bowden was going to defy Carlen and call the play anyway, but the other assistant coaches intervened. Carlen also recalled having to force Bowden to get on the telephone to call Coach Darrell Royal down in Texas, hoping to learn about the wishbone before West Virginia's Peach Bowl game against South Carolina. "He didn't want to do it and I said, 'Bobby, we're going to do it. We've got running backs here,'" said Carlen.

Soon after Bowden took over from Carlen, he hired Houston linebacker coach Howard Tippett to run West Virginia's defense. Tippett had spent one year in Morgantown, coaching the freshmen in 1966, and when he returned for the 1970 season, he had inherited West Virginia's smallish, more mobile defensive players that Carlen preferred using. In fact, not a single Mountaineer defensive lineman in 1970 weighed more than 220 pounds (right end Art Holdt was the biggest of the group, at 220). Consequently, Tippett was in the unusual situation of fielding a defense in which the linebackers (Dale Farley, at 240 pounds and Terry King, at 222) were bigger than the guys responsible for keeping the blockers off of them. "We were so little back then," Farley recalled. "Our defensive line was barely 200 pounds. They did their jobs but they were awful small."

WEST VIRGINIA'S LACK OF SIZE EVENTUALLY CAUGHT UP WITH IT AGAINST DUKE.

West Virginia's lack of size eventually caught up with it against Duke, when Farley wasn't able to play after having twisted his knee badly in a blowout win over VMI. Farley's injury was the result of Bowden putting him back into the game in the second half, based on advice he'd gotten from Joe Paterno. Paterno told him that he sometimes put his starters back in the game in the second half during games where he felt like his team wasn't playing sharp. Of course, Paterno had the luxury of doing that because his Penn State teams were much deeper than Bowden's West Virginia teams. Against Duke, the Blue Devils, despite having a good passer in Leo Hart, pounded West Virginia's defense with runs up the middle. Duke finished the game with 236 yards on the ground and came away with an unexpected 21-13 victory. Even more unsettling to West Virginia supporters was Bowden's puzzling decision to punt the football on Duke's 34 yard line late in the second half, with the Mountaineers trailing by just six points. Bowden asked Tippett if his defense could stop Duke if he tried a field goal and it wasn't successful. Tippett said he wasn't sure. So instead of attempting a field goal, Bowden ordered his punter out onto the field, and the football wound up going several rows into the stands, giving Duke the ball at its own 20. Bowden was booed mercilessly. "That was bad," he recalled. "We were down there inside the Duke 20, I don't know how many times, and we didn't get any points," added Cignetti. "The great lesson to me was, hey, you're down there, get those field goals, because we ended up losing a close game."

It was after the Duke game that West Virginia fans started to wonder if Bowden really knew what he was doing.

Seventy-five miles north, in Pittsburgh, Carl DePasqua was in his second season and trying to rebuild a Pitt program that was left in disrepair by Dave Hart, whose teams won just three games over a three-year period, from 1966–68, before the plug was finally pulled on him. Hart had his problems, to be sure, but a lot of Pitt's athletic woes were systemic. DePasqua, a John Michelosen protégé who was the Pittsburgh Steelers' defensive line coach, was Pitt athletic director Cas Myslinski's choice to replace Hart after at least five other coaches turned him down – one being Frank Kush from nearby Windber, Pa. "There was no magic wand to wave," DePasqua said when he was hired.

The new coach said his teams were going to play fundamentally sound football, and that approach helped give Pitt a three-game improvement in the win column in 1969. Still, DePasqua was far from being popular with Panther supporters. The late Dick Polen, WVU's assistant sports information director at the time, once recalled getting a strong dose of DePasqua's effervescence. "We had a press conference up in Pittsburgh before the game where they had a telephone hookup with Bowden and DePasqua," said Polen. "One of the West Virginia writers asked DePasqua a question he didn't like, and he said 'That's the damned dumbest question I've ever heard.' This was right in the middle of the press conference, and you just didn't hear things like that back then."

According to some of his players, DePasqua was notorious for using clichés when he talked to the team, and he would sometimes confuse the meaning of words. Once, he addressed the players, and instead of telling them not to be philistines, they swore he said "Philippines." DePasqua also became enamored with a two-point conversion card Tampa Coach Fran Curci had given him. "It was like the Bible to him," laughed Pitt quarterback Dave Havern. To the Pitt players, it seemed like DePasqua went to that card after just about every Panther touchdown, usually choosing to go for two almost every time he shouldn't have. Havern recalled a tough game with Navy in 1971 when Pitt had finally gotten the lead by 1 point late in the game. Considering DePasqua's preference for going for two, it only seemed logical that DePasqua would choose to do so now, trying to give Pitt a 3-point lead. But Havern remembered lying on the bottom of the pile next to Pitt center Bobby Kuziel after scoring the go-ahead touchdown, and

Kuziel saying, "I bet the dumb bastard kicks the extra point instead of going for two!" Just as Kuziel spoke, out trotted the kicker, who clanked one off the upright, and the Panthers had to sweat out a one-point victory. Pitt was so bad during the seven years Hart and DePasqua coached there that it never once held a lead against Penn State, and it lost five out of seven times to West Virginia. By 1972, things had deteriorated to the point that, after a 1-10 season, Pitt was forced to fire DePasqua and hire Tennessee native Johnny Majors.

"I was coaching at IUP [Indiana University of Pennsylvania] at the time, and I happened to get back for a game in 1972 during DePasqua's last year to see them play Penn State," Havern said. "They were really bad and I was thinking to myself, 'We were bad when I played but this team was horrible.' That's when they brought Majors in."

DePasqua wasn't a huge fan of Jim Carlen, one, because Carlen could come off as being cocky, and two, because he felt that Carlen had run up the score in 1969, when Eddie Williams turned a simple dive play into an 80-yard touchdown run late in the game. The 49-18 win was WVU's largest margin of victory ever against the Panthers at that point. "He was mad and he told Coach Carlen after the game something to the effect that it would never be that bad again," said West Virginia quarterback Mike Sherwood.

DePasqua spoke prophetic words.

Even though Pitt had its problems against West Virginia in three consecutive losses in 1967, 1968 and 1969, the Duke game film was proof that 1970 might be a different story. The Blue Devils ran with ease on West Virginia's undersized defense and administered a pretty good beating on the Mountaineers that left several players bruised and battered – most notably Charlie Fisher, Danny Wilfong, Terry King and Dan Hannahs on defense, and running backs Pete Wood and Bob Gresham on offense. "I played a lot of football games, but I thought Duke hit us harder than anybody," said defensive back Mike Slater. "All they did was run right at us. It was just a hard-hitting game."

Pitt assistant coach Paul Kemp was the man in charge of scouting the Mountaineers, and he delivered this pregame assessment of West Virginia's defense, printed in the Pitt game program that afternoon: "West Virginia plays a basic 4-3 and they are not very big, but make up for this with their quickness. The defensive front four only averages 210 pounds per man, as compared to Pitt's 237-pound average. They play a very steady defense with a limited amount of blitzing. They utilize a zone pass defense, and will not let you go deep."

So, of course, the Panthers started the game by trying to run the ball wide on West Virginia. That played right into the hands of the much quicker Mountaineers on Pitt's fast new Astroturf surface. "I can't understand why they didn't [run the middle] in the first half," Bowden said after the game.

"The first half we made a lot of tackles on the outside because they tried to do some things wide on us. Pitt just wasn't fast enough to do that," said Slater.

"We just couldn't get outside against West Virginia," added Havern, who was replacing an injured John Hogan at quarterback. "We were running our normal offense and they were stopping us."

Meanwhile, Eddie Williams and Gresham, as they had done the year before, were gouging Pitt with long runs. With Mike Sherwood mixing in some timely passes, West Virginia built up what seemed to be an insurmountable 35-8 halftime lead. "The wire service guys had already written their stories," said Mickey Furfari. "All they had to do was add the final stats and polish up their leads." Furfari was also inclined to get a head start on his story, because his wife Elizabeth was heading downtown to do some shopping. At halftime, she yelled up to the open-air press box where Mickey was sitting, telling him that she was leaving the game with a friend and would meet up with him later. "And she had all of the credit cards!" Mickey laughed.

Pittsburgh Post-Gazette sports editor Al Abrams was sitting in the stands taking in the game, and when he decided to leave the stadium at halftime with just about everybody else, a Pitt fan whispered to him, "Be kind."

Even some of the West Virginia coaches thought this one was already in the bag. As the team was jogging off the field to the locker room, Bowden felt secure enough to joke with Sherwood. "It looks like you own these guys," Bowden said. Sherwood, who passed for a school-record 416 yards against the Panthers in 1968 and led WVU to an easy win over Pitt in 1969, replied, "For two and a half games anyway, Coach." There was jubilation in the West Virginia locker room at halftime, and Bowden had a tough time getting his team calmed down. "We were just cutting it up and having a good time," Slater admitted.

In the Pitt locker room, DePasqua was trying to figure out what to do for the second half. He didn't give a big rah-rah speech to rally his players; in fact, Havern doesn't recall DePasqua saying much at all. The guy doing all of the talking was defensive tackle John Stevens, who, according to Havern, stood up and yelled, "I'm tired of this crap! I'm going to beat the hell out of my guy! I don't care what I'm supposed to do – I'm just going to beat up my guy!"

The West Virginia players and coaches mistakenly believed that Pitt had given up on the game and they were just going to try and run out the clock to avoid another embarrassing loss. But that's not what happened. Havern says DePasqua decided to use a Power-I running formation at the start of the second half, and to go for it on fourth down every single time. That meant giving the ball to 230-pound Tony Esposito, 220-pound John Moss and 202-pound Denny Ferris on nearly every play. All three runners were bigger than West Virginia's defensive linemen. "Everyone went home at halftime," Ferris said in 2000. "I wanted to go home, too."

Bowden also planned to keep it on the ground, eventually getting his starters out of the game and rested for Colorado State. "He said we were going to just run the ball at them and that we weren't looking to run up the score up, that kind of thing," said Sherwood. Bowden also told backup quarterback Bernie Galiffa to get ready to play in the second half. "There were like two busloads of people from my hometown up there to watch me play," said Galiffa, from nearby Donora, Pa. "At halftime, Coach Bowden comes up to me and he says, 'Mike is going to take the first series – warm up on the sidelines because you're going in.' I'm thinking, alright," Galiffa laughed. "I run out of the tunnel and I turn to some of my people from my hometown and I tell them I'm going in! I never got in. I warmed up on the sidelines for nothing."

Earlier that season, Lou Holtz had accused Bowden of running up the score in Bowden's very first WVU game, against Holtz's outmanned William & Mary team. West Virginia won the contest easily, 43-7, and Holtz, from nearby East Liverpool, Ohio, was hot under the collar because he had friends and family in Morgantown for the game. "For crying out loud, they still had [Jim] Braxton in the game with a minute left," Holtz complained afterward. Holtz's criticism may have unconsciously played a role in Bowden's decision to play things conservatively at the start of the second half against Pitt. Whatever the reason, it was a decision he would forever regret.

Pitt returned West Virginia's opening kickoff to the 42 to begin the second half. The Panthers, now in the Power-I, marched 58 yards in 15 plays to reach the end zone. DePasqua went for the two-point conversion to make the score 35-16. Bowden, confident his team could move the sticks and keep the clock running, called three straight running plays. Havern clearly remembered Pitt's defensive series: "They ran a trap, and Lloyd Weston made a great play on second down and they lost a yard. We stopped them on third down and they had to kick it back to us."

Just as it did on its first drive of the second half, Pitt kept the ball between the tackles and once again methodically marched down the field. This time it took the Panthers 14 plays before Dave Garnett blasted in from the 5. DePasqua tried for two once again, and

Havern used some ingenuity to convert Pitt's second one. "They had me trapped and I'm rolling out the wrong way, so I just flicked the ball underhand to our tight end Joel Klimek – a guy who had just come back from 'Nam and was a Silver Star guy. He makes the catch for the two-point conversion [somehow coming up with the ball between WVU defenders Doug Charley, Mike Slater and Leon Jenkins]. So then I'm thinking it's 35-24 and it's about time something breaks our way.

"It was about that time you could see the West Virginia guys across the field thinking 'Geez, what's going on here?'"

"They went for fourth down six or seven times and made it," Bowden said. "Every time they'd measure for a first down they'd stop the clock, and I was sitting there trying to milk that clock."

At about that point Galiffa finally decided to quit warming up on the sidelines. "I looked up at the scoreboard and said, 'Oh @#$%!' Farley was out of the game, and Coach Bowden put him in for a couple of plays when he was hurt just to try and stop them." Farley, unable to continue, had a helpless feeling standing over on the sidelines. "I kept thinking to myself that there is no way they are going to come back and beat us," he said. "But they just kept scoring and scoring and we couldn't stop them."

"I LOOKED UP AT THE SCOREBOARD AND SAID, 'OH $#(+!'"

Ex-WVU QB Bernie Galiffa

After Pitt's second touchdown, Sherwood said he could sense his teammates getting very concerned on the sidelines. "We tried to go back to the things we were doing in the first half and we just couldn't get it going," he said.

"Football is a game of momentum, and it's an art to be ahead and maintain that momentum," said Sandusky, Ohio, native Eddie Williams, who ran for 199 yards against the Panthers in 1969 and added 118 yards in the 1970 game. Williams thought Farley and Art Holdt being out of the game was also in the back of the players' minds. "Say you've got a couple of key players out and then the game starts getting close and you start seeing the momentum change and now you start to think about the two guys that are not in there. All of that begins to have a mental effect on you."

Meanwhile, Pitt continued pounding away on the ground. Its third drive of the second half covered 70 yards in 14 plays and ended once again in West Virginia's end zone, when Esposito got in from the 1. Havern's conversion pass failed this time, leaving West Virginia up 35-30 lead with less than 10 minutes remaining. Once more, West Virginia couldn't move the sticks and had to punt the football back to Pitt. "The defense didn't play well, but the offense did their part [in aiding Pitt's comeback], too," said Farley.

Pitt got the football back at its own 30 and drove the length of the field, making two fourth-down conversions along the way (the second at the WVU 12, with less than three minutes to go) to reach the West Virginia 5, with only 55 seconds remaining on the clock. Then, on third down, Pitt called a pass play designed for Havern to choose either running back Ferris out in the flat or tight end Bill Pilconis running a release down the middle. Slater said Pilconis was his responsibility. "They flared a guy out of the backfield and our free safety was supposed to take him, but I took one step toward [Ferris] thinking for sure they were going to throw the ball to him, and they threw it over the middle to Pilconis."

"As soon as I let the ball go, I got nailed right in the sciatic [nerve], I went down, and I'm dying," said Havern. "I heard the crowd and I figured he caught it. He was so wide open that there couldn't have been a guy within 10 yards of him."

The *Pittsburgh Post-Gazette* account of the game story made mention of Pilconis "enjoying monastic solitude in the end zone," according to Chuck Klausing's 1997 self-published book, *Never Lost a Game (Time Just Ran Out)*. A once-somber Pitt press box had now become electric. The late Dick Polen, West Virginia's assistant publicist at the time, recalled the mood change that had taken place in the second half. "In the first half when we built up that big lead, all of the West Virginia sportswriters were cheering after the good plays. Dean Billick, Pitt's sports information director at the time, got on the press box PA system and said, 'There will be no more cheering in the press box!' He was really mad," said Polen. "Well, in the second half when Pitt started turning it around and all of the Pittsburgh sportswriters began cheering, Billick just stood up there as silent as a tree."

With Pitt now leading by 1, there was still the matter of the conversion. DePasqua, as unpredictable as ever, inexplicably chose to kick the extra point instead of trying for the two-point conversion to put Pitt up by 3. "DePasqua kicks the extra point, we miss it, and now a field goal beats us," Havern moaned. "So of course West Virginia started marching right down the field and they're inside our 40."

With 19 seconds left, Sherwood hit Wayne Porter for a short gainer over the middle, but he fumbled the football and Pitt's Stevens recovered it. One play later, Havern took a knee and Pitt won the game, 36-35. The final statistics were revealing: Pitt ran a total of 61 plays in the second half and 97 for the game, while West Virginia managed just 10 second half plays before its final drive. Most amazing of all was the fact that Pitt's 27-point comeback victory came without the benefit of a long pass, a long run or a West Virginia turnover. Pitt's longest play of the game covered just 21 yards. "It was a pass down the middle to Doug Gindin," said Havern. Ferris rushed for 144 yards, Garnett had

89 and Esposito finished with 42, while Havern completed 11-of-16 passes for 138 yards. Pitt ran the ball 81 times and had only two plays totaling more than 20 yards. Gresham led all rushers with 149 yards; Williams added 118, and Sherwood passed for 139 yards for the Mountaineers.

After the game, some of the players were quietly sobbing in the West Virginia locker room. "Going into the dressing room after the game was really a sad state," said Slater. "The locker room was so quiet," said Dale Farley. "You could hear a pin drop."

"It was sort of a mixture of sadness and shame," added Eddie Williams. "We knew we should have done better." Some West Virginia fans, however, were feeling more than just sadness and shame. Many were seeing red. Mickey Furfari recalled waiting outside the West Virginia locker room before it was opened up for reporters to go in and talk to the players and coaches. Among them were several dozen West Virginia fans who began pounding on the door yelling, "Come on out, Bobby" and "Bye-bye, Bobby."

"Because the team bused up to Pittsburgh, he took his time in the locker room," said Furfari. "He was smart enough to know not to come out with all those people still around."

"Our fans mobbed my dressing room door after the game," Bowden said years later. "I couldn't come out. They'd probably lynch me."

Mike Sherwood remembers hearing some of the stuff that happened, but he doesn't specifically recall any incidents after the game. "I remember there being talk of it," he said. "There are all kind of bizarre things that kind of grew out of the game like there being players getting into fights and so forth. I really don't recall any of that."

"It was not a pretty picture up there, I can tell you," added Polen, who was down in the locker room after the game. Bowden, who looked as if he had just seen a ghost, told reporters afterward: "This is going to be the most heartbreaking loss I've had in coaching – when I wake up tonight. I've seen games like this before, but I've never been through one. I can't help thinking we did our best. That's what worries me." Naturally, DePasqua was elated. "It's a great day of joy," he said afterward. "In all my 17 years of coaching, this is the most fantastic comeback I've ever experienced."

Tippett offered this assessment of his beleaguered West Virginia defense: "We lined up everything we could line up and still couldn't hold them. Pitt was too strong for us: They knocked us out of there."

Bowden, depressed and upset with the way his team had performed, got another dose of reality when he went home and saw his wife Ann lying on the bed crying. She had been listening to the game on the radio and had heard some of the things people were saying about her husband.

The next day, Furfari tried to make sense of the loss. "What happened to the West Virginia defense?" he wrote. "Where was the marvelous mixture of speed and finesse Bobby Bowden's boys had parlayed into a big lead?

"Pitt simply stole the show after the intermission with an awesome act the likes of which these eyes had never seen. Some weird happenings have taken place in sports down through the years, but this observer can't recall one the equal of this. Never. Never. Never."

Colleague Tony Constantine was equally stunned: "If anything written in this corner today sounds ridiculous, or crazy, blame it on a state of shock," he began. He finished by writing, "The second half is hard to believe."

Three days later, the game was still on the mind of *Charleston Daily Mail* sports editor Bill Smith, a personal witness to the insults being lobbed at Bowden while he was barricaded inside the WVU dressing room. His Tuesday afternoon column turned into a sermon on fan behavior. "Only persons second-rate were outside the dressing room door," he wrote. "The ones inside had nothing to be ashamed of. Fans stunned! Fans disappointed!

"Imagine how the players felt? With fans like those who came out of their holes Saturday, the young athletes don't need enemies. So, sue me!"

Wheeling's Cliff McWilliams, a Bowden basher from that afternoon on, wasn't as kind, writing, "An emotional explanation such as 'we were just killed,' tears in the dressing room, 'it was just unbelievable,' leaves an awful lot to be desired – like cold, clear hard facts and a professional analysis no matter who it hurts . . . so far, nobody has offered an answer."

Beckley's Larry Farley pinned the blame directly on Bowden, writing, "I sincerely believe Jim Carlen could have kept West Virginia from losing to Pitt, and maybe Duke."

Even today, Sherwood believes that West Virginia was the better football team that afternoon. "We felt like we had Pitt's number and we really did. I think it was one of those freak things that happened and there is really no explanation for it. We played Colorado State the very next week and beat them when they had Lawrence McCutcheon, and Pitt didn't have any Lawrence McCutcheons, I'll tell you that."

"You just can't forget that one: It just sticks in your craw for some reason," added Slater.

"When you hear people say 'that's football.' Well, that was what that game was really like," remarked Williams, whose three first-half touchdowns were completely erased by Pitt's second-half comeback. "I don't know whether we relaxed or something happened to us mentally going into that second half."

West Virginia finished the 1970 season with an 8-3 record; a loss to Penn State and upset wins by Duke and Pitt kept WVU from going to back-to-back bowl games. Pitt, meanwhile, managed a .500 record in 1970, snapping a string of six straight losing seasons. The period from 1964 through 1972 is considered among the worst in Pitt football history.

Some West Virginia observers believe bad fortune was the cause for the Pitt defeat in 1970. If WVU had had Farley in the middle, or tackle George Boyd (injured during the Indiana game), then the Panthers wouldn't have been able to exploit the middle of West Virginia's defense so easily. Also, right before the game, Bowden suspended starting right end Art Holdt for missing team curfew. "I would have liked to think I could have made a difference," said Farley. "It's a team effort, so I don't know. When a team gets momentum like that it's hard to stop them."

Slater says he always thinks about that game whenever he sees a big halftime score on television. "We'll be sitting there watching the TV and someone will say the game is over. I say, 'Hey, I've been in a game when they've come back and won it.'

"It's never over."

He knows.

McKenzie Kicks the Hell Out of Pitt

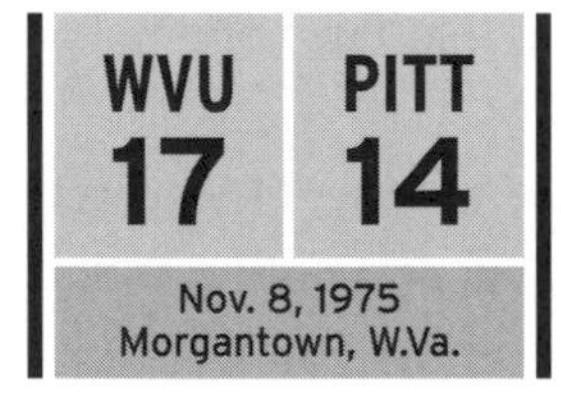

WVU
17
PITT
14
Nov. 8, 1975
Morgantown, W.Va.

The one lasting memory Frank Cignetti has of West Virginia's 1975 victory over Pitt wasn't Bill McKenzie's kick that beat the Panthers on the final play of the game, or the ensuing Sunnyside celebration that left people shocked and awed years before Donald Rumsfeld ever uttered the phrase "Shock and Awe." No, the thing Cignetti remembers most about that unforgettable game was West Virginia's refusal to quit when it had every reason to. It was a lesson Cignetti remembered a few years later when he beat cancer at a time when almost nobody was beating cancer, particularly the form he had, which was so rare it took doctors months to diagnose. Cignetti, retired and living in Indiana, Pa., remembers clearly the circumstances that led to McKenzie's unforgettable game-winning field goal.

"We were on a drive with two or three minutes left on the clock," he recalled. "We were going to run out the clock and set up a field goal that would have won the game. But Ron Lee fumbled the football. It would have been easy for that defense to start bitching about Ron Lee fumbling the football, but no, they went in there and did their job and stuffed Pitt on three downs and forced a punt. Then, the offensive team went out there and did what it had to do to win the game."

It was a victory no one in West Virginia at the time really expected. Running back Artie Owens, whose four years in Morgantown were spent playing in the shadow of Pitt All-American Tony Dorsett, remembered a supremely confident Panther team that strolled into West Virginia's ancient stadium that overcast Saturday afternoon in early November.

"They had so much confidence that they would come in here and take over in our own backyard in our little stadium," Owens recalled. Growing up in eastern Pennsylvania, Owens knew next to nothing about the WVU-Pitt game before he came to Morgantown in 1972. "I only experienced during the years that I was there how intense and how much this game means in the different neighborhoods and things like that," Owens said. "It reminded me of when I was in high school. It had the same type of atmosphere and hype."

In 1973, Johnny Majors pulled the Pitt football program out of the dumpster after years of neglect. "They were terrible in the late 1960s and early 1970s," recalled West Virginia defensive end Gary Lombard, a native of Perryopolis, Pa. Lombard remembered the air being sucked out of his living room when Pitt recruiter Bimbo Cecconi showed up at his house to talk about the Panther program.

"He basically just spoke with me and he said, 'Oh by the way, here's an application. Please fill this out and we'll see if you can get accepted into Pitt.' I can't say I actually ever had another coach say that," Lombard said. "I had a pretty good grade point average, but they approached things a little bit differently at Pitt in the early 1970s."

Fox Chapel's Andy Peters also got an inside peek at what was going on up at Pitt in the late 1960s and early 1970s. "I moved to Pittsburgh in 1964 and [Pitt star player] Paul Martha married my cousin," Peters said. "When he found out I was getting recruited, he was still playing for the Steelers and he said, 'Andy, Carl DePasqua does not have a good program and I cannot tell you in good conscience that you should go to Pitt.' So when Coach Bowden came and sat in my living room and sold my parents and me on West Virginia, it was the logical choice."

When Pitt fired DePasqua after a 1-10 season in 1972, the Panthers – specifically the Golden Panthers (Pitt's fundraising group, today called The Panthers Club) – opened up their wallets and hired Iowa State's Johnny Majors. Everything Majors asked Pitt athletic director Cas Myslinski he forgot. When he wanted Pitt to pull out of the "Big Four" – a loose confederation consisting of Penn State, Syracuse, Pitt and West Virginia that regulated such things as scheduling, officiating, redshirting and scholarship limitations – Pitt let him do it. Majors wanted to redshirt players and sign those big recruiting classes some of the renegade programs in the South and Southwest were bringing in, which is exactly what Coach Jim Carlen had wanted to do at West Virginia before he departed for Texas Tech after the 1969 Peach Bowl. The WVU Athletic Council had refused to let Carlen do it out of fear of jeopardizing longstanding relationships with Pitt, Syracuse and Penn State, and also because of how expensive it would be. In Majors's case, Myslinski acquiesced.

Majors wound up signing somewhere between 75 and 87 players in his first recruiting class in 1973, among them Tony Dorsett, Al Romano, J.C. Pelusi, Jim Corbett, Joe Stone, Arnie Weatherington and kicker Carson Long – all members of the 1976 national championship team. The funding for the extra scholarships came from a trust established for Pitt football players that had been created for their post-graduate education. "The big thing that helped them when Coach Majors came in there was he was able to beat the new legislation on numbers," said Cignetti. "His first year, there are all kind of stories on the number of players he brought in, and I can't say exactly how many. That gave them a leg up right there, and one of them was Tony Dorsett."

Gary Lombard missed Majors by one year, or he likely would have been in that big Pitt recruiting class as well. "There were guys that I played against in high school that I was kind of friends with who were at Pitt at the time, and it was a big transition," Lombard remembered. "A lot of people got run off and a lot of new faces came in. If Majors brought you in you were going to stay there, but if you were there before, he axed a lot of those guys."

"They were recruiting me and I remember talking to people there and they said they had signed between 80 and a hundred players [in 1972] because there were no rules regulating that stuff back then," remembered quarterback Dan Kendra. "I played in the Big 33 game with Randy Holloway and a couple of other guys and I'd say to them 'My god, are you guys going to school or working up there?'"

"With that many players coming in, you've only got to hit on 30 percent of them," explained former Clemson Coach Tommy Bowden, who played wide receiver for his father at WVU in the mid-1970s. "The guys that were left were really, really good players. You could go up there and hit and scrimmage and get 'em hurt and run 'em off and weed it down to the good ones, and that's surely what they did. It was a heck of a plan by Coach Majors."

Majors stopped Pitt's 10-year losing streak in its tracks in 1973 with a 6-5-1 record that included the school's first bowl trip in 16 years. In 1974, Majors led the Panthers to a 7-4 record during a season that featured wins over Georgia Tech, Syracuse and Temple, and competitive losses to USC and Notre Dame. Pitt's two victories over West Virginia in those same years were blowouts: 35-7 in Morgantown in 1973 and 31-14 in Pittsburgh in 1974. Dorsett played a big role in both games, running for 150 yards and three touchdowns (all three scores coming in the second half) in the 1973 game and producing 145 yards and a TD in the 1974 Pitt win. In the 1974 loss, what irked the West Virginia players more than Dorsett's showboating and constant jawing were the three cheap scores the Panthers got in the fourth quarter.

MAJORS STOPPED PITT'S 10-YEAR LOSING STREAK IN ITS TRACKS IN 1973.

And the defeats were beginning to pile up for the Mountaineers that year – seven in all during a season that almost completely turned the West Virginia fan base against their coach. Some of the discontent actually began during Bowden's first year, 1970, when he inherited a strong team from Jim Carlen that featured Jim Braxton, Bob Gresham, Eddie Williams and Mike Sherwood – all offensive stars on the '69 Peach Bowl team. West Virginia began the year in *Sports Illustrated's* Top 20 for the first time in school history. In two consecutive weeks, though, Bowden made two crucial missteps that hardened the opinions of his critics: Choosing to punt deep in Duke territory during a tight game that his team ended up losing (the backup punter sailed the ball well out of the end zone instead of kicking it out of bounds), and going conservative after leading Pitt 35-8 at halftime, in a game the Panthers wound up winning 36-35. Many fans never forgave Bowden for those two blunders. After the 1970 Pitt loss, Tommy Bowden learned quickly just how important beating the Panthers was to the people of West Virginia – and to the continued well-being of his family. "At that particular stage of my father's coaching career – and us as children being considerably younger – the death threats and things of that nature brought it down to a little more personal level, and you kind of understood the intensity of the rivalry much better," Tommy recalled.

Unfortunately, the difficulties continued for the Bowdens. A strong start to the '71 season was eventually derailed by injuries and a lack of depth, with the team's 6-1 record through the first seven games ending at 7-4. In 1972, Bowden took the Mountaineers back to the Peach Bowl, but they were embarrassed by North Carolina State, 49-13. Purported player misbehavior down in Atlanta was blamed for the loss, and many Mountaineer fans drove back from the game with "Fire Bowden" signs in the back windows of their cars. Bowden, a devout Christian, was stung by the perception that he was running a loose ship, and he immediately instituted more stringent rules for his team after that loss. The military fatigues, long hair and mustaches that were popular in the 1970s were no longer allowed. Bowden also began sequestering his football team the night before home games.

"The next two years we took Bluebird buses to Kingwood and stayed the night there before home games at a place called Mamie's Hotel," said Lombard. "Now let me tell you, whenever you came back the next morning on a Bluebird bus on those country roads, you weren't feeling too good by the time you got to the stadium."

The players weren't the only ones suffering from motion sickness. The fans were also getting sick of the rollercoaster ride their football team was on. After winning its first three games of the '73 season against Maryland, Virginia Tech and Illinois to get back into the national rankings, West Virginia promptly dropped four in a row, including losses to Indiana and Richmond that started to turn the heat up on Bowden. Back-to-back season-ending victories over Virginia and Syracuse did little to subdue the criticism that resumed in 1974, the vitriol eventually growing so intense that Bowden thought he might get fired after the Virginia Tech game that would end the season. But true freshman quarterback Dan Kendra led the Mountaineers to a late score, and Hokie kicker Wayne Latimer missed two very makeable field goal tries that wound up saving Bowden's job.

"I got on the bus after the game and [Bowden] grabbed me by the arm as I was going to my seat and he said, 'Boy, you might have saved me!' I was a freshman and I had no idea what he was talking about," Kendra said. "Now, years later when you think back on it, he felt if he would have lost that game he was going to get fired."

The pressure that season eventually got to Bowden, who in a rare moment of frustration waved letters of support written by WVU President James Harlow and Athletic Director Leland Byrd to some of his critics in the press after one disappointing home loss. "The great thing about West Virginia University was the president, the athletic director and the Athletic Council all came to me and said, 'Bobby, don't pay any attention to them [his critics]. You are our coach and we are staying with you,'" Bowden recalled in 2010.

"That year was so bad because the coaches made our offense geared around Danny Buggs and he got hurt," added tight end Randy Swinson. "In '74, the mindset was 'This is Danny Buggs's team.' That didn't feel good at all. You're like, coach, I can do this, but that was Danny Buggs's team and it showed when he got hurt and he missed four or five games. We were crushed."

Defensive end Andy Peters thought Buggs's injury was only part of the problem. "We had more talent in '73 and '74 than we did in '75, but we just didn't have a Danny Kendra and it was a shame because with Buggs, Marshall Mills and some of the great receivers we had – and the running backs – if we would have had a quarterback, we would have been really dangerous," Peters said.

Hoppy Kercheval, then a student at WVU and writing for the student newspaper *The Daily Athenaeum*, recalled WVU students at that time falling into two different camps when it came to Bowden – those who supported the coach and those who didn't. There was very little gray.

"I'm embarrassed to say that I was on the side of Bowden being a bumbling incompetent," said Kercheval, now vice president of operations at West Virginia Radio Corporation and host of the popular Talkline radio show that is broadcast daily throughout the state. "That was the side I was on, which was the side of convenience and ignorance."

Kercheval recalled once taking some shots at Bowden and the team in a scathing column. "I remember making fun of Bowden and making fun of the failures of the football team during their lean years," he said. "I was a smart-ass student and thought I knew something that I really didn't. That was a mistake, because obviously he turned out to be a really good coach. Of course coaches are always better when they have better players."

In Cignetti's opinion, the program's most pressing problem throughout the 1970s was the lack of depth on the offensive and defensive lines. "I think the biggest difference we probably faced at West Virginia was what you had after your best 22 players on the field," Cignetti said. "We had depth at certain positions. We had depth at running back. Where we were thin when I was there was the offensive and defensive lines. We didn't have the numbers there. It wasn't the first 22 players that we put on the field – it was what we had on the field after the injuries where we ran into problems."

Because it was next to impossible for West Virginia to out-recruit Penn State, Ohio State and Michigan for top linemen in those days (those difficulties still continue to this day), Bowden chose to continue running the veer offense Carlen wanted Bowden to install in 1969. "It was an offense that you didn't have to have the greatest offensive line in the world to run because you blocked low and you blocked at people's feet," Bowden once explained. "When you start blocking high you've got to be strong to knock them out of the way."

As Bowden's offensive coordinator, Cignetti quickly became an expert in the veer, and he later kept it when he became West Virginia's head coach. "The veer is basically inside-outside, so the blocking schemes are really predicated on the [defensive] linemen," Cignetti explained. "You had about four basic plays, so in terms of a game plan what you're going to do really depended upon the alignment of the defense. It's not a strategy you would use today in attacking defenses."

On the other side of the ball, West Virginia's veteran defensive coordinator Chuck Klausing was having problems of his own, particularly against the pass. Like most schools at that time, West Virginia was running the 50 defense, which featured a middle guard flanked by a pair of defensive tackles and two defensive ends on the outside. Behind them were two linebackers and a secondary that traditionally played three-deep coverage, with a free safety in the middle of the field and a strong safety near the line of scrimmage. But in 1974, Klausing decided to play a new cover-two configuration in the secondary, which required the two corners to play up on the receivers at the line of scrimmage and placed the safeties behind them, splitting the field in half. "We were probably more innovative for that time period," admitted Donnie Young, who coached the Mountaineer linebackers then.

"WE WERE PROBABLY MORE INNOVATIVE FOR THAT TIME PERIOD."

Ex-WVU Linebacker Coach Donnie Young

In retrospect, what West Virginia was doing defensively in 1974 may have been a little too cutting-edge for the players to handle. The secondary that year allowed opposing QBs to complete 59.4 percent of their pass attempts, an extraordinarily high figure for that period of time. So to fix that, in 1975, two things happened. One, during the off-season the defensive coaches visited Klausing's old buddy Larry Jones down at Tennessee, where Jones had the nation's No. 1 ranked pass defense. Out of those meetings came the decision to have West Virginia's defensive tackles do more angling and shading to make it more difficult for offenses to block them. The second development was that Greg Williams was hired to coach the defensive secondary. Williams earned the immediate respect of the players and brought the toughness to the defense that it was lacking in 1974. "[Williams] could really get those kids to play," recalled Young.

While Williams injected youth and enthusiasm into the defense, it was Klausing's steady hand and experience that melded it all together. Klausing was an outstanding tactician who, since retirement, has written several books on football strategy and conducted yearly football clinics well into the new millennium. At West Virginia, Klausing coached the defensive ends, and he would frequently have them off to the side of the field, where he meticulously walked them through all the things they would encounter on Saturdays.

"Coach Klausing was so good at getting defenses prepared," said Peters. "When the tight end would take his helmet and block down, I knew the top three plays that were coming at me. If he looped around to the outside, same thing. If he came straight at me, boom, boom, boom . . . and that stuff always played true."

Klausing was also a very clever coach (some would even say devious, in the best sense of the word, of course), using whatever information he could get his hands on to get an advantage. And Klausing got information on just about everything. Somehow, he found out that Lombard was working at a downtown bar to make a few extra bucks, so he called his defensive end into the office one morning to find out what was going on. Lombard explained that he needed the extra money to help make ends meet during the off-season. Klausing listened to Lombard's story before telling one of his own.

"You know, Gary, there are NCAA rules that say you can't have a job while you are on scholarship," Klausing began. Then he proceeded to tell Lombard about his days as a college student, going over to Canton, Ohio, on Sundays to play football for the professional Canton Bulldogs under an assumed name. When Klausing finished his story and their meeting was over, Klausing had Lombard so confused that he wasn't sure whether he was supposed to quit his bouncing job or not.

Tony Dorsett reached 1,000 yards during Pitt's eighth game of the '75 season – a 38-0 whitewashing of Syracuse – the third of four consecutive 1,000-yard campaigns for the 1976 Heisman Trophy winner. The 20th-ranked Panthers played the Syracuse game without their starting quarterback, Robert Haygood, who suffered a badly bruised hip in Pitt's 17-0 loss to Navy. Taking Haygood's place in the lineup against the Orangemen was sophomore Matt Cavanaugh, who completed six-of-nine passes for 167 yards and three touchdowns. Cavanaugh was going to make his second career start against West Virginia in Morgantown.

The Mountaineers had started off the 1975 campaign impressively with road victories at Cal and SMU, reaching the Top 10 for the first time in more than two decades before suffering a deflating 39-0 defeat at Penn State. Artie Owens hurt his shoulder against the Nittany Lions and was not available for the following week's game against Tulane, which turned out to be a 16-14 setback. The Mountaineers recovered with back-to-back wins over Virginia Tech and Kent State, boosting their record to 6-2 as they headed into the Pitt game. Still, no one thought West Virginia had much of a chance against the Panthers. In fact, all but one of *The Charleston Gazette's* Fearless Forecasters had predicted a Pitt victory. Bob Fretwell, Bob Baker, Skip Johnson, S.J. Easterling, Danny Wells, Paul

Wallace, Terry Marchal and the Associated Press's "Piggy" (yes, that was a nickname all liked the Panthers as 12-point favorites. Wells and Wallace thought so little of West Virginia's chances that they had Pittsburgh winning the game by two touchdowns. The only *Gazette* writer to side with the Mountaineers was Mike Whiteford, who predicted a 24-17 upset.

Gazette sports editor Shorty Hardman didn't make a prediction, but he also didn't give Gold and Blue rooters much to hope for with his pregame assessment: "According to the experts, there is no way West Virginia's Mountaineers can beat Pitt Saturday when these two old rivals come together in Morgantown," Shorty wrote. "We're not experts by any stretch of the imagination, but we wouldn't argue that this appraisal of the game is just about correct."

The West Virginia players were arguing, too – not about the lack of faith being shown in the local press – but instead about who was going to be introduced on television before the game. ABC was airing the contest to a regional audience; it was the Mountaineers' first regular season TV appearance since losing 28-19 to 11th-ranked Penn State in Morgantown in 1972. Many of the defensive players took a conspiratorial view, believing that Bowden was lobbying to get the offensive players introduced before the game because the offensive side of the field was where he spent most of his time. In reality, ABC's intention clearly was to introduce the WVU defense because the star of the game was Pitt's Dorsett. So during pregame warm-ups, the eleven West Virginia defensive starters walked over to the press box side of the field and stood in a straight line next to the Pitt offense while ABC announcer Bill Fleming introduced the starters from both teams.

"I can remember Coach Bowden made a rule that no one was going to play if their hair was sticking out of their helmets," said Lombard. "A bunch of us got our hair cut. I remember Artie Owens gave me my haircut."

"They lined you up eleven across and I was the first one," added Peters. "You didn't say anything. They just showed your picture and said who you were."

Dan Kendra doesn't recall the pregame introductions, but he does remember the ridiculous yellow blazers the ABC announcers were required to wear. Kendra recalled making a comment about those awful jackets to Bill Fleming, who was down on the field during pregame warm-ups. "I remember running by him and saying to him, 'Man, those are some ugly sport coats.' He just turned around and started laughing," said Kendra. "I bet he heard that a thousand times."

Pregame proved to be more exciting than the first half, which immediately developed into a siege as both teams dug in near midfield. Almost the entire first half was played with both teams' offenses stuck on their own side of the 50, with Pitt's deepest penetration reaching the Mountaineer 35, and West Virginia's longest march ending at the Pitt 39. A pair of losses and an illegal procedure penalty ruined Pitt's best drive, while some scattershot passing by Kendra and Danny Williams ended West Virginia's deepest push.

Twice Bowden tried fake punts and both were almost comical in their failures. At the WVU 46, punter Jeff Fette took off running and got all of 7 yards before being dragged down by Pitt's Dennis Moorhead – a mere 15 yards short of the first down marker. Then, late in the first half, Bowden called a "Bowdenrooski" on his own 40 with 32 seconds remaining on the clock (it was the same play he famously ran 13 years later in a big Florida State come-from-behind win at Clemson). The trick play called for the football to be snapped to the up-back, who hides the ball between his legs until a teammate takes it out and runs with it. Paul Jordan was the ball carrier for this fake punt – not FSU's Leroy Butler, who pulled off the memorable fake for the Seminoles many years later against the Tigers. The first one Bowden tried didn't quite work out as well.

Perhaps the most exciting play of the first half came early in the second quarter, when Pitt's Gordon Jones fielded a punt at his own 5, gave ground into his own end zone (where West Virginia's Ken Braswell, Dave Riley and Paul Jordan all had clear shots to tackle him for a safety), but then somehow pirouetted his way out of danger before being dragged down at the 7. The tattered game film clearly shows Pitt's "Kamikaze Kid" Chuck Bonasorte putting a punctuation mark on the play with an after-the-whistle forearm to the throat of West Virginia's Greg Dorn, whom Bowden mistakenly called "Phil" for most his career. (Bowden was notoriously bad with names, later rectifying that at Florida State by simply choosing to call everyone he didn't know "Buddy.")

At halftime, West Virginia had a 138-114 advantage in total yardage and a 6-3 edge in first downs, but neither team could light up the scoreboard. Still, Swinson remembers a calm WVU locker room at intermission. "All I remember is Coach Bowden saying 'We're going to do this' and 'Guys, this is what y'all have got to do.' We came out of the locker room slapping each other upside the helmet saying, 'Come on, this is what we've got to do,'" Swinson said. Cignetti also decided to keep his play calling conservative, because West Virginia's defense was performing so well. "Our defense played great that day," Cignetti said. "You talk about shutting down a high-powered offense . . . and maybe as great a running back as there has ever been in college football."

Klausing did some tinkering with his defense to slow down Dorsett. Instead of playing his normal 5-2-4 alignment, he had his guys in a 5-3-2-1 configuration that afternoon, with the nose guard (Ken Culbertson), the two tackles (Rich Lukowski and Chuck Smith) and one linebacker (Steve Dunlap) handling the dive while the safeties Tommy Pridemore and Mark Burke looked after Cavanaugh on the option. That left Lombard, Peters, and linebacker Ray Marshall on an island to try and contain Dorsett on the pitch. "I asked our ends, 'Can you run 4 yards as fast as Tony Dorsett can run 8 yards?'" Klausing recalled in 2005. "I wanted them to go straight up field when they pitched the ball to Dorsett so they would be waiting on him."

The tackles also helped the ends by angling, slanting and extending their gaps toward the sidelines to use them to their advantage. "The philosophy always was one player covers one hole and you would stretch your hole out as far as you could to the sidelines to try and keep their speedsters from getting to the corner," explained Chuck Smith. "It worked for us." As well as the defense played, there were still mistakes that Pitt took advantage of. One came late in the third quarter, when Dunlap lost track of Dorsett on a swing pass out in the flat that resulted in Pitt's second touchdown of the game, tying the score at 14. "In that defense I played in the middle over the center," said Dunlap. "We got down to the goal line and we were playing man-to-man, and they came out in a split backfield and Tony lined up behind the offensive tackle."

Dunlap thought about cheating a couple steps to his right in case Pitt tried to throw the ball out in the flat to Dorsett, but he was afraid to do so because linebackers coach Donnie Young was against his players doing any freelancing. So Dunlap remained where he was, Cavanaugh threw the ball to Dorsett exactly as Dunlap thought he would and all Dunlap could do was chase the Pitt running back into the end zone. "I come off to the sidelines and I say, 'Coach, I couldn't get to him. He lined up behind the tackle,'" Dunlap recalled. "Donnie said, 'Why didn't you move out there?' I'm thinking to myself, 'What do you mean why didn't I move out there? You would have killed me!'"

Pitt's other score came as a result of a Gordon Jones 28-yard touchdown catch early in the fourth quarter when he got behind Mark Burke and Johnny Schell for a pretty over-the-shoulder TD grab, pulling it in before stepping out of the back of the end zone.

At the beginning of the second half, a good kickoff return by Dwayne Woods gave West Virginia outstanding field position at the Mountaineer 33. Danny Williams was put into the game to give the offense a boost, and he promptly marched the team right down the field. A 25-yard pass to tight end Bubba Coker on third and 8 got the ball to the Pitt 14. "That was a dump to the tight end when you get them coming up and forcing the option," explained Cignetti. "That was Danny Williams's stuff right there." But three plays later, Panther defensive tackle Randy Holloway recovered Williams's fumble at the five. West Virginia's defense reciprocated two plays later when Dorsett was separated from the football at the 16 and Marshall out-fought everyone for the ball at the bottom of the pile. Kendra came back into the game and handed off eight straight times, the last time to Ron Lee on fourth and goal from the 1, where he carried Pitt linebacker Cecil Johnson into the end zone for the game's first score.

West Virginia's second touchdown came as a result of its best drive of the afternoon, with the Mountaineers consuming 73 yards on just six plays. After a short Lee run got the ball to the Pitt 31, Kendra loosened up the Panther defense with a 16-yard pass to Swinson, getting to the WVU 47. Lee barreled for 12 more to the Pitt 41, and Owens tacked on 13 additional yards to get to the 28. A Lee smash to the Panther 23 set up Owens's beautiful TD run on a counter play that was perfectly executed by blockers Bob Kaminski, Steve Earley and Al Gluchoski. When Owens broke through the line of scrimmage, all that was standing in his way was Pitt's Tom Perko. "It was like he was the only thing between me and the goal line, and I just made a move on him and all of a sudden he just disappeared," recalled Owens.

His touchdown run sent a jolt of electricity through the stadium, its occupants for the first time really believing that their team might just be able to pull off the big upset. Even after Pitt tied the game with 7:55 to go and was later driving for the go-ahead score, the defense's performance kept the fans optimistic.

Pitt appeared to be in business when Dorsett took a pitch from Cavanaugh and raced 22 yards to the West Virginia 28, where he was knocked into the WVU bench by Chuck Braswell. Team captain Dave Van Halanger remembers the Mountaineer players on the sidelines giving it to Dorsett, and as he turned around to go back on to the field, Dorsett let his West Virginia hecklers know which team he thought was No. 1 by putting both hands behind his back, concealing his two extended middle fingers from the TV cameras. "He was cocky," said Van Halanger, "but what a great football player!"

Then, Tommy Pridemore made a great play on Dorsett for a 7-yard loss; Pitt was flagged 15 yards for clipping on the play, pushing the ball all the way back to the 49. Three plays after that, the Mountaineer defense came up with a huge turnover when a Cavanaugh pass toward the Pitt sideline ricocheted off of the back of Braswell's shoulder pads right into the arms of Dunlap. When Dunlap got up to celebrate his momentum-changing interception at the West Virginia 35, Dorsett was right there to slap the football out of his hands. "I don't remember him doing that," laughed Dunlap. "You're talking about more than 35 years ago. Hell, I can't remember what I did yesterday."

Dunlap's pick and two Kendra-to-Tommy Bowden passes totaling 39 yards moved the ball to the Pitt 30 – those two Bowden catches would prove instrumental in setting up Randy Swinson's reception down the far sideline, which in turn put McKenzie into position to kick the game-winning field goal. "The basic thing was Randy would run a flat route to stretch the defender toward the sideline so Tommy could run the curl behind him," explained Cignetti. "The curl is like a 15-, 18-yard route and then he turns it in. Basically, the quarterback's options were first to the curl and if it's not there then he can hit the check-down over the ball, or, if he's getting quick pressure he can unload it to Randy in the flat."

Three plays after Bowden's second grab got West Virginia closer for a McKenzie field goal try that would have put West Virginia back in the lead, disaster struck: With 57 seconds left in the game, Ron Lee fumbled. Romano made a great play to strip the ball, and Perko recovered it at the Panther 17. Pitt could have run out the clock and left Morgantown with a tie, but Majors had a great kicker in Carson Long, and he only needed about 45 yards to get into field goal range. But on first down, WVU defensive tackle Rich Lukowski threw Dorsett for a 1-yard loss, and then two more unsuccessful plays left Pitt with a fourth and 2 at the 25. There was confusion on Pitt's sideline, Cavanaugh believing it was still third down and remaining on the field. Pitt offensive line coach Joe Avezzano frantically ran onto the field to get everyone straightened out and was flagged 15 yards for an unsportsmanlike conduct penalty, moving the ball back to the 10. That forced Pitt's Larry Swider to punt from his own end zone instead of the 13 yard line, and, more importantly, it stopped the clock with 18 seconds left.

"SO I JUST SAID IN THE HUDDLE, 'LET'S GIVE IT A SHOT, WHAT THE HECK?'"

Ex-WVU QB Dan Kendra

Swider's punt was fielded by Burke, who bobbled the ball momentarily before being tackled at midfield with just 10 seconds remaining. West Virginia needed some sort of miracle play to get the ball into a reasonable position for McKenzie to try a game-winning field goal. Kendra knew they needed at least 25 yards, so as the team broke the huddle, he quickly grabbed Swinson by the arm and told him to turn his flat pattern into an out-and-up. "I just remember the corner being on [Swinson's] back the couple of times we ran that, and I figured he would bite again," explained Kendra. "So I just said in the huddle, 'Let's give it a shot, what the heck?' With that amount of time it was sort of all or nothing, because if we didn't complete it we figured the next play was just going to be a grenade – just throw it up and hope for a prayer," said Kendra.

"He wanted to give them something they hadn't seen at all," Swinson added. "They probably knew the formation with Tommy being the flanker, and when they saw our action that's what they thought it was."

The beauty of Kendra's suggestion was that it didn't affect any other player. The line still blocked the same way, Artie Owens still carried out his fake the same way, and Tommy Bowden still ran his route the same way. All that changed was Swinson running a quick out and then turning his pattern up the far sideline. It was the only time Swinson could ever recall Kendra doing anything like that, before or afterward. "I don't know whether he told Randy to do that or the staff did," said Tommy Bowden, adding that it was very uncommon for players to have the freedom to do things like that back then.

When Kendra dropped back to pass, Randy Holloway, Randy Cozens and Ed Wilamowski were all in his face, and just as Wilamowski was about to unload on him, the quarterback was able to loft a high-arching pass down the far sideline in the general direction of Swinson. "All I knew was when I turned up that sideline and looked back toward him I saw the ball," said Swinson. "All I was supposed to do was go up and catch it. I didn't know where I was catching it at. I didn't know how far I had gotten down the field. I didn't see any defender – nothing. I just did what he told me to do; he threw it to me and I had to catch the ball."

Just as Swinson hauled in the pass, free safety Jeff Delaney was there to knock him out of bounds at the Pitt 22. The play covered 26 yards, and, just as importantly, it took only six seconds. Out came Bill McKenzie, either to be remembered for eternity by Mountaineer fans for kicking the game-winning field goal, or to be forever blamed as the reason West Virginia tied Pitt that afternoon. Most of his teammates were confident McKenzie could make the kick, yet many of them kept their fingers crossed anyway. "I was on the sidelines just standing there, and I wouldn't look at the kick," said Kendra. "I just stared across the field at their coaches."

"We never really had a good kicker when I was there," added Peters. "The last good kicker we had was Frank Nester. Bill had this straight-on style, he was a nice guy, but none of us really hung out with him or really knew him that well. I can't say I had a lot of confidence in him and it was a fairly long kick, so I had to say I was surprised that he made it."

"Billy was a clutch kid," said Chuck Smith. "He had a great foot and he put it through the uprights. When Randy stepped out of bounds with four seconds to go, I said 'Billy's got this. No problem.'"

Swinson, the left end on the protection team, also wasn't surprised that McKenzie made it. "We had all the confidence in the world in him – 'Hey, you are my teammate and this is what we have to do,'" said Swinson. "But it wasn't a gimme because he was on the left hash mark. He wasn't lined up in the middle of the post."

What Swinson remembers most about McKenzie was the way he tied his shoe laces to the first spike on his right cleat so he could pull his square-toed kicking shoe up into the air as high as it could go. He secured his laces by wrapping them around his ankle. "He was the last guy I ever saw kick straight-on," said Swinson.

All McKenzie could do until he was called out onto the field was stand off to the side by himself, with his thumbs sticking out of his pants. He didn't have an opportunity to loosen up his leg because he couldn't – there was no room on the sidelines to do anything. "You stretch around and run in place a little bit, but there wasn't any room for kicking nets, even if they had them back then," said McKenzie in 2007.

Klausing, the architect of West Virginia's terrific defensive performance that afternoon, also happened to coach the kickers. He gave all of them one very sound piece of advice: Always keep your head down before you kick the ball. McKenzie also got a nice little tip from Nester, who was hanging around town that year helping out the kickers as a student assistant coach. Nester wore two-inch thick glasses and he could barely see his hands in front of him without them. "One of the things Frank showed me was to paint a big arrow on the kicking tee and when you go out on the field, point that arrow at the middle of the goal post and then just follow it down and put it on the ground," McKenzie said. "When you look at the ground and you see the arrow, you know where the goal posts are."

Of course, McKenzie did everything he was told – placing the arrow toward the goal post, keeping his head down all of the way through the kick and driving the ball comfortably between the goal posts as the clock wound down to zero. (A later-discovered Polaroid picture of Mckenzie's kick, taken from behind the end zone, showed the flight of the football perfectly centered between the two posts.) It was after McKenzie's kick that everything became a blur. Some WVU students were already on the field when McKenzie's boot landed in the stands. Then, a large mass of humanity quickly converged on the players at the 22 yard line.

"I thought I was going to die," said Swinson. "I could not breathe. The whole team was on top of us. That is one helluva feeling. You're happy, but when you're caught in that position and your teammates pile on top of you, that is some serious weight."

Smith went out onto the field to celebrate with his teammates, but he was soon distracted by a WVU student under the influence who was walking around searching for his glasses. Smith noticed a busted pair lying on the ground, picked them up and gave them to him. "The guy put those broken glasses back on and said, 'Thanks, man! This is the greatest day of my life!'" Smith chuckled. "I'm looking at him and I said, 'Good for you!'" Smith would always tell this story to his teammates whenever they got together for reunions, and each time he told it they would cast a wary eye toward him. Then, many years later, he was finally able to prove that his act of kindness wasn't some flight of fantasy.

"I got a copy of the highlight video, and it shows the pile going on and you can see me giving the kid his glasses," said Smith. "The guys would always say, 'That's what you did at such a moment?' I said, 'Well . . . I gave the kid his glasses!'"

Hoppy Kercheval was among the mass of humanity out on the field that November afternoon, although he had briefly considered watching the game on TV back at his apartment on McLane Avenue. "Because I had a vicious hangover and the game was on TV – which was very rare for a Mountaineer game at that time – I said 'Let's go back to the house and watch it on television.' My friends were like, 'No, no let's stay.' Well, I stayed when I came very close to not being there," he said.

Dave Van Halanger, former strength and conditioning coach at Georgia after spending many years on Bobby Bowden's staff at Florida State, said the '75 win over Pitt remains one of the most exhilarating moments of his life. "I can still hear Jack Fleming's call . . . 'There's a mob scene on the field. You haven't seen anything like it!'" said Van Halanger. "I gave two people heart attacks that day because I squeezed them too hard. One was an Episcopal priest that would come and pray for us before the games, and the other was Jack Hines's dad. They both ended up in the hospital after the game because I hugged them so hard."

The '75 Pitt game also permanently split up part of Van Halanger's family. "My dad got my uncle Tony tickets to the game and he was rooting against me – he liked Pitt," laughed Van Halanger. "I never invited him back to my house again after that. Later, he choked on some food during a cruise and went to eternity."

Some of the players joined the many celebrations going on in Sunnyside later that night – a few of the parties even lasted well into the following week. Gary Lombard remembers trying to steer his beat-up Volkswagen Beetle through a mob of students as some of them converged on his car and began to rock it.

"I knew one of the guys doing it and I yelled, 'What are you doing?' He recognized me and he yelled to his buddies, 'Hey, that's Gary Lombard! Let him go through!' This happened right there at the intersection of University Avenue and Stewart Street," Lombard laughed.

Dan Kendra was with his girlfriend's parents as they tried to navigate their car through the humanity lingering outside the stadium. "We got into the car to drive away and they saw our Pennsylvania plates and they started shaking the car," Kendra laughed. "I popped my head out of the window and I said, 'Hey, I'm a West Virginia player. I'm Dan Kendra, the quarterback!' They go, 'Oh no, let them through! Let them through!' It was just total chaos."

"The celebration moved from the field right up to Sunnyside," Kercheval recalled. "Of course there were a number of bars there – there was the College Inn, Choosy Mothers and a couple of other bars up there, and people were spilling out from the bars into the streets because the weather was warm enough. You could kind of see everybody getting more festive and it just rolled into this surreal celebration that lasted long into the night."

Randy Swinson said he was right there with them. Others, such as Artie Owens, weren't really into hanging out that much and just went back to their dorm rooms and listened to all the commotion going on outside. Chuck Smith, bruised, sore and tired after the game, used what remaining energy he had left to climb up on top of the porch roof of a friend's house in Sunnyside to watch the show that was going on below them.

And what a show it was!

Tony D Gets Tossed

PITT	WVU
24	16
Nov. 13, 1976 Pittsburgh	

Tony Dorsett, the coolest cat on the football field, had finally lost his cool. Pitt's soon-to-be Heisman Trophy winner had just carried the football for a fifth straight time as the clock was winding down toward the Panthers' 10th victory of the season, a much-more-competitive-than-expected 24-16 win over a 4-5 West Virginia team that was playing out its season. Dorsett's runs of 5, 11, 8, 7 and 3 yards forced the Mountaineers to burn their final timeout with 29 seconds remaining on the clock. The ball was at the Pitt 43 when play resumed.

Dorsett took the next pitchout from quarterback Matt Cavanaugh and ran toward the Pitt sideline, where West Virginia's Robin Meeley took off after him. When Meeley reached Dorsett, the running back was almost on the ground, but instead of letting up, Meeley charged into him and took out an afternoon's worth of frustration on him. The hit was probably late, but exactly where and how Meeley hit Dorsett is a matter of opinion. Dorsett thought Meeley was going for his head, so he got up and threw the football at him. A free-for-all erupted. Eventually order was restored, the two teams were flagged for unsportsmanlike conduct penalties, and both Dorsett and Meeley were thrown out of the game. Had Dorsett's 2-yard run stood up, it would have been an NCAA-record third consecutive 200-yard rushing performance for the senior. As it was, Dorsett finished the game with 199 yards, and when play resumed, Cavanaugh, who had run for 124 yards mostly on option keepers, took a knee to end the game.

More than two decades later, Dorsett said four years of pent-up frustration from playing against West Virginia had finally erupted on that one play. "That team . . . they would agitate me all game long it seemed like for four years, and I was just getting fed up with it," Dorsett said in a 2007 interview for Fox Sports Pittsburgh. "During the game, they would tackle me, and I'm on the ground and they would press their hands on my helmet to get themselves up, pinch me, grab me in my crotch, and I'm like, 'Oh man!' So finally, I just got fed up and I exploded. There was a big brawl on the bench."

Dorsett teammate J.C. Pelusi had a similar recollection. "Tony came around the right side and somebody hit him late out of bounds, and he took the football and threw it at some kid's face," said Pelusi. "The next thing you know, tempers are flaring and it didn't take a whole lot to get people excited about starting something there."

West Virginia defensive tackle Chuck Smith, who was right in the middle of the melee, has a different take on things. "That was propaganda," he said of Pitt's accusations of West Virginia cheap shots. "I remember helping him up seven or eight times after I tackled him, and never once did I do anything to him. I might say, 'See if you can do a little better next time.' We used to taunt each other and there might have been a late hit here or there, but there wasn't anything cheap. That was hyped up a little bit."

"I remember they had police escorting him off the field and everything," recalled Garrett Ford, an assistant coach for the Mountaineers that year. "Then the fans got involved in it. It was exciting, but it was a mess."

Dorsett, however, was far from being an innocent victim. Some of the things that happened to him during the game he brought on himself. Before the opening kickoff, when the starters for both teams were being introduced for television, Dorsett theatrically gave a No. 1 salute to the crowd before turning around and doing the same to the West Virginia players standing on the other side of the field (Pitt had reached No. 1 in the AP poll the prior week, when top-ranked Michigan was upset by Purdue). Then, he took off and ran down the middle of the field by himself, motioning for some of the West Virginia players to come and get him before turning around and running back to the

Panther sidelines. The Pitt fans roared with approval. Asked after the game why he gave the No. 1 sign to the Mountaineers, he said, "We are No. 1."

He was right – the Panthers were.

Standing on the Pitt sidelines and decked out in a suit and topcoat was the nation's No. 1 high school running back, who also just happened to be West Virginia's top recruiting target: Charleston's Robert Alexander. And the man personally responsible for Alexander's recruitment, Garrett Ford, was more than a little concerned at seeing Alexander cavorting with the enemy. "Robert was on Pitt's sideline that day," Ford recalled. "Then, after the game they had a press conference where Robert was sitting there with Dorsett."

West Virginia really had no business even hanging around with Pitt that year. The Panthers were clearly the better football team, having won 10 straight games dating back to the 1975 season. Pitt's average margin of victory heading into the West Virginia game was 22.1 points. The Panthers beat Notre Dame by 21 points to start the year, and then in succession knocked off Georgia Tech, Temple, Duke, Louisville, Miami, Fla., Navy, Syracuse and Army. The closest Pitt came to losing was against Syracuse, when the Orangemen had a fourth and 1 at the Pitt 20 midway through the fourth quarter, in a game the Panthers were leading by just a touchdown, 20-13. But Pitt stuffed Syracuse, and a long Dorsett run set up a Carson Long field goal to give Pitt a 23-13 victory.

West Virginia's season had not gone quite so smoothly. Offensive coordinator Frank Cignetti was named Bobby Bowden's replacement on January 19, 1976, and when he took the job the first thing he emphasized to the fans was unity. "Whether you like me or not, the important thing is the program," Cignetti said. "You've got to be behind it. Otherwise, we can't do the job."

Many West Virginia fans thought Cignetti played things too conservatively as West Virginia's play caller under Bowden, and they were frequently critical of his choice of plays when he later became WVU's head coach. "As offensive coordinator I have been subjected to some criticism," Cignetti said when he was hired. "But some people lose sight of the philosophy of winning football.

IN 1976, WEST VIRGINIA WAS IN A REBUILDING MODE.

"What they have to understand is that it takes more than offense to win in football – it takes offense and specialty teams. The name of the game is defense. It's important, though, that the offense complement the defense."

In 1976, West Virginia was in a rebuilding mode. Thirty-two seniors were gone from Bowden's '75 team that had won nine games and defeated North Carolina State in the

Peach Bowl. Paul Lumley, Dwayne Woods, true freshman Walter Easley and Dave Riley handled the running game, while Steve Lewis had nearly three times as many receptions as West Virginia's next closest player, tight end Ben McDay. Peach Bowl MVP Dan Kendra didn't quite have the same supporting cast to work with during his junior season, in 1976, and through nine games Kendra was completing less than 50 percent of his passes while throwing 17 interceptions.

After beating Villanova 28-7 to start the season, West Virginia lost back-to-back games to Maryland and Kentucky before topping Richmond on a late Bill McKenzie field goal. Then, a 42-0 win at Temple was wiped out by three straight losses to Boston College, Penn State and Virginia Tech. Kendra played well in West Virginia's 34-28 win at Tulane, completing nine-of-14 passes for 133 yards and a touchdown. He also ran for 35 yards, including the game-winning score with 34 seconds left on the clock. Lumley had a good game against the Green Wave as well, accumulating 122 yards and two TDs on 26 carries.

The '76 Pitt game was just the second time in school history West Virginia was facing college football's top-ranked team. The first time came against Army in 1946, when the Mountaineers lost 19-0. Back then, as the story goes, Army coach Earl Blaik thought so little of West Virginia that he didn't even go to the game, choosing instead to scout Notre Dame's game against Navy.

But Johnny Majors would be at this one.

For the second straight year, the West Virginia-Pitt game was being televised by ABC. It was just the sixth regular season television appearance for the Mountaineers in a span of 17 years. Getting on the tube in the 1970s was next to impossible for schools like West Virginia. For decades, television deals were the sole domain of Walter Byers, the NCAA's powerful executive director, who served in that capacity from 1951-88. Byers turned the NCAA into a very formidable organization, in part because of his skills as a television negotiator. By the late 1970s, however, most of college football's top programs were unhappy with Byers's spread-the-wealth approach to TV. They wanted more opportunities for exposure and more input in television negotiations. "Walter Byers controlled all of that," recalled Leland Byrd, West Virginia's athletic director from 1972–78. "You only had one network that was carrying games back then. They had four regionals and a game of the week, so you only had about five choices at that particular time."

Byrd was only able to get three regular season games on TV during his WVU tenure: One game against Penn State in 1972 and two against Pitt in 1975–76. "In the East, for example, Pitt and Penn State were the superpowers at that time, and they got almost all of the television spots," Byrd explained. "The best we could do was one game with either Pitt or Penn State; the same thing with Syracuse and Boston College. If they got one then that was about it. Until ESPN came along, there was not a whole lot you could do about it."

Athletic departments in the mid-1970s were also feeling the effects of crippling inflation and an energy crisis that was consuming the country, forcing schools big and small to take a hard look at their finances. At different times through the years, athletic departments have tried unsuccessfully to get a handle on expenses. In the 1960s, the Big Ten was the first conference to pass a rule limiting football signing classes to just 30 players per year. In the early 1970s, the Big Eight, the SEC and the Southwest Conference agreed to limit signing classes to 45 players per year, with the provision that schools could "bank" or "borrow" additional recruits, enabling the wealthiest schools to essentially continue conducting business as usual.

Former West Virginia coach Jim Carlen saw college football's inequities firsthand when he was an assistant coach at Georgia Tech in the mid-1960s. Tech Coach Bobby Dodd and Alabama's Bear Bryant were good friends who rarely disagreed on anything, except when the conversation turned to scholarships. Carlen remembered listening to Dodd bitterly complain to Bryant about the huge scholarship discrepancies between the two schools. "Coach Dodd said, 'Paul, I want you to get your pencil out because I want you to put these numbers down. You're signing 55 players a year and I'm signing 32 players a year on average. Then, you redshirt your eight or 10 players like we redshirt our eight or 10 players – not necessarily because they are going to play well but because our academics are so tough – and we're never over our total of 120 and we're on the cusp all of the time.' We were bringing in our 32 to their 55, and this has got to stop," Carlen said. But it didn't, so Georgia Tech and Tulane decided to get out of the SEC in 1966.

Johnny Majors was able to do something similar when he went to Pitt in 1972, and many of those players wound up forming the nucleus of the 1976 team. "Johnny was able to go in there and take advantage of that," said Cignetti. "He might have recruited a hundred football players. After that year, the rules changed nationally. As far as academically, it was equal across the board. For conference and independents, your eligibility was based on the test score and your grade point average. That was based on the population of your student body."

That was one advantage West Virginia had over other schools in the region until the rule was changed during Cignetti's first year, in 1976. "With the Big Ten, Big Eight and the Atlantic Coast Conference – people that would recruit in our area – they had a higher [grade point average] rule," said Cignetti. "Then that was all wiped out the year I got the job there." Consequently, some of the good players Corum, Carlen and Bowden were able to get into school in years prior were no longer admitted to West Virginia University under Cignetti. "That was a crushing blow," recalled Bill Kirelawich, who coached for one year with Cignetti, in 1979.

Change in college athletics was happening at a warp-speed pace in the mid-1970s. The so-called cost-cutting conventions of 1973 and 1975 were the result of the smaller schools in the NCAA uniting behind Byers, who frequently used them as leverage to keep the bigger schools in line. During those two conventions, the biggest schools were forced to accept limitations in scholarships, coaching staff sizes and recruiting expenditures. Further cuts in 1975 reduced football scholarships from 105 to 95, eliminated the $15 per month in expense money (frequently referred to as "laundry money") and made additional cuts in recruiting expenditures. Byers estimated the cuts would save approximately $15 million nationally. But Long Beach State president Dr. Stephen Horn didn't think the reductions went far enough and campaigned for more sweeping changes, drawing the ire of the bigger schools. Horn proposed reducing scholarships to 65 over a three-year period, and limiting travel rosters to 48 players. He also wanted 50 percent of television revenue to be distributed equally among all Division I schools, with the other 50 percent going to Division II and Division III programs. The big schools mockingly began calling Horn's suggestions "the Robin Hood plan." Many coaches argued that the smaller schools had no business telling them how to spend their money, and what Horn's plan actually achieved was the unification of the bigger schools, eventually pushing them toward the creation of the College Football Association (CFA) in 1976. The CFA provided a means for the bigger schools to have more of a say in their own destinies.

Cignetti had two major concerns heading into the 1976 Pitt game. First, he didn't want his team to give up a couple of cheap touchdowns early in the game and get demoralized, and second, he was worried that Pitt might try and pour it on if it got the chance, in an effort to impress bowl scouts and keep Tony Dorsett on the minds of Heisman Trophy voters. Cignetti had studied the film of the prior week's game against Army, and he had watched Pitt kick a meaningless field goal with eight seconds remaining to make the final score 37-7. Also, it was no big secret that Majors and his Panther players were not too pleased with the massive celebration that went on down in Morgantown the year prior, when Bill McKenzie's kick on the final play of the game gave West Virginia a 17-14 victory. “Our players didn’t like what happened and I didn’t either,” said Majors before the ’76 contest.

The game began, cloudy and cold, with a stiff wind making the 36-degree temperature seem much colder than it actually was. West Virginia won the toss and elected to receive, but two unsuccessful runs and a Randy Holloway sack of Kendra forced the Mountaineers to punt. Pitt took over at the West Virginia 44 and tried three straight passes, two incomplete and one going for just 3 yards to Gordon Jones. The Mountaineers retook possession at their own 20, couldn’t move the sticks and had to give the ball back to the Panthers. It was starting to look like a repeat of the 1975 game, when neither team could move the ball past midfield.

But Cavanaugh got things going for Pitt with a 9-yard pass to tight end Jim Corbett for the game’s initial first down. Then another pass for first down yardage to Willie Taylor opened up some room for Dorsett, who took a sweep 11 yards to the West Virginia 30. A Cavanaugh option keeper for 8, and fullback Bob Hutton’s dive up the middle for 5, set up Dorsett’s 17-yard touchdown run, the senior cutting around the right side and hugging the sideline for the game’s first score. Carson Long’s PAT gave the Panthers a 7-0 lead.

Following an exchange of possessions, West Virginia got a big break when James Wilson fumbled Jeff Fette’s punt and the ball was recovered at the Pitt 22. The Mountaineers got to the 6 before Kendra’s third-down pass to tight end Ben McDay fell incomplete. McKenzie came in to kick a 22-yard field goal, making it 7-3, Panthers. Pitt then responded with a 10-play, 69-yard drive (all on the ground) – Cavanaugh getting 44 of those yards on option keepers and rollouts – before Dorsett went over right guard from the 2 for his second touchdown of the afternoon. Long’s conversion gave Pitt a 14-3 lead with 2 1/2 minutes gone in the second quarter, but fumbles were Pitt’s nemesis all afternoon, ruining at least two more first-half scoring opportunities.

“We hurt ourselves a lot offensively with mistakes and just bad execution,” said Majors after the game. “Part of this was caused by West Virginia’s aggressiveness on defense.”

On third and 11 from the West Virginia 34, Cavanaugh was hit while attempting to pass, fumbled, and was able to recover the ball back at the 45. Two possessions later, at the Pitt 49, Cavanaugh fumbled again, but this one was pounced on by Chuck Smith at the 43. Then Kendra gave the ball right back to Pitt on the very next play when he was chased out of the pocket and his pass intended for Lumley was picked off by Wilson at the Pitt 31. With 47 seconds remaining in the first half, Cavanaugh was moving the Panthers into field goal range when his completed pass for first down yardage was fumbled by Corbett at the West Virginia 40. Two plays later, Kendra tried to connect with McDay on a long pass down the middle of the field, but it was broken up by Wilson as time expired. Pitt completely dominated the first half statistically, outgaining the Mountaineers 207-41 and limiting Kendra to just 2-of-10 passing for 8 yards.

Pitt expanded its lead on the opening possession of the second half, moving the football from its own 35 to the West Virginia 10 on runs by Cavanaugh and Dorsett. On third and 11 at the WVU 18, Cavanaugh found Corbett cutting left out in the flat, but he was tracked down 3 yards shy of the sticks. Long came on to kick a 27-yard field goal to give the Panthers a 17-3 lead. Then Pitt's fourth fumble, at the West Virginia 43, set up the Mountaineers' first touchdown of the game. Kendra got the offense moving with a third down completion to Steve Lewis for 10 yards, putting the ball at the Pitt 47. He hit Lewis again for 17 yards down the middle to take the ball to the Panther 28, and after three Walter Easley runs gave West Virginia a first down at the Pitt 17, Kendra rolled right and kept the ball for 11 yards to the Pitt 6. Holloway's sack of Kendra moved the ball back to the 14, where the quarterback hooked up with Lewis in the corner of the end zone for a touchdown with 10:57 remaining in the third quarter. McKenzie's conversion made it a 7-point game. The score remained that way heading into the fourth quarter.

A key moment came early in the fourth quarter, when West Virginia had Pitt stopped at the 46, forcing a Larry Swider punt. As Swider's punt rolled slowly toward the goal line, Tommy Pridemore pushed a Pitt player in the back in an effort to keep him from downing the ball at the one. West Virginia was flagged 15 yards for clipping, and Pitt was able to retain possession of the football at the WVU 31. Two plays later, Dorsett took off to his left, weaved his way through four potential tacklers and high-stepped into the end zone for a 30-yard touchdown. The showboating Dorsett held the ball high above his head during the final 10 yards of his jaunt.

Afterward, Cignetti pointed to the clipping penalty as one of two crucial plays of the game. "I felt that the two key points in the game were when we recovered the fumble and then threw an interception on first down, and then when we were called for clipping on the punt," Cignetti said.

Yet another Pitt fumble, Cavanaugh's third and the team's fifth, gave the Mountaineers new life at the Panther 34. West Virginia eventually scored from the nine when Kendra hooked up with Lewis once again, but the two-point conversion try to make it a 6-point game was unsuccessful. His team leading by eight with 3:11 still showing on the clock, Majors decided to quit messing around and gave the ball to Dorsett five straight times to keep the clock moving. Dorsett's final carry of the game resulted in the fight.

"Eight points isn't that big of a margin, but I'll take it in a game like this any day," said Majors. "Both teams played sky high with a lot of pride – just like it is every year between these two fine teams."

Years later, while being interviewed for a television special commemorating the 100th anniversary of the series, J.C. Pelusi talked about his true feelings for West Virginia. "Beating West Virginia is great," he said. "You can't beat them by enough points as far as I'm concerned." Pelusi said there were always hard feelings on both sides. "In a lot of cases, and I even hate to admit this kind of stuff, but you really didn't care about winning the game. All you cared about was really hurting the people on the other side of the football field. They didn't like us a whole lot and we didn't like them a whole lot and there wasn't a whole lot of respect."

Kendra said the talking that went on usually stopped when the game was on the line. "Everybody, instead of talking and worrying about the other stuff, they thought, 'Yeah, we better get our heads into this game.' They would say stuff to me because I was married. They were saying stuff about my wife and I always had a wonderful response for them." Kendra would not elaborate on his response.

Majors, raised on Tennessee football, learned quickly how volatile the West Virginia-Pitt games could get. "When I came to Pittsburgh, it didn't take me long to realize that Penn State was awfully big historically," Majors said. "But my friends who loved Pitt told me, 'Oh, man, you're going to hate West Virginia.' So I quickly learned the importance of beating West Virginia. It sounded very exciting to me, and it turned out to be a very exciting rivalry."

Farewell, Old Mountaineer Field

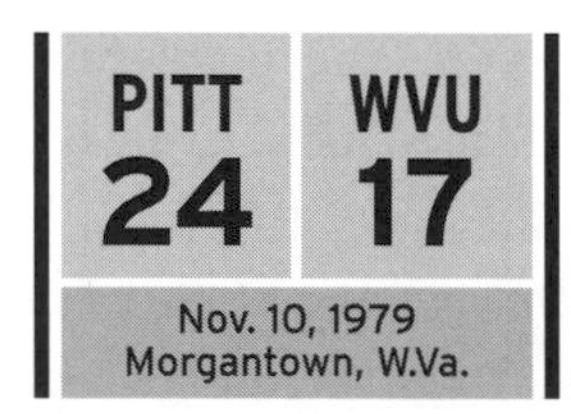

PITT
24
WVU
17
Nov. 10, 1979
Morgantown, W.Va.

Ancient Mountaineer Field was being prepared for the wrecking ball when Pitt arrived for the final game in the aging edifice, on November 10, 1979. For the nostalgic, the stadium was quaint and inviting. To the practical, its better days were in the rearview mirror. "We used to call it the snake pit," laughed linebacker Darryl Talley. "The fans could reach right out and touch you on the head."

Former Coach Bobby Bowden enjoyed coaching there when his teams were winning. And when they weren't? "You could hear everything they were callin' you," Bowden once said. In 1975, following Bowden's Peach Bowl victory over North Carolina State, then athletic director Leland Byrd got an alarming report from the school's physical plant: Mountaineer Field was falling apart. There were only two options – renovate the stadium at a substantial cost or build a new one at another location.

Eventually it was determined that the most practical solution was to build a new stadium on the site of the old nine-hole Morgantown Country Club out in Evansdale, near the medical center. That meant that the remaining years of old Mountaineer Field's existence were spent in disrepair. The wood on the bleachers was rotted and splintered. Trash, broken bottles and garbage were strewn about. The white paint on the stadium was chipped and faded, and large chunks of concrete could be seen on the ground. The Astroturf surface installed in 1969 was in critical condition. By 1979, the T, V and I in the "West Virginia" painted in the bowl end zone were barely visible. More ominously, the turf was becoming a hazard to the players.

"The Astroturf stuck going in one direction and it slid like hell going in the other direction, and they weren't going to replace it because they were building the new stadium," recalled linebacker Mike Dawson, now a high school coach in Ritchie County. "It was terrible and hard – oh my god."

Talley said the wall separating the crowd from the action was so close to the field that the players could actually have conversations with the fans while the game was going on. "You could sit there and talk to somebody about your math class," Talley said. "You could talk to them and not get in trouble because the coaches were up in front and were farther away from you than the fans were."

"As a quarterback you couldn't warm up on the sidelines," explained Oliver Luck. "You couldn't throw behind the bench because there was literally no room. The students could reach out and knock down the ball."

Players were often told to get down on one knee to watch the game because the fans in the first three rows could not see the action. "You'd hear this guy yell, 'Hey 65, sit down! We can't see!'" said defensive tackle Dave Oblak. "Those first three rows were so low to the ground and they couldn't see over the players."

Inside the stadium it was far worse. "There were all of these cubby holes," said Luck. "It was all tucked back in there. You would take three steps and take a left, and another three steps and you took a right. I think there was a dirt floor in the weight room at one time."

Dave Johnson, a freshman tight end in 1979, recalled the makeshift team meeting room the tight ends and tackles had to use. It was right underneath the bleachers. "You could see the framework of the old stadium and there was dirt on the floor," said Johnson. "They just pulled an extension cord out there so they could plug a film projector in."

The defensive players would get taped in the training room and then walk across the field and meet in the visiting locker room on the other side of the stadium. "When the coaches came up they would tell us to come on [to practice]. Well, one time we went up there and the coaches decided that they were not going to meet and half the team was asleep on the [tackling] dummies," laughed Dawson. "Everybody just left the guys that went to sleep. Later, the coaches went up there and found those guys sleeping and just went nuts on them."

The team meeting room was so small that coach Frank Cignetti could barely get his players all in there at one time. If he wanted to talk to the entire squad, it was far easier to assemble them in the locker room. "We had one little section that we squeezed them into but you didn't have meeting rooms down there or anything," he said. Cignetti knew what he was getting himself into when he took the West Virginia head coaching job because his very first experience at the stadium, in 1970, was an unforgettable one. "At the time I was coaching at Princeton University in the Ivy League when Jim [Carlen] left to go to Texas Tech and Bobby got the [WVU] job. I had previously coached at the University of Pittsburgh, was involved in the Pittsburgh-West Virginia rivalry, and started out as a high school coach in Western Pennsylvania.

"I'll never forget, I'm driving down for the interview to see Bobby, my wife came with me, and it was at old Mountaineer Field and all of the plumbing was frozen. My wife had to go to the bathroom and nothing was working. Well, after we had talked and Bobby offered me a job, we're driving back to Princeton and Marlene says, 'Frank, there is no way I'm going to Morgantown!'

"So I accepted the job, we came to Morgantown and believe me, if you ask my wife the best place she's ever been she will say Morgantown, [at] West Virginia University."

Talley remembers working out in the dark, dingy weight room at the bowl end of the stadium, underneath the iron bridge where the students walked across from Sunnyside to get to class. The room was so small that the position players had to come in small groups or else they couldn't fit inside to lift. If you missed your lifting time, then you were out of luck. "Could you imagine being in a cave?" asked Talley. "The weight room was literally a cave underneath the bridge, and you walked in there and it was like a dungeon. You could see the kids walking to school right above you. It was like something you would see out of *The Hunchback of Notre Dame*."

"There was a little peephole that you could see out of," added Oblak. "Nobody knew we were down there, but we knew they were out there and we could see them going to class." That included the pretty WVU co-eds dressed in short miniskirts during warmer weather, and the players sometimes stopped their lifting so they could watch the girls walk across campus. Many times concrete would fall from the ceiling when the players slammed down their weights. And the one constant sound, regardless of where you were inside the stadium, was the drip, drip, drip of water.

"It was like you were in an alley in New York City at night time," recalled Oblak.

Talley and many of the defensive players actually rallied around their dreadful conditions. He remembered once getting a good laugh while watching Penn State linemen Matt Millen and Bruce Clark getting off the team bus and taking their first look at the stadium. "They were wearing their gray pants and blue blazers," said Talley. "They fit so tightly it looked like they had them sprayed on. The group of guys that I played with was not really that materialistic."

Luck wasn't nearly as enthusiastic about the team's modest surroundings. "The only advantage to old Mountaineer Field was that the football players could park their cars there for classes," he laughed.

Well, at least some of the players. "That wasn't the case for me," mentioned Johnson. "Let me tell you, Oliver had a much better parking spot than the rest of us!"

Luck recalled getting a lightning-quick tour of the stadium on his recruiting visit in 1977. His teammates said that happened a lot in the late 1970s. "I'm in the passenger seat of [assistant coach] Gary Stevens's car and he drives down Beechurst and floors the gas pedal when we drive past old Mountaineer Field," Luck said. "He says, 'Yeah that's where the old field is, but let's drive out to the new venue.' He takes me right out to the golf course and there is nothing there!" Luck said. "They had this big poster they put up on an easel and he said, 'Just visualize what this will look like.' We spent 40 minutes out at the golf course and they wouldn't even take you to Mountaineer Field."

"We had all types of creative ways of recruiting during the winter," laughed Cignetti. "It was one thing to see Mountaineer Field on game day with all of the enthusiasm and the fans packed in there. Well, it didn't look so good in the middle of the winter."

Cignetti tirelessly promoted the construction of a new football stadium because he understood that, without a new one, the football program didn't have a chance of surviving. "You look at the whole surroundings in the East back then," Cignetti said. "Penn State had it going great then, Maryland had it going, and that's why facilities were the key to the future of West Virginia football. That new stadium and all of the facilities that go with it was the key."

For a variety of reasons, West Virginia football was struggling mightily in the late 1970s. The Mountaineers had three straight losing seasons in 1976, 1977 and 1978, and the team was headed toward a fourth one after dropping their first three games of the '79 campaign. Then the schedule lightened up, and West Virginia won five of its next six games, including tough wins against Kentucky, Boston College and Virginia Tech.

The Virginia Tech victory was particularly nerve-racking. In the span of 51 seconds, West Virginia had turned a 6-3 lead into a 23-6 deficit. Three consecutive fumbles gave the Hokies 18 straight points. Then the Mountaineers scored 31 unanswered points in the second half to pull out a stomach-churning 34-23 victory. The Tech win gave West Virginia a 5-4 record with games remaining against 12th-ranked Pitt and Arizona State. Before the season, new athletic director Dick Martin had said that Cignetti needed to have a winning record to get his contract renewed. Some players (such as Mike Dawson) understood that their coach was in trouble, while others were not nearly as aware of his dire situation.

WEST VIRGINIA FOOTBALL WAS STRUGGLING MIGHTILY IN THE LATE 1970S.

"Players know when a coach is struggling and fans are upset and all of that, but the only information we had back then was reading the Morgantown paper," Luck said. "There was no Internet, Rivals and all of that nonsense. We kind of lived in our own world. We were going to class and going to school and doing the best that we could on the field."

Talley recalled absorbing some beatings as a 200-pound freshman defensive end before his personal epiphany came during a 31-6 loss at Penn State. He remembered getting hit so hard by fullback Matt Suhey on a sweep that he was chasing the ball carrier down the field without his helmet. "I remember going back to the huddle and looking at [linebacker] Dennis Fowlkes, and he said, 'We ain't ever letting anyone beat us up like this again,'" said Talley.

"There were a lot of guys forced into playing that weren't ready to play," added Dawson, who turned down offers from Ohio State and Penn State for the chance at early playing time at West Virginia.

"Woody [Hayes, of OSU] visited our house and he sat down in my dad's chair, and nobody sat down in my dad's recliner," said Dawson. "So he plopped down in my dad's recliner, nobody said a word, and then he looked at Alex Gibbs [the Ohio State assistant coach in charge of Dawson's recruitment] and he said, 'Alex, turn that goddamn TV down – if that's OK with you, Mrs. Dawson.' If I would have gone to Ohio State my dad would have died."

Earlier that day, West Virginia's recruiting coordinator Ed Pastilong was sitting in the coaches' office at Magnolia High School, waiting to talk to Dawson after his fourth period class, when Hayes arrived in town. Pastilong heard over the school's loudspeaker the announcement that all students were required to report to the gymnasium immediately to listen to Coach Hayes address the student body.

"I'm sitting down there thinking to myself, 'Geezee-peezee, how do you top that?'" Pastilong laughed. "Here I am waiting to talk to Dawson, and Woody shows up and they call everyone out of class so he can make a speech to the entire school. I figured I might as well go up to the gym and listen to what he had to say. Turns out he ended up giving a pretty good speech."

Darryl Talley – the best player the Mountaineer program has produced in the last 40 years – was hiding under a rock when Gary Stevens discovered him. "He was recruited, but they didn't see what I saw in this guy," Stevens said. "They weren't pounding him. I was pounding him. He could run like crazy – all you had to do was watch him. I studied every film and I said, 'This kid is going to make it as a player.' It turned out he was."

By the time of the Pitt game, Cignetti had made the choice to play younger players – even if that meant it was likely going to benefit the next football coach. Only two seniors were in the Mountaineer starting lineup against the Panthers – offensive guard Jim Himic and free safety Jerry Holmes. True freshman tight end Mark Raugh was forced to step in for Rich Duggan, who was out for the year with a broken cheek bone, and four sophomores were in the regular lineup on offense, including Luck and split end Darrell "Coast to Coast" Miller. And the defense was even younger, with four freshmen starting, one of them 204-pound nose guard Dave Oblak.

"I'm in high school and I'm looking at all of the magazines and I'm seeing names and pictures of guys I had grown up watching, and then two months later, I'm in the action right there with them," said Oblak. "I'm there. I'm playing against guys with mustaches and full beards."

"Dave Oblak comes in as a true freshman and he's starting at nose guard. Calvin Turner started out at linebacker and they moved him down [to defensive line]," said Dawson. "On my side was a first-year tackle, a true freshman nose guard; Darryl Talley was playing defensive end in his second year and I'm a second-year player – and we're going up against Pitt!"

The Panthers in 1979 were a year away from having one of the best teams in college football (many, including Bobby Bowden, who faced them that season, believe that the 1980 Pitt squad was one of the most talented teams in college football history). The offense featured two future all-pros up front in Russ Grimm and Mark May, Benjie Pryor was a very good tight end, and the backfield had two big playmakers in Rooster Jones and Randy McMillan. At quarterback, making his second career start that afternoon was freshman Dan Marino. He had been playing behind starter Rick Trocano.

"You watched Marino all of the time on the Pittsburgh news, and you wondered just how good he was," said Dawson, who grew up about two hours south of the Steel City in New Martinsville. "Well, I'm on the hash and my job when the ball is on the hash [in passing situations] was to back straight up, and when he set his feet I was supposed to set my feet.

"This guy goes back and he's holding the ball down around his waist like Joe Namath, and I swear, he threw this ball from out of his hip pocket and you could hear the laces – even with the crowd," Dawson said. "I get one step and put my hand out and the guy caught it about two yards in front of me. The ball was a laser beam. I knew he was the real deal after that."

But the young quarterback was bothered by the boisterous West Virginia crowd, fumbling twice and throwing an interception. "This place is crazy," Marino said to reporters after the game.

"He used to hate the crowd at West Virginia because they used to always get on him," said Talley. "He called us 'the Hoopies.' But we had some fun, though."

As good as Pitt's offense was, the Panther defense was even better. Pitt had the best pair of defensive ends in the country in Hugh Green and Rickey Jackson. Both came from the Deep South – Green from Natchez, Miss., and Jackson from Pahokee, Fla. "Those guys recruited size and speed, and they figured they could teach you how to play," Talley recalled.

Cignetti thought those Pitt defenses from 1977–81 were easily the best that he ever faced. "You take Pitt from about '77 when Johnny [Majors] left there, and you look at their football team until about '81, and that might have been the best defense ever in college football," he admitted. "I've always felt that way. You look at the hall of famers. You're talking about Rickey Jackson, Hugh Green, [(Greg] Meisner . . . you're talking about guys that were outstanding NFL players.

"They had great, great talent. They were doing a great job of recruiting, and they were doing it nationally," Cignetti added. "They were into Florida and all over the south and the East, into Ohio – great, talented football teams, and they did a great job of coaching them."

More than three decades later, Dave Johnson can still remember with fine detail his introduction to big-time college football against Pitt, in 1979. Johnson was one of the gunners on the punt team, and it was his job to chase down the returner once the football was airborne. Johnson ran down the field as fast as he could, angling toward the sideline where the football was headed when, all of a sudden, he got blindsided. "It just felt like I had gotten hit by a truck," Johnson chuckled. "It was right around the hash and the old turf was worn out and wet. I got hit so hard that I slid right through Pitt's bench and hit the wall where the fans were. I can remember going across the turf thinking, 'What just hit me?'" When Johnson turned around he saw a yellow flag on the ground, and standing next to it looking like the cat that ate the canary was Hugh Green. Johnson wasn't the only player Green got. "I don't know what point of the game it was, but I had to scramble around and I'm looking downfield like a quarterback should," Luck said. "I completely missed Hugh Green, and he puts his helmet right into my sternum. He flattened me out to the point where my mother thought I was dead."

The 12th-ranked Panthers may have been a prohibitive favorite against West Virginia, but the Mountaineers had one clear advantage – some of the wildest fans in college football. Three thousand more than old Mountaineer Field's 35,000-seat capacity showed up for the final game there. The fans standing on the sideline and in the end zone were at least eight deep in some places. The athletic department had to beef up security after receiving a phone call from a 10-year season ticket holder who said he planned on bringing a saw to the stadium so he could cut out his seat for a souvenir. It was that crazy. Pitt offensive tackle Mark May said he never went on the field in Morgantown without his helmet on. "Their fans just hated us with a passion," May once said. "The night before the game, out in the parking lot at the hotel, people were making noise until four in the morning. They were partying, yelling . . . anything they could do to try and disturb us."

The administration also thought it necessary to separate the rowdy students from the regular spectators, so a chicken-wire fence was erected that was high enough to keep the students away from the paying customers. Dawson once watched the WVU students greet Syracuse players with some frozen oranges during his freshman year, in 1978. "It's freezing cold and those oranges were like missiles," Dawson laughed. "When the team came out of the tunnel, those students just pelted them. It was like deer season."

Years later, when he was in the pros, Talley remembered having conversations with opposing players who complained about some of their harrowing experiences at the old stadium. "Some of the guys from Temple would ask me 'What is wrong with your fans?' I'd say, 'Well, they're just here to protect us!'" Talley chuckled.

Jackie Sherrill actually enjoyed walking into the lion's den. He won all five times he played West Virginia, including triumphs at Mountaineer Field in 1977 and 1979. Pitt sports historian Sam Sciullo, Jr. was a student traveling with the team back then, and he said Sherrill used to get a kick out of the rabid WVU fans who would often heckle him. "I remember Jackie Sherrill walking around the Holiday Inn parking lot wearing a little button with a derogatory remark about Pitt [likely suggesting that they eat something] that was being distributed around Morgantown," said Sciullo. "He really enjoyed those types of things."

Bill Hillgrove, Pitt's longtime radio voice, wrote in 2007 that his infant daughter discovered a new cheer at one of the WVU-Pitt games at old Mountaineer Field. Hillgrove's wife decided to take their young daughter down to the game in Morgantown on a bus excursion financed by the Golden Panthers, and on the return trip their daughter began to entertain the occupants with a new chant she had just learned: "Eat $#(+ Pitt!" His wife unsuccessfully tried to get her to cheer "Let's Go Pitt" instead.

Before the game, Sciullo was in the Pitt radio booth, and he noticed in an adjacent booth Sandy Yakim, Jack Fleming's daughter, sobbing uncontrollably when the Pride of West Virginia was doing its pre-game show. Former WVU assistant coach Joel Hicks also had a difficult time controlling his emotions. Cignetti asked Hicks if he would like to say a few words to the team before the players took the field for their last game at the stadium, but he got so choked up with emotion that he couldn't speak. "He started shaking and that was it," Dawson said. "He just turned around and left." The most poignant moment for Dawson came near the conclusion of the pre-game prayer, just before the 'amen,' when linebacker John Garcia got up and yelled, "Let's kill the bastards!" The entire team jumped up and took off out of the locker room.

The Panthers were clearly the superior team, but through sheer willpower and determination, West Virginia somehow managed to stay in the game. After trailing 10-0 at the half and then falling behind 17-3 at the start of the fourth quarter, the Mountaineers rallied. WVU drove 80 yards in 13 plays to make the score 17-10, and after a third Pitt touchdown, West Virginia answered with another 13-play scoring drive that covered 60 yards. Luck's 1-yard TD run with 4:07 remaining kept West Virginia's upset hopes alive. Pitt had a chance to run out the clock deep in West Virginia territory, but Talley forced Freddy Jacobs to fumble at the 20, where Calvin Turner recovered it. Luck tried two passes, both incomplete, and then was thrown for a 4-yard loss. On fourth down, Jeff Pelusi made an interception, but he fumbled the ball right back to West Virginia.

Another desperation Luck pass was intercepted by Jo Jo Heath – his second turnover and the team's fifth, allowing Marino to take a knee to end the game. The final score was 24 to 17 – a much closer game than anyone ever expected (Pitt won the two prior games against West Virginia by a combined score of 96-10).

The '79 season played out the following week at Arizona State, when West Virginia lost 42-7 to the Sun Devils, giving Cignetti his fourth losing campaign in as many years. During the week leading up to the game, speculation in Morgantown had new athletic director Dick Martin making a coaching change after the season. All during the Arizona State game, Martin tried to avoid reporters, but he was eventually cornered in the back of the press box by Charleston's Shorty Hardman, who asked Martin if he was going to can Cignetti after the game. "Shorty, if you ask me that again I'm going to punch you in the nose," Martin angrily replied. Two days later, Martin fired Cignetti.

"It was a shame they let Frank go, but they let him go," said Gary Stevens, an assistant coach for the Miami Hurricanes and then later the Miami Dolphins. "I'm going to tell you something, Frank was a good coach. He's the guy that got that stadium built. He was the guy that pushed for it and he really worked recruiting."

For Luck, New Mountaineer Field was the key to putting the West Virginia program on a more equal footing with Pitt and Penn State. "From my class and the class behind that with Robert Alexander and Fulton Walker, I think the new stadium was crucial to the recruiting process," Luck said. "If the new stadium hadn't been on the drawing board, I doubt West Virginia would have gotten the classes that graduated in '81 and '82."

"[Cignetti's successor Don Nehlen] won with our players," said Stevens. "And from that winning, he got better ballplayers with a new facility, so now you've got a winner – and not only that, you take Pennsylvania, you take Ohio – it's a two-three-hour drive to come down with their family.

"To me, if the university was really going to develop a top-notch football program year in and year out, a massive upgrading to the facilities needed to take place," added Luck. "It was fun to play in old Mountaineer Field, and I've got some fond memories of my first college game – it was quaint and very intimate – but it was not conducive to developing the program."

Still, many WVU players had a soft spot in their heart for that old stadium – the broken whisky bottles, the splinters, the falling concrete, the dog-sized rats and all. "I think Mountaineer Field is a great place to play and I loved it, but there was something about that old stadium," Dawson added. "Everybody was right on top of you."

Talley said old Mountaineer Field was always an intimidating place for opposing teams to play in. "Once we got you on that field, you were surrounded, you couldn't go anywhere," Talley said. "It was like being thrown into a snake pit and you couldn't get out. Our crazy fans were running around yelling at you. We had some rowdy fans, I will admit that, but they were good to us."

For most of its 55-year existence, the old stadium right in the middle of campus was also good to West Virginia University football.

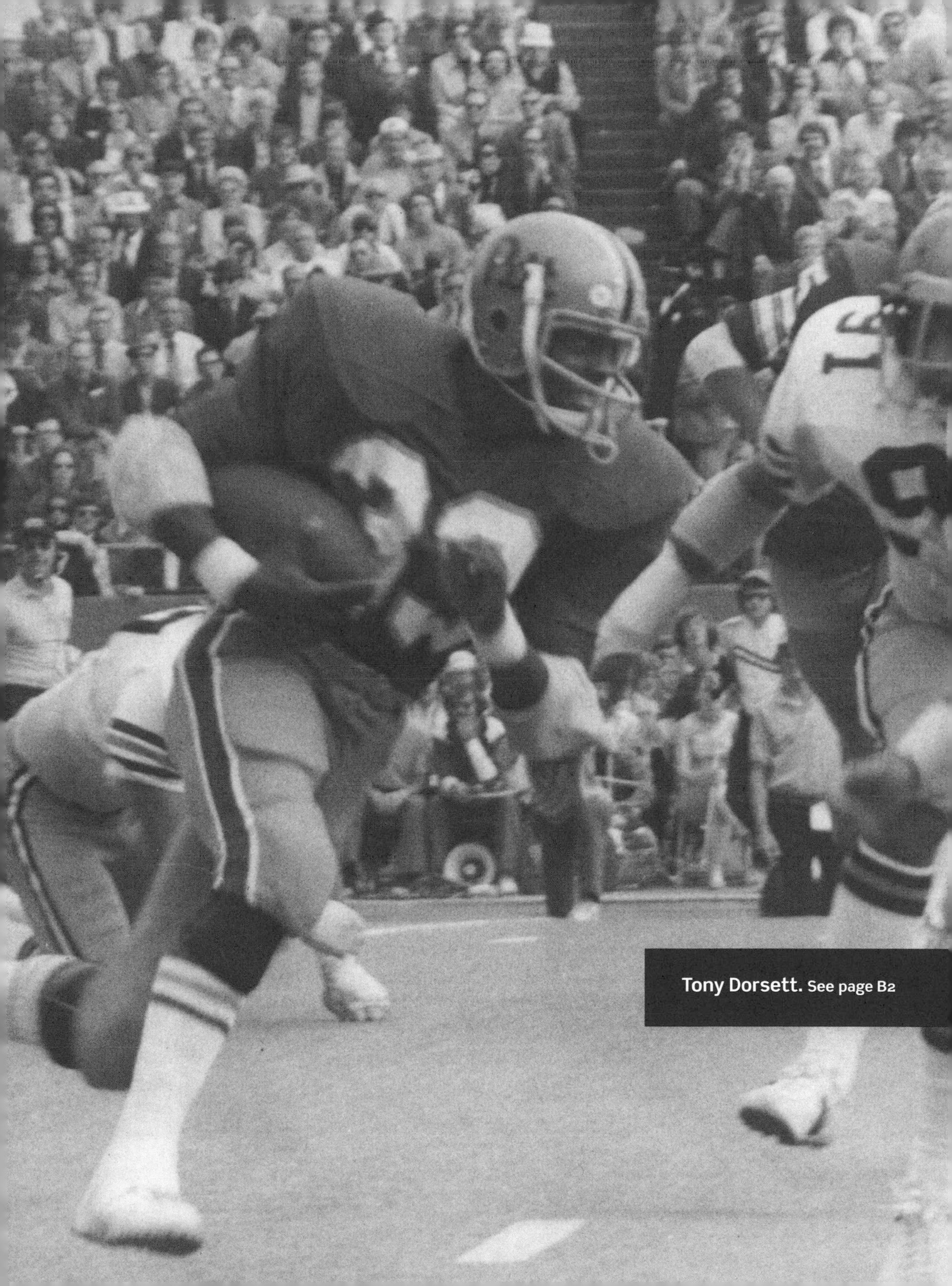

Tony Dorsett. See page B2

Coach Don Nehlen. See page B6

1982-1991
A CHANGING OF THE GUARD

A Classic Comeback

PITT	WVU
16	13
Oct. 2, 1982 Pittsburgh	

Sometime during the 1979 season, Dick Martin made up his mind that a change was needed in the West Virginia University football program. The Mountaineers lost the first three games of the '79 campaign to Temple, Syracuse and North Carolina State by more than two-touchdown margins, rallied to win four of five in the middle of the year, and then dropped a tough 24-17 decision to 12th-ranked Pitt in the final game played at old Mountaineer Field, giving WVU a 5-5 record with one game remaining at Arizona State.

Martin had said publically before the start of the season that he needed to see some progress in the football program with a new stadium on the horizon – namely, a winning record. Coach Frank Cignetti, likable and very popular with the media and the rest of the athletic staff, was not so popular with the fans and some of the boosters seeking more victories. He had coached the team to three straight losing seasons in 1976, 1977 and 1978, and he was stricken with a rare form of cancer that was ravaging his body by the end of the '78 campaign. In fact, Cignetti nearly died on the operating table during an exploratory operation to find out what was wrong with him. He eventually recovered and was healthy enough to coach the team in 1979, but while some progress was being made, it wasn't enough to save his job. Martin decided a coaching change was in order after watching West Virginia perform miserably in a 42-7 loss at Arizona State to end the season.

Martin had been hired as West Virginia University's athletic director at the same time as Cignetti was in the hospital, and the new AD was in the difficult position of having to treat Cignetti's delicate health situation compassionately. There was even some talk in the summer of 1979 of bringing former Colorado coach Bill Mallory in to coach the team if Cignetti was not fully recovered. Martin had a football background, coaching high school in Terre Haute, Ind., before taking over the Washington (Missouri) University program in 1968. Eventually, Martin landed a job at the Big Eight Conference as an assistant commissioner, and then in 1978, West Virginia University president Gene Budig hired him to replace Leland Byrd as the school's athletic director. Martin said the brand new football stadium under construction was a compelling reason for him to take the WVU AD job.

"If you could build a stadium I saw . . . the depiction of that stadium in Morgantown, West Virginia, and within a 200-mile radius have some really outstanding football players . . . [and] the road system was improving coming into Morgantown – all of that together made the West Virginia job an interesting one," Martin recalled in 2006, two years before his death.

What Martin believed the program needed was an energetic football coach who could sell the new stadium to recruits and also galvanize the West Virginia fan base, which had grown apathetic after witnessing losing campaigns in five of the prior six seasons, dating back to 1974 under Bobby Bowden. Martin then discovered Michigan assistant coach Don Nehlen through their mutual friendship with Bob Marcum, a Marshall University graduate then serving as associate athletic director at Iowa State.

"Bob was the first one to mention Don to me," Martin said. "I was working at that time at the Big Eight office, and Bob was the associate AD at Iowa State and then became athletic director down at Kansas. Bob and I were good friends and he recommended Don to me.

"I just kind of did the research from there."

Don Nehlen had several good seasons at Bowling Green before the ship finally ran aground in 1976. "We won six football games in a row, but every week we lost another football player," Nehlen said. "I got what I thought we'd get – we lost them all and we ended up 6-5. The president said to me, 'Don, I don't know how a team can win six in a row and then lose their last five.' Of course I made a real big mistake, because I had heard through the grapevine that all of his vice presidents had quit because he was such a knucklehead, [and] I said, 'I can't understand how a president can lose all of his vice presidents because they can't stand to work for the guy.' He got me in an emotional situation – this was 15 minutes after our last loss and he came into the locker room," Nehlen said. "Had it been an hour later, I probably wouldn't have said what I said."

Nehlen realized then that it was time to look for another job, so, in search of a life preserver, he called an old friend.

"[Michigan coach] Bo Schembechler was a good friend of mine, and I called him up and said, 'Bo, here's my situation here. The president doesn't like me and he wants to cut my recruiting budget down to nothing.' He said, 'Don, I think Gary Moeller is going to get the Illinois job. If he gets the Illinois job you tell that guy to shove that job because you're coming to Michigan.' I went home and told [my wife] Merry Ann, start praying for Gary Moeller. Well lo and behold if he didn't get the job, and Bo called me up and that's how I got the Michigan job."

It was at Michigan where Nehlen learned that football was as much a mind game as it was about tactics and talent. "When you have a bunch of kids who believe in themselves and believe in the program, you have a chance to win," Nehlen explained. "While I was there, I said to myself that if I ever get the chance to be a head coach again I'll be good because what I was doing at Bowling Green was good. But I wasn't real sure I believed it because I didn't have anything to compare it with."

As soon as he arrived at Michigan, Nehlen got an immediate dose of the supreme confidence the Wolverine players had. "I coached the quarterbacks, and Rick Leach was my quarterback," Nehlen said. "Ricky was about 6 feet tall and 180 pounds, but he thought he could conquer the world. He said, 'Coach you've got to understand this is Michigan. At Michigan we do nothing but win.'" Once, before a game against struggling Northwestern, Nehlen was upset with the way the offense nonchalantly went through their pregame warm-ups and went after his quarterback in the locker room right before kickoff. "Hey you guys," Nehlen growled. "Northwestern is not going to lie over and play dead. You better get yourself ready to play!"

Then Leach spoke up. "Don't worry, Coach, we'll be ahead by 35 or 40 at halftime and Bo can take the rest of the guys out," he said. "That's the way we think. We know we're going to win and those guys hope they're going to win."

It was a lesson in self-confidence Nehlen never forgot.

One crisp December morning in 1979, Nehlen walked into the Michigan football complex after returning from a recruiting trip in Louisville trying to chase down offensive lineman Bubba Paris. Schembechler saw Nehlen in the hallway and asked him to come into his office.

"Hey boy, are you interested in West Virginia?" Schembechler asked.

"No."

"Hey Don, don't give me that stuff," Schembechler said.

"Bo, if I was interested in West Virginia the first guy I would come to is you. I couldn't get that job without your approval."

"Well, this guy Martin called, and I've known you since you were 17 and this guy knows more about you than I do," Schembechler said.

Martin and Nehlen had a long phone conversation, and then Martin convinced him to meet the selection committee in the Pittsburgh airport for a formal interview. Nehlen and the committee hit it off immediately.

"The thing that came across to me most about Don was his sincerity and honesty, and I thought he could really relate to the players," Martin said.

Martin also did a good job of selling West Virginia to Nehlen. "When I told Bo I was going to take the West Virginia job, he said, 'Don, you're crazy.' He looked at our schedule and he saw Oklahoma on there," Nehlen recalled. "He saw Penn State and he saw Pitt. He said, 'You've got about four, five or six losses on here right away. Every coach that's ever coached there – if they win, they leave, and if they lose, they get fired. I just think this is a big mistake. You're making good money; we go to the Rose Bowl every year, and in two or three years I'll get you a good job.'"

Nehlen disagreed. He took out a map and showed Schembechler all of the major cities surrounding Morgantown. "Bo, there are a ton of football players within 300 miles of Morgantown," Nehlen said. "I got a feeling I can get me 15 of those guys a year."

Quarterback Oliver Luck remembered the first meeting the team had with their new football coach, in an empty room downstairs in the Towers dormitory. Guys had baseball caps pulled down over their heads, feet were propped up on empty table tops and some of the players were slouched down in their chairs. It had the look of a room full of losers. Nehlen walked inside, noticed one of the players with his feet propped up and went right over and kicked them off the table. "Right then we realized it was going to be a different regime," Luck laughed.

Linebacker Darryl Talley recalled that first meeting as well. "He started telling everybody, 'Regardless of how you guys got here, now all of you are my guys now. No matter what anybody says, you're all mine,'" Talley said. "I said to myself, 'Here's a guy who doesn't know ace from apple butter going to tell me I'm his guy? Well, we're going to see about that.' So I watched him and paid attention to everything he was doing and everything he said he was going to do. And he did it. Immediately, I realized I could trust the guy, and I just went on from there."

But Nehlen wasn't so sure about Talley (who was elected into the College Football Hall of Fame in 2011). The coach remembered once being handed a photograph of his star linebacker sitting on the bench during a game – asleep.

"We were playing Pitt in the snake pit [old Mountaineer Field], and I was sleeping, I'll admit it," Talley said. "I went to sleep. I couldn't play and they weren't going to let me do anything, and back then I was a kid from the city and I believed that I could play as well as anybody out there, and I didn't feel I was given a chance to play. I got mad and I went down on the end of the bench and I went to sleep."

Talley was like a wild thoroughbred that needed broken in. When the linebackers were tired, they would often have Talley go over the dummies first because they knew he would plow right through them and scatter them everywhere. The time it took rearranging the dummies gave the other linebackers an opportunity to catch their breath. Nehlen's linebacker coach Bob Simmons was the person who was really able to tap Talley's huge reservoir of talent.

DARRYL TALLEY WAS LIKE A WILD THOROUGHBRED THAT NEEDED BROKEN IN.

"Coach Simmons taught me how to use my hat and hands," Talley explained. "I was a forearm player beforehand."

Because Talley was tall and somewhat gangly, Simmons drew a line on the wall inside the stadium and had his linebacker stand low and hit that wall with his hands every day in practice, teaching him how to play with leverage. "He taught me how to explode into people and then get off them," Talley said. "He taught me how to read steps, lead the hat, get my hands on him, step with him and stay under him. Gary Tranquill and Bob Simmons is where I got all of my technique from. Then I got stronger, and after that it was just a matter of going out and playing football."

Cornerback Steve Newberry recalled receiving the wrath of Talley at Hawaii during his freshman year, in 1980. Newberry had suffered a concussion in the first quarter and was running around in a daze, once or twice even heading toward Hawaii's huddle, when Talley grabbed hold of Newberry's facemask and lit into him with a barrage of expletives. Right then Newberry came to. "His looks back then were enough to make anybody snap out of whatever state they were in," Newberry laughed.

The coaches Nehlen hired, especially on defense, were young and aggressive, and they wanted a team full of tough guys. It wasn't considered a good football practice unless there were at least three or four fights that had to be broken up.

"I think we took on the personality of our coaches," Newberry said. "Our coaches were aggressive, and they taught an aggressive style of defense – flying around and hitting everything that moved."

Nehlen's first season in 1980 wasn't a winning one, but it wasn't a losing one either, with the Mountaineers going 6-6 despite a foolish midseason trip to Hawaii right before a pair of big games against key rivals Pitt and Penn State. The moment Nehlen first saw the '80 schedule, he tried to get out of the Hawaii game, but too much had been invested into the trip to buy it out.

"We have Hawaii and then we have to play Pitt and Penn State back to back my first year," Nehlen said. "In '79, '78, '77 and '76, not a single kid I had inherited had ever played on a winning team, and we have those guys back to back after coming home losing an entire day traveling. It takes you two days to recover, and it was just a mess. We played Penn State pretty well, but we got killed by Pitt."

The 1981 season was much better, with West Virginia winning nine games and finishing ranked 17th in the final AP poll. A 26-6 victory over Florida in the Peach Bowl capped a fabulous season. "Our kids are champing at the bit," recalled Nehlen. "At the press conference, [Florida coach] Charley Pell didn't know my name – he called me 'Nellun.' He said, 'This new guy Nellun has done a pretty good job with this West Virginia program.' My two captains are snorting when they get out of there. We leave the press conference and [tight end] Mark Raugh comes up to me and he says, 'Coach, I'm going to tell you one thing – Charley Pell is going to know your name at the end of the game.'"

Nine months later, Nehlen topped the Florida victory by going out and beating ninth-ranked Oklahoma to begin the 1982 season. The coach spent the offseason preparing his team for what they were going to face in Norman, and he also had a surprise for the Sooners when quarterback Jeff Hostetler became eligible one year after transferring from Penn State.

"Our coaching staff did a great job of preseason planning," Nehlen recalled. "At the end of every practice, we spent 25 minutes working just on the wishbone. And Jeff was just terrific. We executed beautifully, and that stupid draw play I always called just ruined them."

"It all started with Oklahoma because we didn't have a chance, and that's what everybody was saying – we were going to go out there and kill their horse (Sooner Schooner) because he was going to be running around the field so much [because Oklahoma was going to score so many points against West Virginia]," said Hostetler. "It was a respect thing, and nobody had respect for us – except for the guys sitting in our locker room."

"I think we really turned the corner, especially with that stretch," Newberry added. "Finishing up the '81 season with the Peach Bowl win that everybody thought we weren't supposed to win, and then coming back and carrying that momentum into the start of the '82 year and playing at Oklahoma . . . that was a special time in our program's history."

Wins over Maryland (against all-ACC quarterback Boomer Esiason) and Richmond gave West Virginia a 3-0 record and a No. 14 ranking in both the AP and UPI polls. On the horizon was undefeated Pitt, ranked first in the UPI poll and second in the AP poll. It was the first time since 1955 that West Virginia and Pitt were nationally ranked while playing each other. The Panthers were good, but just how good no one knew for certain.

Just a couple of weeks after leading Pitt to a 24-20 victory over Georgia in the Sugar Bowl, Coach Jackie Sherrill rocked the Pitt campus by agreeing to Texas A&M's offer to assume the dual role of head football coach and athletic director. The contract Sherrill agreed to was the most lucrative in college football at the time, drawing widespread national criticism from professors and educators complaining about the growing exorbitance of the sport. What Sherrill walked away from at Pitt was one of the best football teams in the country, with the bulk of the players returning from the '81 squad that defeated Georgia in the Sugar Bowl, including quarterback Dan Marino.

Sherrill was a masterful recruiter who left no stone unturned, which is how he was able to procure some of the most talented football players in Pitt history. When Jeff Hostetler made himself available to college recruiters once again in 1981 after two unhappy seasons at Penn State, Sherrill came after him with both guns blazing. Sherrill knew everything there was to know about Hostetler, including the fact that he was a devout Christian who wasn't interested in the party scene. Other schools pursuing Hostetler didn't quite do their homework the way Sherrill did.

"The guy they had take me around campus was a Christian guy, number one. Number two, they knew everything about me," Hostetler said. The quarterback recalled being taken to one of Sherrill's favorite Italian restaurants in Oakland and being led to a dimly lit back room. He could see this figure sitting all the way in the back of the room, just like a scene out of the movie *The Godfather*. It was Sherrill.

"He said, 'Hey, we've got Marino here, and he's got one year left, and if you come here you can be our starter after Danny, and you would have a great career here. We would make everything right for you,'" Hostetler recalled. "It was really enticing and they almost had me, but I didn't fit in the city."

The Pitt situation in the early 1980s was one full of mystery and intrigue, and surprisingly similar to what West Virginia encountered in 2007 when Rich Rodriguez left for Michigan. Sherrill was a three-year starter for Bear Bryant at Alabama from 1964–66 and later latched on with Johnny Majors at Iowa State in 1970, becoming his defensive coordinator and assistant head coach – a title he maintained when Majors took the Pitt job in 1972. It was Sherrill who was responsible for recruiting Tony Dorsett to Pitt and fielding those dominant defenses that helped the Panthers quickly ascend to Top 20 status. In 1976, Sherrill was hired to coach Washington State during Pitt's national championship run, but after just one year in Pullman, he was enticed to return to Pittsburgh following Majors's pre-Sugar Bowl announcement that he was leaving for Tennessee. Sherrill's five seasons coaching the Panthers, from 1977–81, were the best by a Panther coach since the Sutherland days, and as Sherrill was building Pitt into a yearly national title contender, he had also forged a close working relationship with Pitt athletic director Cas Myslinski.

Myslinski, an All-American center at Army who was selling real estate in California at the time Pitt hired him in 1968, had one of the most successful athletic tenures of any Pitt AD. Myslinski hired both Majors and Sherrill, was responsible for merging four separate fundraising groups into the Golden Panthers (one of the prior groups was called "The Prowling Panthers"), successfully fought those who wanted to move Pitt's home games to Three Rivers Stadium, and made the controversial decision (and the correct one) of ending "Tiger" Paul Auslander's antics at Pitt basketball games. Myslinski, a 22-year military man, was once described as being always at attention – even when he slept. Myslinski had little time for small talk, and he occasionally ended staff meetings by saying to his subordinates, "As you were."

But Myslinski's powers were being stripped away in the early 1980s, and Sherrill was growing concerned. According to a 2007 account of that period by columnist Bob Smizik in the *Pittsburgh Post-Gazette*, Sherrill wanted a meeting with Chancellor Wesley Posvar before Pitt's Sugar Bowl appearance against Georgia so he could address some of his concerns with the program, but Posvar refused to see him. Sherrill took that as a personal affront, and as Myslinski's authority was further eroding (eventually he was forced out in favor of Posvar lieutenant Ed Bozik in the spring of '82), the die was cast. Sherrill got a hefty raise and the authority he desired at Texas A&M, and Pitt, stung by the back-to-back departures of Majors and Sherrill within a five-year span, opted to go with one of its own by promoting defensive coordinator Serafino "Foge" Fazio to head coach. In Fazio, Pitt had a guy it believed was willing to stick it out for the long haul.

Fazio, the son of Italian immigrants, was born in West Virginia and lived in a mining camp near Clarksburg until he was four, when his father moved the family to Coraopolis, Pa., after breaking his leg in a mining accident. Fazio starred at Coraopolis High and then at Pitt, in the late 1950s. After a brief stint with the Boston Patriots he returned to Pitt to complete his master's degree. Fazio later got into coaching, first at the high school level, and then on to the college ranks at Boston University and Harvard, before making a second return to Pitt as a member of Carl DePasqua's staff. When DePasqua was fired after the 1972 season, Fazio was the only coach retained by Johnny Majors, but after only a month and a half with Majors, Fazio decided to join Tony Mason's staff at Cincinnati. Four years later, when Mason left for Arizona, Fazio was passed over for the Bearcat head coaching job, so he made yet another return to Pitt, in 1977, when Sherrill was hired to replace Majors. Fazio had become assistant head coach and defensive coordinator by the time Sherrill was wooed to Texas A&M.

Fazio was popular with the players and the media, and he often enjoyed poking fun at himself. "My first name is 'Serafino,' which I guess all of you realize is Italian for angel," he would say. "And my middle name is 'Dante,' the same as that guy down there in Hades . . . I guess what that all means is that you can call me a helluvan angel."

What Pitt fans were really looking for was a helluva coach to continue what Majors and Sherrill had started. Despite the transition to a new coach, Pitt was voted No. 1 in both major preseason polls. The easygoing and fun-loving Fazio was now under a lot of pressure to win, and a difficult early schedule that included games against fifth-ranked North Carolina, Florida State and 19th-ranked Illinois only added to the pressure. Pitt won all three games, but the offense wasn't clicking; Marino was completing only 54 percent of his passes, for 473 yards with four touchdown passes and nine interceptions – four of those picks coming in the red zone.

However, the Panther defense was as good as ever, sacking quarterback Tony Eason 10 times in a 20-3 victory at Illinois. Two defensive starters were out for that game – linebacker Rich Kraynak and defensive end Al Wenglikowski – but Pitt didn't miss a beat with their replacements, Caesar Aldisert and Chris Doleman.

Don Nehlen could poor-mouth with the best of them, and when he was asked to give his opinion of the Pitt team he was studying on film, he gushed like Mount Vesuvius. "What do I think of Pitt? Let me put it this way. The pro scouts tell me when they go to Pitt there are 17 kids they have to look at. When they come here, they don't even turn on the projector," he said. Now on a roll, Nehlen didn't stop there. "Offensively they can do it all. Defensively, they're even better. When I look at that team I get a little jealous."

Fazio was pretty good at poor-mouthing, too. "It surely looks like West Virginia knows how to win," he began. "They have a lot of experience and probably one of the best defensive teams in the country this year. They have good personnel on offense, and quarterback Jeff Hostetler knows how to run the offense.

"That Don Nehlen," Fazio continued, "he's sitting down there in Morgantown, smiling away, keeping quiet, when, in fact, he's got outstanding personnel this year. It's his personnel that makes the big difference."

The biggest difference between the two teams was Pitt's offensive and defensive lines. The Pitt O-line featured three future pros in Jimbo Covert, Jim Sweeney and Bill Fralic, and the defensive front was just as impressive with Bill Maas, Chris Doleman, Dave Puzzuoli, Jay Pelusi and Michael Woods starting up front.

"My left tackle had a real tough time trying to block Chris Doleman and Bill Maas," Nehlen recalled. "We didn't stack up with them, but our kids just laid it on the line. It was amazing the way those kids just laid it on the line in that game."

Especially quarterback Jeff Hostetler, who was so beaten and battered after the game that Nehlen blocked the door to the training room to keep reporters from talking to his quarterback. Hostetler was in that much pain. "I think Jeff about got killed that game," Nehlen said. "We had to carry him into the locker room, and then we had to carry him onto the bus."

> **"IN ALL MY YEARS OF PLAYING, I NEVER FELT AS BADLY [AFTER A GAME]."**
>
> *Ex-WVU QB Jeff Hostetler*

"The following day my roommate, Dave Johnson, had to help me out of bed and get me up to the stadium [for treatments]," Hostetler said. "In all my years of playing, I never felt as badly [after a game]. I think the first play of the game, either the backside guard or the backside tackle, left Chris Doleman [unblocked] and he hit me full blast, and I felt like my head was going to explode."

The guys watching from the sidelines said Hostetler was hit by a Pitt player every single time he dropped back to pass that afternoon. "As the game wore on, those guys were hitting me and they were starting to help me up because they could see the beating that I was taking," Hostetler chuckled. "I can't remember which one of them said it, but one of them said, 'Man, you're taking a beating,' and he helped me off the ground. Not only was that physically a tough day, but to be beating them the whole game and then to lose at the end was difficult too."

As tough as things were for Hostetler, the opposite could be said for Talley, who had a terrific all-around game. In fact, it was a performance that really launched his career by showcasing to the country what a wonderful all-around football player he was. Everywhere the ball went, it seemed as if Talley was right there, whether he was dropping back in coverage to make an interception, chasing down the ball carrier from behind, or even recovering his own punt block in the Pitt end zone at the start of the fourth quarter for West Virginia's only touchdown. Nehlen wanted to go for a two-point conversion to try and make the score 14-0, but the players were celebrating so hard that he couldn't get the conversion unit onto the field in time.

In Talley, West Virginia had a tough, 6-foot-4-inch, 220-pound player who could run like the wind, and the defensive coaches took advantage of it by lining him up almost anywhere on the field. "We were playing what we called 'tough coverage,' where we took Talley and put him out on the split end and over-shifted to try and stop their passing game," Nehlen recalled.

Talley said he lined up at almost every defensive position that afternoon, with the exception of the two safety spots. "I even lined up at nose guard," he said.

Bill Kirelawich recalled Nehlen not being a big fan of moving Talley away from the line of scrimmage to cover Pitt's wide receivers. "I remember him being pissed off, saying 'You guys have my best football player out playing cornerback!'" Kirelawich laughed. "Talley was unbelievable that game. He played the game of his life."

Oliver Luck, a rookie quarterback for the Houston Oilers, happened to be standing on the sidelines watching that afternoon, because the NFL was on strike that year. Luck rarely concentrated on one player when he watched games, and if he did, it was usually an offensive player. But on this afternoon, his eyes were trained on Talley like a bug attracted to light. "He was just a one-man wrecking crew," Luck recalled. "I remember thinking to myself, because I was playing pro ball and I had an eye for pro players, 'Yeah, he's going to be a hell of an NFL player.'"

"He made play after play," added Hostetler. "Darryl's number was called and he came up big against a very, very talented team. If you looked across the board, that team was just stacked."

After Talley's TD gave West Virginia a 13-0 lead early in the fourth quarter, finger pointing and yelling could be seen going on over on the Pitt sidelines. "To be up on Pitt

13-0 going into the fourth quarter, and then looking over at the Pitt sidelines and seeing Dan Marino punching his players because he didn't want to lose . . . yeah, we thought we were going to win," recalled kicker Paul Woodside.

But that's when Marino took matters into his own hands. He marched the Panthers 83 yards in nine plays, completing passes of 18 yards to Dwight Collins and 10 yards to Keith Williams before Bryan Thomas took it into the end zone from the 3 for Pitt's first score.

"Being down 13-0, it was a real struggle," Fazio recalled in 2005, four years before his death. "I remember the guys on the sidelines kept saying 'Come on, keep hanging in there! Don't let them score! We're going to come back!'"

Two possessions after Pitt's TD, the Panthers got a huge break when Hostetler didn't get a firm grasp of Billy Legg's snap at the West Virginia 45, and strong safety Dan "Peep" Short was able to come out of the pile with the football. It was the first play of the game for the injured Legg, who was forced to come in at a key moment when regular center Dave Johnson went out with an injury. Right away Marino went to work, finding Collins for 16 yards on a third-and-5 play that took the ball to the WVU 27. Two plays after that, on another third and 5 at the 22, Marino hit tight end John Brown for 14 yards to get to the 8. Then, Marino hooked up with flanker Julius Dawkins on a quick slant for a 6-yard touchdown to give the Panthers a 14-13 lead with 3:23 remaining in the game. "Marino hit three or four great passes on us," Nehlen recalled. "They were [all] that 12-to-15-yard curl."

"Danny just got hot," Fazio recalled. "We got into a rhythm, and once you get into a rhythm you can run the ball a little bit, and with Danny throwing the ball, you can keep them off balance. And then we were good enough to shut them out the rest of the way."

Perhaps, but it was not without some tense moments on the Panther sideline. Hostetler was sacked by Maas for a safety with 41 seconds left, giving Pitt a 16-13 lead, and on the ensuing free kick, Woodside was able to recover his own kick at the West Virginia 31. Backup quarterback Kevin White came in to try one pass, which bounced on the turf in front of Wayne Brown, before Hostetler returned for even more punishment. After a holding call moved the ball back to the WVU 21, "Hoss" was able find tight end Mark Raugh for 21 yards to get to the 42. Fifteen additional yards were tacked on to the end of the play when a roughing the passer penalty was called on Pitt. Another quick Hostetler pass to backup tight end Rob Bennett got West Virginia 8 yards closer, setting Woodside up for a 52-yard field goal try. He had already made two that afternoon and was just one field goal away from making his 16th in a row, which would have tied Steve Little's 1979 NCAA record for consecutive field goals made. Woodside's kick was right down the middle, but it landed just beneath the crossbar. "That kick . . . son of a gun I thought it was going through," said Nehlen. "I fell right down to the ground to my knees when it went right underneath that cross bar."

"Tom Flynn was going to jump up and bat it away, but pulled his hand back just at the end because he didn't want to knock it through," Woodside said. "He said it grazed the cross bar."

Marino then took a knee at the 36 yard line, and the game was over. "It was a sensational football game," Nehlen said. "It was such a hard fought game. I remember it being such a beautiful fall day. It was just a gorgeous day in Pittsburgh.

"The amazing thing about that game was three years before that, we were one of the worst football teams in America," Nehlen said.

"Even though we lost in '82, I think that was one of those wake-up calls [for Pitt] where a team that was stacked like they were could lose to us – and we should have beat them," said Hostetler. "We had them. To hold that team [to 16 points] was a real eye-opener. But, of course, you have to get the win."

"I think the big thing was it was one of those deals where you were playing against West Virginia, and I don't care what the teams' record[s were] because there were times when West Virginia was a big favorite and Pitt won, and there were times when Pitt was a big favorite and West Virginia won," said Fazio. "It was one of those days. West Virginia was a much better football team than people at the time were giving them credit for."

According to Fazio, in the early 1980s it was extremely difficult to get Pitt boosters and supporters to realize that the West Virginia program under Nehlen was rapidly improving.

"Whenever I was coaching there, we had Penn State," Fazio explained. "A lot of people thought, 'Well, we're going to beat West Virginia and there is nothing to worry about there. Let's worry about Notre Dame and Penn State.' Not so much the players – but the fans and boosters who sometimes buy into what they read in the papers."

Nehlen thought the performance at Pitt, the wins against Oklahoma and Maryland, and the Florida victory in the 1981 Peach Bowl all combined to really put his young program on the map.

"From 1982 on this football program joined the upper echelon of college football, and we've been able to maintain that to a decent degree ever since," he said.

For Talley, the '82 loss to Pitt was the game that really advanced his college career. It was largely based on this performance, witnessed by a large proportion of the country on ABC, that he went on to become the school's third consensus All-American player.

Joe Boczek, West Virginia's assistant sports information director at the time, remembered that, as he walked out of Pitt Stadium with Talley, Fazio made a point of coming over and seeking out the linebacker to compliment him on the great game he had played. "Foge looks up at him, and he says, 'Darryl, I have to tell you, you are one hell of a football player, son,'" Boczek recalled.

"That game is part of what drove me in the NFL because I had tried every way in the world to beat Dan Marino when he was at Pitt," Talley admitted. "I just wanted to beat Pitt so bad. We tried everything in the world to beat them. Delbert [Fowler] was a track star coming out of Ohio – he was the 220-yard sprint champ – and I'm like, we can do this! We're just as big as they are and we're just as fast.

"I tried everything for three years to beat their asses and I could not do it. I just decided if I've got to do it by myself, then I'm going to do it."

And he almost did.

"Let's Do It!"

WVU
24
PITT
21
Oct. 1, 1983
Morgantown, W.Va.

Don Nehlen's defensive coordinator Dennis Brown walked up to the chalkboard, grabbed a small, dusty piece of chalk and scratched out, in big block letters, "WE BEAT PITT". He turned around, looked at the team and guaranteed they would win the football game. It wasn't exactly a Joe Namath moment, but the guys in the locker room got the message.

In a game the Mountaineers should have been winning, West Virginia was trailing the Panthers 21-14 at the half. But in 1983, wins against Pitt were almost impossible to come by, especially if you were the West Virginia Mountaineers. One of the first questions WVU fans asked Don Nehlen when he was hired, in December, 1979, was how long he thought it would take before West Virginia could finally beat rivals Pitt and Penn State. Generations of Mountaineer football fans had not enjoyed a victory over Penn State – the last one coming in 1955, when Dwight Eisenhower was still in the White House. Pitt was also enjoying great success against WVU, beating the Mountaineers by scores of 24-16 in 1976, 44-3 in 1977, 52-7 in 1978 and 24-17 in 1979.

"The first thing the fans wanted to know was when we were finally going to beat Pitt and Penn State," Nehlen recalled. "I told them, 'Let's not worry about Pitt and Penn

State right away – let's try and beat those other teams on the schedule first before we can worry about them.'"

That may have been what Nehlen was telling the fans outside the locker room, but inside, he was indoctrinating each and every one of his players about the importance of the Pitt game. It was one of the many little tricks he had learned from the master of tricks, Bo Schembechler.

"I can remember when Nehlen took the job, the first thing he told those kids was about fighting out of the well [to beat the Panthers]," said assistant coach Bill Kirelawich. "Every kid that came to West Virginia during his 21 years here was hit with that story and was made to understand that Pitt was THE rivalry. Seventy-five miles up the road was the big game, and you were brought here to beat their asses, and that's what your job was."

"He was a guy who said it like it was," said Jeff Hostetler. "No matter what you think, guys respond to that. He can tell you something and you may not like it, but at least you knew exactly where he was coming from. You may look at it like [it was contrived], but he meant it and it was true."

But Nehlen knew success against Pitt and Penn State was not going to come overnight. And it didn't. Pitt beat West Virginia 42-14 in 1980, just seven days after West Virginia foolishly took a trip out to Hawaii to face the Rainbows in a midseason game that didn't kick off until 1 a.m., East Coast time. After absorbing their 28-point beating at Pitt, the West Virginia players got the pleasure of seeing the message "A Coal Miner's Slaughter" plastered on the Pitt Stadium scoreboard as they walked to their locker room (*Coal Miner's Daughter* was a popular movie from that year about the life of country music singer Loretta Lynn). Nehlen fared much better in his first crack against Penn State, coming within a touchdown of knocking off the Nittany Lions in Morgantown. But the losses to both schools continued in 1981 and 1982.

"When I came here, Pitt and Penn State were two of the best teams in America, and they were right in our backyard," said Nehlen. "And of course Ohio State was always there, and we couldn't beat those guys for any players. So I decided that we were going to take good kids; we were going to keep them for five years, and maybe they won't play their fourth or fifth year, but we can keep the program moving, and they will be plenty good enough for us to win with."

Nehlen brought other things from Michigan with him to West Virginia, including the reliance on a structured weight training program. Naturally, there is a physical boost that comes from any strength program, but there are also psychological benefits to having stronger football players. In many respects, Nehlen thought that was just as important as the physical strength they were gaining.

"I had linemen that could run five miles and couldn't bench press 200 pounds," Nehlen said. "I'm playing Pitt and Penn State. I told [strength coach] Dave Van Halanger, 'I don't give a damn if these kids can run from here to the refrigerator, we've got to increase their strength by 30 percent or we're going to get killed.'"

Nehlen knew that once the team started noticing the gains they were making in the weight room, they would become more confident football players on the field. Nehlen had Van Halanger measure every part of a player's body, and he wasn't against telling his strength coach to fudge the measurements every once in a while, creating the perception that each player was getting stronger – even if they weren't. Nehlen was a technically sound football coach, and like most coaches of his era, he believed that teams that played great defense, could run the football and were solid in the kicking game would win most of the time.

But what separated Nehlen from most of his contemporaries, and from where his true greatness as a football coach came, was his ability to motivate his players and get them to do things they didn't think they were capable of doing. All-American offensive lineman Brian Jozwiak recalled Nehlen's pregame speech before the team's 1984 win over Penn State being one the most positive and uplifting presentations he had ever heard. Two decades later, Jozwiak could still recite the words.

"The night before when we were out at Lakeview, we would go into a room and all of our guys would bring their pillows and lie around on the floor and watch a movie," he recalled in 2007. "But this was a little different. Before the movie, Nehlen came in, and he walked up to the podium with all of the lights off.

"While he was getting everything together, he just turned on the little light there at the podium. He talked about the game and he played it right out right in front of us," Jozwiak said. "He called guys' names out. We went through a mental exercise that night that was so intense; he allowed us to literally see into the future – see your block, envision this play, envision 56 off the right side – and we're going to toss that ball to Pat Randolph and Scottie Barrows is going to turn the corner and wipe out that safety, and Pat is going to run for a touchdown. He said this stuff. And then he said, 'Woody [kicker Paul Woodside], you're going to seal the deal for us, baby!' He actually called the game the night before it happened."

The players on the 1981 Peach Bowl team still talk about the way Nehlen worked over offensive tackle Keith Jones; it was like Angelo Dundee getting Muhammad Ali ready for the George Foreman fight. Each day during practice, Nehlen reminded Jones that he was blocking Florida All-American tackle David Galloway, and if he didn't get after it, Galloway was going to absolutely embarrass him. By game time, Jones was fit to be tied, and West Virginia defeated Florida 26-6 in one of the most stunning upsets of the year.

"Don Nehlen did a marvelous job of motivating us," said quarterback Oliver Luck. "He was a smart man, and the older I get the more I credit him. He did a very smart job of, if anything could be termed an injustice or even the slightest sign of a lack of respect, Don would jump all over it."

Luck recalled a game up at Boston College when Nehlen got his hands on a game program that had West Virginians depicted as a bunch of drunken hillbillies. "Nehlen came into the locker room and started waving that thing around, saying Boston College just thinks we're a bunch of hillbillies," Luck said. "He was just masterful."

More Nehlen psychology helped West Virginia come from behind to upset Oklahoma in the 1982 season opener. In back to back games over a nine-month span, the Mountaineers had taken down two heavyweight programs, demonstrating Nehlen's insistence on "beating those other teams" on West Virginia's schedule before taking on Pitt and Penn State. During the locker room celebration after West Virginia's 41-27 win over the Sooners, linebacker Dennis Fowlkes shouted out, "You can tell them there are three teams in the East now!"

It was a clear reminder to everyone that Pitt and Penn State were never too far from the players' minds, even in the midst of such a momentous victory. The fans, too, gauged the response Pittsburgh media gave those two huge victories over Florida and Oklahoma. Did they recognize West Virginia as a program to be reckoned with? Could our Mountaineers finally be taken seriously?

Less than a month after the Oklahoma win, West Virginia gave the second-ranked Panthers the scare of their lives in Pittsburgh, when Pitt was forced to make a 13-point fourth quarter comeback to pull out a 16-13 victory. It was the only time during Dan Marino's magnificent college career that he led his team to a fourth-quarter comeback win. West Virginia had a chance to tie the game at the end, but Woodside's 52-yard field goal try fell just below the crossbar. Nehlen, squatting on the sidelines and hoping the ball would somehow clear the goalpost, fell to his knees when he realized the kick was no good. His team, despite the enormous odds against it, had almost pulled off another monumental performance.

Nehlen would sometimes exaggerate just how bad the West Virginia football program was when he was first hired. The difference between a 5-6 record in 1979 and a

6-6 season in 1980 was really negligible, more a matter of playing an extra game. The coaches on Frank Cignetti's staff were convinced that they had already turned the corner with the construction of the new football stadium and the boost they were getting in recruiting.

But the way Nehlen wisely downplayed expectations – and played up the obstacles he had to overcome – left everyone convinced that he was the man who, in time, could lead the program to much greater heights. Of course Cignetti never had the luxury of time. And Nehlen was not the first West Virginia coach to do a little exaggerating. Art Lewis had almost everyone (especially his players) thinking that the Mountaineer program really began in 1950; the same goes for Jim Carlen in 1966.

It's true that none of the players Nehlen inherited had ever played on a winning college team, and that creating a winning atmosphere was of the utmost importance, but Cignetti had left behind several very talented players: Darryl Talley, Oliver Luck, Fulton Walker, Walter Easley and Dennis Fowlkes turned out to be among the best players Nehlen coached at West Virginia. And having two quarterbacks in a row as intelligent and as talented as Oliver Luck and Jeff Hostetler made the transition much easier. "If you've got two players, give me the one with the intelligence because they understand what you're talking about," said Gary Stevens, a Cignetti assistant coach who later earned fame coordinating offenses for the Miami Hurricanes and the Miami Dolphins. "You get a talent and he's dumb, all he understands is 'Give me the ball; give me the ball.' There are some kids that you can talk goals and how you're going to get there, and they don't have a clue what you're talking about. All they want to know is how many times am I going to carry the ball?"

Nehlen had Luck when he arrived at West Virginia, but after him there was no heir apparent at quarterback. Then Jeff Hostetler became disenchanted at Penn State, deciding to transfer after the team's Fiesta Bowl win over Ohio State. Hostetler, in his autobiography *One Giant Leap*, said his older brother Doug first encouraged him to take a look at West Virginia. Doug was in the insurance business, and one of the towns he frequently visited was Morgantown, where West Virginia had just built a 50,000-seat football stadium and also had the 14,000-seat WVU Coliseum for its basketball team – two clear signs of the school's commitment to big-time college athletics. Hostetler knew a little about WVU, getting the bulk of the playing time in Penn State's 1980 20-15 win over West Virginia in Morgantown, and he was impressed by the Mountaineers' rabid fan base.

"As we walked down before the game, there were fans in the stadium saying stuff about us and yelling stuff, and I remember turning to one of my teammates from Penn

State and saying, 'Look at these people – this would be a great place to play.' At the time I never dreamed of it happening, but the people there impressed me so much," Hostetler said.

Hostetler was intrigued by WVU, and when he realized there was a clear path to the starting quarterback job after Luck graduated, it was too good an opportunity to pass up. Hostetler had another compelling reason to choose West Virginia. "The head coach had a really good looking daughter, too," he joked.

And Hoss was a big hit from the moment he first took the field, passing for 321 yards and four touchdowns in West Virginia's impressive win over Oklahoma. Hostetler threw for 285 more a week later in West Virginia's 19-18 over Maryland, and by the end of the season, he had passed for nearly 2,000 yards and 10 touchdowns despite various ailments that kept him out of a few games. "Had Jeff not transferred in, we would have never turned the program because there were no other quarterbacks in the program of that caliber, and we couldn't recruit any," Nehlen explained.

It was at the end of his first season that Hostetler began dating Nehlen's daughter, Vicky, the two eventually marrying when Hostetler graduated from WVU. Nehlen was once asked what he thought of his star quarterback dating his daughter: "It has its advantages," he said. "At least I know where he is."

West Virginia sports information director Mike Ballweg decided a promotional campaign was in order for Hostetler in 1983, so he dressed his quarterback up in a cowboy outfit and stood him next to a horse. The glossy color photograph was mailed out to sportswriters around the country. To go with the photo, a song to the theme of *Bonanza* was also made and distributed. It was gimmicky, to be sure, but those were the types of things publicity people were doing to get their star athletes recognized back then. And Hostetler was a bona fide star – the school's first true Heisman Trophy candidate.

Hoss led West Virginia to a pair of easy wins over Ohio and Pacific, and then two tough triumphs on the road at Maryland and Boston College got the Mountaineers to No. 7 in the national rankings. It was West Virginia's highest ascent in the polls in 28 years. Ironically, the last time West Virginia had been this high in the polls was November 12, 1955, when the sixth-ranked Mountaineers lost 26-7 at Pitt.

The Panthers were next up on the schedule.

Despite losing to Pitt seven games in a row (and nine out of its last 10) dating back to 1973, West Virginia was a one-touchdown favorite against the Panthers, based primarily on West Virginia's 31-21 win at Maryland and Pitt's 13-7 loss to the Terps. It was the first time West Virginia had been favored against Pitt since 1972, when Bobby Bowden was in his third season coaching the Mountaineers and Carl DePasqua was nearing the end of his Pitt coaching tenure.

In 1983, Foge Fazio was in his second season as Jackie Sherrill's replacement, and there was growing concern in Oakland that Fazio wasn't quite up to the task. Pitt still had one of the best defenses in the country, with the Panthers not allowing a single rushing touchdown in the month of September in games against Tennessee (win), Temple (win) and Maryland (loss), but an erratic offense led by sophomore quarterback John Congemi had everyone concerned.

In the days leading up to the game, it was becoming almost a foregone conclusion that West Virginia was going beat to the Panthers. One West Virginia sports columnist, who also happened to be a Pitt graduate, pointed out the similarities between Pitt's 1976 national championship team and Nehlen's 1983 team. The comparison was absurd, even reading it today.

In the press, Nehlen downplayed the importance of the Pitt game. "I don't know what all the fuss is about over an itty, bitty little football game like this," he said in jest. "Sure, Pitt has a great football team. They haven't given up a touchdown all year. And we're going to have to play our best game to date, and probably the best we're capable of playing, if we're going to have a chance to beat them. But it's still just another football game . . . one of 11 we have to play this year. What am I supposed to do, put on a silver hat and run up and down the halls?"

He wasn't finished.

"A guy on my call-in show last week said he didn't care if we lost the other 10 games, just as long as we beat Pitt," Nehlen said. "I'm glad the guy isn't coaching the football team. What happens if you gear up all year to win one football game and then you lose that one? What do you tell your kids after it's over?"

What really irked Nehlen were the obscene buttons and slogans the West Virginia fans were wearing to Pitt games. He thought it was time for the fans to move on to something more constructive.

"A couple of years ago, Jackie Sherrill came up to me Friday before we went to practice, and I saw that [obscene] button and I got sick," said Nehlen. "And all of his players had them on. We don't need that."

Of course a lot of this was just a diversion to keep the pressure off the players. Nehlen knew what the game meant to his football program and what a win over Pitt would do for it; what he was telling the press was completely different from what he was telling his team. Still, veteran UPI sportswriter Dan Hose thought it necessary to remind

West Virginia fans (and the Mountaineers' football coach) of the importance of the Pitt game. He recalled a growing ambivalence among the younger reporters covering the West Virginia-Pitt game in the late 1960s, when Pitt was terrible – something the late Bill Evans of the *Fairmont Times* would have quickly rectified. "Bill said he didn't care if Pitt never won a game, each victory over Pitt was something special," Hose wrote. "If those younger guys had been around when Pitt was rubbing the Mountaineers' noses in it, and treating them like dirt in the process, they would relish and cherish every single victory over the city slickers from up north. . . .

"Perhaps part of Don Nehlen's job as coach of WVU is to try to treat this as just another game. It's for sure he doesn't have to take any measures to get his players excited about playing Pitt.

"But, it is not just another game. It's West Virginia against Pitt.

"Bill Evans would love this one."

It was an unseasonably warm day for October – 70 degrees – when Steve Superick kicked off to begin the 76th game of the series. More than 64,000 fans filled Mountaineer Field, and millions more were watching on CBS. After stopping Pitt on its opening drive, West Virginia wasted no time in going after Pitt's No. 1-ranked defense. Hostetler passed 26 yards to tight end Rob Bennett; running back King Harvey (playing in place of injured starter Tommy Gray) and fullback Ron Wolfley picked up 10 more on runs; then Hostetler hooked up with Wayne Brown, who made a sliding catch for a 19-yard touchdown.

Minutes later, Pitt's defense tied the game when Hostetler was blindsided by Bill Maas and the ball popped into the arms of defensive tackle Tim Quense, who returned it 75 yards for a touchdown. "The fumble by Hoss was unfortunate," Nehlen explained afterward. "We had called an 'automatic,' but the noise was so loud that one of our linemen didn't hear the call. He missed his assignment and let his man come flying through."

Another freak play helped give Pitt a 14-7 lead. West Virginia's coverage team thought Superick's punt was blown dead at the Panther 38, but it wasn't, and Pitt safety Tom Flynn alertly picked up the ball and ran 49 yards to the West Virginia 13. A clipping penalty called on the play moved the ball back to the 28, but it was still outstanding field position for Pitt's struggling offense. Two plays later, freshman tailback Chuck Scales found an opening through the right side and ran 22 yards for a touchdown – it was the very first carry of his college career.

"It was designed to bounce outside," Scales said. "The play opened right up, and I saw the end zone right away. After that it was just a race."

Scales was also responsible for the game's next touchdown when he fumbled at the Panther 24, setting up King Harvey's 1-yard plunge that tied the score at 14. Again, an electric Mountaineer Field had caused the turnover. "The play was an audible, but I heard it and went the right way," Scales said. "The fullback didn't hear the call, so when I got the ball I had no lead blocker. I got hit as soon as I got the ball."

Pitt retook the lead right before the half when Congemi went to the air, hooking up with flanker Matt Stennett for 16 yards and then hitting Billy Wallace down the middle of the field for a 35-yard touchdown. The only third-quarter score – by either team – was a Paul Woodside 49-yard field goal to pull the Mountaineers to within four points, 21-17. The scene was set for an unforgettable fourth quarter.

West Virginia forced Pitt to punt with 12:27 remaining in the game, and following a clipping penalty on Willie Drewery's return, the Mountaineers had the ball at their own 10. Hostetler walked into the huddle and told his guys, "We've got 90 yards to go. Let's do it!"

For the next six minutes, the Mountaineers did to Pitt what the Panthers had done so many times before to West Virginia – ran the football right down their throats – and they did it against Fazio's pride and joy, the highly rated Panther defense. West Virginia went the length of the field in 14 plays. Thirteen of them came on the ground in one of the few times anyone then could remember a West Virginia football team simply lining up and teeing off on Pitt. No tricks, no gimmicks: "Here we are, big boys, and here we come!" Nehlen said the winning drive was the result of the hard work his team had done in the weight room in the off-season. "Honestly, I would guess that we won this game last January, February and March, not today, because the strength of our football team showed," he said after the game.

The guys up front blocking on the drive included tight end Rob Bennett, right tackle Kurt Kehl, right guard Dave DeJarnett, center Bill Legg, left guard Scott Barrows and left tackle Brian Jozwiak. Ron Wolfley and Pat Randolph were in the backfield with Hostetler. Between the tackles was where Nehlen decided the football game was going to be won. Wolfley carried four times for 31 yards, and Randolph took it four times for 24 yards, with the rest coming from Hostetler, including a pretty bootleg fake for the go ahead 6-yard touchdown. When Hostetler crossed the goal line, the eruption in the stadium was so loud that people sitting on their porches all the way across the river in Granville could hear the applause.

"We drive 90 yards on a defense that is absolutely loaded with professional football players," said Nehlen. "On the scoring play I know Foge Fazio is going to have everyone coming down inside like you won't believe, and Jeff waltzed into that end zone absolutely unmolested."

"The thing I remember most from the game was a moment when I dived for a first down and slid out of bounds," Hostetler wrote in 1991. "My three brothers had all somehow managed to finagle their way onto the sidelines. . . .

"I lunged for the extra yards and went down right in front of them. Instantly, I felt six hands all over my body as they physically lifted me to my feet."

All four Hostetler boys were reunited right there at Mountaineer Field, just as if they were playing again in their backyard up in Holsopple. Hostetler's scramble was the key play of the drive, his third and 10 run covering 10 1/2 yards and moving the sticks with 8:24 showing on the clock.

ALL OF THOSE INSIDE RUNS HAD SET THE PANTHERS UP FOR THE BOOTLEG.

All of those inside runs had set the Panthers up for the bootleg. "We knew after pounding, pounding and pounding that it was there," said Hostetler. "I had seen it earlier and wanted to run it."

But Nehlen didn't want to waste it on just any play – he wanted it to be the dagger in Pitt's heart. "They had seen it up above [in the coaches' box], and it was one of those things where you wait and you wait and you call it at the right time," Hostetler said. "That was the right time."

On Hostetler's go-ahead TD run, it was Randolph who made the key block. The freshman admitted that he had no idea what he was doing, or where he was supposed to be. "To tell you the truth, I didn't really know who I was supposed to block on the play," he told reporters after the game. "I turned around and the only person I saw was the short cornerback. I hit him and Hoss went in behind me."

When Hostetler crossed the goal line, he sank to one knee and pointed toward the sky as the stadium exploded. The local newspaper described the WVU student section turning into "one gigantic high-five." Still, there were six minutes left for West Virginia to deal with. A Steve Newberry interception at midfield gave the Mountaineers an opportunity to run out the clock, and with time still remaining for a Pitt comeback, West Virginia was confronted with a fourth down at the Panther 29. Nehlen could have gone to Woodside for a 46-yard field goal to put West Virginia ahead by 6, or he could run another play and keep the clock moving.

Nehlen chose to stick with his hot-footed quarterback, who scrambled 5 yards to make the first down. West Virginia was on the Pitt 7 when the game ended. Defensive tackle Jim Merritts and linebacker Scott Dixon hoisted Nehlen up on their shoulders and carried the coach across the field to meet Fazio. Fans everywhere rushed the field, first to celebrate at the stadium, and then later to celebrate a little harder downtown.

"Anytime a team takes the ball and drives it 90 yards, it deserves to win," said Fazio after the game. "I said all week we had to get to No. 15 [Hostetler], and we didn't do it."

West Virginia outgained Pitt 355 yards to 197, with Hostetler accounting for 164 through the air and another 51 on the ground. "He's the best all-around threat at quarterback I've played against," said Pitt safety Tom Flynn after the game. "His throwing is good, but what really makes him a threat is that he can scramble."

After the game, there were more words written on the locker room chalkboard for everyone to see, including reporters let in to talk to the players. In thick block letters, someone wrote "90 YARDS – TOUCHDOWN."

If WVU's performance up at Pitt in 1982 could be likened to the Battle of the Coral Sea, then the 1983 win over the Panthers was the Mountaineers' Midway. WVU under Nehlen had outstanding wins against Oklahoma and Florida, as well as triumphs against Maryland and Boston College that were also very important. In the eyes of the fans, though, the '83 victory over Pitt was the one that put Nehlen's program over the top. After that triumph the Mountaineers no longer took a backseat to the Panthers, winning 17 of the next 27 games (with two ties) through the 2011 season. Plus, in the vast majority of the WVU-Pitt games since 1983, West Virginia has been the favorite. Three times since then, the Mountaineers have been in contention for the national title while playing in five major bowls and 21 bowl games overall.

The year 1983 also marked the end of the last remnants of Jackie Sherrill's powerhouse program. After the West Virginia loss, the Panthers went undefeated for the remainder of the regular season, beating Florida State, Syracuse and Notre Dame, and tying Penn State before losing to Ohio State in the Fiesta Bowl. But Pitt lost seven games in 1984, and after a five-win season in 1985, Fazio was fired. The Panthers have gone through seven different football coaches since then in an attempt to rediscover the magic Majors and Sherrill brought to the Pitt program in the late 1970s and early 1980s. During much of that same time, Nehlen coached at West Virginia through the 2000 season before retiring. Six years later, he was inducted into the College Football Hall of Fame.

"I think Don Nehlen put West Virginia on the modern map," said former WVU and Florida State coach Bobby Bowden in 2009. "Sam Huff, Bruce Bosley and Freddy Wyant…

all those guys that played back in the early 1950s, they put West Virginia on the map also, but then it seemed like Don Nehlen put the modern West Virginia on the map."

Bowden was right. Nehlen did.

A Tie and a Sigh

PITT	WVU
10	10
Sept. 28, 1985 Morgantown, W.Va.	

PITT	WVU
6	3
Sept. 26, 1987 Morgantown, W.Va.	

Don Nehlen's football program was stuck in idle. The coach's West Virginia record was an impressive 40-16 after the Mountaineers defeated Penn State 17-14 at Mountaineer Field on October 27, 1984, ending nearly three decades' worth of frustration against the Nittany Lions. After the Penn State victory, West Virginia was knocking on the door of the Top 10, but decimating injuries and a lack of depth led to consecutive regular season losses to Virginia, Rutgers and Temple, turning what could have been a great season into just a good one.

A year later, in 1985, West Virginia won the games it was supposed to win and lost the others badly – 28-0 at Maryland, 27-0 at Penn State and 27-7 at Virginia. In 1986, West Virginia's record sank to 4-7 (Nehlen's first losing campaign at WVU) as the Mountaineers dropped six in a row during one stretch from late September to early November. The losing trend continued at the start of 1987, when a turnover-prone offense self-destructed in road losses at Ohio State and Maryland. The defeat to the Terrapins was particularly disturbing considering that the Mountaineers had jumped out to a quick 14-0 lead before losing 25-20. Nehlen's post-Penn State record was just 13-16 over his next 29 games, spanning two and a half years. Lumped into this streak were two of the most lackluster West Virginia-Pitt games ever played in the series, in 1985 and 1987, in Morgantown.

Over both games, the two teams crossed the goal line just twice and combined for only 29 points. West Virginia came back from 10 points down to tie the Panthers 10-10 in 1985, and Pitt used a late Mountaineer turnover to pull out a 6-3 victory in 1987. The Panthers' winning drive in 1987 actually went backwards 2 yards before culminating in a game-winning field goal.

The longest play from scrimmage by either team in those two games was a 38-yard run by A.B. Brown, who was then playing for Pitt in 1985, but who eventually switched sides to play for the Mountaineers in 1987 (Brown had a 14-yard run in the '87 game). The longest pass from scrimmage came in the '87 game – a 30-yarder by freshman quarterback Major Harris, who had also chosen to switch sides and play for West Virginia, despite growing up within walking distance of the Pitt campus in Oakland. The 275 total plays run from scrimmage in those two games netted just 1,140 yards, for an average of 4.1 yards per play. The two teams were running in the mud.

Actually, the punters and refs got most of the work: Pitt and West Virginia were flagged 33 times for 286 yards, and the teams' punters kicked the ball a combined 28 times. Obviously, these two games were far from epics.

West Virginia's problems were clearly on the offensive side of the football. Nehlen caught a big break when he came to West Virginia, first inheriting quarterback Oliver Luck from the previous coaching regime and then a year later convincing Jeff Hostetler to transfer from Penn State. Luck led West Virginia to records of 6-6 in 1980 and 9-3 in 1981 before Hostetler steered WVU to a pair of 9-3 seasons in 1982 and 1983. Kevin White came after Luck and Hostetler, and he turned out to be better than Nehlen ever expected, leading the Mountaineers to an 8-4 record and a victory over TCU in the Bluebonnet Bowl in 1984.

"Kevin was a kid out in Arizona who happened to play for a high school coach [WVU assistant coach] Bill Kirelawich knew," Nehlen recalled. "The guy comes in 5-11 and 160 pounds, and I'm saying, 'Holy mackerel, who are we going to beat with this guy?'"

"I was not a hot commodity in the recruiting market at 5-foot-11 and 160 pounds," White laughed. "I played for a very unsuccessful high school team, and I shared in our lack of success – with lots of support, I might add."

If it weren't for White's high school coach John Kashner, there is no way he would have played major college football. "My high school coach took it upon himself that he was going to go out and sell Kevin White to every coach he knew on the East Coast over his Christmas break," White, now a judge in Arizona, recalled. "That guy went from college to college, and of course he was also making his contacts and having a good time with all of his old coaching buddies.

"So he made the rounds and visited West Virginia, made his spiel and they expressed interest in me, but really they had a lot of guys in front of me," White continued. "Then lo and behold, on signing day they had a couple of guys back out and I was the last little puppy in the litter, and they called me up after the signing date and asked me if I wanted to come."

White may have exceeded everyone's wildest expectations, but the quarterbacks who followed were nowhere close to what Mountaineers fans had grown accustomed to when Luck and Hostetler were in the lineup. In fact, West Virginia was swinging and missing on a bunch of good high school quarterbacks. Nehlen's first signing class in 1980 had two quarterbacks: Bruce Gillard from Zanesville, Ohio, and Mark Introcaso from Church Creek, Md., and neither ever saw the field. In 1981, White was a last-minute sign, and the quarterback group in 1982 included Tony Reda from Mt. Lebanon, Pa., and Mike Filkill from Westlake, Ohio. In 1983, the Mountaineers landed Steve Grober from Somerville, N.J., John Talley from East Cleveland, Ohio, and Mike Timko from Euclid, Ohio. And after failing to sign a high school quarterback in 1984, WVU went out and inked Chuck LeVinus from Peoria, Ariz., in 1985. A very concerned Nehlen also instructed recruiting coordinator Donnie Young to go out and find a junior college quarterback, and Young came up with Benny Reed from Northeast Oklahoma Junior College.

During that period, the Mountaineers were late to pull the trigger on Bernie Kosar from Youngstown, Ohio, and he ended up going to the University of Miami. "I can still remember [Ohio recruiter] Mike Jacobs pounding the table all pissed off that we didn't take Bernie Kosar," said Kirelawich. "Bernie was Jake's guy, and that was one of the dumbest turns of events that ever happened here."

Shortly afterward, Nehlen chose to make some systemic changes in the way quarterbacks were recruited, with Nehlen now overseeing the approval process for all potential recruits. Eventually, he was able to straighten things out, and in 1986 he managed to sign a pair of outstanding high school quarterbacks in Major Harris and Browning Nagle.

What Nehlen had encountered trying to recruit top-quality quarterbacks was nothing new at WVU. Previous coaches Bobby Bowden and Frank Cignetti also had trouble landing top-shelf quarterbacks, particularly tall ones. After Mike Sherwood in 1970, and then Bernie Galiffa in 1972 (both were outstanding quarterbacks but small in stature), Bowden's next good prospect didn't come along until Dan Kendra, who was forced to play in his freshman season, in 1974. After that, it was Oliver Luck four years later in 1978.

The cumulative effect of West Virginia's inability to sign quality quarterbacks was beginning to show up on the football field by 1985. The Mountaineers that season scored just 21 offensive touchdowns, were blanked twice (by Maryland and Penn State), and failed to tally more than 13 points six times; in 1986, West Virginia was a little better, only getting blanked once by Penn State and scoring 10 points or less four times. During the '85 campaign, Nehlen tried three different guys under center, starting the season with the athletic John Talley before switching to Reda, and then finally going to Timko at the end of the year when Reda was injured in the Boston College game.

Talley, Timko and Reda were three completely different quarterbacks. Talley was big, at 6-foot-6 and weighing nearly 225 pounds, athletic, and possessed a very strong arm. However, he frequently threw the ball when he should have run it, forced passes he shouldn't have thrown and displayed little touch on the shorter ones. The decision was later made to move Talley to wide receiver when it became apparent that things were not going to work out at quarterback. Reda was a much more accurate passer and could move the team when he was on the field, but he was small (barely 6-feet tall) and was frequently injured. Timko was an intelligent quarterback and could be proficient in the pocket when he had time to pass, but he lacked mobility and sometimes struggled when under pressure. In 1985, the three combined to complete 145-of-281 passes for 1,626 yards with nine touchdowns and 12 interceptions.

"An old coach once told me if you've got to play three quarterbacks, that means you don't have a quarterback," Nehlen said that season. "I'm afraid he's right."

In 1986, five different guys tried passes, including position players Harvey Smith and Pat Randolph. Once again, West Virginia's quarterbacks threw more interceptions than touchdown passes (14 picks to 11 TDs). One of the popular jokes going around the state at the time compared Nehlen to famous evangelist Billy Graham: "Question: Name the only two people who can make a crowd of 65,000 West Virginians stand up and praise the Lord? Answer: Rev. Graham and the next quarterback that damned Nehlen puts into the game!"

Fans also began joking that the best way to keep Nehlen from getting into his house was by drawing a goal line across his front door. Growing desperate in late 1986, Nehlen turned to former junior college QB Benny Reed in a last-ditch attempt to turn around his first losing season at WVU. Reed, today a Hollywood actor with credits in several successful television shows and feature films, possessed movie star good looks and the charisma to match, but his passing could sometimes be erratic. Undeterred, Reed loved showing his old Northeast Oklahoma film to the other quarterbacks in the meeting room, and he would grab the clicker and run back and forth through his rollout passes, repeatedly asking his teammates, "Have you ever seen anyone roll out and throw like that? Who have you ever seen around here who can throw like that?" After watching the charade for a couple of minutes, another quarterback finally got up and replied, "Hey Ben, have you ever heard of a guy named Jeff Hostetler?"

Nehlen would have loved to have Hoss or Luck under center for the '85 season, but both were playing in the NFL. West Virginia fans were not sure what type of football team they had after WVU's first two games, a 52-13 blowout win over Louisville in the opener and a too-close-for-comfort 20-18 victory over ACC cellar dweller Duke the following week. But the team cleared that up in game three, at Maryland, when the Terps completely ran West Virginia off the field in a 28-0 whitewash on national TV. Fans were upset with just about everything, including Nehlen's decision to give announcers Lindsey Nelson and Paul Hornung the first three plays from the offensive script to reveal on the game telecast. "If I thought they would give the plays to the other team, I wouldn't tell them," growled Nehlen, adding, "we give the plays to our kids, practice them all week, go to the line of scrimmage, and they forget them. If [Maryland] knew them on the other side of the line, they must have a bunch of Einsteins." It was the first time Nehlen had really experienced significant criticism as West Virginia's football coach.

Foge Fazio's seat was also getting warm. Pitt had the best record of any team in the country (71-12-1) from 1976–82, the nation's third-best winning percentage from 1978-82 (.855), finished in the Top 10 six out of seven years and went to nine straight bowls from 1975–83. Then, the Panthers went 3-7-1 during Fazio's third season, in 1984, including an unexpected 28-10 shellacking at the hands of West Virginia. The '84 win over Pitt holds a special place in Bill Kirelawich's heart because of what his young defensive line went up against that afternoon in Pittsburgh.

"They had [Bill] Fralic and [Jimbo] Covert on the offensive line, and I started two freshmen and a sophomore," Kirelawich recalled. "In my mind we were the absolute underdogs, and there was no way in hell we should have won that game. But we did.

"After the game, I'm at home in my living room watching the Pittsburgh news, and here is Brad Hunt telling everyone that Fralic and Covert weren't that tough, and I about fell off my chair when he said that," Kirelawich laughed. "Here were two NFL No. 1 draft picks and my guy is saying that, but our kids just played their asses off that day."

Joe Boczek, West Virginia's sports information director, was also feeling pretty good about the way the way things were going for the Mountaineers up in Oakland that day. Boczek was standing on the West Virginia sideline as the clock was winding down, and he yelled across the field to Fralic in a voice loud enough for everyone to hear, "Hey Fralic, why don't you put that Heisman in the trunk of my car [at the time, Fralic was being touted as a Heisman Trophy candidate at offensive line]?" Fralic flashed Boczek a glare that he never forgot. "I never had anybody give me a look like that," Boczek recalled. "My heart just went into my throat. I thought he was going to come across the field and kill me."

In 1985, Fazio was headed toward even more misery, with consecutive losses to Ohio State and Boston College after opening the year with a 31-30 win against Purdue; Purdue fell short at the end when Boilermaker quarterback Jim Everett bounced his two-point conversion pass in front of a wide open receiver. After the BC loss, a disgruntled fan called into the Panther Hotline on WTAE to complain that a talented Pitt team had become "mesmerized by [Fazio's] incompetence."

Fazio blamed Pitt's problems on some bad breaks and couple of stupid mistakes, pointing out that two players were in the wrong defense when Kelvin Martin scored his game-winning 51-yard touchdown reception. Not exactly music to the ears of Pitt fans. Some coaches under the gun begin referring to themselves in the third person, as Fazio did to *Pittsburgh Post-Gazette* writer Tom McMillan before the West Virginia game: "We had some unfortunate things happen, a lot of adversity, but we faced up to that. So don't worry; Foge Fazio can take care of himself."

FAZIO BLAMED PITT'S PROBLEMS ON SOME BAD BREAKS AND COUPLE OF STUPID MISTAKES.

Adding spice to things was WVU assistant coach Russ Jacques's decision to switch sides by joining Fazio's Panther staff for the '85 season. Jacques coached for three years with Nehlen at Bowling Green and then five more at WVU before resigning after the 1984 season. Jacques had recruited some of West Virginia's better players (such as offensive tackle Brian Jozwiak, defensive back Stacy Smith and quarterback John Talley), he knew the team's personnel, and even more alarming to Nehlen, he knew the Mountaineer playbook like the back of his hand. WVU fans couldn't blame Nehlen for giving out the script against Pitt because Jacques knew it anyway. "He put our playbook on Foge's desk," said Kirelawich. "It was a big deal. It was huge. I think that was the last game we ever gave out playbooks. After that, the playbook was in our heads."

The Panther defense certainly played like it knew West Virginia's plays, blanking the Mountaineers in the first half and holding them to just four first downs and 84 yards of offense. Pitt led 10-0 on a Mark Brasco 20-yard field goal and a John Congemi 1-yard touchdown run. At the beginning of the second half, Nehlen put Reda into the game at quarterback, and the senior led the Mountaineers to a third-quarter field goal; later, in the fourth quarter, he notched a disputed touchdown when he leapt into the end zone from a yard out, on fourth down, with 4:38 remaining in the game. Fazio bitterly protested the touchdown on the field and outside the team locker room after the game.

"I hope to God he was in," Fazio snapped. "If he wasn't, that borders on being criminal. The films better show Reda was conclusively over the goal line. If they don't, I'm going to raise hell."

He probably wasn't, but Nehlen correctly pointed out that fullback Chris Peccon crossed the goal line on second down, and that John Gay got in on third down. Nehlen was also miffed that a call wasn't made on a fourth-down pass play at the goal line on the previous drive.

"I might ask Foge what he thought about that fourth down pass from the five we threw to Tommy Gray," Nehlen commented afterward in his column for the *Charleston Daily Mail*. "It definitely was interference. Gray was hit while the ball was still in the air."

Both teams had little to show for their 10-10 tie. Pitt went up and down the field on West Virginia's defense, accumulating 22 first downs and 412 yards of offense while managing to hold on to the football for five more minutes than the Mountaineers. Three fumbles, an interception and seven penalties were Pitt's undoing. Two Congemi fumbles on the center-quarterback exchange deep in WVU territory ruined sure-fire scoring opportunities for the Panthers, and Brasco missed a pair of makeable field goals to keep WVU in the game. "It was a contest neither team deserved to win," recalled Pitt radio announcer Bill Hillgrove. A couple of conservative decisions by Nehlen led to postgame second guessing by critics. Fans were upset that Nehlen chose to go for it from the Pitt 5 with 11:35 left in the game and with the Mountaineers trailing 10-3 (the pass interference play Nehlen referenced in his column). West Virginia's Reda eventually scored a touchdown seven minutes later to make the score 10-9, but some were miffed when Nehlen chose to kick the PAT to tie instead of going for the two-point conversion to try and take the lead.

"There was no decision to make there," Nehlen explained. "There was still 4:38 to go. Plenty of time."

The circumstances were very similar when West Virginia played host to Pitt at Mountaineer Field in 1987. The Mountaineers were searching for an offensive identity with freshman quarterback Major Harris under center. His first college completion went for a 40-yard touchdown in the '87 opener against Ohio University, but he connected on only seven of his next 28 passes in road losses to Ohio State and Maryland. Harris's backup, Mike Timko, was even worse, completing 15 passes – 10 of them to his teammates and five to the other team. West Virginia turned the ball over 17 times in its first three games, including eight in a 24-3 giveaway against the Buckeyes in the second week of the season. Turnovers (six) were also the culprit in the Mountaineers' 25-20 loss at Maryland after West Virginia had taken an early 14-0 lead. "We've self-destructed," lamented Nehlen before the Pitt game. "We've been our own worst enemy. We'll move 50 or 60 yards on a drive and then we'll drop the football. You can't do that."

Pitt, too, was having a tough time getting its offense on track under second-year coach Mike Gottfried, a guy with a reputation for being an offensive innovator, who was brought in to reinvigorate the Panther program in 1986. Gottfried's record in 1986 was the same as fired coach Foge Fazio's record in 1985 – 5-5-1, with both coaches enduring blowout losses to rival Penn State. Gottfried, however, scored a big win over West Virginia in the 1986 Backyard Brawl. In that game, senior quarterback John Congemi was able to take advantage of West Virginia's banged-up secondary to throw for 260 yards and three touchdowns, leading the Panthers to a 48-16 victory. But Congemi was gone in 1987, and the Pitt offense was now in the hands of junior college transfer Sal Genilla, who led the Panthers to early wins over BYU and North Carolina State before dropping a disappointing 24-21 decision to Temple the week before the West Virginia game. Pitt's biggest offensive weapon was 260-pound fullback Craig "Ironhead" Heyward, who ran for more than 100 yards in each of Pitt's first three games.

With Pitt having an inexperienced quarterback and a workhorse runner, and with West Virginia overly concerned about turnovers, both teams were not going to take too many chances; plus, both were eager to start the game on defense. West Virginia won the toss and elected to defer until the second half, but instead of taking the ball, Pitt chose to kick anyway — Gottfried wanted to play with the sun in their favor. That meant West Virginia would get the football at the start of the game and also at the beginning of the second half. "I kept thinking that in the second half we would be kicking into the sun," Gottfried said after the game. "I wanted to prevent that."

It didn't matter. Pitt could have kicked off to West Virginia all day and the Mountaineers would not have crossed the goal line against the Panther defense. West Virginia got past the 50 just once in the second half, reaching the Pitt 26 late in the third quarter. But Eugene Napoleon, who ran 22 yards on the previous play, fumbled his first down carry, leaving the ball to be recovered by Pitt defensive lineman Tony Siragusa at the 28.

West Virginia's second fumble was even more damaging. It came with 4:50 left in the game, at the Mountaineer 27, when Burt Grossman grabbed Harris's arm as Harris was about to make an option pitch, knocking the ball loose, and linebacker Zeke Gadson pounced on the ball at the 21. Gottfried took no chances, running three straight times to get his kicker Jeff Van Horne into prime position to kick the go-ahead field goal. He did, from 40 yards, and Pitt pulled ahead to a 6-3 lead with only 2:45 showing on the clock.

After taking over at its own 20, West Virginia's best offensive play of the game ended up covering just a portion of the distance it might have, when Napoleon's long run up the near sideline was ruled out of bounds at the Mountaineer 37. On the next three plays, Pitt's defense mercilessly pressured Harris, forcing him to throw an incomplete pass to John Talley on first down, running him out of bounds for a loss of 1 on second, and then forcing him to dump off short to Talley on third down. Harris's fourth down pass attempt never left his hand as Gadson blew right through the middle of the line, hauling him down for a 14-yard loss. Game over.

"The defensive coaches wanted to blitz to prevent anything from developing downfield," Gottfried explained.

Added Gadson, "In a key situation like that, I would think they would think we were coming with the blitz and would pick me up. But they didn't, and I just made the big play at the right time."

Two plays prior to Van Horne's 41-yard field goal at the end of the first quarter, Genilla completed a 9-yard touchdown pass to Heyward coming out of the backfield, but the play was waved off because of a clipping penalty called on Bill Cherpak.

This was the closest either team came to reaching the end zone.

Kissing Your Sister; Clubbing Your Neighbor

WVU	PITT
31	31
Sept. 30, 1989 Morgantown, W.Va.	

To West Virginia fans, this was one tie that sure felt like a loss. The year was 1989, and the ninth-ranked Mountaineers had built a seemingly insurmountable 31-9 lead with 9:20 left in the game, only to see the 10th-ranked Panthers storm back to score 22 unanswered points, tying the game at 31. When the clock wound down to zero, the Panther players stormed the field and celebrated with their fans like they had just won the national championship.

"It was one of those games when at halftime you thought this one is in the bag," recalled WVU play-by-play man Tony Caridi.

Afterward, Don Nehlen was at a loss for words, taking only a few questions before abruptly ending his news conference. "What do you want me to say?" he growled. "We blew it. It's that simple. The game would have been in the bag if we had played smart. But we weren't smart.

"What do we feel like? Well, our players aren't jumping up and down and swinging from the rafters. How in the hell do you think they feel?"

After that, he walked out of the interview room.

A day later, after closely studying the game film, Nehlen said there were at least nine different opportunities for his team to put away the game, and each time, they couldn't do it. He counted at least four dropped interceptions by his defense; a critical formation mix-up that wiped out a first down play that would have let West Virginia kill the clock; a fumble; three dropped passes; and a botched defensive assignment that enabled Pitt to complete a short pass and get out of bounds, leaving enough time for Ed Frazier to kick the game-tying 42-yard field goal.

Despite allowing a 17-play, 80-yard drive ending in an Adam Walker 1-yard touchdown run (after which Pitt missed the two-point try), the Mountaineers were still in good shape with 9:20 remaining – they led by 16 points, 31-15.

But right away, a personal foul penalty on backup quarterback Greg Jones during James Jett's kickoff return put the ball back at the West Virginia eight. A Major Harris-to-Reggie Rembert 16-yard pass got the Mountaineers out of a hole, and a Eugene Napoleon 10-yard run on third and 1 got West Virginia to the 37. Then, on Napoleon's next carry, he fumbled, allowing Pitt to recover the ball at the West Virginia 39.

The Panthers took over with 6:51 left, and they needed a 17-yard completion on third-and-10 from quarterback Alex Van Pelt to tight end Eric Seaman to get the ball to the West Virginia 22. Two plays later, Van Pelt found Henry Tuten open in the end zone for a 9-yard touchdown. The two-point conversion failed, leaving West Virginia with a 10-point lead with just 4:50 to go. West Virginia sent its "hands team" out onto the field, expecting an onside kick, and it got one – the ball ricocheted off Preston Waters's shoulder pads, and the Panthers pounced on the ball to secure great field position. Later, Waters made an even bigger mistake, running into kicker Ed Frazier as Frazier attempted a 29-yard field goal. The kick was good, but Pitt Coach Mike Gottfried chose to take the points off the scoreboard when the penalty yardage was walked off, giving the Panthers a first and goal at the 6. From there, Curvin Richards scored, and Frazier's conversion made it a three-point game: 31-28.

Still, with less than two minutes remaining and possessing the ball at their own 17, West Virginia could have put the game away. Harris completed a third-down pass to fullback Aaron Evans out in the flat for a 15-yard gain, but West Virginia was called for an ineligible player down field. Tight end Adrian Moss had mistakenly lined up in the backfield instead of on the line of scrimmage.

"We had the perfect play called and it was a completion," said Nehlen. "We just screwed up and got in the wrong formation. It was an option run or pass. It was a safe call. In that situation, we felt we had to get the ball on the perimeter to move it.

"We had the best quarterback in America to execute it. We just didn't count on getting in the wrong formation," Nehlen said.

Following the penalty, Harris's third and 11 pass to Reggie Rembert from the West Virginia 12 fell incomplete. After Greg Hertzog's 48-yard punt was downed at the Pitt 40, the Panthers had only 49 seconds left to get into field goal range. A Ronald Redmon run netted only 2 yards, and two straight incomplete passes by Van Pelt (both nearly intercepted by West Virginia defenders) made it fourth and 8 at the 42. Then Tuten somehow got loose for a 25-yard reception to bring the ball down to the West Virginia 33, where Van Pelt hustled his teammates to the line of scrimmage and spiked the ball to stop the clock. The quarterback got the football 8 yards closer on a completion to tight end Tom Huebner, setting up Frazier's game-tying field goal.

The stadium fell eerily silent when Frazier's kick sailed between the goal posts; the only noise came from the north end zone, where the Pittsburgh mascot, cheerleaders, and fans celebrated their improbable comeback. West Virginia players fell to the ground, shocked and stunned that they had let another victory over Pitt slip through their hands. "It hurts whenever you tie a game you know you should have won," said Napoleon, a former Panther player who had transferred to West Virginia. "I'm sick to my stomach. It's a big disappointment . . . I'll remember this game probably for the rest of my life."

"We're taking it hard, like a loss," added Harris. "This is like a blemish on our record."

"It was a loss," said assistant coach Bill Kirelawich. "We ran out of defensive backs in that game. We didn't have anybody left. All of our kids were cramping over on the bench."

The reaction in the Pitt locker room was dramatically different. "We're satisfied with the tie," said Van Pelt. "When we got down, we said to ourselves that we were going to come back. It was exciting to look up and see the crowd as big as it was [silenced]."

West Virginia played the first three quarters of the Pitt game like a team headed to another major bowl appearance. The Mountaineers had the nation's longest regular season winning streak at 15 games after an 11-0 campaign in 1988 saw West Virginia play Notre Dame in the Fiesta Bowl for the national championship.

WVU had produced good teams before but none quite like the '88 squad. Nehlen had built that team through redshirting and some shrewd recruiting, including the school's first sustained foray into the state of Florida. He had recruited Florida a little bit when he was at Michigan, but the coach gave the Sunshine State little thought when he first took the West Virginia job. Then, while speaking at a high school coaching clinic in the spring of 1982, Nehlen was cornered by Rick Perry, a West Virginia alumnus then coaching at Stranahan High School in Ft. Lauderdale.

"He told me, 'Don, I'm telling you there are so many kids down here, and Miami, Florida and Florida State can't take them all. You could come down here and get a ton of kids that could be really good football players,'" Nehlen recalled.

The problem, as Nehlen explained to Perry, was that he didn't have the manpower or the resources to recruit a state so far from West Virginia. Perry told Nehlen he didn't have to recruit the entire state. "He said, 'Just pick out 50 schools here in Dade and Broward County,'" Nehlen said. "We started out with 50 schools and [assistant coach] Doc [Holliday] became a household name in those schools because those were the only schools we recruited. We didn't go to Tampa or Gainesville, Jacksonville or the West coast. We just stayed right there, and slowly but surely we started to get players."

Holliday's first attempt at signing Florida players, in 1983, was a disaster. "We had kids visit, but we couldn't get anybody to sign," said Nehlen. The ice was finally broken when Perry delivered running back Undra Johnson, who became a solid four-year player for the Mountaineers. "I think the biggest reason I came here was because my high school coach bugged me about Doc all the time, and Doc was always at my school," Johnson recalled. "I visited Florida, Missouri and Iowa.

"The only time I had doubts was flying down from Pittsburgh to Morgantown and seeing that airport in Morgantown. I'm thinking, 'This is the Twilight Zone landing in there.'"

Once Holliday was able to persuade Johnson to come to West Virginia, other players soon followed. By the time West Virginia played Notre Dame in the national championship game, West Virginia had 15 Florida players on its roster, and included among them were several starters. "At that point, that really solidified us in Florida, and other schools saw what happened with those Florida kids," Holliday said. "They were all starters and they played for a national championship at a place nobody thought it could be done. From then on, it kind of snowballed with the good and the bad. The bad thing was we got a lot of publicity from the national championship game, and then you started seeing everybody else going down there."

When Holliday first started recruiting Florida, the only other out-of-state schools he recalled working the state as hard as he was were Iowa State and Michigan. "We tried to go after kids that we felt could help us," Holliday said. "They may have had some schools after them, but it wasn't the competition in recruiting as what you have down there now. You only had to deal with Miami, Florida and Florida State at that time."

Florida may have helped provide West Virginia with some excellent running backs, wide receivers, defensive backs and linebackers, but what the program was in desperate need of in the mid-1980s was a playmaking quarterback. Nehlen had had two good ones in a row, in Oliver Luck and Jeff Hostetler; plus, Kevin White led West Virginia to a Bluebonnet Bowl victory over TCU in 1984, but once White graduated, the cupboard was bare. By 1986, following a 4-7 season – Nehlen's first losing season at West Virginia – he was growing desperate.

Major Harris grew up in Pittsburgh's Hill District, not far from the Pitt campus, and he became a year-round sandlot legend on The Hill – wiffleball in the summer, football in the fall and basketball (his first love) in the wintertime. But he lost interest in baseball at age 12 when he was hit in the face with a ball thrown by a teammate, leaving football and basketball as his top two sports. He played on two city league basketball championship teams at Brashear High and was probably good enough to play small college hoops, but football was his calling.

Harris became the team's starting quarterback as a junior, and he never lost a City League game. "You give him a bowling ball and he could probably bowl a 250 game," said one high school coach of Harris's athletic prowess. There were two standout plays at Brashear that demonstrated what a terrific all-around player Harris was. One came on a game's final play during his junior year, when he threw a 71-yard pass (in the air) for a touchdown to beat Indiana Area High School. Another came against Allderdice High when he missed a handoff and then took off for a 30-yard touchdown run. Twice he was named City League Player of the Year, and had Foge Fazio still been the coach at Pitt when Harris was a senior (Fazio was fired after the '85 season), Harris would likely have been a Pitt Panther. But Fazio wasn't around, and new Pitt Coach Mike Gottfried wasn't really that interested in Harris because he didn't fit in with the offensive system he was running. Gottfried sent his assistant coach Tommie Liggins over to Brashear to meet Harris and his high school coach, but the meeting did not go well. Liggins was more interested in Harris playing defensive back, while Harris was adamant that he wanted to play quarterback in college.

"Major a defensive back?" his high school coach Ron Wabby told *Sports Illustrated* writer Ralph Wiley. "Major couldn't hit a teddy bear without apologizing."

Don Nehlen had no problem with Harris playing quarterback. "We had Major in our football camp, and people didn't recruit Major as a quarterback, but we did. I watched him play touch football and I thought if nobody could touch him they were going to have a heck of a time tackling him," Nehlen said.

Harris remembered reading about West Virginia in the papers when he was still in middle school and learning more about the Mountaineer program then. "Growing up and being from Pittsburgh, I heard things about West Virginia. I knew that Jeff Hostetler had transferred there," he said. "We get a lot of Penn State news in Pittsburgh, and I just remember West Virginia was in the process of building a program to a national level to where they could compete with Penn State, Pitt and stuff like that."

When Nehlen convinced Harris that he would be able to play quarterback at West Virginia, Harris decided to become his quarterback – even if he wasn't totally sure who his coach was. "It was funny because when I first met him, I got him mixed up with his son [Danny, West Virginia's equipment manager] because they looked so much alike," Harris laughed. Meanwhile, to cover his tracks, Nehlen had also recruited another good high school quarterback, from Florida, named Browning Nagle, and the coach had a difficult choice to make after redshirting both in 1986.

"We felt with the type of football we played, [Major] would fit the rest of our team better than Browning Nagle, a drop-back passer," Nehlen recalled. "We had running backs and we had fullbacks – those were the type of kids we recruited – and we wanted to throw the ball off the option. Major was able to run the option.

"To be honest, I wouldn't say we didn't know the drop-back passing game, but we didn't know it near as well as we knew the power offense, the option and the option passing game like we did at Michigan."

Nehlen called Nagle into his office after spring practice and explained the situation to him. "I said, 'Hey Browning, this is a tough thing for me because you are a great quarterback in your own right, and you ought to go someplace where they drop back and throw it.' He said, 'Coach, Louisville does that with Howard Schnellenberger.' I said, 'Hey, let's help you get there,' and that's how he got there," said Nehlen.

When Harris finally got on the field in 1987, his career began miserably in games against Ohio and Ohio State, and soon he lost his confidence when the team's record dipped to 1-3 as a result of his late fumble that led to Pitt's game-winning field goal. "If you are out with an easy schedule, you're building confidence," Harris explained. "Well, we came out with Ohio U. and then we played Ohio State and already you are behind the eight-ball because they are favored to win. Then it was Maryland and Pitt back to back. So we came out against some tough opponents. After that, the schedule started to ease up a little bit."

Major's epiphany came before the Rutgers game when he had overslept and missed the team breakfast. Quarterbacks coach Dwight Wallace, growing tired of Major's carefree attitude and immaturity, stormed up to his room and got on him while he was still lying in bed – literally.

"I'm in the room laying there and he comes in the room mad at me because I'm a young quarterback, struggling, and stuff like that," Harris recalled. "Well, he jumped on me while I'm under the covers and I couldn't even move. He really got on me. It was like a Bobby Knight thing. I look back on that now and it's funny, but to be honest, it lit a fire under me is what it did."

Harris passed for 196 yards against Rutgers and ran for 108 more, including an amazing touchdown jaunt when he leapt over a Rutgers tackler, to lead the Mountaineers to a 37-13 victory. Harris played well in West Virginia's last game of the regular season against undefeated Syracuse, as well as in the Sun Bowl loss to Oklahoma State, setting up West Virginia's improbable run in 1988.

"I remember seeing Don Nehlen during Major's redshirt freshman year when I was in Morgantown working a game, and he said, 'Mike, wait until you see the kid I got for a quarterback next year . . . he's a good one,'" recalled ESPN's Mike Patrick. "I was working one of Major's first games as a starter, and he took the snap from center and scrambled around the backfield. A receiver was way down the field, wide open 55 or 60 yards, and basically quit running because he felt the quarterback was not going to throw the ball to him. Major stopped on a dead run and threw it down the field 10 yards over his head."

The play that sealed the Legend of Major Harris came against Penn State in 1988, when he went the wrong way and faked out the entire Nittany Lion defense for a 26-yard touchdown in a 51-30 victory. "The play clock was running down and I didn't want to call timeout," Harris said. "I called the play and I was going up to the line and getting everybody ready, and I forgot which way the play was going. I knew it was an option, I just forgot which way.

"To be honest, it was like a bootleg where the guys go one way and the quarterback goes the other," he said.

Patrick, a Clarksburg native, recalled watching that Harris run on television and immediately realizing the significance of West Virginia's victory over Penn State – just its second in 33 years. "For all the long-suffering WVU fans to watch the way he played in that game, it took 25 years of frustration away," Patrick said. "He made one of the greatest runs of all time, the circumstances and who it was against, that is what made it so special."

Harris led West Virginia to an undefeated regular season and a great chance of winning its first-ever national title, against Notre Dame in the 1989 Fiesta Bowl, but a shoulder injury on the game's third play did Harris and the Mountaineers in. "We go into the game and my left guard Bobby Kovach goes down, then my right guard John Stroia goes down. Then Major goes down," said Nehlen. "We couldn't afford to play Notre Dame with four starters out of the game, but I think we could've got by had Major not been hurt.

"Major was so durable, he never got a bump all season, and we decided to put a lot of stuff in for him that Notre Dame had never seen," said Nehlen. "We had some great stuff, and lo and behold, the third play of the game he comes off the field and he says, 'Coach, I don't think I can throw.' I'm thinking, 'Oh brother, what did I do to deserve this?'"

"I had never had an injury like that, so you don't know how you're going to react," said Harris. "It wasn't a play where I got hit hard. It was really a fluke accident. It was a play where I got hit low and as I was falling the guy just jumped on my back. I kind of relaxed and my arm couldn't withstand the instant weight that was put on me."

Harris finished fifth in the Heisman Trophy balloting in 1988 and was a leading contender to win the award as a junior in 1989. Despite losing 25 seniors from the Fiesta Bowl team, West Virginia was ranked 17th in the country to begin the 1989 season, primarily because of Harris. The Mountaineers had easy wins over Ball State and South Carolina, and tough victories against Maryland and Louisville. Harris led the Mountaineers to a 14-10 comeback win over the Terps in 90-degree heat, passing for 150 yards and running for 64 more to set up Garrett Ford's game-winning touchdown run.

But difficulties followed at Louisville. The Mountaineers fell behind, 21-10, in the third quarter, and they needed a 17-point fourth quarter comeback to pull out a 30-21 victory. Harris made a miraculous 23-yard touchdown pass to Greg Dykes – everyone's jaws dropped to the ground when he somehow completed the pass to Dykes while falling on his back. Nehlen was pleased with that particular play, but he was upset with the way his team played, especially its lack of poise. West Virginia turned over the ball several times and made mental errors that would eventually come back to haunt it against Pitt.

The Panthers were off to a good start under Gottfried, in his fourth year after leading Pitt to back-to-back winning seasons in 1987 and 1988, a run that included a Bluebonnet Bowl appearance against Texas in 1987. Gottfried revamped his coaching staff after a 6-5 record in 1988, bringing in four new assistant coaches, including new offensive (Paul Hackett) and defensive (Bob Valesente) coordinators. He also had to break in a new quarterback in redshirt freshman Alex Van Pelt after regular quarterback Darnell Dickerson was ruled academically ineligible.

Van Pelt had actually played at two West Virginia high schools, North Marion and Grafton, before moving to San Antonio, Texas, to live with his mother. He grew up following West Virginia, but despite repeated phone calls by his father Greg to the Mountaineer football office, the coaching staff showed little interest.

Representatives from Pitt stumbled on to Van Pelt while in Texas recruiting running back Curvin Richards, and they were surprised when Van Pelt approached them about returning to the Northeast.

"We hadn't heard of Alex Van Pelt, but that changed quickly when we saw some film on him," said Gottfried before the West Virginia game in 1989. "Our coaches liked him and we committed to him quickly. And he committed to us quickly."

Van Pelt played well in Pitt's three wins over Pacific, Boston College and Syracuse, completing 76.1 percent of his passes for 633 yards. In Pitt's victory over the 10th-ranked Orangemen, he completed 25-of-32 passes for 306 yards and a touchdown in a 30-23 win. In a yet another twist to the Backyard Brawl, a Pittsburgher was quarterbacking West Virginia, while a West Virginian was quarterbacking the Panthers.

For three quarters Harris played flawlessly, getting most of his 250 yards passing and all four touchdown passes that night. Van Pelt, meanwhile, played miserably in the first half, completing just five passes (seven if you count the two he threw to West Virginia) in 18 attempts for 108 yards. But Van Pelt got hot in the second half and finished the game with 366 yards.

Frazier, who kicked the game-tying field goal, redeemed himself after missing two field goals against Syracuse and putting himself on a short leash heading into the West Virginia game. He began the year as the team's No. 3 kicker, but he beat out the two guys ahead of him because he was better at kicking without a tee (a new NCAA rule prohibited kickers from using tees for the 1989 season). Richards led all ball carriers, with 128 yards and two touchdowns on 20 carries; Pitt had a 176-127 advantage on the ground, which is why West Virginia couldn't run out the clock and had to pass late in the game.

"Pitt had everybody up on the line of scrimmage, and when you have 275-pounders running down your throat, you aren't going to get much yardage," Nehlen wrote in his Monday column for the *Charleston Daily Mail*. "Where are you going to run?

"I told my offensive coaches in the fourth quarter, 'We can't just run the ball up the middle. Keep mixing it up,'" Nehlen explained. "It is very difficult to run the ball against Pitt."

"Maj, bless his heart, didn't manage the clock well in that game," recalled Caridi.

Gottfried tried hard to keep from referring to the tie as a win, but judging from the way his players celebrated on the field and in the locker room after the game, it was as close to a win as any tie will ever get.

IT WAS AS CLOSE TO A WIN AS ANY TIE WILL EVER GET.

"Normally I don't like a tie, but to get a tie down here, in front of this crowd, and considering the circumstances of having to come back, is an accomplishment," Gottfried said. "I considered going for the win at the end, but with the way we fought back, I wanted to come away with something. And I think we did."

The Charleston Gazette's Bob Baker, like every other reporter working under a very tight deadline in the press box that night, was forced to keep changing his lead paragraph as Pitt began to mount its fourth-quarter comeback . . . starting with West Virginia recording a "smashing victory" to "a decisive victory" to "a narrow victory" to, finally, a tie. The first run of the *Pittsburgh Post-Gazette* had West Virginia still leading the Panthers 31-28 – a score West Virginia fans would have gladly accepted.

In the short run, the 31-31 tie did more damage to West Virginia's season than to Pitt's. The Mountaineers, unable to overcome the lingering psychological effects, lost 12-10 to Virginia Tech the next weekend, on homecoming. But the Mountaineers recovered to win four of their five remaining regular season games, before falling to Clemson in the Gator Bowl.

Pitt won its next two games against Temple and Navy to reach No. 7 in the polls, before losing 45-7 at Notre Dame. The Panthers were also blown out by Miami and lost a 3-point decision to Penn State to end the regular season with a 7-3-1 record. Gottfried and Pitt Athletic Director Ed Bozik had a falling out during the year, and Gottfried was eventually fired before Pitt played Texas A&M in the John Hancock Sun Bowl. Hackett was named interim coach and was later elevated to full-time coach after the Panthers upset the Aggies 31-28.

West Virginia's poor performance at the Gator Bowl brought out into the open a growing rift between Nehlen and Harris; the discord became clear to everyone when, during the game, Harris's mother Sandra bitterly complained about Nehlen's play calling on national television. "I didn't see it, but years later it was brought to my attention," Harris recalled. "They said, 'Maj your mom said to turn pro.' She didn't know any better. She's seeing her son getting sacked, and as a mom, she's like, 'He can't get hurt,' and in her mind she's probably thinking, well, if he's going to get hurt he might as well try and make money, and it probably came across wrong."

By then it was clear that Harris wasn't going to return for a fourth season in Morgantown. In February, 1990, two anonymous players told a United Press International reporter that Harris was planning to sign with a Los Angeles sports agent and make himself available for the draft. A week after that, Harris confirmed he was going pro in a hastily arranged press conference at the WVU Coliseum. Harris said negative press was one of the reasons he chose to leave school early.

"People started putting in the paper that me and Nehlen had a feud, and that kind of burned the bridge," said Harris at the time. "There's so much stuff going on that I know I can't come back."

Two decades later, Harris confirmed that he had signed with an agent right after the Gator Bowl. "After the game, I end up taking a flight out to California to meet with an agent," Harris said. "I had no money. So I go out there and sign with an agent. Now, when I look back on it, if that agent really had my best interests at heart he would have told me to go back with the team and he will get up with me later. But when you're young, sometimes you can get caught up in the mix."

Harris finished third in the Heisman Trophy balloting in 1989, after becoming just the second player in NCAA history to pass for more than 5,000 yards and run for more than 2,000 yards during his college career. He was taken in the 12th round by the Los Angeles Raiders, never played in the NFL and lasted only one year in the Canadian Football League before winding up his pro career in the Arena League. Leaving school early was a mistake Harris still regrets.

"Looking back on it, I probably wouldn't have come out, but when you are young and not realizing what is actually going on or where you might come out . . . now they have a thing where you apply [for the draft]," said Harris. "If it doesn't work out, you can go back to school. I wish they would have had that when I was in school.

"The way I did it was wrong," he added. "When you get older and you look back on it now, you can see it better. But when you are young and you play for a national championship, you are nominated for the Heisman and you are an All-American, so to speak, you look around the country and you see guys leaving whose résumé might not be as good as yours, so you are basically following suit.

"The one thing I regret the most was that I didn't really go to Coach Nehlen and sit down and listen to what he thought about it. You've got people in your ear telling you different things. I think I wasn't getting the right advice from the right people, but you don't realize that when you're young."

"When he played for us, he was somewhat of a folk hero, and that never seemed to bother him; I don't think he even knew he was a hero in this state," said Nehlen. "I think our kids really respected Major because he never changed. What you see is what you get, and that's why they really respected him and really followed him."

ESPN's Ivan Maisel, who covered Harris when he was still working at the *Dallas Morning News*, credits Harris with being the player that turned West Virginia into a national program.

"We now expect quarterbacks to have the ability to run and to pass. But in the late 1980s, Harris became a revelation," said Maisel. "Defenses didn't know how to handle him. His stewardship of the Mountaineers in those wonderful seasons of 1988–89 turned West Virginia from a regional team into a national team. The Mountaineers have been taken seriously ever since."

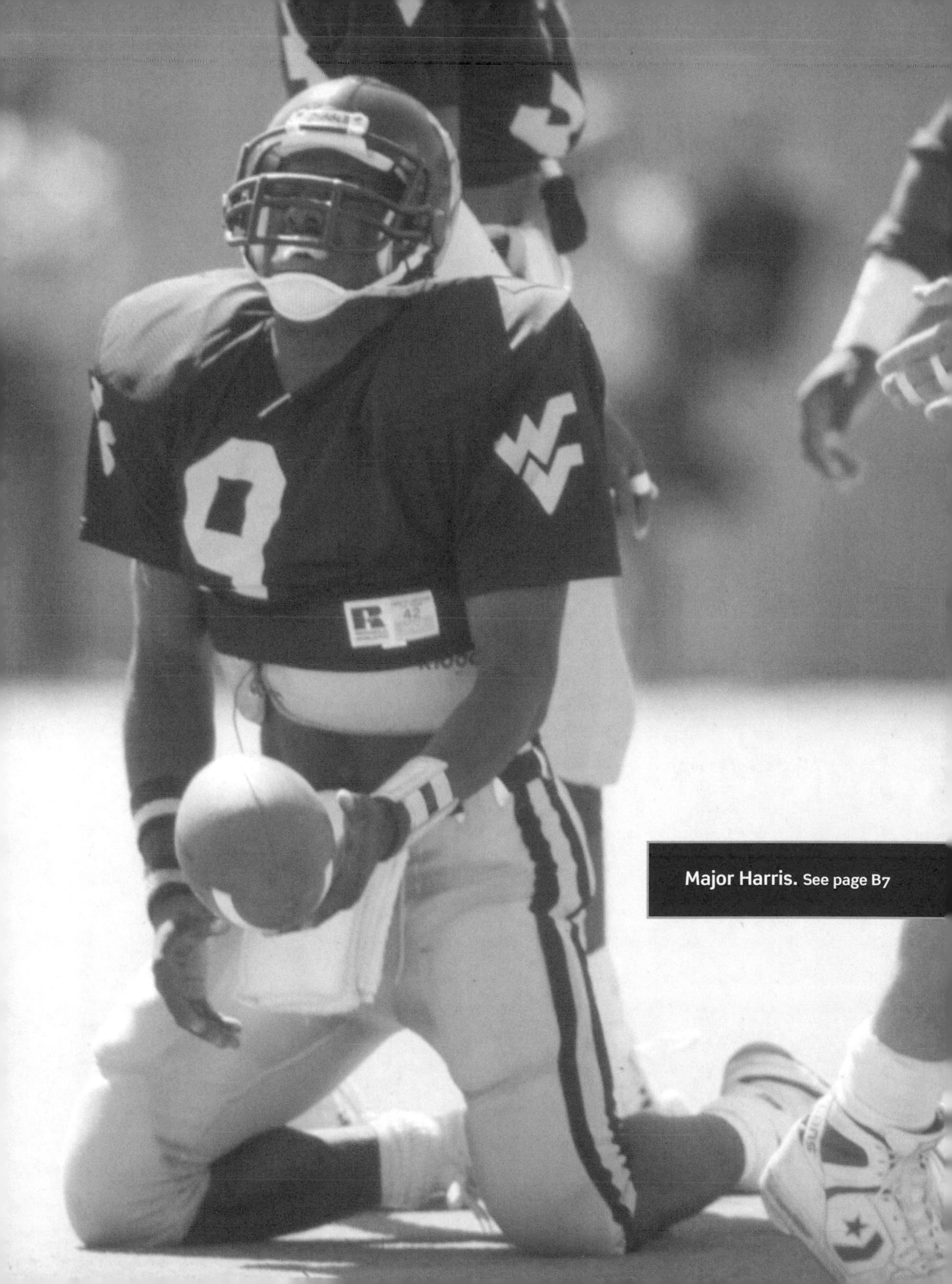

Major Harris. See page B7

Zach Abraham. See page B10

1991-2011 THE BIG EAST YEARS

A Big East Blowout

PITT
34
WVU
3
August 31, 1991
Morgantown, W.Va.

Paul Hackett, Pitt's second-year football coach, was sitting on an airplane next to West Virginia's mammoth offensive tackle John Ray – all 6-feet-10, 320 pounds of him – as the two were flying from Pittsburgh to Newark, N.J., for the first-ever Big East football media day, at Giants Stadium. Hackett struck up a light conversation with Ray about their upcoming game as members of the new Big East Football Conference.

Hackett admitted to Ray that he was a little concerned about the environment down in Morgantown, particularly considering that it was a Saturday night game. He knew Mountaineer fans would have plenty of time to get sauced up before the big game. Ray looked at Hackett and, with a straight face, told him that he didn't know the half of it.

"Coach Hackett, they start early in the morning partying for that game, and quite frankly, I have to be honest, they even scare me!" Ray said, only half-jokingly. Hackett recalled the conversation he had with Ray during his Monday morning media teleconference the week of the game.

"It's a major, major hostile environment," Hackett said, referring to what his team would encounter down in Morgantown as a "semi-out-of-control situation."

The West Virginia-Pitt game was originally scheduled to be played on November 16, between West Virginia's season-ending road dates at Miami and Syracuse, but it was moved to August 31 to help kick off the newly formed league. Rutgers and Boston College were to play the first-ever Big East game that afternoon, but the bright lights of national television (ESPN) would be in Morgantown to showcase the conference's two oldest and most bitter rivals.

The brief history of Big East football can actually be traced to State College, Pa., oddly enough. Penn State, under the late Joe Paterno, had become the marquee football program in the Northeast, with the Nittany Lions winning national championships in 1982 and 1986 and having five undefeated (and untied) seasons between 1968 and 1994. In the late 1960s and into the early 1970s, Penn State, Syracuse, Pittsburgh and West Virginia were part of an association referred to as the "Big Four," which basically oversaw scheduling, officiating and also had limited jurisdiction over redshirting, travel rosters and other athletic personnel issues. Then, the Big Four abruptly disbanded in 1973 when Johnny Majors was hired to take over the Pitt program. The last thing Majors wanted was restrictions on how to build his football program, especially when those restrictions were coming from Penn State and its sometimes sanctimonious football coach. All four schools continued to play each other as independents throughout the 1980s, despite frequent disagreements between Pitt and Penn State.

Their biggest dispute came in the spring of 1981, when Paterno, then doubling as Penn State's athletic director, tried to help organize an eastern all-sports conference. What Paterno envisioned was a league consisting of Penn State, Pitt, Syracuse, West Virginia, Boston College, Rutgers, Temple, the service academies Army and Navy, and possibly even Maryland, bringing them in from the Atlantic Coast Conference. What appeared to be a pretty appealing concept soon became bogged down in details, with the biggest hurdle being revenue sharing. Penn State proposed that the new conference acquire the bulk of its money through the sharing of bowl and television revenue; meanwhile, Pitt, then a national program frequently going to major bowl games, wanted a more equitable distribution of gate receipts, pointing out that Penn State typically sold out all of its football games at Beaver Stadium. "We were within a decimal point of having an eastern all-sports conference," recalled the late West Virginia athletic director Fred Schaus in 2003.

"The feeling was if Penn State and Pitt could have resolved their differences, then the rest of the East would have followed along," added Leland Byrd, West Virginia's former athletic director, who at the time was executive director of the Eastern 8 Conference.

In the meantime, Syracuse athletic director Jake Crouthamel was keenly interested in preserving the Big East basketball conference, which he had played a major role in creating along with his Dartmouth College roommate Dave Gavitt, then the athletic director at Providence College. Crouthamel wanted to protect the high profile Syracuse basketball program that Jim Boeheim had built. The model the Big East had chosen to adopt for its new basketball league was to attract schools from major media markets in the Northeast, and to use television (particularly ESPN, which was just getting started at the time) to help grow the conference.

Naturally, Paterno's new eastern sports league would have removed Boston College and Syracuse from the Big East equation and put the infant basketball conference in great peril. Penn State had tried to get its basketball program into the Big East, but it was rejected by a 5-3 vote because Nittany Lion basketball at the time was simply not up to par with their regional competitors. Instead, the Big East chose to invite Pitt, which in the words of Crouthamel "checkmated" Penn State's eastern sports conference. Had Rutgers chosen to go to the Big East in basketball instead of sticking with Penn State in the Eastern 8 (the Scarlet Knights were the Big East's first choice, and when they declined, Seton Hall replaced them), Penn State basketball might have gotten into the Big East. At the time, the decision not to invite Penn State proved to be a boon for Big East basketball in the mid-1980s, but it would have devastating implications for the overall stability of the conference two decades later.

According to David Jones of *The Harrisburg Patriot-News*, Penn State had first inquired about joining the Big Ten Conference in 1980 under then-president Jack Oswald, but no action was taken. Then, in the spring of 1989, Penn State president Bryce Jordan called Illinois president Stanley Ikenberry, a former colleague of Jordan's at Penn State, to see if the Big Ten was still interested in the Lions. This time Penn State had a staunch ally in Ikenberry, and he began to work discreetly on getting the other presidents in the conference to come on board. Nine months later, in December, 1989, the Big Ten presidents voted 7-3 to admit Penn State as the 11th member of the conference (later, the vote was retaken, with a unanimous result). For the first time in nearly 40 years, a team was added to the Big Ten, and it was done without the consultation of the faculty, athletic directors or coaches. On the day of the announcement, the Big Ten athletic directors were tracked down, and commissioner Jim Delany informed them that a conference call would take place later that afternoon to announce that the Nittany Lions would be joining the conference. Michigan's Bo Schembechler, well-known football coach and the school's athletic director at the time, told Jones that the news hit him "right between the eyes." It surprised everybody.

The one guy not totally floored by Penn State's westward move was longtime West Virginia sportswriter Mickey Furfari, who through the years had developed a cordial relationship with Penn State athletic director Jim Tarman. The two were having a friendly conversation during the 1989 Atlantic 10 basketball tournament at the Palestra, in Philadelphia, when Tarman casually mentioned that Penn State might be playing in another conference in the near future. "This time next year, we may be in the Big Ten," Tarman confided to Furfari.

THE BIG EAST HAS EXPERIENCED A MUSICAL-CHAIRS EXISTENCE.

"Do you really think so, Jim?" Furfari asked.

"Maybe."

Taken aback by Tarman's candor, Furfari decided to sit on the bombshell and wait and see how things played out. "And I missed the scoop of my life!" Furfari groaned.

Penn State's move triggered a chain of events that permanently changed the landscape of college athletics. The Southeastern Conference expanded for the first time in its history, in 1991, adding Arkansas and South Carolina with the goal of creating a lucrative football championship game. The Atlantic Coast Conference added its first new member in 13 years when Florida State came aboard in 1991; the Southwest Conference imploded, with the Big 12 Conference coming out of the rubble; and the Big East Conference, in another move of self-preservation, opted to get into the football business by persuading Miami (Florida) to join the league (Miami was looking to bolster its struggling basketball program). An offshoot of Miami's Big East all-sports membership was a separate, football-only configuration that included West Virginia, Rutgers, Temple and Virginia Tech – the Hokies had been looking for a landing place for their athletic program since the Metro Conference had disbanded. The Big East had to act quickly to stave off Charlotte-based Raycom Sports's 16-school super conference proposal, which would have merged eastern football independents with the Metro Conference schools and comprised 35 percent of the television markets in the country. The league would have been divided into two divisions: in the North would be Boston College, Cincinnati, Pitt, Rutgers, Syracuse, Temple, Virginia Tech and West Virginia; in the South would be East Carolina, Florida State, Louisville, Memphis State, Miami, South Carolina, Southern Mississippi and Tulane. The idea died when Miami chose to stick with the Big East and Florida State opted to go to the ACC.

It took two years for the Big East to clear off schedules and make the football league a reality. By 1993, the conference was playing a full round-robin grid slate. A year later, in 1994, the Big East entered into television negotiations with CBS, which was eager to get into college sports after losing its NFL rights to Fox. Because Big East football and basketball were configured separately, the football schools were unwilling to represent the non-football schools in the television discussions. It became apparent to the football schools that the conference could only remain intact through expansion, but seven of the 10 Big East member schools had to vote in favor for the conference to add more football schools. The four football playing schools, plus Villanova and Connecticut – both contemplating a jump to Division I football (Connecticut eventually did) – were in favor of expansion. That left one more school to convince, and St. John's, understanding the long-term implications of being aligned with major college football programs and the value football added to the league's television inventory, became the deciding vote in favor of expansion. West Virginia and Rutgers were added as the 11th and 12th members, and Notre Dame joined the Big East in all sports except football, giving the conference 13 schools.

Since then, the league has experienced a musical chair existence: Virginia Tech eventually joined as an all-sports member in 2002; Temple football was ousted in 2004 because of a lack of fan support and interest; and Miami and Virginia Tech departed for the Atlantic Coast Conference after the 2003 season, with Boston College following a year later. The conference replaced those schools with Cincinnati, DePaul, Louisville, Marquette and South Florida in 2005, only to seek additional replacements six years later, in 2011, when Pitt and Syracuse left to join the ACC and West Virginia departed for the Big 12.

Television markets, revenue sharing and conference realignment were the last things on the minds of the West Virginia football players getting prepared to face the Pitt Panthers in their very first Big East game, at Mountaineer Field on Saturday, August 31, 1991. It was the 100th anniversary of Mountaineer football, with the school celebrating its century of gridiron play by producing a book, a video and decorating the cover of the media guide with historical memorabilia.

Adding to the interest and intrigue was veteran Coach Don Nehlen's decision to close portions of preseason practice to the media in order to work on some secret plays. With a new quarterback in sophomore Darren Studstill, and facing a bitter rival to open the season, Nehlen was intent on keeping a lid on any information Pitt could get its hands on. This meant that, at specific times during practice, the handful of reporters observing practice from the sidelines were escorted outside the stadium until the all-clear was given by football administrator Mike Kerin. Those reporters who wanted to come back and watch the remainder of practice could then return.

What West Virginia was working on was a no-huddle shotgun offense to try and catch Pitt off guard. West Virginia thought it might be something to throw at Pitt early in the game when the Panthers were not prepared for it. Unfortunately for the Mountaineers, those plans went out the window early in the second quarter when Studstill injured his shoulder. At the time of his injury, West Virginia was trailing just 7-3 – WVU had taken an early 3-0 lead on a Mark Johnson 21-yard field goal, but the coverage unit allowed Steve Israel to return the ensuing kick 73 yards to set up Pitt fullback Glenn Deveaux's 1-yard touchdown run. Pitt tacked on a second quarter touchdown to make it 14-3, but the Mountaineers were still very much in the game, moving the ball successfully between the 20s while racking up a 170-100 advantage in total yardage by halftime.

"I remember Alex Van Pelt was the quarterback and all through the game I was thinking, 'How can a kid from Grafton go to Pitt and beat West Virginia?'" said Caridi.

However, things began to unravel for West Virginia in the third quarter. The Panthers tacked on a field goal and then got a 45-yard TD catch by Chad Askew to make the score 24-3. The nail in the coffin came with 1:18 left in the third quarter, when Sean Gilbert intercepted backup quarterback Chris Gray's pass out in the flat, and the big defensive tackle rumbled 26 yards for the touchdown. Pitt added on a fourth quarter field goal to make the final score 34-3. "I thought I could get the ball to Jett, but we weren't on the same page," Gray said of the interception he threw.

Gray, a senior from Manalapan, N.J., was getting his first extended action after serving in a backup capacity behind Major Harris and Greg Jones. He patiently answered several tough questions afterward, doing so with frankness and a self-deprecating sense of humor that was appreciated by the reporters struggling to meet their deadlines.

"On my first series, I was in a daze," he admitted. "Apparently I didn't prepare very well. Mentally, you've got to be ready to go, and I wasn't."

He continued.

"I had played one down of college football, and there I was on national television," Gray said. "But that's not an excuse. I had a job to do, and I didn't do it."

Gray finished the game completing 12 of his 17 pass attempts for 108 yards against a tough Panther defense, but he was picked off for a TD and sacked twice, and his longest completion was only 18 yards to tight end Alex Shook.

"As a quarterback, you're supposed to be able to make a third-down conversion, motivate the team and not turn the ball over," he said. "I didn't do any of those things."

Naturally, Gray was being overly hard on himself. Tall, blond and handsome, and with a razor-sharp wit to match, Gray was among the most popular players on the team.

He appeared in eight games during his senior season in 1991, leading the Mountaineers to a 24-17 victory over Bowling Green by passing for 175 yards and a touchdown, and he finished the season with 400 yards through the air. Yet it was Gray's goal line fumble late in the Virginia Tech game that is probably most remembered by West Virginia fans. His turnover prevented West Virginia from defeating the Hokies in a game the Mountaineers lost 20-14, and once again, Gray showed the stand-up guy he was by not shying away from the press, taking full responsibility for his miscue after the game.

Years later, he would humorously reenact that play whenever he was around friends and teammates at bars and tailgates.

After graduating from WVU in 1994, Chris eventually landed a job as a foreign exchange broker at Cantor Fitzgerald, in New York City. He was in his office on the 105th floor of the North Tower of the World Trade Center on the morning of September 11, 2001, when terrorists flew two airplanes into the complex. Chris was one of the 658 Cantor Fitzgerald employees who lost their lives on that bleak Tuesday morning. Months after the attack, when it was apparent that he didn't survive (his remains were never recovered), the West Virginia Legislature passed a resolution in his honor, and the athletic department conducted a memorial service for him at the Milan Puskar Center. A scholarship to benefit future WVU athletes was established in Chris's name by his family and the Mountaineer Athletic Club. "He was a great kid, with a great personality," said West Virginia coach Don Nehlen. "He always had a grin on his face and lit up every room he walked into. He was a solid player to coach – the kind of player that every team needs to have."

Chris Gray was just 32 when he died.

E-I-E-I-O, Tractors and Corncob Pipes

WVU
PITT
47
41
Oct. 15, 1994
Pittsburgh

All signs pointed to a low-scoring game when West Virginia boarded four chartered buses and traveled up I-79 to face Pitt in a mid-October Big East Conference clash at Pitt Stadium. So far that season, the Mountaineers had managed just 89 yards of offense in a season-opening 31-0 loss to No. 1 Nebraska, scored 16 points against Ball State, 12 in a defeat at Rutgers, 13 in a loss to Maryland and only 6 in a blowout defeat at Virginia Tech.

West Virginia was ranked last in the Big East and 95th in the country in scoring offense, averaging an anemic 13.5 points per game. And just ahead of WVU was Pitt, averaging an equally lackluster 17.7 points per game – not exactly the type of scores that keep ticket offices busy. The Panthers were all growl and little bite during Johnny Majors's return to Pitt. His first team, in 1993, lost eight games against an impossibly difficult schedule, and his second, in 1994, dropped five of its first six heading into the West Virginia game.

Typically there was a buzz whenever West Virginia and Pitt got together on the football field, but that was not the case for this one. Pitt was practically giving away tickets to try and get people to come to the game – the Panthers had last sold out 56,500-seat Pitt Stadium three years prior, against Penn State in 1991, before the Lions bolted for the Big Ten. Veteran Pittsburgh Associated Press sports writer Alan Robinson called the WVU-Pitt game "an afterthought" and asked the question, "Where have you gone, Dan Marino? Tony Dorsett?"

Majors joked of his team's 1-5 record, saying "So far, we've been a boost to other people's confidence."

West Virginia wasn't much better, even though the Mountaineers were coming off a Sugar Bowl appearance in 1993 – Don Nehlen's second undefeated, untied regular season in five years. The sting following the team's 41-7 loss to Florida in the Sugar Bowl had barely subsided when WVU got drilled by eventual national champion Nebraska in the Kickoff Classic. Although nowhere near as talented as his first undefeated team, in 1988, Nehlen's '93 squad continued to improve as the season wore on. By the end of the year, the Mountaineers had knocked off fourth-ranked Miami, and, a week later, entered the national championship picture by beating nationally ranked Boston College on the road (BC had upset No. 1-ranked Notre Dame on the same day West Virginia defeated Miami).

Yet, barely 10 months later, after sustaining massive losses on both sides of the football, Nehlen was staring at the possibility of having the worst record of his coaching career. West Virginia's 1-4 record was its worst start since 1978, when the Mountaineers ended up going 2-9, and the team's 47 points through their first five games were the fewest scored since West Virginia's winless season in 1960. Nehlen had always preferred to begin each year with an easy game or two to give his team some confidence, but that wasn't an option when the school was offered $700,000 to face Nebraska in the Kickoff Classic to open the 1994 college football season.

"We needed some Dairy Queen to play in the opener, not Nebraska," said Nehlen years later. "My best player Mike Logan gets a broken arm, and another kid blows out a knee in the tunnel before we even get out onto the field before the kickoff. I say to myself, 'Boy, we're off to a great start.'"

"We had a function where the two teams ate together, and I just remember looking at those Nebraska guys and thinking, 'My goodness what do they feed those guys?'" said wide receiver Zach Abraham. "I'm looking at their linemen and I'm looking at our linemen, and I'm thinking, "Now what's different here?" Their linemen were big and muscular with not an ounce of fat on them. Our guys were big, too, but we had a couple of guys who didn't really care too much about their midsections."

Nehlen, too, noticed the substantial discrepancies between the two teams. Nebraska coach Tom Osborne had asked Nehlen to come out and speak at Nebraska's football banquet, observe practice, and tour the facilities the spring before the two teams were scheduled to play. "I called Tom up and I said, 'Hey Tom, since we scheduled this game, maybe you don't want me to come,'" Nehlen recalled in 2011. "He said, 'Don, I've used the same playbook for 22 years, and I'm not going to change for you guys.' So I go there and he walks me around spring practice, and I met every one of his players. You talk about being sick.

"When I came back to West Virginia, I told our coaches, 'We don't have a kid on our team that even looks like those guys.'"

West Virginia's sophomore quarterback Chad Johnston started the Nebraska game and completed just two-of-six passes for 19 yards before being pulled in favor of Michigan transfer Eric Boykin, who wasn't much better. But Boykin did move the offense enough against the Cornhuskers to earn more playing time in the team's next two games, against Ball State and Rutgers. Losses followed against Maryland and Virginia Tech, and that's when the coaching staff decided to go back to Johnston for good.

"My first start against Ball State would have been much better than my first start being against Nebraska, which ended up winning the national championship that year," Johnston admitted. "Really, if you go back and look at the record they had that season, we lost 31-0, and it was actually one of their closer games."

Johnston played well in West Virginia's 34-10 victory at Missouri by completing 17-of-25 passes for 291 yards and a pair of touchdowns. "That game kind of cemented it for me, and from that point I was the starting quarterback," Johnston recalled.

"That seemed to be the changing point of the season, for whatever reason," added Abraham. "I don't know if that was because we finally started to stick with one person [at quarterback]."

Johnston thought West Virginia's football program in the mid-1990s was undergoing some major philosophical changes. Nehlen had grown up on Midwestern football and was influenced by Doyt Perry, Woody Hayes and Bo Schembechler, preferring to run the ball, call play-action passes off the running game and play great defense. When Nehlen took the West Virginia job in 1980, it would have taken an act of Congress for him to even consider putting four wide receivers in the game at the same time. By the middle of the 1994 season, however, Nehlen was beginning to change his tune after watching his defense struggle to stop other teams using four-receiver sets and throwing the football all over the field.

"We did what we could do with what we had," explained Nehlen. "When we got there we had a certain kind of player and we recruited a certain kind of player, and then when we had Major Harris he was an option-running, play-action-off-the-option type guy, and then we run into Chad, who can't do much of that at all, but he can throw the ball, and we started to recruit a couple of receivers."

Once, confronted with the choice of starting drop-back passer Browning Nagle over Harris in 1987, Nehlen chose Harris, in part, because he was more comfortable coaching the option game. When the same situation came up seven years later with Johnston and Boykin, he picked the drop-back passer.

"I think it just took some time for them to figure out that that was where we needed to go," said Johnston. "It was probably a three-to-four-year process to get to that point. We went from pounding the football and playing defense with that '93 team, to my years being the transition to the stuff they were doing when Marc Bulger got there with all those good receivers."

"What really pushed us was Marc Bulger," added Nehlen. "I had never seen a kid as accurate as Marc Bulger. He could hit you in either eye. To be honest, [assistant coaches] Billy Legg and Doc Holliday started to sit on that [grease] board and stretch them out here and stretch them out there and say, 'Hey, they've got to remove this linebacker, and if they don't remove this linebacker' . . . so we started to do a little bit of that. When Rich [Rodriguez] came here, his offense was my third down offense."

It also took the coaches some time to figure out who their best players were – one of them being walk-on wide receiver Zach Abraham from Wheeling. Abraham passed on some smaller local colleges to take a shot at the big time at WVU, knowing he was going to have to prove himself every day just to get noticed.

"There was one practice when I was on the scout team when [linebacker] Steve Grant was still there, and I just remember spinning guys around," said Abraham. "The defensive coaches were so pissed, and I thought the defensive guys were going to kill me that day. It was then that I just thought, you know what, I can play with these guys."

Abraham also very quickly understood that playing time was often just a simple matter of economics. There was a lot of money sunk into scholarship players, from their recruiting visits to the full ride that they received, and it was going to take something pretty special for a walk-on player to sit down a scholarship player.

"I just realized if I'm going to play, every practice I've just got to make guys look dumb," Abraham said. "Now that didn't work all the time, but eventually, I found out, hey, they're watching film every day. They're seeing this stuff. Whether they like it or not, they're seeing it and they can't ignore it. That was my way to combat that."

Abraham said there were no "eureka" moments for him – just a lot of hard work and persistence that eventually paid off. "There is no way a kid like me, coming out of nowhere, getting no money, is going to beat out a top-ranked recruit from Florida," he said. "It's just not going to happen. So I just got that mindset that I'm going to out-work them and I'm going to do everything I can to prove to them that I can do it. That took a long time."

Abraham believes he finally secured his scholarship when he ran into Nehlen in the hallway while the coach was on his way to the team's training table, where meals were served to the staff and scholarship players.

"I was one of the last guys upstairs, and Coach Nehlen was just coming out of his office. I was heading out the door to go get some dinner, and coach was like, 'Hey Zach, where are you going? Aren't you going to get something to eat?' I said, 'Coach, I don't have a scholarship, and I can't eat in the training table.'"

Nehlen gave Abraham a puzzled look. Then he grabbed his wide receiver by the arm and took him back into his office, where he had several bushel baskets full of vegetables sitting on the floor. "He said, 'We have a fan who insists on giving me some of his good vegetables, and he brings me so much that I don't know what to do with it. I give it away to the coaches.' Well, he loaded me up with enough vegetables for me and my roommate to eat for a week, and I had to walk about a mile to my apartment with all those vegetables," Abraham said. "Not too long after that, I was put on full scholarship . . ."

Nehlen was one upset football coach heading into the Pitt game. Not only was his team performing so poorly, but he also had to deal with some off-the-cuff remarks his flaky punter Todd Sauerbrun had made to a *Sports Illustrated* writer. Nehlen was never a big fan of the magazine – he believed its reporters always went out of their way to take below-the-belt shots at his program and the people of West Virginia.

During the undefeated 1988 season, Nehlen had let the aptly-named Doug Looney of *SI* spend a week with his team to get an inside look at the program, and what Looney came up with after West Virginia's home win over Maryland was another story littered with the Appalachian stereotypes that seem to give West Virginians a perpetual inferiority complex. However, this time it was Sauerbrun who fanned the flames, claiming that he rooted for the offense to fail so he had more opportunities to try and add to his 50.7-yard punting average. Naturally, his remarks went over like a dead cat in the punch bowl once his teammates got their hands on the magazine. Earlier in 1994, Sauerbrun had become somewhat of a minor celebrity after his 90-yard punt against Nebraska on national television earned him Player of the Game honors.

"I remember him once saying the reason he came to West Virginia was because we were good enough to go to bowl games, but the offense was always bad enough for him to kick a lot," Johnston laughed. "That was just Todd."

As Sauerbrun began to rise in the national punting rankings, he somehow got his hands on the telephone number to the press box, and he would frequently call after home games to find out what his punting average was. Sauerbrun and Mike Vanderjagt came to West Virginia at the same time, and the coaching staff knew so much about the kicking game that they decided to have the man who would become the most accurate placekicker in NFL history (Vanderjagt) begin his career as a punter, while having one of the best punters in college football history (Sauerbrun) start his career as a placekicker. Soon, after watching Sauerbrun duck-hook field goals and Vanderjagt's shank punts, it became apparent to everyone that a change was in order.

Once, after a game at Boston College when Sauerbrun was just a freshman, he decided to go home to Long Island instead of returning to Morgantown on the team charter. It wasn't until two days later, as the team was about to start practice with some special teams work, that the coaches realized that Sauerbrun had not come back with the team. Another time, Nehlen wanted to get in some situational kicking work with Sauerbrun, having him try some long field goals at the end of practice. By then, Bryan Baumann had taken over regular placekicking duties, but Sauerbrun's leg was much stronger than Baumann's. Nehlen always wanted to have Sauerbrun try some kicks with the entire team on the field distracting him, in case that situation ever came up late in a game. Nehlen blew his whistled and yelled for Todd. No answer. He blew his whistle again. More silence.

"Where in the hell is Sauerbrun?" one of the assistants asked.

Finally, one of the players looked up toward the bowl end of the stadium where the lights to the training table were on, and sure enough, Sauerbrun was the only player up there loading up his plate with food. "Nehlen saw him up there and he just burst out into laughter," Johnston recalled. "Right then he ended practice."

Nehlen had a strict rule that, when the team traveled, all players had to bring a sport coat for the team dinner the night before the game. Once, during a trip to Syracuse, Sauerbrun forgot his jacket, and as the players were filing into the hotel ballroom for their meals, a coatless Sauerbrun walked right past Nehlen. The coach stopped his punter and asked him where his jacket was. Sauerbrun told him he forgot it.

NEHLEN DUG BOTH HANDS DEEP INTO HIS TROUSERS AND PULLED OUT A PAIR OF RABBIT EARS.

"Well, Todd, if you don't have a coat then you can't eat with the team – that's the rule," Nehlen said.

"OK. Give me some money and I'll go to the Burger King across the street and get some dinner," Sauerbrun answered.

Nehlen dug both hands deep into his trousers and pulled out a pair of rabbit ears. "Todd, I'm the West Virginia football coach. I don't have any money!" Nehlen said.

His teammates said Sauerbrun got a lot of mileage out of that story.

During Tuesday practice in the week leading up to the Pitt game, the WVU players noticed the coaches coming up with some new things to try on offense. One play had Johnston faking a reverse to Abraham and then throwing a pass downfield to speedy receiver Rahsaan Vanterpool. The receivers were also asked to do more double moves than usual.

"Before that game, we would do deep comebacks or deep outs, and I think Pitt looked at that and decided they were going to jump these hard because they didn't think we could throw the ball down the field, because we hadn't," said Abraham. "We sort of knew from watching film that they were [going to jump the outs]. They were kind of like us. They were really mediocre. That was at a time when they were trying to get the program back up, and they were fighting some things with a new coaching staff."

It was a beautiful, sunny fall afternoon in Pittsburgh when the two teams took the field on October 15, 1994. Pitt got the ball first but couldn't get a first down, so they punted the ball back to West Virginia. The Mountaineers marched from their own 23 to the Panther 24, where Baumann made a 41-yard field goal. On Pitt's next possession, West Virginia scored the game's first touchdown – Dave Merrick's 41-yard field goal try was blocked and returned by Harold Kidd for the score. This play served as a harbinger of the bizarre things to come.

Shortly afterward, Rahsaan Vanterpool returned the favor when he muffed Nate Cochran's punt at the West Virginia 8 – the ball was recovered by Pitt defensive back Eric Kasperowicz at the 2. (This was one of the few plays a Panther DB actually made that afternoon.) Kasperowicz's recovery set up Billy West's 2-yard touchdown run, but Merrick missed the PAT, making the score 10-6, West Virginia.

The Mountaineers scored the next three times they had the football, taking what appeared to be a commanding 31-6 lead with 5:44 left in the first half: Johnston hooked up with Abraham for a 40-yard touchdown pass; All-American defensive back Aaron Beasley stepped in front of a John Ryan pass and returned it 50 yards for another score; and Johnston hit Vanterpool for a 46-yard TD on that pretty fake-reverse pass the team had been working on earlier in the week.

Beasley said it was pressure by linebacker Matt Taffoni that allowed him to jump in front of Ryan's pass and get the interception. "Matt came up to me and said, 'Hey Bease, I'm going to get to the quarterback and you sit on this route and take it to the end zone.' Man, I knew it was a three-step and I just sat," said Beasley. "I actually had to wait for the ball to get there. It was like I caught it behind me."

West Virginia even got points when Pitt scored. Right after Vanterpool's TD catch, Ryan connected with speedster Dietrich Jells for an 80-yard touchdown, but the Pitt QB's two-point conversion pass was picked off by Taffoni, who raced the length of the field to give the Mountaineers two additional points, bringing the score to 33-12.

Four minutes later, Pitt got on the board once more when Ryan found split end Billy Davis open for a 34-yard touchdown. Merrick was successful on his PAT to pull the Panthers to within two scores, 33-19. Pitt actually got the ball once more before the end of the half, with an opportunity to cut even deeper into West Virginia's lead, but Ryan's third-down pass from midfield was broken up by Kidd as the half ended.

At halftime, both teams had 253 yards of offense, but neither team could run the ball – this was a recipe for disaster for a team like West Virginia, which still preferred to control the clock whenever it had the lead. Nehlen tried to do so on his team's opening possession of the second half, burning off nearly seven minutes before having to punt at the Pitt 41. Unfortunately for West Virginia, it took Pitt a much shorter amount of time to score when Jells got behind the secondary a second time, for a 63-yard touchdown. "Our defense played pretty well, but what Pitt did was, in the second half, they went to an empty backfield on offense," Johnston explained. "Of course now everybody does empty sets all the time, but we just couldn't handle it."

After Pitt's fourth TD, both offenses took another little hiatus for about the next six minutes, until late in the third quarter when linebacker Elige Longino set up West

West Virginia tailback Artie Owens looks for running room during West Virginia's 17-14 victory over Pitt at Mountaineer Field in 1975. Also pictured are Pitt's Randy Holloway (77) and Arnie Weatherington (59).

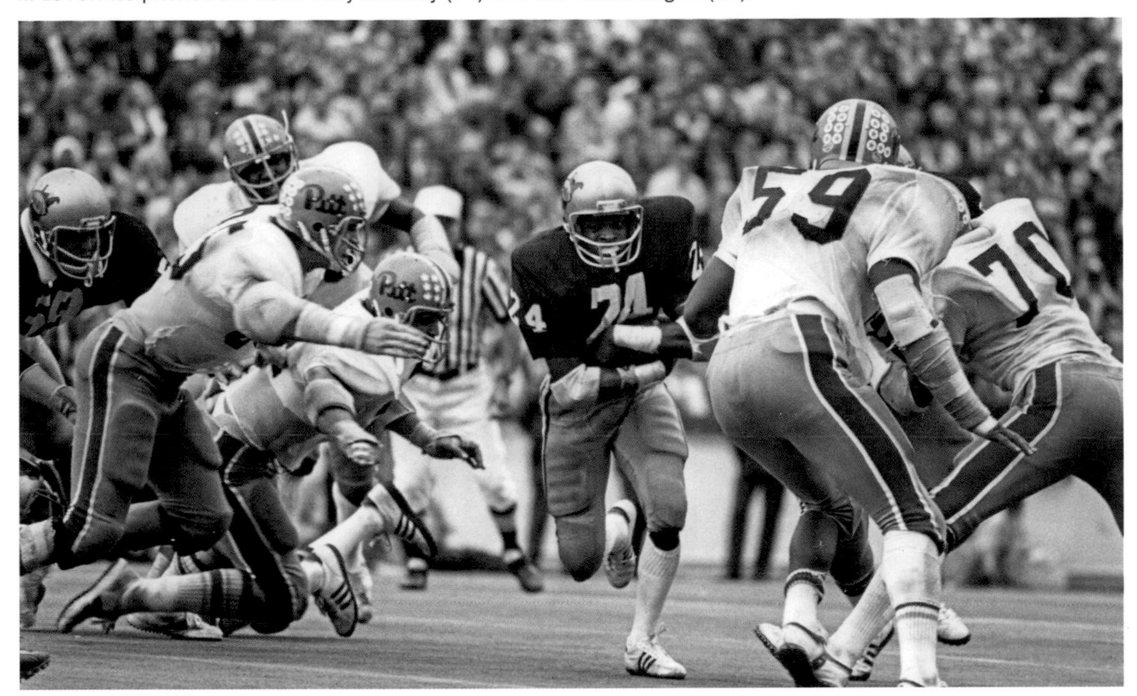

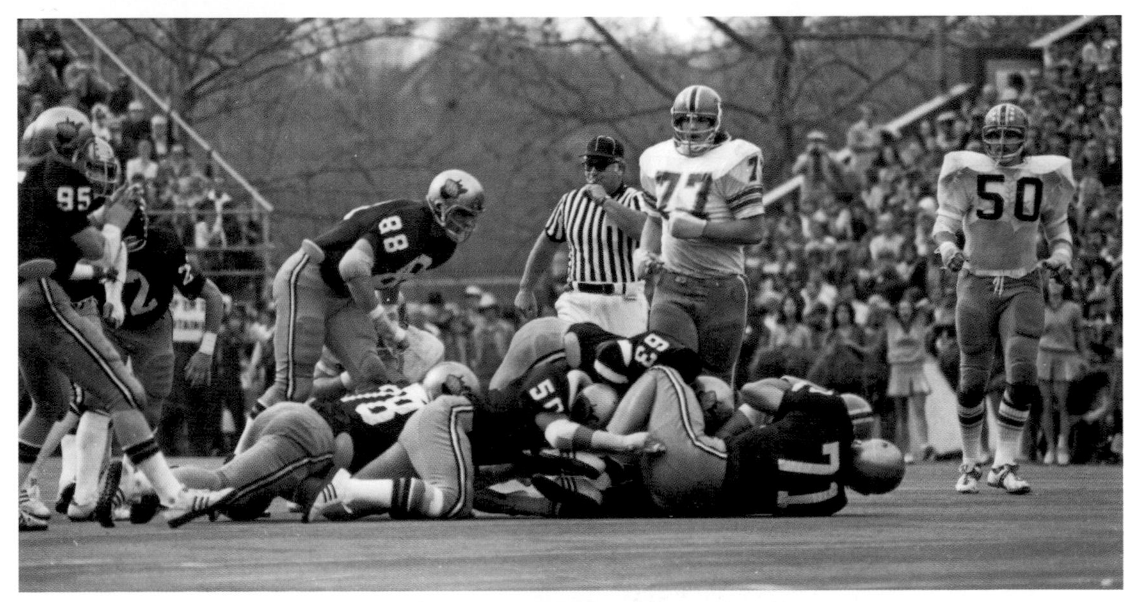

West Virginia's defense was superb against Pitt in 1975, holding the Panthers to only 11 first downs and limiting All-American running back Tony Dorsett to just 107 yards rushing. On the ground making the tackle for the Mountaineers are Ken Culbertson (50), Rich Lukowski (71), Ray Marshall (63) and Chuck Smith (78). Also pictured are Gary Lombard (88), Andy Peters (95) and Tom Pridemore (22) of West Virginia, while trailing the play are Pitt offensive linemen Matt Carroll (77) and John Pelusi (50).

A snapshot of Bill McKenzie's 1975 game-winning field goal against Pitt, taken from the end zone by Dr. Carolyn Peluso Atkins, now a professor in WVU's College of Human Resources & Education. (Courtesy of Dr. Carolyn Peluso Atkins)

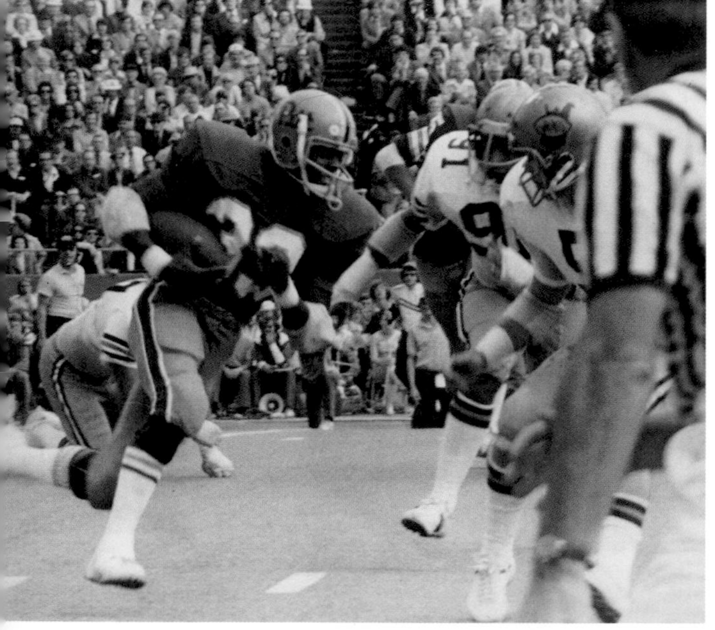

Tony Dorsett, pictured here in 1974, ran for a game-high 199 yards on 38 carries, scoring three touchdowns in Pitt's 24-16 win over West Virginia in 1976. Dorsett would have set an NCAA record for consecutive 200-yard rushing games that afternoon had he not been ejected near the end of the game for throwing a football at West Virginia's Robin Meeley, an act that incited a bench-clearing brawl. Chasing Dorsett in this photograph are John Spraggins (91) and Jack Eastwood (5).

Quarterback Matt Cavanaugh did most of his damage on the ground against West Virginia, carrying 19 times for 124 yards. Cavanaugh would set up three Tony Dorsett touchdown runs in top-ranked Pitt's 24-16 victory over the Mountaineers at Pitt Stadium on Nov. 13, 1976. Giving chase is West Virginia linebacker Jeff Macerelli (55).

Quarterback Jeff Hostetler scores the go-ahead touchdown during West Virginia's 24-21 victory against Pitt, at Mountaineer Field in 1983, snapping the Panthers' seven-game winning streak over the Mountaineers. When Hoss crossed the goal line, the eruption in the stadium was so loud that it could be heard all the way across the river in Granville. Also pictured are West Virginia's Pat Randolph (24), and Pitt's Troy Hill (22) and Al Wenglikowski (6).

Coach Don Nehlen gets a ride off the field following West Virginia's 24-21 victory over Pitt at Mountaineer Field on Oct. 1, 1983. More than 64,000 packed into Mountaineer Field to witness West Virginia's historic victory.

Major Harris, a Pittsburgh native and top 100 prep prospect, found a home at West Virginia University when other schools were unwilling to recruit him as a quarterback. Harris went on to lead the Mountaineers to the brink of a national championship in 1989, and he was later elected into the College Football Hall of Fame. (George Gojkovich photo)

A.B. Brown owns the unique distinction of playing on both sides of the Backyard Brawl in 1985 for Pitt and 1987 and 1988 for West Virginia. Also pictured are Pitt's Marc Spindler (93), Billy Owens (1) and Jerry Wall (51), and West Virginia's John Stroia (75) and Kevin Koken (57). (George Gojkovich photo)

Ed Frazier kicks a field goal on the final play of the game, capping a 22-point fourth quarter Panthers comeback at Mountaineer Field. Though the result was a 31-31 tie, most West Virginia fans consider this game to be a loss. (Joedy McKown photo)

Pitt quarterback Alex Van Pelt, originally from Grafton, W.Va., passed for 366 yards and a touchdown in this 1989 game in Morgantown. Later, in 1991, Van Pelt led the Panthers to a 34-3 victory in Morgantown. (Joedy McKown photo)

Quarterback Darren Studstill was supposed to run a new no-huddle shotgun attack against Pitt in the 1991 season opener (which also happened to be the inaugural Big East game for both schools), but a shoulder injury forced him to the sidelines. West Virginia had to scrap its top secret plans. (Bill Amatucci photo)

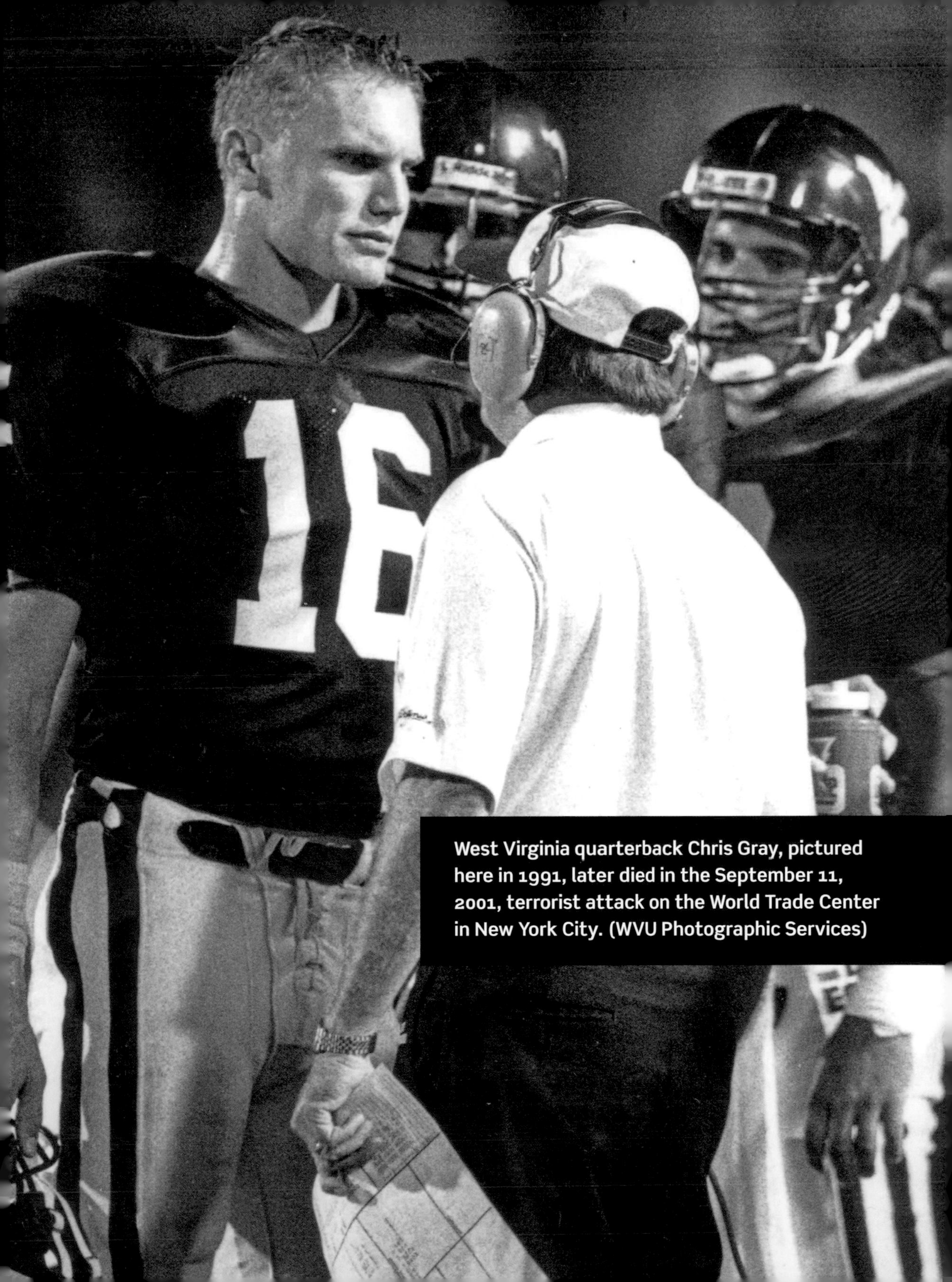
West Virginia quarterback Chris Gray, pictured here in 1991, later died in the September 11, 2001, terrorist attack on the World Trade Center in New York City. (WVU Photographic Services)

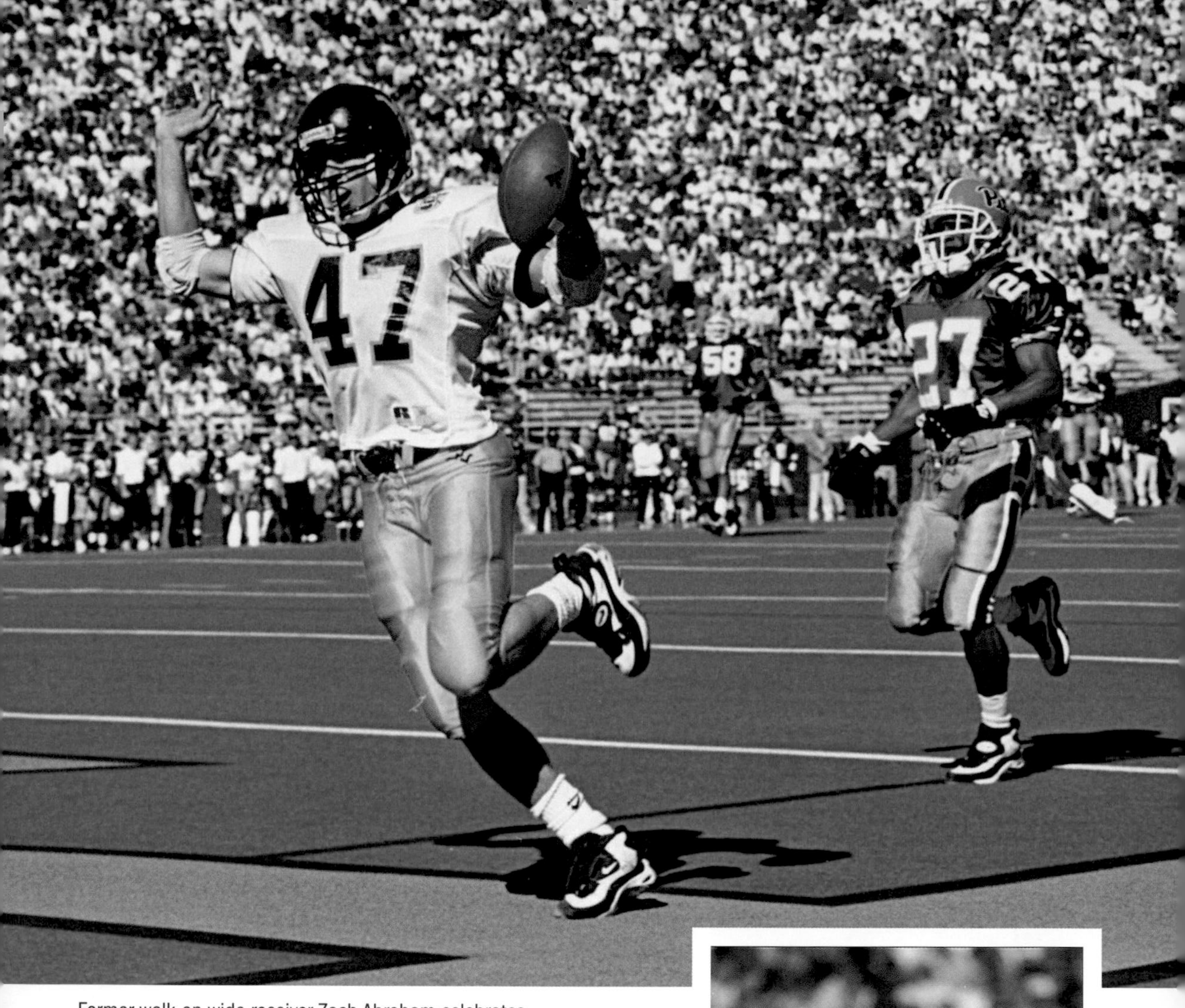

Former walk-on wide receiver Zach Abraham celebrates his 40-yard touchdown reception in the first quarter of West Virginia's 1994 game at Pitt. Abraham later won the game on a 60-yard touchdown catch with 15 seconds left. Trailing on this play is Pitt defensive back Derrick Parker. (All-Pro Photography/Dale Sparks)

No West Virginia quarterback enjoyed more success against the Panthers than Marc Bulger. Bulger completed 73-of-113 passes for 1,097 yards and 11 touchdowns in four career games against Pitt, with victories over the Panthers in 1996, 1998 and 1999. (Bill Amatucci photo)

Amos Zereoue ran for 153 yards and scored three touchdowns against Pitt in 1997, but it was his overtime fumble that aided the Panthers in their 41-38 triple-overtime victory at Mountaineer Field. It was the first overtime game in Mountaineer Field history. (WVU Photographic Services/M.G. Ellis photo)

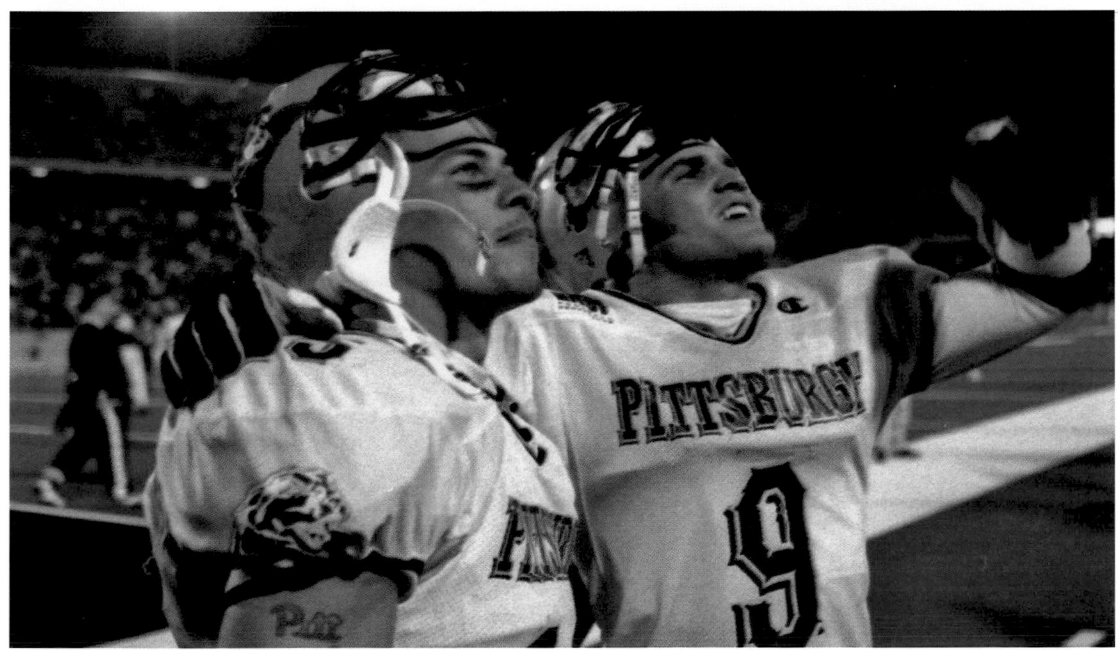

Panthers players John Jenkins and Jake Hoffart celebrate with a contingent of Pitt fans at Mountaineer Field. The 41-38 triple-overtime win in 1997 snapped the Mountaineers' five-game winning streak in the series. (WVU Photographic Services/M.G. Ellis photo)

Hidden among all of this humanity is running back Avon Cobourne, who somehow twisted his way out of this predicament to score a 2-yard touchdown, putting West Virginia ahead, 17-10, against Pitt in 2002. (All-Pro Photography/Dale Sparks)

Phil Braxton of Connellsville, Pa., gets behind Pitt defensive back Torrie Cox for a 79-yard touchdown, giving West Virginia a two-touchdown lead in this 2002 game at Heinz Field. (All-Pro Photography/Dale Sparks)

Quarterback Rasheed Marshall's Pittsburgh homecoming in 2002 was an enjoyable one as the sophomore led West Virginia to a 24-17 victory over 17th-rated Pitt at Heinz Field. Marshall threw a touchdown pass and ran for another while accounting for 153 yards of total offense. (All-Pro Photography/Dale Sparks)

Coach Rich Rodriguez works the sidelines during West Virginia's 13-9 loss to Pitt at Milan Puskar Stadium, in 2007. Two weeks later, Rodriguez left West Virginia to take the Michigan job. (All-Pro Photography/Dale Sparks)

Running back LeSean McCoy carried 38 times for 148 yards in Pitt's 13-9 upset victory over West Virginia in 2007 at Milan Puskar Stadium. Getting blocked is West Virginia's Johnny Dingle (92). (All-Pro Photography/Dale Sparks)

Cornerback Larry Williams sits in disbelief on the turf at Milan Puskar Stadium, after 28-½-point underdog Pitt defeated West Virginia 13-9 to knock the Mountaineers out of the 2007 national championship picture. (All-Pro Photography/Dale Sparks)

An old-school trap play springs Noel Devine free for an 88-yard touchdown, helping West Virginia knock off eighth-ranked Pitt, 19-16, at Mountaineer Field in 2009. Giving chase is Pitt free safety Jarred Holley. (WVU Photographic Services/Brian Persinger)

Tyler Bitancurt's field goal sails past a leaping Jon Baldwin to give West Virginia a 19-16 victory over Pitt on the final play of the game in 2009. (WVU Photographic Services/Brian Persinger)

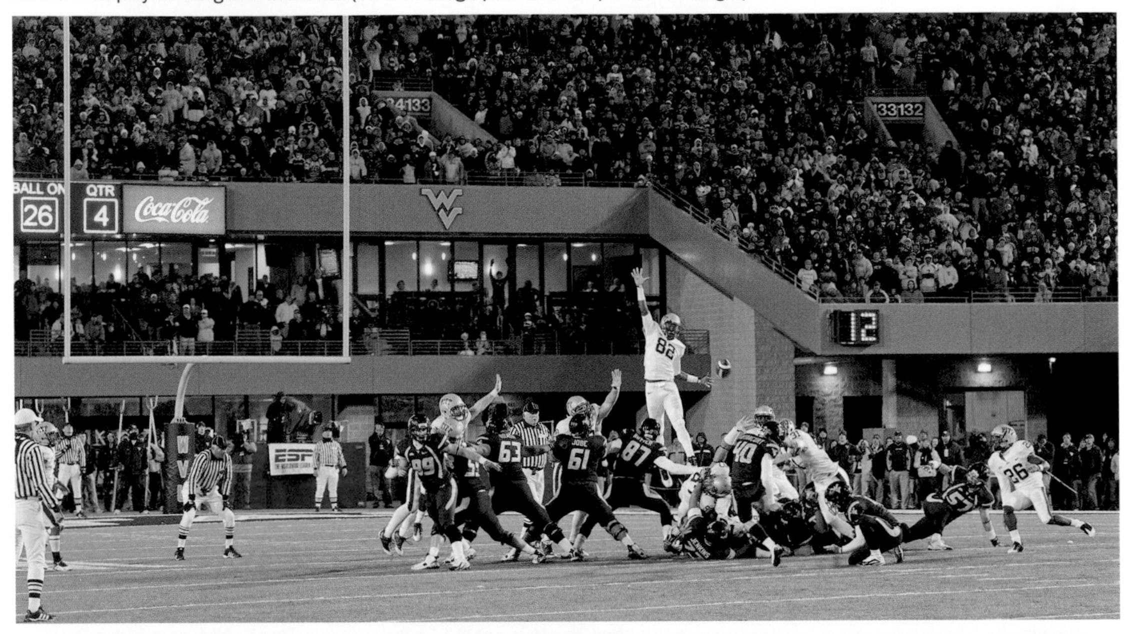

West Virginia quarterback Geno Smith eludes pressure against Pitt in this 2011 game at Milan Puskar Stadium - possibly the final Backyard Brawl to be played for a while. (Pete Emerson photo)

Virginia deep in Pitt territory, forcing Denorse Mosley to fumble Sauerbrun's punt. Scott Bailey was there to recover the ball at the Panther 23. Once again, Nehlen tried to slow down the game and restore some order by running the football. But at the start of the fourth quarter, a Kantroy Barber run up the middle on third and 9 got nowhere, and Nehlen sent out his field goal team, content to make it a two-score game. But Baumann's 39-yard field goal try was blocked by Chad Askew, and Pitt defensive tackle Tom Barndt came up with the ball at the 47. The only two West Virginia players with a shot of tackling Barndt were Baumann and holder Brian West.

It took Barndt what seemed like forever to weave his way down the field to score the tying touchdown, with West and Baumann running after him like a pair of school kids playing chase at recess. It was obvious to those watching the play that neither West nor Baumann were really all that interested in trying to bring down the 275-pound tackle.

The score was now tied at 33, West Virginia having blown a 25-point first half lead – and there was still 14:08 left to play. Nehlen had heard all about Bobby Bowden's epic collapse at Pitt in 1970, and he had had a pretty fair collapse of his own against the Panthers in 1989, when Pitt stormed back from 22 points down in the fourth quarter to tie the Mountaineers. This time, he wasn't ready to add another of those games to the history books.

"I thought about that 1970 game up there when WVU blew a 35-8 halftime lead and wound up losing 36-35," Nehlen said after the game. "I said to myself, 'I heard about that game and how mad everybody was at Bobby Bowden.' Then I said to myself, 'Well, I think Bobby is going to have a friend.'"

Meanwhile, as West Virginia's defense was melting down, Pitt public address announcer Don Ireland began giving it to the Mountaineer fans up in the stands. At one point in the first half, the wisecracking Ireland made an announcement that a tractor parked outside with West Virginia license plate number "E-I-E-I-O" had its lights on. Later, he read the stadium's non-smoking policy, before adding, ". . . and that includes cigarettes, cigars and corncob pipes." Most took Ireland's ribbing for what it was – good-natured fun – but others were appalled that the University of Pittsburgh would allow its public address announcer to treat their guests with such insensitivity. Soon after the game, Ireland chose to give up his PA duties.

With 2:30 remaining and the score still tied, West Virginia was finally able to take advantage of Pitt's all-out blitzing – a tactic Panther defensive coordinator Chuck Driesbach had decided to put in place for the entire second half, keeping the pressure on Johnston. On third and 11 from the Mountaineer 19, Johnston could see right away that

Pitt was coming with the house, because West Virginia had the Panthers spread out with a four-wide receiver set, a formation that forced the Pitt defense to declare what it was planning. Vanterpool had man coverage on the outside, so he broke off his pattern. Johnston delivered the ball about 15 yards downfield to Vanterpool, who ran the remaining 66 yards for an 81-yard touchdown, giving West Virginia a 40-33 lead with just 1:32 showing on the clock. Johnston said backup center Derrick Bell was the main reason the play was a success.

"They blitzed from the outside and Derrick Bell was the only uncovered guy, and he had to go all the way out past the left tackle to pick up the backside linebacker," Johnston explained. "He picked him up to allow me to step up and throw the ball to Vanterpool."

However, for a game like this, there was still too much time left on the clock, especially with the way the two defenses were playing. And Pitt went right to work. On first and 10 at his own 20, Ryan hit Askew for 18 yards. Another Ryan pass to Davis for 9 yards got the ball to the 47. Ryan then ran 16 yards to the West Virginia 37 before finding Askew open for 20, taking Pitt to the 17.

A West Virginia pass interference penalty stopped the clock and gave Pitt a first and goal at the 5, where Ryan hit Askew for a touchdown, pulling Pitt to within one point, 40-39. Majors opted to go for the two-point conversion, and his quarterback was able to cross the goal line on a rollout to his right, giving the Panthers a 41-40 lead. It looked like another big Pitt comeback victory over West Virginia was about to be added to the record books; all Pitt's defense had to do was hold West Virginia for 54 seconds.

Vanterpool returned Todd Barton's kick to the WVU 28, giving the Mountaineers about 30 yards to go before they could get into range for Sauerbrun to try a long field goal – at least that's what Johnston was thinking when he broke the huddle. "I had seen him before in practice kick a 70-yard field goal, so I just thought, if we could get downfield and get into a position to kick a field goal, maybe we can win the ballgame," Johnston said.

On first down, another Pitt blitz forced Johnston to scramble out of the pocket for 12 yards, taking WVU to the 40. Johnston's run turned out to be the critical play of the game, because it perfectly set up the next play – four streaks down the field, with Vanterpool on one side and Abraham on the other. "They were playing so aggressively the entire game and were taking chances," Abraham said. "During the last series, it was all streaks."

Once again, Pitt came with pressure from the outside, forcing Johnston to step up in the pocket. His first thought was to hit tight end Lovett Purnell running a deep drag down near the Pitt 40. That would easily have been enough yardage to give Sauerbrun a reasonable try at kicking a game-winning field goal, but out of the corner of his eye he saw Abraham running even with Panther defensive back Denorse Mosley, who had no safety help.

"I got flushed and had to step up, and I didn't have time to set my feet and throw it," said Johnston. Those three or four steps toward the line of scrimmage Johnston took in the pocket caused Mosley to hesitate just enough to let Abraham run past him.

"It was a perfectly thrown ball, and it was one of those things when you think to yourself, 'What is that person doing?'" said Abraham. "They were playing prevent and he squatted, and I was like, are you kidding me? As soon as he did that, I turned and looked and the ball was in the air. I'm thinking, 'Man, I better not drop this one.'"

The ball traveled 50 yards in the air before hitting Abraham perfectly in stride. He ran the remaining 10 yards for a 60-yard touchdown and the go-ahead score. There were just 23 seconds left on the clock when Abraham reached the end zone. "When I stepped up and I saw Zach out of the corner of my eye, I saw that he was running even and we always used to say, 'If he's even, he's leavin'.' I wasn't sure if he was going to be leavin' or not, but I had to give it a shot," said Johnston.

When the Pitt offense returned to the field, it still had 15 seconds left to score, and on the final play of the game, Ryan actually completed a 41-yard pass to Jells before Beasley was able to drag him down at the West Virginia 39. "You talk about an exhausting game," said Abraham. "I never felt so drained in my life. That was just a long game."

It was much longer for the coaches, particularly Majors. "It was a great example of Murphy's Law: Whatever can go wrong will go wrong," he said.

"Somebody might call that the greatest game ever, but for a guy that coaches football, it certainly was not," added Nehlen.

Even today, Nehlen still shakes his head when recalling that game. "It was the greatest game for the fans and the worst for the football coaches," he said. "We got ahead by 21 or 24 points and absolutely played terrible."

The 1994 Pitt game will forever be etched in Bill Kirelawich's mind. He drove his young son Billy up to Pittsburgh to watch from the sidelines, and Billy was there to share in the joy of a great comeback victory. Afterward, the two drove down I-79, replaying Abraham's miraculous touchdown catch all the way into West Virginia. When Kirelawich pulled into his driveway, his wife Maggie was there waiting to tell him that his father had died that afternoon.

"He died right about the time [of Abraham's touchdown catch], and all I could think about was Zach Abraham getting behind that corner being divine intervention," Kirelawich recalled. "So I go into the house, and Billy and my wife are outside – Billy is only a little kid then – and he looks at her and he says, 'He was so happy. Why did you have to have to tell him that?'"

Johnston threw for a career-high 396 yards with four touchdowns, but 23 of his 39 attempts were incomplete passes. And only three WVU players caught passes that afternoon: Vanterpool's nine for 205 yards, Abraham's six for 180 yards and Purnell's one for 11 yards. "Honestly, I probably should have had about 600 yards passing," said Johnston. "They would either be off a fingertip or they would be one step away. When you go man and they blitz, everything has to be short. It's not like when you're against zone. You have to throw it a little bit quicker to a spot, and your guy has to break his route off a little quicker, so it's not a nice, neat, timing passing game that you get when you get zone coverage."

Ryan, Pitt's backup to regular quarterback Sean Fitzgerald, finished the game completing 20-of-37 passes for 433 yards and four touchdowns; Ryan and Fitzgerald threw for a combined 480 total yards that afternoon. Had it not been for Abraham's touchdown catch, Ryan would have been remembered in the same way as quarterback Dave Havern for leading Pitt's comeback victory in 1970.

Abraham vividly remembers his post-game discussion with the late Bill Van Horne, sports editor of his hometown newspaper in Wheeling. Van Horne told him he would always be remembered for that catch. "I remembered saying to him, 'Yeah, but hopefully they will remember some other catches as well,'" laughed Abraham. "Well, he was right."

Abraham, Johnston and Vanterpool – the three stars of the game – were standing outside the locker room, talking to reporters who were still trying to make some sense out of what they had just witnessed. As they spoke, the four West Virginia team buses pulled out of the parking lot and headed down the hill, on the way out of town. Nehlen, in his haste to get out of Dodge, had forgotten his three remaining players. Johnston was able to get a ride back to Morgantown with his parents, while the two receivers caught a ride home with the team's associate sports information director in his beat-up Honda Civic – Abraham sat in the front seat, curled up around a large box of game programs, and Vanterpool sprawled in the back seat with an ice bag on his knee and his left foot dangling inches from the driver's head.

I know that because I just happened to be the guy driving them home. Despite the remarkable victory and the unforgettable ending, neither player uttered a single word the entire way down I-79. Both were sound asleep.

For the Love of Pete

PITT	WVU
41	38

Nov. 28, 1997
Morgantown, W.Va.

West Virginia was listed by the oddsmakers as 13-point favorites for its game against Pitt in Morgantown, despite a leaky secondary and a linebacker corps that was down to its last healthy guy. First, Damon Cogdell was shelved with a broken hip during the Mountaineers' 40-10 loss at Syracuse, and then a week later, Gary Stills suffered a broken kneecap in the first quarter of West Virginia's 21-14 loss at Notre Dame.

Meanwhile, starting inside linebacker John Hadley was playing with torn cartilage in his knee, which would eventually require off-season surgery. Steve Lippe, Cogdell's replacement, was battling sore ribs. Jamie Sweeney was also dealing with a bum knee. The only healthy linebacker Coach Don Nehlen could put on the field was sophomore Ryan Brady - Stills's replacement. "Whoever can walk Friday will play," Nehlen said before the game. "That's the only test for the linebackers now."

West Virginia's growing injury list and a secondary that sometimes left receivers uncovered – coupled with Pitt's offensive resurgence under first-year coach Walt Harris – had finally injected some life back into a football series that was losing its appeal, especially in Pittsburgh. Two of the three prior WVU-Pitt games played in the Steel City failed to draw more than 42,000 fans, and only 38,293 came out to watch one of the most exciting games ever played between the two schools, in 1994, the outcome of which was eventually decided on a late touchdown catch by Zach Abraham. A year later, just 38,795 showed up in Morgantown to watch a pillow fight that the Mountaineers won by three touchdowns. By 1997, the pendulum of momentum in the series had completely swung in West Virginia's favor.

WVU recorded back-to-back shutouts against Pitt in 1995 and 1996, and the team won five straight from 1992–96, by a combined score of 188-68. That still remains the best five-year stretch of success West Virginia has ever enjoyed against Pitt, exceeding the Mountaineers' three-year victory run against the Panthers from 1967–69. (This earlier streak actually should have been six in a row, but Bobby Bowden squandered a 35-8 halftime lead, losing 36-35 to the Panthers in Pittsburgh in 1970.)

In early October, it appeared that Pitt was on its way to another losing campaign, with the Panthers dropping early conference games to Temple and Boston College, and needing a late score in overtime to defeat woeful Rutgers. But Pitt coach Walt Harris got his players regrouped, losing a 1-point game to Syracuse before knocking off defending Big East champion Virginia Tech, evening the team's record to 5-5 and giving it a shot of earning Pitt's first bowl bid in eight years – that is, if they could beat West Virginia. The early 1990s were not exactly a Golden Era of Pitt football, with Paul Hackett's 3-9 record in 1992 followed up by Johnny Majors's four years of disappointment, before time ran out on him after the 1996 season. Considering the recent futility Pitt had endured, for the Panthers to still be in bowl contention this late in the season was a pretty big deal.

"If anything has happened this year, it is, I think, the heart this football team, and primarily our seniors, have demonstrated [, which] is something many of us may not have seen a year ago," said Harris. "I'm not blaming anybody. I can only see what I've seen, and we have played some good football against people who have more size, speed and numbers than we have, yet we have fought tooth for tooth. I think that has a lot to do with the kind of program we're running, the kind of expectations we have and the kind of character and grit our football players have."

Nehlen, who never missed a chance to build up his opponent (with a straight face, he once referred to a winless Temple team as "flat-out scary . . . to a degree"), naturally gave Harris high marks for reviving the Pitt program. "For my money, their coaches have done just an outstanding job – as good as anybody in the country, that's for sure," Nehlen said.

Senior quarterback Pete Gonzalez was the primary reason Pitt was playing better. Until 1997, Gonzalez's Pitt career was nondescript and headed for the scrapheap of history. As a sophomore in 1995, he had briefly replaced starter John Ryan at midseason before going down with a knee injury. Matt Lytle stepped in and played the remaining two games that season, won the starting job in 1996, and was then replaced by Gonzalez at midseason until Gonzalez got hurt again. When Harris arrived at Pitt, he wanted to go with one guy under center, and he waited until August to name Gonzalez his guy.

It was a wise choice. Heading into the final game of the year, Gonzalez was completing 57 percent of his passes for nearly 2,400 yards and 25 touchdowns, giving Pitt the most lethal passing attack in the Big East. "We would not be where we're at if it wasn't for Pete's contribution," Harris said.

"All I know is Gonzalez is doing everything they want him to do," Nehlen said. "And Pitt does everything known to man on offense. You name it, they do it."

Not a good prescription for an ailing Mountaineer secondary that already had problems sticking to their men, or for a linebacker corps held together with duct tape.

You name it, and West Virginia's Amos Zereoue did it in 1997. He had burst onto the scene against Pitt as a freshman in 1996, taking his very first collegiate carry 69 yards for a touchdown. He finished the game with 135 yards (on just 12 carries) and ended his freshman season with 1,035 yards rushing.

In year two, Zereoue got off to a great start when he ran for 174 yards in the season opener against Marshall – and it only got better after that. He torched Miami for 206 yards and two touchdowns in West Virginia's 28-17 win down in Florida, and two months later, Zereoue exceeded his Miami effort with a 234-yard, two-touchdown performance at Notre Dame. Zereoue, born in the Ivory Coast before moving to Hempstead, N.Y., to live with his father Bonde, was the nation's second-leading rusher heading into the Backyard Brawl. "He, along with [Syracuse quarterback] Donovan McNabb, is the most dominant player in our conference," said Harris of Zereoue. "He can win a game. [West Virginia] is very physical up front and he doesn't need much of a hole, and he doesn't need [a block] held very long.

"I don't know if we can keep him under 200 yards," Harris added. "But we've got to keep him out of the end zone. Winning is about scoring defense, not yardage defense."

Quarterback Marc Bulger, from Pittsburgh, was another outstanding player Pitt had to deal with. Bulger, barely weighing 170 pounds in high school, attracted very little interest from recruiters, despite leading the same Central Catholic program that Dan Marino had led two decades prior. All college recruiters had to go off of was Bulger's senior film, but that was enough for Nehlen to see the lightning-quick release, the feathery touch and his amazing accuracy. The other West Virginia coaches were concerned about Bulger's size, but not Nehlen, himself a former malnourished college quarterback. "Being the head coach, I have the only vote that counts," Nehlen said.

Bulger, despite playing just a few miles from the Pitt campus, never got a sniff from the Panthers. "I didn't get any interest from Pitt. There was no visit, no offer," he said. "I was surprised a little bit since one of my high school coaches was from there and told them about me."

There were additional offensive weapons: Shawn Foreman, from the fertile Tidewater, Va., area, had hands the size of bread loaves and in 1997 became only the second player in school history to catch more than 70 passes in a season (David Saunders was the first, in 1996). Foreman was the focal point of the passing game that year after Saunders suffered a season-ending knee injury during preseason training camp. On down the list of Mountaineer pass catchers in 1997 was a pair of future pros in tight end

Anthony Becht and wide receiver Jerry Porter. Despite the firepower West Virginia had assembled, particularly on offense, the Mountaineers were 7-3 heading into the Pitt game – some considered this underachieving. Walt Harris would give Nehlen detractors some added ammo once they read his comments in the papers about the talent he saw on West Virginia's roster. "I understand the depth of the program at West Virginia," Harris commented. "We know we have a long way to go in order to be at the level West Virginia is at – physically, athletically, emotionally and record-wise."

A trap had been set.

Pitt's redshirt junior defensive end Marlin Young was asked his opinion of the West Virginia-Pitt rivalry. "I've been through a couple of games – a couple real ugly ones," he said. "I've grown to, I wouldn't say hate them, but I have a taste in my mouth that I need to get rid of."

Harris, too, made it a point to ratchet up the rhetoric during practice. He had never coached or played in the game, so he took some time to have the seniors lecture the team on the importance of beating West Virginia. One important speaker was defensive back John Jenkins, from North Versailles, Pa. "I've been a Pitt fan my whole life, and if you've been around here for a while, you realize that there's no bigger game than the West Virginia game," he said. "You prepare just the same for the other games, but you keep an eye and an ear on the television to see what West Virginia did.

"The guys from California and Florida, they might not know how big it is. I've known it my whole life."

Then Harris threw in his two cents. "What I've gathered is that we're 0-5 the last five years, and I've gathered a rivalry is based on one side winning and the other side winning," Harris said. "So right now I don't think we've done our part to make it a very big rivalry."

There was one more little piece of information at Harris's disposal: Before the game, Amos Zereoue had stated that in order for it to be a rivalry, the other team had to hold up its end of the bargain. Zereoue's comments were noted in the Pitt locker room.

West Virginia scored on the game's opening possession by driving 80 yards in 13 plays. Bulger completed a pass of 23 yards to Pat Greene and another of 13 yards to Foreman, moving the ball into Pitt territory. Then, a 24-yard Bulger pass to Foreman got the ball to the Panther 18. From there, Zereoue took over, carrying six straight times to reach the end zone and give the Mountaineers an early lead.

Pitt's opening possession of the game ended with a turnover when safety Gary Thompkins picked off a Gonzalez pass at the WVU 10. But Pitt's defense forced West Virginia to punt, and Bryan Baumann's short kick gave the Panthers great field position at the WVU 28. Three plays later, Billy West, playing in place of injured starter Dwayne Schulters, went wide left for a 13-yard touchdown to tie the game. Four minutes later, Pitt reached the end zone once again, when Gonzalez hooked up with Jake Hoffart for a 16-yard score, completing a seven-play, 74-yard drive for the Panthers. Another Gonzalez TD pass, this one to Terry Murphy for 27 yards, came before halftime and after Jay Taylor's 47-yard field goal for West Virginia, giving Pitt a 21-10 lead at the break. Nehlen thought his team had played sluggishly in the first half and made that point to them at halftime. "I don't know if you could print what I said. In effect, I told them I didn't care whether they even came out for the second half," Nehlen explained. "I said, 'This is supposed to be a big game, and you guys are playing like you don't even know that.'"

His team got the message. The defense forced Pitt to punt on its opening possession of the second half, and the offense marched right down the field, getting a pair of first down runs from Zereoue before Bulger found Greene down the near sideline for 56 yards to the Panther 5. After an illegal shift penalty moved the ball back to the 10, Zereoue skirted up the middle to reach pay dirt. Bulger's two-point conversion pass to Foreman was successful, pulling West Virginia to within a field goal, 21-18.

After an exchange of possessions, another poor Baumann punt gave Pitt the ball in Mountaineer territory with 5:25 remaining in the third quarter. On third down, Gonzalez found Kevan Barlow out of the backfield for 12 yards to the WVU, and a 15-yard personal foul penalty on the Mountaineers got the ball to the 25. Three plays later, Gonzalez hit Terry Murphy for a 10-yard touchdown to once again put the Panthers up by 10.

Gonzales also contributed on the ground, rushing for 42 and making himself Pitt's second-leading rusher for the game."I think my running slowed down their pass rush," Gonzalez said. "I think I hurt them in the first half, and they were susceptible to that. Them two big boys up front [John Thornton and Henry Slay] weren't coming like they had. They weren't talking that noise like they were."

With the clock winding down in the third quarter, short Bulger throws to Foreman and Becht were sandwiched between an 18-yard Zereoue run. Another Zereoue carry took the ball to the Pitt 3, and on the first play of the fourth quarter, he reached the end zone to make it a field goal game. The Panthers answered with a 12-play drive that consumed 4:57 of the clock and ended in the end zone when Gonzalez found Juan Williams for a 9-yard touchdown. On the drive, Gonzalez completed two key third down passes, one to Hoffart for 17 yards on third and 15 to the Pitt 30, and the second for 18 yards, also to Hoffart, on third and 12, taking Pitt to the Mountaineer nine.

The Mountaineers took possession of the football with 10 minutes remaining, and Bulger immediately went to the air, using short passes to Zereoue, Greene, Porter and Foreman to advance to the 47. From there, Bulger took a shot down the field, in the vicinity of Greene and Pitt strong safety Curtis McGhee. What looked like a sure interception by McGhee turned into a 53-yard touchdown pass when Greene somehow came up with the ball and ran into the end zone. "I was there, I was in position to make the play," said McGhee. "It must have gone through my hands. We were both right there going for it. I heard the crowd going wild, and I was like, 'Man, he caught it.' I thought I at least knocked it down. I was asking people on the sidelines what happened."

The Greene score breathed life into the Mountaineers, and two minutes later, Thompkins recovered Hoffart's fumble at the WVU 37. Hoffart's miscue set up Taylor's game-tying 34-yard field goal with 1:19 left. Both teams still had a chance to win it in regulation. Pitt was forced to punt the ball back to West Virginia, and the Mountaineers had two cracks from the Panther 45 with 12 seconds remaining to get into field goal range. Both Bulger passes to Greene fell incomplete.

THE GREENE SCORE BREATHED LIFE INTO THE MOUNTAINEERS.

A year earlier, this game would have ended in a tie, but a new overtime rule had been adopted in 1997, making this the first overtime game in Mountaineer Field history. The Mountaineers' first opportunity to unknot the score was unsuccessful, with Taylor's 37-yard field goal try sailing left of the goal post. Pitt's attempt to win on its possession was denied, too, when Jerry Porter got a piece of Chris Ferencik's 41-yard field goal try.

Both teams' possessions in the second overtime ended with turnovers. WVU safety David Lightcap stepped in front of Gonzalez's pass in the end zone for an interception. On the WVU side, Zereoue fumbled, allowing the Panthers to get the ball. "We had the game won," said Zereoue later. "The ball was in my hands, I fumbled and we lost. Big players make big plays and I didn't make the big play this time."

West Virginia took its first and only lead of the game in the third overtime, when Taylor booted a career long 52-yard field goal – the drive had actually traveled 10 yards backward. Then Pitt took over at the Mountaineer 25. West's first-down run gained 3 to the 22; Gonzalez's second down pass to Hoffart fell incomplete; and on third down, Ryan Brady was able to get Gonzalez to the ground for a 10-yard sack back to the 32, setting up a fourth and 17. Harris called timeout and came back with a pass play the Panthers had called several times throughout the game, a deep square-in to Jake Hoffart. Gonzalez was able to escape pressure from the outside, stepped up, and hit Hoffart for 20 yards right in front of WVU safety Gary Thompkins.

"We thought we knew what they would do, and they did it," explained Nehlen. "Our kid just didn't get the job done. As soon as the Pitt kid caught the ball, our kid tackles him. If he had just lined up where he was supposed to be, it would have been an interception.

"We played 'Cover 2' and we played 'hole,' which means we stacked the safeties, which means on the drawing board they can't do what they did," Nehlen said. "With 17 yards to go, you figure they're not going to throw an out. That's just a little too far and they don't have quite the time, so you figure they're going to try to get it between the zones."

"[West Virginia] was in a coverage that should have been a single safety robbing the crossing area, along with the deep safety," Harris later told author Sam Sciullo, Jr. "What happened was they busted; both guys went deep. There was nobody right there. Jake Hoffart beat his man and Pete made the throw."

"Had they done something else, then we wouldn't have felt so bad," added Nehlen.

Two plays after the fourth down conversion, Gonzalez found Murphy for a 12-yard touchdown to win the game, 41-38.

Gonzalez finished the game completing 22-of-34 passes for 273 yards and five touchdowns. Hoffart caught nine passes for 124 yards, while Murphy added six catches for 78 yards. West ran 22 times for 87 yards and a touchdown, and Pitt finished the game with 436 yards of offense.

For West Virginia, Bulger completed 26-of-43 passes for 348 yards and a touchdown; Greene caught a career-high 11 passes for 205 yards and Zereoue finished with a career-best 41 carries for 151 yards and three scores. The Mountaineers had 482 yards, giving the two teams a combined 918 yards of offense.

"It's tough to take, real tough," said linebacker Steve Lippe afterward. "It's not the Backyard Brawl stuff that makes the loss hurt; it's just that the seniors had never lost to them and we wanted to keep it that way."

"This is one of those games that even after the clock runs out, you can't forget about it," said cornerback Perlo Bastien. "This is unbelievable."

Tony Caridi was calling Mountaineer games on a full-time basis for the first time that year, and he recalled the feeling of disbelief that West Virginia had lost the game. "I remember I had to leave for San Juan, Puerto Rico to work a basketball tournament the

Mountaineers were in, and I remember twisting and turning in bed dreaming, 'Did this just happen? Did West Virginia actually lose the game?'"

Gonzalez, who had waited a long time to beat the Mountaineers, couldn't resist getting in a few digs against Pitt's rediscovered rivals. "I think Zamos, or whatever, 'Famous Zamos' – he said something in the paper about this isn't a brawl when you're beating somebody all the time, or something," said Gonzalez, clearly knowing Zereoue's name but also clearly not caring that he was mispronouncing it. "Well, I think we just made it a brawl."

Yes, they did.

Collins Steals the Show

WVU	PITT
24	17
Nov. 30, 2002 Pittsburgh	

"Hold the rope." That was the slogan West Virginia Coach Rich Rodriguez came up with for the 2002 football season. The one he used in 2001 – "Play like your hair is on fire" – flamed out in the second quarter of the season opener against Boston College, a depressing 34-10 loss. Four straight defeats to Maryland, Virginia Tech, Notre Dame and Miami, and another three-game losing streak to Syracuse, Temple and Pitt, left Rodriguez's first season in smoldering ruins. For those expecting big things right away from the 38-year-old Rodriguez, it was a splash of cold water in the face.

When, after a 31-27 loss to Syracuse, Don Nehlen had made the surprising announcement that the 2000 season would be his last at West Virginia, attention immediately turned to Rodriguez, whose offenses he'd led under Coach Tommy Bowden had rewritten the record books at Tulane and Clemson.

Rodriguez was a highly sought-after assistant who turned down at least four solid job offers from other major schools, including a fairly public courting by Texas Tech in 1999. "The Texas Tech decision was the most difficult professional decision I've ever made in my life," Rodriguez said in 2000. "I didn't sleep for a couple weeks after that thing."

When Nehlen announced he was done after his 21st season at WVU, Director of Athletics Ed Pastilong and President David C. Hardesty's chief of staff David Satterfield went undercover and quickly zeroed in on Rodriguez, meeting with him on three separate occasions, including a trip to his home in Clemson, S.C. The pair had also met with Tennessee Titans assistant head coach George Henshaw and former Auburn coach (and ABC football analyst) Terry Bowden at the Pittsburgh airport. Rodriguez, though, was always their No. 1 target.

"When Coach Nehlen's resignation took place, quite frankly, I called Rich Rodriguez. He was my first call. I asked if he was interested; he said he very much was," Pastilong told *Charleston Gazette* sports editor Mitch Vingle in 2000. After word began to leak that Rodriguez was going to take the job, a day before West Virginia's 38-28 loss to Pitt, a Monday afternoon press conference was eventually arranged at the Milan Puskar Center. The announcement was a huge pick-me-up for Mountaineer Nation, still smarting from Pitt QB Kevan Barlow's 272-yard, four-touchdown decimation of the WVU defense up at Three Rivers Stadium.

Rodriguez, wearing a plaid sport coat, a patterned tie and dark pants, walked into a crowded room holding the hand of his wife Rita. With them were their two small children, Raquel and Rhett, in the arms of Rodriguez's parents Arleen and Vince. Four-year-old Raquel became so enamored with what her daddy was saying that she fell asleep shortly after his press conference began. What Rodriguez had to say, and what he was planning to do with the Mountaineer football program, was the complete opposite of what West Virginia fans had grown accustomed to under Nehlen. For the first time since Bobby Bowden in the mid-1970s, WVU had a coach who planned to make offensive football the centerpiece of his program. And like Bowden, Rodriguez had a southern, down-home, country-style way of talking that entertained people. He talked about becoming the youngest head football coach in the country, at age 24, and then a year later, when Salem College dropped its football program, becoming the youngest fired head football coach, at age 25. He also discussed what happened two years later, when he became the head coach at Glenville State, describing the impossible job of convincing players to attend the small West Virginia Conference school.

"We used to bring recruits in at night and have them sleep in the car on the way," Rodriguez said. "When they woke up the next day, they were in Glenville, and they looked around and wondered why there was nobody around. We told them it was spring break. They said 'Coach, it's January.' We said, 'Yeah, isn't that great. We have five spring breaks!'"

Rodriguez really had them laughing when he told the story about his freshman quarterback, "Freddie," who only got into the game as a last resort when the starting quarterback and the backup both went down with injuries. Freddie's job was to run three safe plays so the team could punt. "We were on our own 3, so I told him to run three quarterback sneaks," Rodriguez said. "The first sneak gained about 35 yards; the next one about the same thing. The third time he ran that sneak he got to about their 3.

"We were screaming and yelling from the sidelines to get Freddie's attention, but he just waved us off and said, 'I know, Coach, I know.' Well, damned if he doesn't line up in the shotgun, take the snap from center and punt the ball through the end zone right out of the stadium.

"I was mad, man, was I mad. I screamed at Freddie, 'What were you thinking?' He just looked at me kind of strangely and said, 'I'm thinking I've got the dumbest coach in America.'"

Mountaineer fans loved it. And while everyone loved his stories, it took some of them a little longer to be convinced that Rodriguez was the right guy to be wearing the headset for the Mountaineers. Most of the players he inherited were more suited for Nehlen's style of play, and the defense he chose to run under veteran defensive coordinator Phil Elmassian was downright awful. The Mountaineers led the country in pass defense that year, but only because teams would have been foolish to do anything other than run the ball against West Virginia. Six of 11 opponents gained more than 200 yards on the ground against the Mountaineers, with BC running for 325 yards in the opener and Notre Dame later gouging the WVU defense for 345 yards. In fact, WVU's run-stopping unit was so bad that free safety Rick Sherrod led the country in tackles, with an average of 15.6 per game.

Elmassian had a spectacular résumé and his most recent stop at LSU had been a successful one, but he had a difficult time at WVU. His attacking eight-man fronts just didn't suit the defensive personnel in the Mountaineer program at the time. So Rodriguez cut ties with Elmassian after one year and promoted Todd Graham and Jeff Casteel to co-defensive coordinators; Graham handled the defensive calls and the schemes while Casteel oversaw the personnel and scouting.

Rodriguez instructed them to go down to South Carolina to learn the 3-3 stack defense, which had given him fits when he had prepared to face it as Clemson's offensive coordinator. The 3-3 stack is basically a 3-4 defense with an extra defensive back that can walk up to the line of scrimmage to play the run, or back off and help in the passing game. Not only is it unorthodox and difficult to prepare for, but it also doesn't require many defensive tackles, which Rodriguez felt were difficult to recruit at West Virginia.

"We never had any problems [with the dual role] that year," said Casteel. "The thing was every week we were still finding our way with our kids in the odd front. We were really concerned with all of the coaches we were facing in the Big East at that time: Paul Pasqualoni was at Syracuse, Frank Beamer at Virginia Tech, Butch Davis at Miami – there were just so many good coaches in that league, and we were like, 'Geez, what are they going to do to us next?'"

Rodriguez also tinkered with his spread offense, changing from a 50-50 run-pass philosophy in 2001 to a more heavily run-oriented attack in 2002. He had two outstanding tailbacks in Avon Cobourne and Quincy Wilson, and instead of alternating them, he decided to play them both at the same time. Rodriguez had a nimble quarterback in Rasheed Marshall, who got more playing time late in the 2001 season after recovering from a broken wrist in the opener against Boston College. "With my running ability, they basically said they were going to make this thing work on the ground," Marshall recalled. "Then we're going to go over top [of] people off of that."

Marshall believed the offense could have been more effective in 2001 had they had more time to get used to Rodriguez's unique system. "We knew we could have been better in '01, but it was the whole installation and getting comfortable with the offense and everything he was trying to do that first year. I think that delayed the process."

It also didn't help that regular quarterback Brad Lewis was more suited to run the traditional offense that Nehlen had used in 2000. His five touchdown passes in the 2000 Music City Bowl were the most ever thrown by a Mountaineer quarterback in a bowl game at the time, and his 308 yards passing against Ole Miss in that game included 216 in the first half on only seven completions. "You need a guy who is athletic, can improvise and can kind of make plays on the run and make things out of nothing," Marshall explained. "It starts with the quarterback in this offense. If you don't have a guy that can do those things, the offense is going to be more limited because he is not going to be able to do the things that [Rodriguez] wants him to do out of different sets. Certain things set up other things, and you need a guy who can do it all."

The first key moment of the 2002 season came on the road at Cincinnati in mid-September. The Mountaineers were not a very good road team in 2001, losing all five away games by an average of nearly 20 points per game, and the team was taking a seven-game road losing streak into the Queen City. West Virginia's offense churned out 523 yards, including 334 on the ground, but the Mountaineers needed a missed 49-yard field goal by Jonathan Ruffin on the final play of the game to escape with a 35-32 victory. Another key road tilt came in the next month, at Rutgers, when West Virginia blanked the Scarlet Knights 40-0 a week after getting blown out by Maryland, 48-17. It was the first shutout victory in five years for a beleaguered defense that was beginning to show signs of improvement. The defense only permitted a third-quarter touchdown and 242 yards of offense the following week against Syracuse, and in early November, they limited a nine-win Boston College team to just two touchdowns in a 24-14 Mountaineer victory. The BC triumph set up a pair of season-ending road finales against 12th-ranked Virginia Tech and 17th-ranked Pitt.

In the Tech game, the defense came up with two huge fourth-quarter goal line stands, and the offense produced 263 yards on the ground against Tech's nationally ranked defense, pulling out a 21-18 victory. It was West Virginia's first win over a ranked team in four years, and its first on the road against a ranked team since 1993. This win had set up the most meaningful Backyard Brawl since 1982. The Panthers were enjoying their best season in more than a decade, and their three losses heading into the West Virginia game were by margins of only 2 points against Texas A&M, 8 points against Notre Dame and just 7 points against Miami. Pitt had one of the most dynamic offensive weapons in the country in wide receiver Larry Fitzgerald, but the Panthers' calling card in 2002 was a smothering defense that was ranked among the nation's Top 20 in total yards and scoring. Only No. 1-ranked Miami was able to score more than 25 points against Pitt's defense, in a 28-21 Hurricane victory that the Panther players felt Pittsburgh should have won. Pitt captured the prior two games against West Virginia, in Pittsburgh in 2000 and in Morgantown in 2001 – the 6-point win in 2001 was decided by a 27-yard touchdown catch by Antonio Bryant, who finished the game with 11 grabs for 186 yards. Bryant had had added motivation to do well against the Mountaineers after hearing the trash-talking coming from West Virginia's Richard Bryant. "During that week, he said he would be the best Bryant on the field," Marshall recalled.

THIS WIN HAD SET UP THE MOST MEANINGFUL BACKYARD BRAWL SINCE 1982.

Marshall said that the following year, in 2002, Rodriguez issued a gag order for the players in the days leading up to the Pitt game. "At that time, we had been on a roll and we just wanted to keep it up and take the humble approach, as always, and go up there and do what we needed to do."

Rodriguez was especially concerned about his sophomore quarterback, who was returning home to play in front of friends and family for the first time as a college player. Marshall was also facing the quarterback (Pitt's Rod Rutherford) who had gotten the best of him every time they played each other in high school. "I don't even remember the scores," Marshall said. "I just know it was bad."

Marshall remembered some of the Pitt defensive players snickering and talking trash when he entered the game as a freshman in 2001. "Brad ended up getting hurt, and I knew I was going to get into the game, and they were like, 'Oh yeah, bring on Brashear (Marshall had faced some of them while playing at Brashear High School in Pittsburgh) and all that trash talk stuff," Marshall said. "I was hyped up. I had a bunch of family there and a bunch of friends."

West Virginia got back into the national rankings, at No. 24, after the Virginia Tech win. With Pitt at No. 17, it marked the first time in 12 years that both teams were nationally ranked when they met. It showed at the box office. Pitt had its first sellout ever at Heinz Field: with an extra 2,000 bleacher seats added underneath the scoreboard to accommodate the overflow crowd, attendance was announced at 66,731, marking the biggest crowd in modern Panther sports history. Even when Pitt was doing well under Johnny Majors and Jackie Sherrill in the 1970s, Pitt rarely drew big crowds unless it was playing West Virginia, Penn State or Notre Dame. Pitt athletic director Steve Pederson announced that extra security would be added to combat unruly behavior. "I have no reason to believe our fans won't react in a great fashion," Pederson said. "We just don't want anything to mar this event."

Pitt scored on its opening possession to take a 7-0 lead, marching 63 yards in just six plays, with Rutherford finding Fitzgerald behind the WVU defense for a 32-yard touchdown. West Virginia answered Pitt's score by moving the ball into Panther territory, where Todd James booted a career-long 42-yard field goal to reduce Pitt's lead to 7-3 with 7:06 left in the first quarter. Later in the quarter, WVU took its first lead of the game when Marshall directed a nine-play, 66-yard drive that ended in the end zone. Marshall called his own number to score.

"It was one of our normal plays that we could run in any situation," said Marshall of his 19-yard touchdown gallop. "Closer to the red zone is when Coach Rod always liked to run, because if I got 10 yards like that, there was a possibility that I could get into the end zone. It's one guy to beat and the linebacker is sitting there, and I was in the secondary like that, and [Pitt DB] Torrie Cox was running over and he got a good lick on me, and I think I fell into the end zone."

Pitt kicker David Abdul knotted the score at 10 with a 33-yard field goal on Pitt's first possession of the second quarter. Then, an Angel Estrada interception at the WVU 26 late in the quarter not only killed a Pitt scoring opportunity, but also set the stage for West Virginia's 64-yard scoring march. Marshall showed his versatility on the drive, running once for a short gain, hooking up with Phil Braxton for 29 yards, and then catching a 25-yard pass from backup quarterback Danny Embick on a reverse pass.

"We'd been talking about it all week," Embick said after the game. "We weren't sure if we'd use it. I'd made a few warm-up throws before I went in."

While signaling a play, Rodriguez had Embick enter the field when the offensive players were near West Virginia's sideline. "My objective was to sneak onto the field without them noticing," Embick said. Marshall took the snap and handed the ball off to Embick, who ran to Marshall's right on a reverse. Then Rasheed drifted down the left sideline away from the pursuit. "It opened up really nice," Embick said. Marshall was dragged down at the Pitt 9, setting up Cobourne's 2-yard touchdown run – Cobourne ran into the middle of the Pitt defense and appeared to be stopped short of the goal line. But he kept his legs moving, doing a pirouette to his right and sneaking into the end zone standing up.

"He finished all of the runs," said Pitt coach Walt Harris of Cobourne's 104-yard rushing performance. Cobourne's TD gave West Virginia the 17-10 lead it enjoyed at halftime.

Early in the third quarter, when it appeared that Pitt was poised to tie, West Virginia's 200-pound middle linebacker Ben Collins was able to come up with a big fumble recovery at the West Virginia 16. Rutherford had attempted an option pitch toward Pitt tailback Brandon Miree, but the ball struck fullback Lousaka Polite's head and fell to the ground, where Collins dug through the pile to come up with the football. "I got chop-blocked by a guard," Collins said. "When I got up, the ball was bouncing around. I just got on it and got it away from two guys."

Casteel said he was shocked to learn at the end of the season just how small Collins was. "We used to weigh them in on Monday in the weight room, and he would put five-pound weights in his pocket just so he could weigh in at 205 or 210," said Casteel. "We were thinking he was about 210, and I think he told me later that he was 194 or 195 pounds the week of that game."

"Here is Ben Collins from North Marion High School, and here you are thinking about that and then looking at the other guys on the other side that he's playing against," recalled Tony Caridi. "It's like going to the Greenbrier and seeing all these guys pulling up in their Maseratis, and here comes old Ben driving up in his Impala."

Three plays after Collins's fumble recovery, Marshall found Phil Braxton open for a 79-yard touchdown on a third-and-5 play from the 21. Marshall was able to elude pressure from Pitt defensive end Claude Harriott by faking a pass, giving him enough time to locate Braxton streaking down the field. "It was one of our main play-action plays off of that zone [play]," Marshall explained. "Earlier in the game, something happened where I'm not sure if I got on the edge and one of their guys got to me, but I kept thinking to myself, 'If we come back with that same play . . .' I guess it was the way their guys were aligned."

Marshall knew if he could get past the defensive end he might be able to produce a big play. "As the play developed, I saw the guy sitting out there, and I had [tight end] Tory Johnson dragging across," Marshall said. "When I pulled up, I was actually about to throw it to Tory, and for whatever reason, I pulled it back down and kept going to the sidelines, and I saw Phil streaking with his hand up waving to me."

Braxton was the last option on the play. "It was almost like a long drag," Marshall said. "Normally it happens so fast that you won't even get a chance to hit that play, but with the pump fake buying more time, I was able to let him come open."

"The Braxton play was the kind of play we needed to win the game in the conditions that we were playing in," said Caridi. "Here is Phil Braxton from Uniontown and he is making the big play to beat Pitt."

Braxton caught the football at the Pitt 44 and beat Cox to the end zone for West Virginia's longest scoring play of the year. More importantly, it gave the Mountaineers a two-touchdown advantage with 6:55 remaining in the third quarter. At that start of the fourth quarter, the Panther offense finally quit shooting itself in the foot and got its act together, with Rutherford and Fitzgerald connecting for a 25-yard touchdown. The TD was set up by an 8-yard James punt that gave the Panthers possession of the football at midfield.

Minutes later, Pitt could have had the ball right back in good field position when Mark Fazzolari's short punt struck Pitt's Josh Lay near the Panther 40, but Ben Collins was there to jump on the football once again. West Virginia couldn't do anything with Pitt's fourth turnover, although it did manage to burn some precious time off of the clock. After exchanging possessions, Pitt took over at the 7 and marched deep into Mountaineer territory. Facing a third and 13 at the West Virginia 14, Rutherford appeared to have Fitzgerald open in the end zone for their third TD connection. But Rutherford's pass was a little beyond Fitzgerald and he wasn't able to hold onto it for the tying score. It wouldn't have been an easy catch, but it was one college football's top receiver was certainly capable of making. "On the last play thrown to me, there was no excuse," Fitzgerald said after the game. "It hit me in the hands and I did not make the play."

"They would get down to the red zone and they would just throw jump balls [to Fitzgerald], and I don't know if anybody defended that until our guys did," said Casteel. "We would double up and he never got one on us. I don't think he ever got one on us down in the red zone the whole time he played against us. He got them down the field, but as soon as they would get down inside the 15, they would put him on the single receiver side and go one on one with your corner."

Rutherford's fourth-down pass intended for tight end Kris Wilson was knocked down by Collins in the back of the end zone. "I could have tried to catch it, but I was kind of off-balance," Collins explained. "I didn't want to tip it into the air, so I just batted it straight down to the ground."

Marshall came back onto the field to take a knee and run off the remaining 12 seconds before the West Virginia players ran onto the field in celebration. "To completely turn it around in one year with some new starters and a first-year quarterback starting would have been on the high end of the optimism scale – peaking the limit," said Rodriguez after the game.

"That was a great game, and Walt Harris was, and still is, a good football coach," added Casteel. "One of the things Walt did, and [that] we still work on to this day, is he would get into a lot of unbalanced sets and then [run] the ball back weak on us. Whenever we start practice, the third day is always working on the unbalanced set, weakside run because of that."

Watching it all unfold from the press box was athletic director Ed Pastilong. It was Pastilong who chose to add another year to Rodriguez's initial deal after his 3-8 season, and the AD took considerable heat for doing so.

"I thought we had a chance to be on the plus side this year, record-wise, and go to a bowl," Pastilong said. "Get six wins, maybe get into the seven range, and then even eight. But getting nine wins was icing on the cake." Pastilong knew Rodriguez had all of the qualities necessary to become an outstanding college football coach. "He's smart. He works hard. He relates to the players," Pastilong said. "He has compassion. He keeps up with the game."

At the time, Pastilong also recalled that first meeting with Rodriguez before hiring him to replace Don Nehlen. "When we sat down with him, we figured to talk about an hour," Pastilong said. "One hour led to two and two to three. Every subject that was brought up, he had a plan for it. And he gave a great explanation about how he'd handle the situation."

"That was when Rich's program was really starting to pick up momentum and began to roll," remembered Caridi.

Indeed, the Rich Rodriguez era of Mountaineer football had officially begun.

Miracle in the Mountains

PITT
13
WVU
9
Dec. 1, 2007
Morgantown, W.Va.

The conspiracy theories were running wild in West Virginia, as they naturally would when a 28-1/2-point favorite loses to its biggest rival in a game that would have put the Mountaineers into the national championship contest. Who could have ever imagined West Virginia losing to Pitt in the Backyard Brawl after the way, the week before, WVU had completely dismantled 20th-ranked UConn 66-21 to lock up the Big East title?

One of the more popular and off-the-wall theories going around the Mountain State had Rich Rodriguez sandbagging the Pitt game because he already had the Michigan job in his hip pocket. Well, anyone who saw Rodriguez after the Pitt loss or watched his post-game press conference knew how distraught he was, and could tell just how ridiculous those theories were.

This one was easy to explain – West Virginia simply got whipped up front by Pitt's Joe Clermond, Greg Romeus, Scott McKillop, Mick Williams, John Malecki, Rashaad Duncan and Tommie Duhart, and the game film clearly showed that. In fact, Panther defensive coordinator Paul Rhoads was so thrilled with the way his players performed that he agreed to sit down with *Pittsburgh Tribune-Review* columnist Joe Starkey the following week to review the game tape. After all, Pitt had nothing else to do, having finished its season with a 5-7 record. According to Starkey and Rhoads, instead of WVU "playing its worst offensive game in years" (words Rodriguez used after the game), it was more a matter of the Pitt defense dominating the line of scrimmage and playing near-flawless football. Rhoads said Pitt's defensive players missed two tackles the entire game. Two. Pitt decided to blitz West Virginia more than usual, and to disguise its defenses until the last possible moment, making it more difficult for the Mountaineers to change their plays from the coaches' box. Rhoads jumped all over his defense during its walkthrough the day before the game after a couple of players went the wrong way on a blitz. "I had the kids turn around," Rhoads told Starkey. "There was nothing back there but turf, and I said, 'Understand everybody's responsibility. If we don't get it done, the back judge isn't going to tackle anybody.'"

One play Rhoads was particularly concerned about was West Virginia's bubble screen; Rhoads wasn't worried so much about quarterback Pat White passing the football, but rather about the threat he posed running it when the linebackers had vacated the middle of the field to help with the pass receivers. Time and again in 2005 and

2006, White burned the Panthers on that particular play, so Rhoads decided to send blitzers at White whenever he felt that play was coming – a very risky proposition, to be sure, because if they missed, White had nothing but open field in front of him. "We ran one and only one defense the whole second half," McKillop told Starkey in 2011. "I don't know if that fact is out there. I guess I'll spill the beans. We had one adjustment based on where the running back lined up. I was thinking, 'Are they ever going to pick up on this?'"

Earlier that season against Navy's option offense, Pitt had had a miserable time trying to stop the Midshipmen, with Navy running all over the Panthers for 331 yards in a 48-45 double-overtime victory at Heinz Field. And Pitt's defensive performances against West Virginia in their two previous games were just as bad.

In 2006, the Panthers chose to shadow running back Steve Slaton with their fastest defensive player, high school sprint champion Tommie Campbell. Campbell was an awful shadow, chasing Slaton all night but never catching him. Slaton and White each ran for more than 200 yards, becoming only the third duo in NCAA history to accomplish that feat. In fact, White had so much fun during West Virginia's 45-27 romp over Pitt that he would meow on the bench whenever the Panther growl was put on the public address system; he was caught in the act by an ESPN cameraman, and the clip eventually found its way onto YouTube, where Pitt players undoubtedly watched it.

PAT WHITE WOULD MEOW ON THE BENCH WHENEVER THE PANTHER GROWL WAS PUT ON THE PUBLIC ADDRESS SYSTEM.

White and Slaton had come to West Virginia under somewhat similar circumstances. White verbally committed to LSU, but he soon changed his mind when he wasn't certain that the Tigers were as committed to him playing quarterback as he was. Slaton first chose Maryland but then found out from a reporter that the Terps had rescinded his scholarship offer after receiving commitments from other running back recruits. "I committed; I was already there," Slaton said in 2006. "Upcoming program. They were pretty close to home. I liked my family coming to games, and that was a pretty big reason to go there."

Slaton said Maryland asked him if he wanted to try defensive back, as did Boston College, but his heart was set on playing running back in college. Rodriguez had no problem with that. "I liked him from the first two minutes I saw him on film – everybody else looked like they were going in slow motion," Rodriguez said. "I certainly never wavered."

For Rodriguez, it was love at first sight when he saw White, too. "I saw tape on him, and I thought, 'Man, this guy is perfect for what we do,'" Rodriguez recalled. After White signed with West Virginia, Rodriguez still had one more obstacle to overcome to get him on campus – professional baseball. White was drafted as a center fielder in the fourth round by the Los Angeles Angels, and he was given second-round money ($400,000) because the Angels did not have many high draft picks ahead of him. Rodriguez flew down to White's home in Daphne, Ala., and was able to convince White and his family that a college scholarship to West Virginia University was more valuable to him than a professional baseball contract.

Slaton barely weighed 180 pounds when he arrived at WVU, and he initially took a back seat to high school All-American running back Jason Gwaltney, who had made his announcement to attend West Virginia on national television. Naturally, Gwaltney got most of the attention when the two arrived in 2005, but it was Slaton who distinguished himself in games against Virginia Tech and Rutgers. Slaton then scored six touchdowns in West Virginia's three-overtime victory over Louisville, securing himself a place in the starting lineup.

White also came of age against Louisville. He had been sharing the quarterbacking duties with Adam Bednarik, but he assumed full control of the offense after he brought the Mountaineers back from 17 points down in the fourth quarter to defeat the Cardinals. The duo then led West Virginia to consecutive victories over Connecticut, Cincinnati, Pitt and South Florida, before stunning Georgia 38-35 in the 2006 Nokia Sugar Bowl, where Slaton ran for a Sugar Bowl record 204 yards, scoring on runs of 52, 18 and 52 yards.

In 2006, the White-Slaton tandem gave West Virginia its best one-two offensive punch in school history. Slaton finished fourth in Heisman Trophy voting after rushing for a school-record 1,744 yards and scoring 16 touchdowns. White accounted for more than 2,800 all-purpose yards and 30 touchdowns as a dual-threat quarterback, becoming the first player in school history to run and throw for more than 1,000 yards in the same season. The pair led West Virginia to back-to-back top 10 finishes in 2005 and 2006, and they seemingly had the Mountaineers headed on a run to the BCS title game in the fall of 2007.

As poorly as West Virginia played against the Panthers in the 2007 debacle, it still had plenty of chances to win the game – but two early missed field goals and three fumbles put the Mountaineers in a bind. Plus, White missed most of the second and third quarters with a thumb injury, and a much-bulkier Slaton just didn't have the same burst he had as a sophomore in 2006. Tacklers Slaton had easily run past in his first two seasons at WVU were getting him to the ground in 2007.

Momentum turned in Pitt's favor at the beginning of the third quarter when Vaughn Rivers coughed up the football during his kickoff return, giving it to the Panthers at the WVU 48. A third down Pat Bostick-to-Oderick Turner pass netted 18 yards to the Mountaineer 17, and four plays later, Bostick sneaked into the end zone for a 1-yard touchdown, giving Pitt a 10-7 lead. Although the Panthers failed to score on their second drive of the third quarter (Conor Lee missed on a 35-yard field goal try), Pitt's running game, behind freshman LeSean McCoy, chewed up the clock and kept West Virginia's offense off the field.

"The thing that really got overlooked, especially at Pitt at that time, was the offensive line they had," said West Virginia defensive coordinator Jeff Casteel. "I think three of those kids, and maybe even four, went on to play in the NFL. When you have an NFL tailback and three or four NFL offensive linemen, they were tough to stop."

"They were pretty one-dimensional, and we did a good enough job of stopping them, but not what we needed to do," added defensive line coach Bill Kirelawich. "We needed to shut them down and we didn't."

With 6:17 left in the game, Pitt capitalized on backup quarterback Jarrett Brown's fumble at the West Virginia 17, extending its lead to 13-7 on Lee's 18-yard field goal. Then, White returned to the game and had great field position to work with after Noel Devine took David Brytus's kickoff 48 yards to the Pitt 33. But the Mountaineers couldn't convert a fourth and 2 at the Pitt 26, when Scott McKillop pulled Slaton down a yard short of the sticks with 4:05 remaining. Had Slaton been able to break free, it was a sure touchdown.

With less than three minutes remaining, the Mountaineers once again got deep into Pitt territory, with White hooking up with Darius Reynaud on a bubble screen for 20 yards and taking West Virginia to the Pitt 33. Then White scrambled for 12 more, to the Pitt 21, but once again Pitt's defense held by forcing a pair of incomplete passes, a White sack for minus-7 yards, and another incomplete pass, which turned the ball back over to the Panthers on downs.

Rhoads called all-out blitzes on the final two plays to keep White from getting time to throw, and on the fourth-down play, the Pitt defensive coordinator had 5-foot-8 corner Jovani Chappel walk off West Virginia's 6-foot-8 receiver Wes Lyons to prevent West Virginia from completing a quick fade for first down yardage. When Chappel stepped back, White was forced to wait, allowing the Pitt pressure to get to him. His pass sailed out of the end zone and landed harmlessly on the ground.

With West Virginia out of timeouts and Pitt facing a fourth and 9 from its own 15, West Virginia watched Panther coach Dave Wannstedt opt to run out the clock and take the safety, making the final score 13-9.

"I remember walking off the field two years ago at halftime saying that we needed to run faster," Wannstedt said after the game, referencing an embarrassing halftime interview on national television, when he had tried to explain why his defense couldn't stop the Mountaineers. "Today we ran faster."

Meanwhile, Rodriguez looked like a broken man when he walked to the podium and addressed the media after the game, his words barely audible above the shouting and the celebrating going on in the Pitt locker room behind him. In 2011, McKillop recalled watching Rodriguez's tortured press conference on YouTube.

"You can hear us in the background," McKillop said. "We had no intentions of making the noise heard in Rich Rod's news conference. You can see it bothers him a little bit. If we would have known, I'm sure we would have been 10 times louder."

When Rodriguez was finally ready to speak, he exhaled deeply, wiped his face with a towel that was draped over his shoulder, and tried to remain composed. "Certainly, it was just off all day offensively . . . just off," he said.

"Just off," he repeated.

"It was tough on him," said Casteel. "He got physically ill right after the game. When you work that hard to get to that moment, and you're that close and it slips through your hands, it's tough. That's not only what Rich went through – that's what everybody went through who was involved with West Virginia football that night."

"When something like that happens, you have your own personal misery you go through," said Kirelawich. "Each guy suffers individually. It was one of those things where everybody takes a little bit of the blame."

Wannstedt, recalling the game two years later, in 2009, thought the victory had injected life into his young program. "We had so many recruits that were right on the bubble," he said. "It gave us an opportunity to get one more shot at these guys and say to them] that it will happen, and believe in us. I think it was energizing to our players. I'm sure just for our fans it was a shot in the arm, a little bit of hope – 'Hey, let's hang in there, this is a positive thing.' Let's try to focus on the positives and go forward."

Pitt was able to land several Western Pa. recruits on the basis of that victory, with some even switching sides right after the game. "I remember going out there for pregame warm-ups and the recruits were all lined up on the sidelines, and I looked over and could see all these kids that we were recruiting and they were recruiting," Wannstedt said. "Within 10-14 days [after the game] we got eight commitments. Two or three of those kids that were right there [on West Virginia's sideline] committed with us."

"I like to reiterate the fact that we basically ruined their whole entire college career," McKillop said. "Nothing brings me more pleasure than when I say, '13-9.' The face they give me is just priceless."

"Even now as I sit here, I still think Pat White is going to score one on them," added Casteel. "Pat White always got it done. I really thought until the very end that we would make a play and win it."

Casteel thought the defense missed a big chance to set the tone early in the game, when the Mountaineers couldn't cash in on an early interception. "I think we could have run that back for a score if we would have done a better job of blocking," he said. "We didn't get any points off that, and I think we would have probably got after them if we would have gone down and put some points on the board early, especially off a turnover."

Michigan started the 2007 college football campaign by falling to Appalachian State in a stunning season-opening loss, and four-touchdown favorite West Virginia ended it with an equally stunning defeat at the hands of Pitt. Those two upset losses would bring the two schools together in a way nobody in the Mountain State could have ever imagined.

If a straw poll had been conducted in the fall of 2007 to determine the most popular West Virginian, Rich Rodriguez would have won it, hands down. In fact, Rich Rod was so popular that he probably could have finished second and third in the same poll. In less than a year, Rodriguez's Mountaineers first upset Georgia in the Sugar Bowl to save the Big East football conference (commissioner Mike Tranghese said as much after the game), and then, 11 months later, Rodriguez turned down an offer to coach the Alabama Crimson Tide to remain at his alma mater.

When it became apparent that Rodriguez was Alabama's No. 1 target – Rodriguez and his wife Rita had a very public meeting with Alabama athletic director Mal Moore in New York City before the College Football Hall of Fame induction banquet – West Virginia boosters quickly mobilized to try and sweeten the pot to keep their coach in Morgantown. What came out of those efforts was another substantial raise for Rodriguez, bringing his total compensation to approximately $1.75 million per year. Promises were also made to fund facility improvements and other things he wanted done for the football program.

Just nine months earlier, after his Sugar Bowl victory, Rodriguez had renegotiated his contract to become the first coach in state history to earn more than $1 million per year, with $50,000 raises guaranteed over the next seven years. He was also guaranteed another $600,000 in deferred money if he remained West Virginia's football coach through the 2011 season. The negotiations were sometimes difficult, and when the deal was finally struck, Rodriguez didn't want the terms announced until he was in his car, headed to the beach on his family vacation. When the second agreement was made six months later, Rodriguez this time called a press conference to announce the deal after he had informed the team that he was staying. "Obviously I'm very excited to stay here, and I plan on being here a long time," Rodriguez told a jam-packed team meeting room. "There weren't many reasons to go. It's all about the reasons for staying. I'm biased, this is my school. I think it's a great place to raise a family."

However, by the fall of 2007, Rodriguez was once again unhappy with the support he felt he was getting from WVU. But he was still able to cast that aside, leading West Virginia to the brink of the national championship game. The Mountaineers were rolling along, with wins over Western Michigan, Marshall, Maryland, East Carolina, Syracuse, Mississippi State, Rutgers, Louisville, Cincinnati and Connecticut as they headed into the season finale. West Virginia's lone blemish headed into the Pitt game was a turnover-plagued 21-13 loss at South Florida, when White had missed a portion of the game with a deep thigh bruise. After a 66-21 decapitation of Connecticut, a team that had been vying for a share of the Big East title, the Mountaineers moved up to No. 2 in the AP poll and, for the first time in school history, was ranked No. 1 in the ESPN/USA Today Coaches' Poll. Sitting comfortably at No. 2 in the BCS standings behind top-ranked Missouri, all West Virginia had to do was defeat the Panthers and the Mountaineers would be playing in the national title game. "There were three great teams in college football that year: Ohio State, Southern Cal and Oklahoma," said Kirelawich, who joined Rodriguez's Arizona coaching staff in 2012. "Nobody wanted to play Southern Cal or Oklahoma. You wanted to play Ohio State because they were the weakest of the three. So we lose to Pitt and we ended up playing Oklahoma in the Fiesta Bowl and I'm thinking to myself, 'We're going to get murdered.' You didn't want to play those guys."

Rodriguez was noticeably depressed after the Pitt loss, and he sounded somewhat disconsolate on a media teleconference announcing the matchup against the Sooners for the 2008 Tostitos Fiesta Bowl, to be played in Tempe, Ariz. Then, on December 14, less than two weeks after the Pitt defeat, Internet reports began to trickle out that

Rodriguez, his wife and their financial advisor were in Toledo, Ohio, meeting with Michigan athletic director Bill Martin and school president Mary Sue Coleman. By the time the plane that took Rodriguez and his wife to Toledo had returned to Morgantown's Hart Field early Friday evening, a coterie of photographers and TV reporters was waiting for them. He brushed aside their shouted questions. "I'm going to practice," he said.

The next morning, Rodriguez attended a scheduled Fiesta Bowl news conference in a renovated area of the Milan Puskar Center – a result of his most recent contract renegotiation. Workers were still doing their finishing work on the new academic center and stadium club area when Rodriguez walked in to take some questions from a couple dozen reporters. Immediately, the subject of Michigan came up. "It may be disappointing to you," Rodriguez began, "but I am not going to talk about any innuendos or rumors or jobs; what else is floating out there – not going to talk about it at all. I will talk about this year's team, the bowl game preparations, aspects of recruiting we're involved in right now – the other I don't want to talk about."

When asked another question about Michigan, Rodriguez threatened to leave the room. *The Charleston Gazette's* Dave Hickman, who covered Rodriguez when he was a high school quarterback at North Marion, brought the situation to a head by asking if he planned to coach in the bowl game. Rodriguez flashed an awkward smile, complimented Hickman for his clever question, and shortly after that ended the charade. It was clear to everyone there that Rodriguez was strongly considering an offer to coach the Wolverines. Still, most of the school's big-buck boosters who attended a West Virginia basketball game against Maryland-Baltimore County later that evening remained hopeful that another agreement could be reached with their football coach. But none could be made.

Morgantown that Sunday was gray and cold, with the wind blowing the snow in sideways as Rodriguez pulled his white Mercedes-Benz SUV into the Milan Puskar Center parking lot. In a separate car was his wife Rita. The team was scheduled to practice that afternoon before breaking for Christmas. Veteran sportswriter Bob Hertzel captured the scene: A fully decorated Christmas tree stood in the lobby, providing a pleasant diversion from the storm that was about to blow through the doors. Players were already assembled in the team meeting room when Rodriguez walked in to address them, but instead of wearing his normal coaching gear, he was decked out in trousers and a sweater, and instead of talking about the Oklahoma game, Rodriguez discussed the University of Michigan job he had recently been offered. Rodriguez told them he was taking it.

The emotional meeting lasted less than 10 minutes. Defensive tackle Keilen Dykes got up and walked out of the room, pulling a hooded sweatshirt over his head to protect him from the harsh winter elements outside. "This sucks," he blurted out to the reporters camped out in the lobby as he left the building. That was their confirmation that West Virginia was now searching for a new football coach.

Rodriguez went back into his office and closed the door. His wife was outside in the hallway, accepting congratulatory hugs from friends and family members, when his door reopened. Rodriguez came out, perhaps an hour or so after he had first arrived at the Puskar Center, and with an overnight bag hanging over one shoulder, Rodriguez left through a side entrance to get to his parked car. Staying behind to deliver Rodriguez's letter of resignation was his graduate assistant.

The end to the Rich Rodriguez era at West Virginia University was abrupt and unceremonious. Those supporting the coach were disappointed that more couldn't have been done to keep one of their own happy. Lawsuits and counter lawsuits were filed, the school wanting to ensure that Rodriguez fulfilled his contractual obligation to pay the $4 million buyout clause in his most recent agreement. Rodriguez argued in court that certain promises were not kept and that he didn't owe the money. Eventually, in the summer of 2008, a judge ruled that Rodriguez was required to pay the buyout, which he did with the help of the University of Michigan.

In between, emotions were raw and unfiltered. In all parts of the state, residents felt scorned and betrayed. Newspapers were filled with commentaries and guest commentaries like the one submitted to *The Herald-Dispatch* (Huntington) by Charleston attorney Jon Mani on December 23, 2007: "Rich Rod deals another blow to state's psyche."

"The thing that is most depressing about Rich Rod's departure from the program is that he was the premier emissary for the State of West Virginia," Mani wrote. "Other than perhaps long-time senators Robert Byrd and Jay Rockefeller, Rich Rod is arguably the most recognizable West Virginian on a nationwide basis. What does his departure say about the State (a State he professes to love?).

"His departure has not only set back the Mountaineer football program, but has dealt the people of West Virginia another crushing setback."

Wrote *Charleston Gazette* sports editor Mitch Vingle: "The Colts left Baltimore in the middle of the night. Bobby Petrino told Atlanta Falcon players he was leaving for Arkansas by leaving notes on their lockers. And Rich Rodriguez joined their ranks on Sunday."

U.S. Senator Jay Rockefeller, who was instrumental in the construction of the new football stadium while he was governor, called Rodriguez's decision to leave his team before the bowl game "amoral." Governor Joe Manchin, a lifelong friend of Rodriguez and a fellow Marion County native, issued a lengthy statement criticizing the "high-priced agents" who had turned "dreams into just another back-room business deal." Manchin challenged everyone to "start looking more closely at the system that we've allowed these agents to create, because in the end, it serves no one well but them."

In the months following Rodriguez's departure, it seemed that each week brought a new series of revelations. The Associated Press issued a Freedom of Information request seeking emails and relevant documents from the school pertaining to Rodriguez's departure; this led, in January, 2008, to the publishing of a monthly chronology of the deteriorating relationship between the school and its football coach. Cyberspace was full of anti-Rodriguez videos and ESPN's *Outside the Lines* television program devoted 10 minutes of one show to the backlash Rodriguez was receiving from upset West Virginia fans. Many WVU boosters and supporters, previously unknown to the general public, were being quoted and interviewed on an almost daily basis.

Even former WVU coach Don Nehlen innocently injected himself into the firestorm when he was candid with a Michigan reporter about the allure of coaching the Wolverines. "There are not many Michigans around," said Nehlen. "Naturally, I love West Virginia. I coached there for 21 years and stayed here, but I understand the mystique of Michigan. You talk about Michigan football . . . Let's be honest, that's as good as it gets."

Rodriguez would have a brief three-year coaching tenure at Michigan, with his 2010 Wolverine team winning seven games and reaching the Gator Bowl only to suffer a 38-point loss to Mississippi State. Less than two weeks after the bowl game, Rodriguez was fired. In 2012, he is head coach at the University of Arizona.

It is unlikely that many West Virginians will ever completely forget the way Rodriguez left the program. However, his outstanding contributions to Mountaineer football are undeniable: a 32-5 record over his final three seasons and a 60-26 overall mark; three consecutive Top 10 finishes for the first time in school history; the school's first-ever major bowl victory, over Georgia in the 2006 Nokia Sugar Bowl; the school's first major national award winner in center Dan Mozes, who won the Rimington Award; and winning outright or sharing four Big East titles in his final five seasons at WVU. Those are the things the Rodriguez backers will undoubtedly remember. Naturally, his detractors will always bring up the 2007 Pitt loss and the way he departed.

"After the Fiesta Bowl, when you sit back as coaches and you begin to look back at that Pitt game and realize that we were so close to playing for a national championship

. . . you are aware of it while it was going on, but you really didn't know how close you were to winning a national championship until later – and how hard it is to get to that moment," recalled Casteel, now coaching with Rodriguez at Arizona.

In February 2011, a month after being fired as Michigan's football coach, Rodriguez was a guest on the Colin Cowherd Show on ESPN Radio. Cowherd asked Rodriguez if he regretted leaving West Virginia. Rodriguez's reply was telling. "There are always regrets," he said. "And looking back on it now, the way things worked out, certainly, there's regrets in that regard."

Down to the Wire

WVU	PITT
19	16
Nov. 27, 2009 Morgantown, W.Va.	

WVU	PITT
21	20
Nov. 25, 2011 Morgantown, W.Va.	

As Bill Stewart watched his players jump up and down, celebrating in front of him on the turf at Milan Puskar Stadium, there was one overriding thought going through his mind: *Thank God I gave a kicker a football scholarship.* It was Tyler Bitancurt's 43-yard field goal on the final play of the game that enabled West Virginia to defeat eighth-ranked Pitt 19-16 in the 102nd game of this long and unpredictable football series, which has had more twists and turns than a country road.

Just two years previous, Pitt had turned West Virginia's world upside down on the very same field, upsetting the Mountaineers 13-9 in a game that ruined the Mountaineers' chances of going to the national championship game. A year after that, in 2008, Pitt overcame an eight-point fourth quarter deficit to beat West Virginia 19-15 in Pittsburgh. In both games, it was West Virginia's inability to get the tough yards that led to Panther victories. Defense had made a big comeback at Pitt under Coach Dave Wannstedt. His 2009 unit was one of the best in the country heading into the West Virginia game, allowing just 314.7 yards per contest. It was a unit – especially the front four consisting of Jabaal Sheard, Mick Williams, Gus Mustakas and Greg Romeus – that had Panther fans once again talking about some of Pitt's great defenses of the late 1970s and early 1980s.

"This is five years in the works," explained Stewart during his Tuesday afternoon news conference the week of the game. "It's five years of getting better each year and adding to the repertoire. To me, I see many seniors on this two-deep [roster], and that has been five years in the making."

Wannstedt, a Johnny Majors-era player at Pitt and a Pittsburgh native, was officially introduced as the Panthers' head football coach on December 23, 2004, replacing the offensive-minded Walt Harris, who was essentially pushed out the door to take a similar job at Stanford following the Panthers' bowl game against Utah. Harris had led Pitt to a three-way tie for first place in the Big East, and through tiebreakers, the Panthers were the Big East's representative in the 2005 Fiesta Bowl. Pitt lost the game badly to Utah, and Wannstedt, with his professional football connections and his friendships with many Western Pa high school coaches, was brought in to revive the great Panther tradition of tough, physically dominating football teams. But progress was slow, with his first squad, in 2005, finishing with a 5-6 record, and his second team going 6-6 to finish sixth in the Big East with a 2-5 conference mark. Another lackluster season in 2007, when Pitt finished 5-7, had many Pitt supporters concerned that Wannstedt might be in over his head.

Then Pitt upset No. 1-ranked West Virginia in Morgantown to finish the regular season. A year later, Wannstedt considered the '07 West Virginia victory the life preserver his sinking program badly needed. "I think that win, when you look back on it, it gave us life," Wannstedt admitted. "That would be the way that I would classify it.

"Winning that game, I can remember the first day of the off-season program in January – we had as much enthusiasm, from a team standpoint, to get started and to try and build on that for the next year as any. I'm sure just for our fans it was a shot in the arm, a little bit of hope," he said.

Pitt did make progress in 2008, winning nine regular season games and finishing tied for second in the Big East with a 5-2 league mark. But the Panthers once again stumbled miserably in the Sun Bowl in El Paso, Texas; in brutal weather conditions, Pitt failed to score in a difficult-to-watch 3-0 loss to Oregon State. It was such a disappointing performance that offensive coordinator Matt Cavanaugh took the fall and was replaced by University of California quarterback coach Frank Cignetti Jr., the son of former West Virginia University football coach Frank Cignetti.

With many players returning, particularly on defense, Pitt was the preseason pick to win the Big East title in 2009. The Panthers won their first three games of the season before dropping a shootout at North Carolina State, 38-31. Pitt then went on to win its next six before facing West Virginia in Morgantown. They cracked the national rankings at No. 20 following their 13-point victory at Rutgers; Pitt moved up six more spots after a 27-point win over South Florida at Heinz Field; and two more victories against Syracuse and Notre Dame had the Panthers ranked eighth – their highest spot in the polls in 27 years, dating all the way back to the Marino days, in 1982. Wannstedt and the Panthers were within reach of their first outright Big East title with only two regular season games remaining, against 7-3 West Virginia and 10-0 Cincinnati.

Bill Stewart earned his promotion to head football coach in the Arizona desert following West Virginia's stunning 48-28 victory over third-ranked Oklahoma in the Tostitos Fiesta Bowl. Stewart, then 55 and basically a career assistant coach (with the exception of a brief three-year head coaching tenure at VMI) was one of the West Virginia coaches remaining with the team after Rich Rodriguez had decided to take the Michigan job three weeks earlier. On the day Rodriguez announced his decision to leave, it was Stewart who rallied the players (and coaches) for a scheduled practice up in the Caperton Indoor Practice Facility later that afternoon. Three days later, Athletic Director Ed Pastilong named Stewart interim coach until a full-time replacement could be identified following the bowl game. Stewart said and did all of the right things leading up to the game, even bringing in former Coach Don Nehlen and Gov. Joe Manchin to speak to the team. Although he didn't realize it, each day he was being observed by Pastilong – a sort of three-week-long interview process.

Stewart could kill you with kindness, and he had a politician's gift for remembering names and people's most significant accomplishments. Some of that probably came from his father, Blaine Stewart, who his son claimed turned his back on a promising career in country music to raise his two boys in New Martinsville. "My dad, they say, was the best mandolin player in the country," Stewart recalled proudly. "He was on the fast track. Our next door neighbors were Grandpa Jones [a nationally known banjo player and a cast member of the popular television show *Hee Haw*] and his wife Ramona, and my dad was friends with Patsy Cline, Hawkshaw Hawkins and Cowboy Copas – the three people that were on that plane [that famously crashed in March, 1963]. Dad wasn't playing with them in the big time, but he could have been."

Stewart recalled the many times his father turned down requests to go back on the road and tour with the band. "They said, 'We've got to have you come to the Grand Ole Opry and play with us.' He said, 'I'm not coming.' They said, 'Well why?' He said, 'I'm not leaving New Martinsville. I'm raising these boys.'"

When Stewart was in seventh grade, football entered his life as a means of keeping up with his older brother Ted and one of his early idols, Emo Schupbach, who wound up getting a scholarship to play for Gene Corum at WVU. "I really, really took to the coaches," Stewart said. "They were good men and good role models, and I thought, man, these are really special guys. I've always liked coaches, from Little League baseball and basketball all the way up. I really loved the game and liked those men. From that moment I knew what I wanted to be."

After completing high school in 1969, Stewart spent one year at WVU on the freshman team before realizing that, as a 5' 10-1/2" 177-pound guard, he might fare better by going down a level to nearby Fairmont State. "I thought I was ready to take on the world," Stewart laughed.

When Stewart's career at Fairmont State ended in 1973, he got right into coaching, first spending two years at Sistersville High, and then moving on to small college football at Salem College. Bigger jobs followed at North Carolina, Marshall, William & Mary, Navy and once again North Carolina – each move an advancement in his career. "I never applied for a job," he said proudly.

It was at North Carolina that Stewart realized the business of college football can sometimes be cold, calculated and unforgiving. "We got fired at North Carolina, and I still have a crack in my heart over that," Stewart recalled in 2008. "[North Carolina coach] Dick Crum is a great man and is a great role model for me – the best, greatest and most polished organizer I've ever been around. The loyalty that they preached all the time sometimes wasn't a two-way street – it wasn't 50-50. Most of the time it was 20-80, and that's when I learned about the business." Another difficult lesson for Stewart came nine years later when his three-year coaching tenure at VMI ended abruptly, in 1996. "At VMI, where I was blessed to coach, I was just too demanding and wanted it to happen too soon," Stewart said. "The program had been down for so long, and it was a tough situation. We took a shot at it and I will forever be grateful for the opportunity."

Out of coaching for a full year in 1997, Stewart eventually landed a job in the Canadian Football League, where he spent two seasons before returning to West Virginia as a member of Don Nehlen's staff in 2000. When Nehlen announced his retirement 10 months later, Stewart was the only Nehlen assistant initially retained by Rich Rodriguez. "Rich was good to me," Stewart said. "Rich gave me work for seven years, and in turn, I gave him loyalty for seven years."

Late in the fourth quarter, when it became apparent that West Virginia was going to upset Oklahoma for its biggest victory in school history, the wheels were already in motion to make Stewart West Virginia's 32nd football coach. ESPN's Pat Forde found a smiling Pastilong standing along the sideline, went up to him and asked if the game had altered his coaching search. "Yes," Pastilong said.

Stewart wisely remained in the background in the practices leading up to the game, letting his assistants do their jobs and concentrating mainly on team morale. Standing before his players as they were about to take the field, Stewart jogged his memory to come up with a story that might inspire them. Having lived for two years in Phoenix as an assistant coach at Arizona State, Stewart knew well the tale of the Lost Dutchman's Gold Mine, of how, each year, thousands journeyed into the Superstition Mountains unsuccessfully searching for their pot of gold.

"I just looked up there and saw those Superstition Mountains and it just popped into my head, and I said, "You know, guys, how many people have died out in these Superstition Mountains looking for the Lost Dutchman's Gold Mine?" Stewart said. "They still can't find it today with all this technology. It's there and they can't find it." Stewart told the team that their pot of gold was right behind those doors in the University of Phoenix Stadium. Not only did the team find its pot of gold, but Stewart did so as well.

NOT ONLY DID THE TEAM FIND ITS POT OF GOLD, BUT STEWART DID SO AS WELL.

After celebrating with the players on the field and fulfilling his required postgame media responsibilities, Stewart had expected to spend a quiet evening in his hotel suite with his wife Karen, his son Blaine and other close family members. He was fully prepared to wake up the next day and start looking for a new job. He was going to savor the night with his family, to soak in his good fortune after once moving with his wife seven different times in a span of 10 years, and having worked for most of his adult life on one-year contracts.

Then the phone rang. On the other end was Pastilong.

"I about fell over," Stewart recalled. "I was on such a high and I thought maybe he would say 'Billy, when you get back to Morgantown, maybe we'd like to talk to you.' That's what I thought. Blaine was like, 'Gee whiz, dad, what do you think?' I said maybe they'll give us a chance for an interview and that's all I could ask for. We went back to his room and talked. It was a powerful night."

Pastilong offered Stewart the job, and the following morning the announcement was made public, with the team holding up its chartered flight until a nationally televised news conference at the hotel could be completed. The reaction to Stewart's hiring was mixed. Those closely associated with the program heaved a big sigh of relief, while others, including some national media pundits, were highly skeptical, terming it a "battlefield promotion."

Stewart assembled a defense-oriented coaching staff, keeping defensive coordinator Jeff Casteel and adding two other former defensive coordinators in Steve Dunlap and Dave Lockwood to go along with veteran defensive line coach Bill Kirelawich. The offensive staff was pieced together systematically, with Wake Forest quarterback coach Jeff Mullen being chosen to lead the unit. Stewart was under the gun right away: his 2008 team was considered a national title contender with quarterback Pat White returning for his senior season. But those hopes evaporated after West Virginia lost 24-3 at East Carolina in the second week of the season. A week later, the Mountaineers lost in overtime, at Colorado, 17-14. In a span of two short weeks, West Virginia went from being a national title contender to completely falling out of the Top 25. Mountaineer fans who were unsure of the Stewart hiring became convinced that he wasn't the right guy for the job.

But Stewart rallied the team to five straight wins, including a 34-17 victory over Auburn in Morgantown, before the Mountaineers dropped a 26-23 overtime decision to Cincinnati. Another loss, at Pitt, cost West Virginia a chance at a share of the league title, and the Mountaineers had to settle for a Meineke Car Care Bowl appearance against North Carolina, where West Virginia won 31-30.

Expectations remained sky high in Morgantown at the start of the 2009 season, despite the facts that the Mountaineers were breaking in a new starting quarterback in Jarrett Brown, and that the team would face difficult road games at Auburn, South Florida and Cincinnati. A fourth quarter collapse led to a 41-30 loss at Auburn, turnovers and mistakes caused a 30-19 defeat at South Florida and a replay official's controversial call was a contributing factor in the Mountaineers' 24-21 setback at Cincinnati. When Pitt arrived in Morgantown on Friday night to play West Virginia in the 102nd Backyard Brawl, Stewart and his Mountaineer team were clearly in season-salvaging mode.

After a first half that featured very little offense, things finally opened up in the third quarter when West Virginia's Noel Devine scored the game's first touchdown on an 88-yard run. Before Devine's jaunt, it was a battle to see which team's kicker would miss first. Pitt's Dan Hutchins made field goals of 37 and 30 yards, while West Virginia's Bitancurt kicked field goals of 20 and 43 yards.

Before Devine's run, Pitt had stacked the box against the Mountaineers, who were backed up near their own goal line. The shifty running back was able to break free, angling first toward the WVU sideline before outrunning the rest of the Pitt defense to the end zone. "It was a trap. Woody Hayes, Frank Kush and Don Nehlen – trap. We don't even have it anymore. I'm probably the only coach today who calls a trap in modern-day football, so you're looking at a genius," said Stewart, cryptically, after the game.

"Noel saw the guy squeeze it," Stewart continued. "A good back has to trust his guard. He saw that guy squeeze and he bounced it [the first time West Virginia had tried that play]. [Assistant coach] Chris Beatty told him, 'Do not bounce it again. Even if you see a truck [in front of you], you trust the guard to get movement.' He trusted and I just closed my eyes and heard the crowd, and I saw him come out and I said, 'He's out!'"

Another Bitancurt field goal, with 10:05 left in the game, gave the Mountaineers a 16-6 lead. Then, three minutes later, Hutchins kicked his third field goal, this one from 36 yards, pulling the Panthers to within a touchdown. On its ensuing possession, West Virginia managed to get one first down before being forced to punt the ball back to the Panthers. More than four minutes remained on the clock. Panther quarterback Bill Stull, starting from his own 25, immediately went to work. He found Jon Baldwin for 15 yards to the Pitt 40 and hooked up with Mike Shanahan for 10 more to midfield. He then found Baldwin behind the West Virginia secondary for a 50-yard touchdown, tying the game at 16. The scoring drive covered 75 yards in just three plays, and it consumed only 1:20 of the clock.

That left West Virginia with 2:54 to try to break the tie. Mark Rodgers returned Luke Briggs's kick 29 yards to the West Virginia 32. Two Brown runs netted 14 yards to the 46, and an 11-yard Brown-to-Alric Arnett pass gave the Mountaineers another first down, at the Pitt 45. Two incomplete passes forced a critical third and 10 play. Brown was flushed from the pocket and scrambled for what appeared to be first down yardage at the 35, but he stumbled and came up a yard short of the first down marker. The spot was beyond Bitancurt's field goal range, and punting the ball back to the Panthers with 56.6 seconds still remaining on the clock was clearly out of the question.

It was very similar to short yardage situations that had plagued West Virginia in its two previous losses to the Panthers, as well as in other close defeats to South Florida, Cincinnati and Colorado. Stewart chose to give the ball to 240-pound freshman fullback Ryan Clarke, who used all of his brawn to nudge the football the necessary yard to get the first down. Two more runs, by Clarke and Devine, got the ball to the Pitt 26, where the Mountaineers called timeout with just four seconds left on the clock – the same amount of time remaining when Bill McKenzie kicked his game winner against Pitt in 1975. Stewart, who coached the special teams, treated his freshman kicker the same way a catcher treats a pitcher throwing a no-hitter – he completely avoided him.

"I looked at everybody but him," Stewart said. "I looked at the snapper and said, 'Well, that won't be bad luck.' I snapped when I played – nobody else wanted to do it. I wasn't real good, but I've been in that situation. [Holder] Jeremy Kash came right up to me, and I said, 'Knock it in, big fella.'"

He did. A picture of that kick later showed just how close Pitt's Jon Baldwin came to blocking the field goal, his outstretched hand just underneath the ball as it began to sail through the goal post. When the ball landed, there was no time left on the clock. Mountaineer players ran onto the field to celebrate. "That was a heck of a football game," said Stewart.

"That final possession was orchestrated like a surgeon," said Tony Caridi. "When Tyler made that kick, I remember looking down and seeing Stew look at it, watch all of his players run on the field to celebrate, and him turning and walking over to shake Wannstedt's hand and then walking off the field."

"After the game, it was probably more a feeling of relief [that West Virginia had won]," added Casteel. "Obviously it's always great to beat Pitt, and I think the way that it happened going down to the last play of the game and Tyler getting a chance to win it, it's really hard for all of us when everything goes down to the last play to see how it goes."

West Virginia was able to run for 205 yards against a Pitt defense that came into the game allowing only 102.7 yards on the ground per game. The Mountaineers' 369 total yards were also the most gained against the Panthers since 2006. Brown completed 19-of-31 passes for 164 yards.

On the other side, Stull completed 16-of-30 passes for 179 yards and a touchdown, Baldwin caught eight passes for 127 yards and a TD and freshman running back Dion Lewis finished the game with 155 yards rushing. The win sealed West Virginia's first undefeated home season in 16 years. "I know a lot of them were not signature wins, but they were wins," Stewart said in an obvious jab at his critics.

It was Stewart's first victory against the Panthers, it was the highest-ranked Pitt team any West Virginia coach had ever managed to defeat, and it was only the ninth time in school history a Mountaineer team had defeated a Top 10 team. But for Stewart, that win, coupled with the subsequent blowout victory at Pitt in 2010, was simply a respite. Eventually, on December 15, 2010, new athletic director Oliver Luck made the decision to hire Oklahoma State offensive coordinator Dana Holgorsen as West Virginia's "coach in waiting" for the 2011 season. Since defeating Oklahoma in the 2008 Tostitos Fiesta Bowl, Mountaineer fans had watched Cincinnati (twice) and Connecticut claim BCS berths that they believed were rightfully West Virginia's. Holgorsen was brought in to end that trend.

Pitt, too, watched with dismay as a couple of upstarts were able to achieve what Wannstedt couldn't produce in six seasons with the Panthers – a BCS bowl invite. Wannstedt resigned following a morning meeting with athletic director Steve Pederson on December 6, 2010, ending his Pitt tenure with a 42-31 record that included a 26-12 mark over his final three seasons – the school's most successful period since 1981-83. But Wannstedt couldn't get the Panthers into the big game despite Pitt twice being predicted to win league titles during his tenure, and his team endured embarrassing upset losses to Ohio University and Bowling Green.

Stewart couldn't get the Mountaineers back to the big game, either, despite possessing a 28-12 record that included three consecutive nine-win seasons. Stewart's .700 winning percentage was the second-highest among all coaches with three or more seasons of leading the Mountaineers; College Football Hall of Famer Clarence Spears owns the best record, with an .808 winning rate in his four seasons guiding WVU, from 1921-24. What Stewart's West Virginia teams struggled to do was score a lot of points, topping the 40-point mark just twice, against Villanova in 2008 and against UNLV in 2010 – a stark contrast from Rich Rodriguez's teams, which topped 40 quite frequently during the 2005, 2006 and 2007 campaigns. Defensive coordinator Jeff Casteel thought the offense would have eventually gotten things ironed out with a little bit of constancy at the quarterback position.

"Having three different quarterbacks in three years, those things are tough and it takes a little while to get a little bit of continuity," said Casteel.

When Holgorsen was announced as the school's coach in waiting, the initial plan was for Stewart to coach the 2011 campaign before ceding power to Holgorsen at the end of the season. That arrangement was in place for a time, but Stewart and West Virginia University eventually agreed to part ways on June 10, 2011, making room for Holgorsen to take over on a permanent basis. Sadly, Stewart died suddenly while playing golf at Stonewall Resort on May 21, 2012.

One of Dana Holgorsen's first acts as West Virginia's new head coach was to jump out of an airplane. During a two-day summer getaway in the southern part of the state, Holgorsen went skydiving with the U.S. Army parachute team, making a 10,000-foot jump that had been arranged by the West Virginia State Police. The landing, as seen by thousands of Mountaineer fans on YouTube, wasn't perfect, but he did reach the ground safely. Holgorsen also took a little fishing trip on the Upper New River to contemplate the enormous responsibility that he now shouldered – not just overseeing the West Virginia football program, but also the collective psyche of Mountaineer Nation.

"I was on the river with some pretty good friends, some boosters and a couple of other coaches, which was very peaceful," he said. "There were three people in each boat – one guy knew what he was doing because he was the one rowing that thing, and then there was me and another guy in there, and we didn't have any idea what we were doing. I just took a pole and tried to flip it somewhere and tried not to get it caught in the trees.

"I'm not a good fisherman – this is supposed to be the best small-mouth bass fishing in the United States, and I caught like three, and I was out there for like eight hours. I didn't really care about the fishing, it's all about [thinking] about what's ahead."

Holgorsen, who grew up in Iowa and played small college football at Iowa Wesleyan, is not a collector. His office walls are not full of mementos or memorabilia, and he doesn't waste a lot of time worrying about things that have happened in the past. His compass is always pointing north, and the throttle is usually wide open. "It's all about what's ahead," he repeated.

What was ahead for Holgorsen at WVU in 2011 was a pretty favorable schedule featuring home games against Marshall, Norfolk State, second-ranked LSU, Bowling Green, Connecticut, Louisville and Pitt, and road contests at Maryland, Syracuse, Rutgers, Cincinnati and South Florida. Plus, the Mountaineers were once again predicted to win the Big East.

Holgorsen was able to steer the Mountaineers to another Big East title, but it didn't come without some trials and tribulations. His team was embarrassed at Syracuse in a game televised nationally on ESPN, and it lost a close home contest to Louisville later in the year. But the first-year coach was able to rally his team with narrow wins over Cincinnati, Pitt and South Florida to end the regular season.

The Pitt game presented a couple of interesting subplots. For one, Holgorsen and first-year Panther coach Todd Graham had had some prior run-ins when the two coached in Conference USA, and a lot was made of their personal rivalry. And two, Pitt had made the surprising announcement in mid-September that it was leaving the Big East to become a new member of the Atlantic Coast Conference. A month later, West Virginia announced its intention to join the Big 12, leaving the future of the long-time football series hanging in the balance. However, most of the questions Holgorsen and Graham answered in the days leading up to the game were about their personal feud.

"The media is making a big deal out of the fact that we had competitive games," said Holgorsen. "I have a tremendous amount of respect for him and what he has been able to accomplish, and I assume the respect is mutual on his part, based on the success we've had."

The 69th straight (104th overall) Backyard Brawl was either a classic or a clunker, depending upon which side of the field you were standing on. If you were a West Virginia fan, you saw a great second-half comeback that included a critical fourth-down conversion on the game-winning drive, and you saw 10 sacks by a Mountaineer defense that also limited the Panthers to just 80 second-half yards and a lone field goal, which came as a result of a bobbled punt deep in West Virginia territory.

If you were a Pitt fan, well, you had to get up on Saturday morning and read *Pittsburgh Post-Gazette* columnist Ron Cook write this: "A lot of people will spend a lot of time in the days, weeks and months ahead worrying that there won't be another game in the great Pitt-West Virginia rivalry. I have one question this morning: Why?" Cook went on to describe the game as "hard to watch." (It makes you wonder if Cook felt that way about another hard-to-watch WVU-Pitt game in 2007).

Graham, a football coach who possesses the uncanny ability of continually finding his dream jobs, discovered his next one at Arizona State after just one season at Pitt. Graham had this to say about his first and only Backyard Brawl as Pitt's football coach: "Up until the middle of the fourth quarter, we had everything right where we wanted it. We weren't playing an enormous amount of plays on defense, so everything was going as we planned, but you have to score touchdowns there and we didn't."

Keith Patterson, Graham's defensive coordinator at Pitt (who has since switched sides and now works for West Virginia), said the Panthers' defensive objective that night was to take away Stedman Bailey on deep passes and roll the dice with Tavon Austin on crossing routes. "We just tried to control Tavon," Patterson said. "You're not going to take away Tavon. What we tried to do was take away Sted, so we rolled the coverage to him and just tried to contain Tavon." Holgorsen was so impressed with how well Patterson defended the Mountaineers that evening that he hired him to help run West Virginia's defense in 2012.

West Virginia's victory over Pitt was its third in a row, coming on the heels of the 2009 upset in Morgantown and a 2010 35-10 rout in Pittsburgh that likely contributed to Dave Wannstedt's hasty departure. In that game, as the clock wound down, Stewart showed his merciful side: rather than rubbing it in, he opted to run the ball up the middle four straight times from inside the Pitt 15.

Holgorsen's win over Pitt in 2011 was followed up by an even more impressive triumph at South Florida, giving the Mountaineers another share of the Big East title. A Cincinnati victory over Connecticut the next afternoon enabled WVU to earn the Big

East's BCS bowl berth, lining them up to face ACC champ Clemson in the 2012 Discover Orange Bowl. West Virginia's stunning 70-33 victory over the Tigers in that game will go down as one of the most impressive offensive performances in bowl history.

Luck, the man responsible for bringing Holgorsen to Morgantown, was obviously impressed with the way the Mountaineers performed in Miami. "This came on a big stage," Luck said. "Getting to a BCS bowl is not easy. We've been fortunate to be in the three that we've been in and won all three – big stage, millions of viewers. It's a positive all the way across the board."

Quarterback Geno Smith tied a bowl record with six touchdown passes, and he earned game MVP honors by throwing for 407 yards (he was credited with one additional completion for six yards after the game). Tavon Austin was also terrific, catching 12 passes for 123 yards and four touchdowns. "Never could we imagine that we'd put up 70 points," Smith said afterward.

Nor did West Virginia fans, many of them honking their horns, waving their arms out of their windows and shouting words of encouragement as six chartered buses brought the team through town to the Milan Puskar Center. Construction workers stopped what they were doing to acknowledge the players, a couple of them even taking off their hard hats in appreciation of a job well done. Children in school buses pulled their windows down and stuck out their heads to get a closer look at their passing heroes. You could see, sprinkled among them, some blue Tavon Austin and Geno Smith jerseys. Those kids were undoubtedly still a little sleepy after begging their parents to let them stay up well past midnight so they could watch Rece Davis hand the Orange Bowl championship trophy over to Dana Holgorsen. Several local businesses already had messages of congratulations on their signs, wisely mixing praise with commerce. In most places when traffic is stopped, it's a nuisance, but that afternoon, going through Morgantown was a cause for celebration. This only happens in places where the people care deeply about their program – which also happen to be some of the best places in college football.

And Dana Holgorsen is well aware of this. "I've only been at West Virginia for one year, and for the last seven years, West Virginia has won 70 games and has finished in the Top 25 in six of [those] years," he remarked. "And West Virginia has won three BCS games in the last six years, so a lot has taken place prior to what happened in the Orange Bowl."

That's for sure.

Dana Holgorsen became the first West Virginia coach in the modern era of the Backyard Brawl to defeat Pitt in his first game coaching against the Panthers, in 2011. (Bill Amatucci photo)

EPILOGUE

We all remember 1963 as the year John F. Kennedy was assassinated, but it was also around that same time that the University of Pittsburgh finally agreed to play football games in Morgantown, W.Va., on a regular basis. Before that, the vast majority of West Virginia's games against Pitt were played either at Forbes Field or Pitt Stadium - 40 out of 55 to be exact.

From 1919–1929, all 11 games West Virginia played against Pitt were in Pittsburgh. The same goes for the eight times the two schools played from 1938–1948, as well as the four games played from 1950–1953 and the three played from 1960–62 – and for good reason: the Mountaineers were simply not on par with the Panthers. In fact, West Virginia needed Pitt much more than Pitt needed West Virginia. For many years, WVU's coaches realized that the city of Pittsburgh was the gateway to national attention and respect for their teams: Perform well against the Panthers and recognition and praise will follow. That's why West Virginia continued to play football games in Pittsburgh for so long and on such an unequal basis – and with such passion and great determination.

Pitt won eight mythical national titles during a 22-year period from 1915–37, including four from 1931–37 under legendary coach Jock Sutherland. The Panthers played in four Rose Bowls in 1928, 1930, 1933 and 1937 and had more than 30 All-American players from 1914–37 – one of them being Marshall "Biggie" Goldberg, an Elkins native who crossed enemy lines to become one of the most infamous turncoats in state history. For Mountaineer fans, losing Goldberg to Pitt was a massive psychological blow that lasted for decades.

Back then, the West Virginians who played at Pitt – guys like Goldberg, Parkersburg's Gibby Welch and Benwood's Emil Narick - were referred to as "Snakes" by their Panther teammates; "Snakes" served as WVU's unofficial nickname well into the 1920s, when the school understandably made the official switch to the much more appropriate Mountaineers. Pitt players referring to their West Virginia teammates as "Snakes" was a clear reminder of where they had come from.

Beginning with Pitt's 53-0 win over West Virginia in 1904 (back when Pitt was still being referred to as Western University of Pennsylvania), the Panthers won 38 of 49 games over the next 58 years. The two schools played annually from 1919 until 1939, when the series was interrupted for three years, from 1940-42, as Pitt tried to get into the Big Ten Conference, then known as the Western Conference. When the Panthers began to make room on their schedule to play more Big Ten schools, West Virginia was the local team most expendable, as the WVU-Pitt games were neither competitive nor interesting. But gasoline and rubber rationing during the war years forced the two schools to resume the series in 1943 because of their close geographical proximity, and the two played every year from then until 2011.

Bill Kern ended Pitt's 15-game winning streak in 1947 with a 17-2 victory in the fog and snow up in Pittsburgh, and five years later, Art Lewis surprised everyone by blanking the 18th-ranked Panthers on the very same field. It was the first time that the Mountaineers had defeated a nationally ranked football team. Lewis did it again in 1959 in stunning fashion – this time in Morgantown – with a team that had no business even being on the same field with Pitt. In between, much stronger Lewis teams also won games against Pitt in 1953 and 1957. Finally, West Virginia was beginning to hold its own in the series – and Pitt athletic director Frank Carver took notice.

Carver was Mr. Pitt for nearly 40 years, beginning as a student in 1927 before eventually working his way into the AD's chair on a permanent basis in 1959, when Captain Tom Hamilton left to become commissioner of the Pacific 8 Conference. Carver's path toward a career in athletic administration was born of an aversion for making the steep walk up Cardiac Hill to go to his freshman chemistry lab. Instead, he discovered that a journalism class was being offered at the same time in State Hall (at the bottom of the hill), and from there he found his niche in Pitt's publicity office, working first for Don Saunders and then Fred Turbyville.

Carver became the school's lead publicist in 1931, when Sutherland was beating everybody in America, and it was Carver who very quietly – and very effectively – promoted college football's No. 1 program. When he was younger, Carver used to believe his publicity efforts helped fill the stadium. He realized otherwise when Sutherland left and the Pitt Stadium crowds grew sparse once again. "No publicity man can take the place of a couple of good tacklers," Carver used to say.

Carver was the guy who came up with the slogan "Dream Backfield" to describe Panther greats Goldberg, John Chickerneo and Curly Stebbins, and he also labeled Pitt basketball coach Doc Carlson's innovative offense the "Figure Eight" – today a common basketball term. In the late 1940s, when James Hagan resigned as athletic director, it was Carver who was asked to step in and serve as the school's interim AD. And when Hamilton was finally wooed from the Naval Academy, Carver acquired the nebulous title of graduate manager, which basically meant that he was Hamilton's No. 2 guy. Carver fit that role perfectly, quietly working in the background while riding the train to work every day from his home. It was said that he rarely took his car out of the garage.

"Frank Carver was one of the nicest guys I ever met," said Mickey Furfari. "He was just a great guy and a classy person."

When Carver was athletic director, Furfari recalled Carver once stepping in to resolve a dispute between Tony Constantine and Pitt publicist Beano Cook; Cook would not give Constantine a press credential because he said there were no seats left in the press box. "Tony called Carver and Carver made Beano find him a seat," said Furfari.

By all accounts, Carver was very interested in maintaining good relations with Pitt's neighboring schools, often remarking that good games were good for the series. "It was cliché, but I think he meant it," said Eddie Barrett. Carver was first and foremost a football guy, often to the detriment of the Panther basketball program, but he realized in the early 1960s that times were changing – particularly when it came to West Virginia. It was during Carver's tenure that the football series with Pitt finally became home and home, and it was Carver who made it happen. But why? Why would Carver agree to do that?

"I just think West Virginia said we'd like to play at home more often and [Carver] agreed," said Cook.

"The '63 season was our state Centennial celebration, and Red Brown drummed up a great schedule with Pitt, Navy and Oregon," said Barrett. "I think from that point on, Red said to Frank Carver, 'Look, we're more than competitive against you' – we had beaten them in 1959, 1961 and 1962, and I think Carver went right along with it."

Back then, game contracts were merely handshakes, sometimes over a couple of cocktails at a social gathering. Barrett imagines that that is how Carver and Brown came to an agreement – just a few words about the football game mixed in with a lot of storytelling. "There were no contracts back then, and there were no lawyers," Barrett said. "It was not even a handshake – they just agreed. They both respected each other; now Penn State . . . Pitt regarded them as much more of a rival than West Virginia, and West Virginia was perfectly content to be the country boys against the city boys. The attraction of the contrasting rivalry – the city and the country boys and all that stuff – [Carver] liked that."

"We always played Penn State here because their place only seated 32,000 then, and then when Penn State added to their stadium in the 1960s, it became home and home,"

Cook said. "Pitt was willing to play [West Virginia]. It didn't cost that much [to go down to Morgantown] – it was just different in those days. Now it's all cutthroat and business and everything else."

In 1965, when Carver was getting criticized by everyone (including his SID) for creating an unbalanced basketball schedule that featured just seven home games at Fitzgerald Field House, the AD offered some insight into his scheduling philosophy, including his feelings about West Virginia – which dominated the basketball series against the Panthers back then. "We still plan to play West Virginia," he said. "We have played West Virginia since 1900. Just because we are losing to them now doesn't mean we should kick West Virginia off the schedule."

Carver continued.

"I remember the late 1930s, when every school was taking pot shots at us," he said. "West Virginia never said a word. They stuck by us and I will never forget this. We will play traditional opponents and games which either side has a 50-50 chance of winning."

And 50-50 is just about what the West Virginia-Pitt football series has been since 1963. The Mountaineers have won 25 games, Pitt 22, with two ties. Roughly the same number of points has been scored by both sides – 1,227 for West Virginia and 1,070 for Pitt; Pitt has been shut out three times, West Virginia twice. Pitt won seven games in a row from 1976–82 while West Virginia won five in a row from 1992–96. West Virginia has won 33 times against nationally ranked teams; Pitt has beaten 32 ranked teams.

The series has experienced more than 20 sellouts since 1963, 12 crowds of more than 60,000, 26 of more than 50,000 and at least 32,000 spectators have attended each one (old Mountaineer Field's seating capacity was just 35,000 for several of those years).

"When we played West Virginia, Notre Dame or Southern Cal, the crowds were much bigger and louder," Pitt coach Johnny Majors once recalled.

More than 68,000 packed Mountaineer Field to watch West Virginia and Pitt play the first-ever Big East football game in 1991. In 2002, when both teams were in the national rankings, a record Heinz Field crowd of 66,731 braved frigid temperatures to see West Virginia hang on for a 24-17 victory. The game has been aired on some form of national television 28 times since 1963, including every year from 1995 to 2011, bringing untold millions to the schools' athletic coffers through the years. There have been good games and there have been bad games, to be sure, but all of them have been interesting. Furthermore, the games have been hard-fought and competitive but without many on-field incidents.

Don Nehlen, who grew up in Ohio and observed the Ohio State-Michigan rivalry for three years in person while working the Michigan sidelines, knows a thing or two about rivalry games. "I don't think [Pitt-West Virginia] has quite the national implications that Michigan-Ohio State has, but from a coaching standpoint, it's exactly the same."

"Nothing against pro football, but to me, [rivalries] are what make college football so special," said West Virginia assistant coach Steve Dunlap. "There are all of these rivalries around the country that have been playing for over a hundred years. Pro football wasn't even around then. Now, I'm not talking about the hate thing, but I think that's what makes college football really special. Pitt, with them being just right up the road, is what makes it so fun."

"Every guy that has coached the game – whether they were coaching at West Virginia or coaching at Pitt – gets emotional," said Bill Kirelawich. "I can remember Jack Henry, who was an offensive line coach for Frank [Cignetti], and then he later coached at Pitt [for Johnny Majors in the mid-1990s]. When he was here, they were beating our ass, and when he was there, we were beating their ass. He told me after one game, 'I wish the hell I could get on the right side of this thing!'"

"As a Mountaineer – for my family and for us as a University – it will be sad to see this game disappear," added Jeff Hostetler. "There is nothing like getting a win against Pitt – and you will hear the same thing from their players about us."

Today, West Virginia, Pitt and Penn State – the three schools that used to play for the old Ironsides Trophy and made up three-fourths of the Big Four – have gone their separate ways. Penn State has been a member of the Big Ten Conference since 1993 and hasn't played Pitt since 2000 or West Virginia since 1992; Pitt made the decision to join the Atlantic Coast Conference in September of 2011, and a month after that, West Virginia was voted into the Big 12 Conference.

Three outstanding schools with many outstanding qualities, each within 200 miles of each other, and all three now playing in different conferences in different parts of the country – it kind of makes you wonder what Frank Carver would think of that.

BACKYARD BRAWL COMPLETE HISTORY

Year	Site	Winner	Score
2011	home*	WVU	21-20
2010	away	WVU	35-10
2009	home	WVU	19-16
2008	away	PITT	19-15
2007	home	PITT	13-9
2006	away	WVU	45-27
2005	home	WVU	45-13
2004	away	PITT	16-13
2003	home	WVU	52-31
2002	away	WVU	24-17
2001	home	PITT	23-17
2000	away	PITT	38-28
1999	home	WVU	52-21
1998	away	WVU	52-14
1997	home	PITT	41-38/3OT
1996	away	WVU	34-0
1995	home	WVU	21-0
1994	away	WVU	47-41
1993	home	WVU	42-21
1992	away	WVU	44-6
1991	home	PITT	34-3
1990	away	WVU	38-24
1989	home	tie	31-31
1988	away	WVU	31-10
1987	home	PITT	6-3
1986	away	PITT	48-16
1985	home	tie	10-10
1984	away	WVU	28-10
1983	home	WVU	24-21
1982	away	PITT	16-13
1981	home	PITT	17-0
1980	away	PITT	42-14
1979	home	PITT	24-17
1978	away	PITT	52-7
1977	home	PITT	44-3
1976	away	PITT	24-16
1975	home	WVU	17-14
1974	away	PITT	31-14
1973	home	PITT	35-7
1972	away	WVU	38-20
1971	home	WVU	20-9
1970	away	PITT	36-35
1969	home	WVU	49-18
1968	away	WVU	38-15
1967	home	WVU	15-0
1966	away	PITT	17-14
1965	home	WVU	63-48
1964	away	PITT	14-0
1963	home	PITT	13-10
1962	away	WVU	15-8
1961	away	WVU	20-6
1960	away	PITT	42-0
1959	home	WVU	23-15
1958	away	PITT	15-8
1957	away	WVU	7-6
1956	home	PITT	14-13
1955	away	PITT	26-7
1954	home	PITT	13-10
1953	away	WVU	17-7
1952	away	WVU	16-0
1951	away	PITT	32-12
1950	away	PITT	21-7
1949	home	PITT	20-7
1948	away	PITT	16-6
1947	away	WVU	17-2
1946	away	PITT	33-7
1945	away	PITT	20-0
1944	away	PITT	26-13
1943	away	PITT	20-0
1939	away	PITT	20-0
1938	home	PITT	19-0
1937	home	PITT	20-0
1936	away	PITT	34-0
1935	away	PITT	24-6
1934	home	PITT	27-6
1933	home	PITT	21-0
1932	home	PITT	40-0
1931	away	PITT	34-0
1930	home	PITT	16-0
1929	away	PITT	27-7
1928	away	WVU	9-6
1927	away	PITT	40-0
1926	away	PITT	17-7
1925	away	PITT	15-7
1924	away	PITT	14-7
1923	away	WVU	13-7
1922	away	WVU	9-6
1921	away	PITT	21-13
1920	away	PITT	34-13
1919	away	PITT	26-0
1917	home	PITT	14-9
1913	away	PITT	40-0
1910	away	PITT	38-0
1909	home	tie	0-0
1908	away	PITT	11-0
1907	away	W.U.P.	10-0
1906	away	W.U.P.	17-0
1904	away	W.U.P.	53-0
1903	home	WVU	24-6
1902	away	WVU	23-6
1901	home	W.U.P.	12-0
1900	home	WVU	6-5
1898	at Fairmont	WVU	6-0
1895	at Wheeling	WVU	8-0

* Morgantown

ACKNOWLEDGMENTS

Saying "thank you" has never been a problem for me – my mother taught me the necessity of doing that many, many years ago – but remembering exactly whom to thank . . . well, that is a different story. And since this is a book of stories, I thought the best way to thank everyone is by telling a few more stories to help jar my memory.

Many, many moons ago, when the West Virginia University athletic department was much smaller than it is today (back when you could actually fit all of us into one room for department staff meetings), telling stories was considered an essential respite from those monotonous summer afternoons when it was raining outside and the golf courses were closed.

Keep in mind, when I first began working at WVU, there was no Internet to confine us to our desks, so human interaction entailed much more than just an email or a Facebook post. In fact, during my first year on the job, in 1991, I can remember in fairly clear detail standing as close as I could to Penn State coach Joe Paterno during one of his Friday evening off-the-record "BS sessions" that he enjoyed having with his favorite sportswriters at the Nittany Lion Inn before Penn State home football games. While attempting to eavesdrop on the legendary coach, I imagined someone just like me at Toots Shor's back in the day, doing something similar with Casey Stengel, straining to hear the old ball coach gossiping to his newspaper cronies the way Paterno was doing.

Well, there were no sportswriters around for our department BS sessions, which typically took place in baseball coach Dale Ramsburg's office on the second floor of the WVU Coliseum, and it was there where I really gained an appreciation for storytelling – the kind of stories that made your stomach ache from laughter – and it was there where I also learned how to manage money. That's right, in between the stories, the off-color jokes and the laughs, the subject of personal finance had somehow entered the conversation, most likely by way of Gale Catlett or someone who actually had money, and it was then that I learned the single most valuable lesson of my life.

This particular "Mad Money" discussion had somehow veered off into stocks, bonds, mutual funds and other things that are totally foreign to most 23-year-olds, when Ramsburg, his feet propped up on his desk, hands cupped behind his head with a baseball-sized wad of chewing tobacco stuffed inside his cheek, had finally heard enough from the Jim Cramer wannabes in the room. Rammer spat out the oily blob that was lodged in his jaw, wiped off his mouth, and asked, "Do you guys REALLY want to make money? Well, spend less than you make!"

That's some pretty sound advice that any 23-year-old could understand.

For that and many other things, I will always be grateful to the late WVU baseball coach – one of the best storytellers there ever was – along with Marty Pushkin, Kevin Gilson, John "Tug" McGrath, Craig Turnbull, Terry Deremer, Gale Catlett, Gary McPherson, Ed Pastilong, Craig Walker, Greg Van Zant, the late Carl Bahneman and the rest of the Coliseum gang, who taught me the value of telling a good story . . . and also for teaching me how to save a few bucks along the way. I would have also lumped another great storyteller, Ed Dickson, into the group, but his WVU tenure came a little bit later.

While the laughter and the storytelling usually took place upstairs – along with a lot of great work, I might add – it was downstairs in the Sports Communications Office where the flurry of activity usually happened, rain or shine. It was there where we all learned from Mike Parsons the value of hard work. Mike has a philosophy that has served our department well for many, many years. To paraphrase: "Take the time to get the extra interview, the extra camera shot, or make the extra effort to do the research you need to get it right." The message was clear: Don't settle for less, because your audience deserves more. Yes, more great advice.

The athletic department has enjoyed an unprecedented era of success during the last 25 years, initiated by Fred Schaus, Don Nehlen and Gale Catlett in the 1980s, and advanced by Ed Pastilong, Rich Rodriguez, John Beilein and the late Bill Stewart. Today, that phenomenal success continues under the stewardship of Oliver Luck, Dana Holgorsen and Bob Huggins. Some schools (hint, hint, Pitt) are still searching for their first BCS bowl victory or a trip to the Final Four. I've been a personal witness to three BCS wins in the last six years, and I was also lucky enough to get to see a Final Four from a seat on press row. What a ride it has been so far, with the promise of even bigger things to come now that West Virginia University is headed to the Big 12 Conference.

I am appreciative, too, for the meaningful friendships that I have developed with some really outstanding co-workers: Michael Fragale, Joe Swan, Mike Montoro, Bryan Messerly, Tim Goodenow, Katie Kane, Shannon McNamara, Lisa Ammons, Amy Prunty, Cheryl Maust, Matt Wells, Nathaniel Zinn, Julie Brown, Grant Dovey, Daniel Whitehead, Brian Kuppelweiser, Abby Norman, Ashleigh Pollart, John Riedesel, Gina Sporio and the gang of students we have in the Sports Communications Office today; not to mention Joe Boczek, Shelly Poe, Kevin Keys, Greg McCracken, Marie Morton, David Cline, Erin Anderson, Cathy Dixon, Barbara Henderson, Brian Feldmeier, Jai Giffin, Mark Ragonese, Andy Shultz, Karin Delbuono, Joe Michalski, Courtney Morrison, Kerry Mossburg, Meagan Davis, Jim Dunlap, Tracey Sussman, Lisa Smith, Jo Ellen Fetty (a New Martinsville native!), Brian Lough, Loretta Shaffer, Sarah Gould,

Bob Welsh, Amy Bailey, Leslie Murry, Greg Walker, Amy Townsend, Brian Crane, Katie Landolt, Mendy Nestor, Robin Rupenthal, Brian Reinhardt, Joshua White, Adrienne Mullikin, Phil Hess, Patrick Fischer, Donna Cayton, Gina Magistro, Camille Currie, Adam Zundell, Brandi Bonkowski, Brady Smith, Jason Baum, Dina Karwoski, Rance Berry, Steve Harris, Megan Wilson, Phil Caskey, Scott Castleman, Lainie Guiddy, Jarrod Sudduth, Justin Zackal, Elizabeth Brandt, Allison Hoehn, Chris Marshall, Kelly Tuckwiller, Ira Green, Steve Stone, Tiffany Doolittle, Mickey Glowacky, Tim Roberts, Brad Howe, Chris Boyer, Casey Craig, Mitch Fink and the many others from our department who have since moved on to pursue their careers.

Additionally, a special nod of the cap goes out to Joe Swan, Michael Fragale and Mike Parsons for taking the time to read the manuscript for this book and for steering me clear of unwittingly stepping on any landmines. Joe's eagle-eye editing skills and his great knowledge of sports were particularly helpful. Thanks, too, to Mike Montoro for his help tracking down the national writers and broadcasters that added so much to this book.

When you are hunting for good stories, the athletic trainers and the equipment managers are typically a good place to start. John Spiker, Randy Meader, Dave Kerns and Tony Corley from the athletic training staff, and the equipment guys Bubba Schmidt, Kevin Johnston, Stevie Bierer, Mike Kerin and Danny Nehlen were frequently willing to share a funny story or two. The team doctors, too, have always been right there in the middle of the action, providing splendid medical care for our athletes – plus, a few of them have even felt the urge to give some unsolicited advice to our coaches whenever the circumstances required. I recall standing on the sidelines during a game up at Pitt one fall afternoon when one of the doctors walked behind Don Nehlen during the game and yelled, in a voice loud enough for everyone to hear, "THROW THE BALL, DON!" I looked at strength coach Al Johnson and we both just smiled and shrugged, realizing that he might actually be on to something.

Fundraisers are another place to go for good stories, and we have had several through the years in the Mountaineer Athletic Club. My thanks to all of them, especially Whit Babcock (now athletic director at Cincinnati), for helping me try and get things right.

The same goes for all of the outstanding strength coaches through the years, especially Al Johnson, Mike Barwis and Mike Joseph.

I can't thank enough Donnie Young, Garrett Ford, Delania Bierer, Joyce Bucklew, Tammy Cavender, Ruby Shrout, Cathy Martin, Jay Redmond, George Nedeff, John Twining, the late Russ Sharp, Jan Runner, Debby Travinski, Jerry Bowermaster, Brad

Cox, Lori Rice, Kim Calandrelli, Rose Barko, Brett Kelley, Terri Howes, Keli Cunningham, Michael Szul, Gary Waters, Bill Shultz, Paul Downey, Judy Cress, Cindy Smith, Eleanor Lamb and the entire maintenance gang for their help, and also to the many other athletic department staff members – past and present – who have shared their stories and experiences with me.

Speaking of sharing stories, it's impossible to count the number of times I got the late Eddie Barrett or Mickey Furfari on the telephone – or the late Dick Polen, when he was still living – to confirm a story someone had told me. I am glad Mickey has finally gotten around to writing books, because there is a treasure trove of material locked inside his brain that would have been lost to history if he hadn't. Whenever I'm around Mickey all it usually takes for me to stir his memory is to say . . . *Hey Mick, remember the time Adolph Rupp wouldn't let you have a credential to cover the KIT, or the time Lefty Driesell was beside himself when you wrote that he was controversial* . . . As you can imagine, having Mickey around has always been a big treat for all of us.

Eddie Barrett, too, was usually equipped with a great story or two whenever you needed one. About 10 years ago, Eddie sat down to do an oral history with Tony Constantine of his years covering West Virginia University athletics while he worked for the *Morgantown Post,* and I was able to listen to some of those interviews. Several stories from those discussions are revealed within the pages of this book, so a big thank you goes to Eddie for allowing me to pull a J. Edgar Hoover and listen in on some history in the making.

Tony Constantine was still going strong when I just got started, and I vividly remember the first time he ever reviewed my work. When he was done, what I had written was covered with so much red ink that it looked like someone must have stabbed me with a butcher knife. I learned immediately that it is probably better to have your thoughts organized in your brain before putting them all down on a piece of paper.

I was also fortunate enough to observe a bunch of old-time West Virginia news hawks in action, names such as Shorty Hardman, Bill Smith, Bob Baker, Danny Wells, Bill Van Horne, Doug Huff, Nick Bedway, Jim Mearns, Norm Julian and Cliff Nichols. Those guys passed the baton on to the next wave of reporters, which included Mitch Vingle, Dave Hickman, Jody Jividen, Mike Cherry, Chuck Landon, Rick McCann, Rick Kozlowski, Ed Kracz, Bob Pastin, Rich Gibson, Nick Scala, Joe Koch, Bob Hertzel, Dan Shrensky, Joe Kacik, Jack Bogaczyk, Joedy McCreary, Dave Morrison, Greg Talkington, Don Clegg, Rich Kozlowski, Greg Hunter, Todd Murray and Jim Butta. The newest crop of West Virginia sports scribes is made up of familiar names like Drew Rubenstein, Justin Jackson, Chuck McGill, Mike Casazza, Kevin Kinder, Patrick Southern, Frank Giardina, Jim Elliott, Chip Fontanazza, Garrett Cullen, Scott Grayson, Mike Corley, Geoff Coyle and Vernon Bailey.

For a person growing up in the state's Northern Panhandle, Bill Van Horne was our tour guide to the world – at least to the world of sports. I can still remember like it was yesterday spreading out the *Wheeling News-Register* on the front porch of my parents' house, just to read Bill's afternoon sports column. Bill was never one to spare words, his columns usually jumping three or four times before ending up on the back page of the paper, right next to the strip club advertisements, but he wisely understood that the more names he could stuff into his columns, the more newspapers he would likely sell. Not a bad idea, huh?

I am also grateful to Doug Huff for reviewing this manuscript and offering his historical perspective on the West Virginia-Pitt rivalry. No one in this state has done more to promote high school sports than Doug, and after a long and successful career as the sports editor of the *Wheeling Intelligencer*, Doug is now spending his retirement years honoring the many great achievements of Ohio Valley athletes through the numerous committees and associations he is involved with – and doing a great job of it, too, I might add!

I had the great privilege of getting to know Jack Fleming during the remaining years of his life, and it was a highlight to be able to transcribe those Internet columns he used to write for our website. In addition to being a one-of-a-kind announcer, Jack was also a terrific writer, and for years Mike Parsons tried unsuccessfully to get him to write his memoir. It's a shame he didn't, because that would have been a real keeper for Mountaineer sports fans. Like Fleming, the late Woody O'Hara was another one of my favorites. Woody always had an off-the-cuff remark on the tip of his tongue that kept the mood light and the road trips interesting, and his great sense of humor is sorely missed.

Today, Tony Caridi is providing the same impressive catalogue of memories that thousands of Mountaineer fans through the years enjoyed when Jack was the official "Voice of the Mountaineers." Tony may eschew any references to being West Virginia's "Voice" out of deference to Jack's memory, but make no mistake about it – Tony Caridi has clearly been the voice of Mountaineer sports for the past 15 years. I am certainly biased, but in my opinion there is no one in the business better than Tony Caridi. The same goes for the rest of the guys on the radio network – Dwight Wallace, Hoppy Kercheval, Jeff Jenkins and Dale Miller on the football side, Jay Jacobs and Kyle Wiggs in men's basketball, and Travis Jones with women's basketball. My good buddy, Jed Drenning, also ranks near the top of the list of the best sideline reporters/analysts in the game, even if his stories are sometimes too long and his neckties are frequently too short.

My thanks to all of the great photographers we've had through the years, specifically Dale Sparks, Dan Friend, Greg Ellis, Brian Persinger, Bill Amatucci and Pete Emerson for capturing, frame by frame, some of the greatest moments in school history. Also, a nod of the cap for the great work Mark DeVault has done through the years researching Mountaineer sports history. Mark's website, wvustats.com, is a tremendous asset to all of us hunting for a score or a date to a key game.

I would love to be able to mention all of the television journalists who have covered the Mountaineers during my tenure at WVU, but unfortunately, with small market TV being such a transient business, I cannot for the life of me remember them all. Think Saigon in '68 when considering the number of people who have passed through the front doors of those Clarksburg, Wheeling, Parkersburg, Charleston, Beckley and Huntington TV stations during the last 20 years or so. However, there was one guy who clearly sticks out in my mind – WBOY's Dean Obenauer.

Dean's preppy attire (he frequently wore bow ties on air) stood out in the land of flannel shirts, Levi jeans and Jovan musk, and I can still clearly remember his first year on the WVU beat back in 1991, asking Don Nehlen after a big win at Maryland if he thought the victory would propel the Mountaineers into a bowl game. The date was September 21! Nehlen looked at poor Dean the way LBJ used to look at Bobby Kennedy, and he immediately ended the post-game press conference. Not a single word was uttered by the head football coach about the football game that was just played. There were about 25 furious reporters on deadline, circling Dean like a bunch of wild jackals, when Nehlen started to walk back into the locker room. Another time, Dean asked baseball commissioner Fay Vincent during an on-camera interview if he thought the performances at the 1991 National League Championship Series in Pittsburgh would decide the league MVP award. Vincent gave him a look of bewilderment before blurting out, "Um, the regular season is over, and the voting is already completed."

Even I can't make this stuff up!

A special thank you to all of the great folks at West Virginia University Press, namely Carrie Mullen, Abby Freeland (a fellow New Martinsville native!), Floann Downey, Rachel King, editor Bryan Coyle, art director Than Saffel, and designer extraordinaire Laurence Nozik. This is book No. 2 together, and it seems like we are now really starting to hit our stride.

Sam Sciullo, Jr. has always been my No. 1 go-to guy whenever I had questions about Pitt athletics, and I am forever indebted to him for all of his help through the years. Sam is an outstanding writer and a thorough researcher who never fails to have the pertinent facts at his fingertips, and I highly recommend you check out his work at your local bookstore, or online at Amazon.com. During those rare occasions when Sam was stumped on a Pitt question I had, he usually got me in touch with the right people from the right era – great folks such as Alex Kramer, Beano Cook, Dave Havern and others who helped me try and get the story right.

And while West Virginia-Pitt football games can get heated, the rivalry has NEVER spilled over into the working relationships we have had with Pitt's sports information department through the years. Senior associate athletic director E.J. Borghetti is one of the best PR guys in the business, and if E.J. can't answer your question with an email, then you can rest assured that a phone call will follow. His sidekick, Mendy Nestor, is a rising star in the profession who just happened to get her start in our office, while Greg Hotchkiss does outstanding work promoting Pitt basketball. Before them, Larry Eldridge, Linda Venzon and Sam Sciullo were also first-rate PR professionals.

My appreciation also goes out to all of the Pittsburgh sportswriters who have fanned the flames of the rivalry and kept everyone's blood boiling; this non-inclusive list includes Bob Smizik, the late Bruce Keidan, Alan Robinson (who actually grew up in Sistersville), Gene Collier, Gerry Dulac, Ron Cook, Joe Bendel, Paul Meyer, Joe Starkey, Chuck Finder, Colin Dunlap, Paul Zeise, Jerry DiPaola and Jenn Menendez.

If I missed anyone, it's only because my memory is beginning to fade – not because of a lack of importance.

Growing up in New Martinsville, W.Va., a small river town about two hours south of Pittsburgh, I learned very early the importance of not taking yourself too seriously. Thankfully, I have a bunch of lifelong friends to make sure that never happens, and I will always be grateful for their fellowship and wisdom. To my family, immediate and extended, a heartfelt thanks for your love and support. Sadly, with many of us scattered throughout the country, it seems like the only time we can all get together now is during special occasions.

And finally, to all of the West Virginia players and coaches, and yes, to all of the Pitt Panther players and coaches, too, my appreciation to each and every one of you for making things so interesting around here during the fall.

What do you say we all get together and do it again sometime?

BIBLIOGRAPHY

Articles in Newspapers and Periodicals

"800 Panty Raiders Invade WVU Dorms." United Press, November 11, 1955.
Abrams, Al. "Grim Dave Reveals How It Happened." *Pittsburgh Post-Gazette*, November 28, 1968.
——. "Michelosen to Stay at Pitt, Rumors End." *Pittsburgh Post-Gazette*, December 22, 1963.
——. "Sidelights on Sports." *Pittsburgh Post-Gazette*, October 19, 1970.
"ACC Officials Deny WVU, VPI Will Join." United Press, December 3, 1953.
"All in the Family." *Front Row Magazine*, Winter 2004.
Alyta, Ken. "Plan To Admit West Virginia Is Turned Down." United Press, December 5, 1953.
Anderson, Shelly. "Generation Gap." *Pittsburgh-Post Gazette*, November 28, 1997.
"Anonymous Petition by 22 WVU Players Rekindles Kern-Hawley Controversy." Associated Press, December 1, 1947.
——. "Pitt jumps security for 'Backyard Brawl' sellout." *Pittsburgh Post-Gazette*, November 27, 2002.
"Art Won't Name Starters Until Kickoff." Associated Press, October 16, 1959.
"Attendance Drops Nearly 50 Percent." *The Pittsburgh Press*, December 22, 1940.
Atwater, James. "A Mountaineer Dream is Over." *Sports Illustrated*, November 21, 1955.
Baker, Bob. "For WVU, it was a tie that seemed like a defeat." *The Charleston Gazette*, October 2, 1989.
——. "Harris says 31-31 ties is 'blemish on record.'" *The Charleston Gazette*, October 2, 1989.
——. "Nehlen cites weight training as vital to comeback." *The Charleston Gazette*, October 2, 1983.
Beachler, Eddie. "Pitt, W.Va. Renew Fall Grid Rivalry." *The Pittsburgh Press*, August 3, 1943.
Bendel, Joe. "West Virginia disappointed with defeat." *Pittsburgh Tribune-Review*, November 29, 1997.
"Bill Kern Resigns Post As WVU Football Coach." United Press, November 26, 1947.
"Bowden 'Roasted' For WVU's Loss To Pitt." United Press International, October 20, 1970.
"Bowl Contests, 1st-Year Play High on Agenda." United Press, December 7, 1952.
Buta, Jim. "Rodriguez not talking about job." *Parkersburg News*, December 16, 2007.
Carroll, John. "WV Outplays Panthers." United Press, November 10, 1957.
"College Football: Jolly Roger." *Time*. October 18, 1963.
Conlin, Bill. "Mountaineers' McCune Aerial Artist." *The Evening Bulletin*, December 17, 1964.
Cook, Ron. "Cook: If this was final Backyard Brawl, it was bad on all counts." *Pittsburgh Post-Gazette*, November 26, 2011.
Constantine, Tony. "Carlen Praises Team and Coaches." *Sunday Dominion-Post*, October 8, 1967.
——. "Post Scripts." *Morgantown Post*, October 18, 1970.
Cook, Carroll H. "'When Winning Means Everything, Then I'll Quit.'" *The Miami News* (Florida), February 8, 1965.
Crane, Forrest. "Football Continues . . ." *West Virginia University Alumni Magazine*, Summer 1943.
——. "Football – As Usual." *West Virginia University Alumni Magazine*, Fall 1943.
——. "Maybe This Will Be The Year!" *West Virginia University Alumni Magazine*, Summer 1947.
——Press Release. West Virginia University Department of Intercollegiate Athletics, July 11, 1943.
"Defense's Big Plays, Kicking Please Nehlen." *Charleston Daily Mail*, September 30, 1985.
Dent, James. "Pitt Fans Tear Down Goal Posts." *The Charleston Gazette*, October 31, 1954.
Deweese, Kathy. "Living Through History: Brown v. Board of Education and WVU." *West Virginia University Alumni Magazine*, Fall 2004.
Dolson, Frank. "Indoor Liberty Bowl Is Progress." *The Philadelphia Inquirer*, December 19, 1964.

"Dorsett Ejected For Fighting as Pitt Turns Back Game WVU." United Press International, November 15, 1976.

"Dorsett, Owens Could Make Quarterback Issue Academic." Associated Press, November 6, 1975.

Dulac, Gerry. "Falling Off the Mountain." *Pittsburgh Post-Gazette*, October 13, 1994.

——. "These guys were no Einsteins." *Pittsburgh-Post Gazette*, September 25, 1985.

"Email trail between Rodriguez, West Virginia." Associated Press, January 23, 2008.

Emery, Michael V. "Panthers rally nets deadlock." *Altoona Mirror*, October 1, 1989.

Errington, Chris. "Green has day to remember; Bastien hopes to forget." *The Exponent Telegram* (Clarksburg, W.Va.), November 29, 1997.

Finder, Chuck. "Cook, Furfari can measure depth of WVU-Pitt rivalry." *Pittsburgh Post-Gazette*, November 25, 2007.

"Foge Fazio: Up from melting pot." United Press International, May 15, 1982.

——. "Football: WVU's Slaton has been waiting for Terrapins." *Pittsburgh Post-Gazette*, September 11, 2006.

Franke, Russ. "WVU Wins, 17-14, On Last-Second FG." *The Pittsburgh Press*, November 9, 1975.

"Fumble costs WVU in 6-3 loss to Pitt." Associated Press, September 28, 1987.

Furfari, Mickey. "A Fantastic Game! – But We Lost." *The Dominion Post* (Morgantown, W.Va.), October 18, 1970.

——. "Fan-Fare." *Dominion-News* (Morgantown, W.Va.), December 21, 1964.

——. "Former Coaches Look at 'Backyard Brawl.'" *Bluefield Daily Telegraph*, November 11, 2002.

——. "Morgantown 'still home' to 'The Voice'." *The Dominion Post* (Morgantown, W.Va.), February 1, 1987.

——. "Pastilong rewarded for having patience." *Times West Virginian* (Fairmont, W.Va.), December 2, 2002.

——. "WVU awaits word on bowl bid." *The Register-Herald* (Beckley, W.Va.), November 30, 1997.

——. "WVU Had Poise, Made Fewer Mistakes." *Dominion-News* (Morgantown, W.Va.), October 16, 1961.

"Gloomy Future For Jan. 1 Extravaganzas." United Press, December 17, 1951.

Gorman, Kevin. "Pitt's Defense Has Been Overwhelmed By WVU's Offense The Past 2 Seasons." *Pittsburgh Tribune-Review*, November 30, 2007.

Gilleran, Ed Jr. "Tartan Powerhouse." *College Football Historical Society Newsletter*, May 1997.

Grimsley, Will. "Football's Craftiest Recruiter." *The Saturday Evening Post*, November 10, 1956.

——. "Lewis Defends WV Schedule." *Charleston Daily Mail*, November 11, 1955.

Hardman, Con. "Here We Go Again, Boys . . ." *West Virginia University Alumni Magazine*, Summer 1947.

Hardman, Shorty. "Bill Kern Is Named Grid Coach Of West Virginia University Mountaineers." *The Charleston Gazette*, January 14, 1940.

——. "Close Win." *The Charleston Gazette*, November 14, 1976.

——. "Corum Out of Chaos." *Sunday Gazette-Mail* (Charleston, W.Va.), May 22, 1960.

——. "Corum Won't Forget Seniors of '62." *The Charleston Gazette*, January 19, 1963.

——. "Gov. Barron Hopes To Be 'Luck Charm.'" *The Charleston Gazette*, October 19, 1963.

——. "Hardman of Sports." *The Charleston Gazette*, October 28, 1952.

——. "McCune Had to Take Some Stern Measures." *The Charleston Gazette*, October 4, 1965.

——. "McKenzie Kicks H--- Out of Pitt." *The Charleston Gazette*, November 9, 1975.

——. "Pappy Seems Happy With Scouting Job." *The Charleston Gazette*, April 15, 1962.

——. "Pitt Favored Over WVU in Regional TV Game." *The Charleston Gazette*, November 8, 1975.

——. "Pitt's Boo-Boos Lead to WVU Points, Near Brawl." *The Charleston Gazette*, November 15, 1976.

——. "Sports." *The Charleston Gazette*, November 26, 1947.
——. "Sugar Bowl Showed No Regard for WVU." *The Charleston Gazette*, November 23, 1964.
——. "WVU Humbles Proud Panthers, 23-15." *The Charleston Gazette*, October 18, 1959.
Hertzel, Bob. "Bulger: Being ignored by Pitt OK." *The Dominion Post* (Morgantown, W.Va.), November 28, 1997.
——. "'It's been a rough day.'" *Times West Virginian* (Fairmont, W.Va.), December 17, 2007.
Hickman, Dave. "Big East's 'surprise player.'" *The Charleston Gazette*, November 26, 1997.
Hickman, Dave. "Nehlen Downplays 'Itty, Bitty' Game With Pitt." *Times West Virginian* (Fairmont, W.Va.), September 28, 1983.
——. "Report: Rich talking with Michigan." *The Charleston Gazette*, December 15, 2007.
——. "WVU health check: 'Whoever can walk.'" *The Charleston Gazette*, November 26, 1997.
Hillgrove, Bill. "Backyard Beholdings." *Mountaineer Illustrated*, December 1, 2007.
"Holdinsky Stars as Mountaineers Sweep 20-6 Win." Associated Press, October 15, 1961.
Hose, Dan. "On Deck." United Press International, September 29, 1983.
"Hostetler Offered Thanks After Scoring Winning TD." United Press International, October 3, 1983.
Hudson, Dick. "Lewis Boosts WVU Mountaineers By Keeping State Boys At Home." *Charleston Daily Mail*, December 27, 1953.
——. "Pitt Knocks WVU From Perfect List." *Charleston Daily Mail*, November 13, 1955.
——. "Pitt Wins Thriller In Tough Game." *Charleston Daily Mail*, October 21, 1963.
——. "W.V.U. Starts Search For New Coach." *Charleston Daily Mail*, December 14, 1965.
——. "Warming Up." *Charleston Daily Mail*, November 26, 1947.
——. "Warming Up." *Charleston Daily Mail*, November 23, 1955.
——. "Warming Up." *Charleston Daily Mail*, October 12, 1959.
——. "Warming Up." *Charleston Daily Mail*, October 24, 1959.
——. "Warming Up." *Charleston Daily Mail*, June 14, 1962.
——. "Warming Up." *Charleston Daily Mail*, June 15, 1962.
——. "Warming Up." *Charleston Daily Mail*, October 18, 1963.
——. "Warming Up." *Charleston Daily Mail*, October 21, 1963.
——. "Warming Up." *Charleston Daily Mail*, October 8, 1965.
Hughes, Carl. "Frank Carver Is Silent Man Behind The Scenes For The Panthers." *The Pittsburgh Press*, April 30, 1947.
——. "Pitt Sends Mountaineer Bowl Hopes Tumbling." *The Pittsburgh Press*, November 12, 1955.
"Intensity lapse costly." *Charleston Daily Mail*, October 2, 1989.
Jacobs, David W. "Mr. Kern Comes to Town . . . Former Carnegie Tech Coach Selected for Mountaineer Post." *West Virginia University Alumni Magazine*, Winter 1939–40.
Jividen, Jody. "Randolph Guesses Right On Block For Hoss' TD." *Charleston Daily Mail*, October 3, 1983.
"Jock Sutherland Quits Coaching Job At Pitt." United Press, March 6, 1939.
Jones, David. "Welcome to the Big Ten." *The Patriot-News* (Harrisburg, Pa.), December 11, 1994.
Kriek, Jim. "Sports Notes." *Daily Courier* (Connellsville, Pa.), October 10, 1967.
Labriola, Bob. "Mountaineers Scale Pitt 'D' For Win." *Greensburg Tribune-Review* (Pennsylvania), October 2, 1983.
Lage, Larry. "Nehlen: 'Great opportunity.'" Associated Press, December 17, 2007.
Landon, Chuck. "Did WVU Score? Yes And No." *Charleston Daily Mail*, September 30, 1985.
"Leftridge Could Become WVU's 1st Negro Player." United Press International, November 9, 1961.
"Lewis Given Shower, Says Win No Fluke." Associated Press, October 26, 1952.
"Lewis Rates Pitt Victory 'Great Win.'" Associated Press, October 27, 1952.

"Little things bother Fazio now." United Press International, September 1, 1982.
Mangelsdorf, Phil. " 'Sorry For Kids,' Lewis." *Charleston Daily Mail*, October 31, 1954.
Mani, Jon. "Rich Rod deals another blow to state's psyche." *The Herald-Dispatch* (Huntington, W.Va.), December 23, 2007.
Masaschi, Matt. "Former West Virginia U. quarterback missing in NYC." *The Daily Athenaeum* (Morgantown, W.Va.), September 14, 2001.
McCreary, Joedy. "Money Not an Issue for 'Rod.'" *Wheeling Intelligencer*, November 28, 2000.
McHugh, Roy. "Frank Carver Backed Up His Convictions," *The Pittsburgh Press*, November 28, 1965.
McHugh, Roy. "Hart Played The Game And Paid The Price." *The Pittsburgh Press*, November 26, 1968.
——. "Pitt's Frank Carver Holds A Day In Court." *The Pittsburgh Press*, February 8, 1965.
McMillan, Tom. "Fazio's chair heating up again." *Pittsburgh Post-Gazette*, September 24, 1985.
Meadows, Donald. "Wanted: Fans, Not Viewers." *Raleigh Register* (Beckley, W.Va.), October 17, 1963.
Mehno, John. "Panthers can't feel sorry for themselves today." *Altoona Mirror*, September 26, 1987.
Mellace, Bob. "Ball Larceny Turning Point." *Charleston Daily Mail*, October 31, 1954.
Meyer, Paul. "LB hunts a victory for WVU." *Pittsburgh Post-Gazette*, December 1, 2002.
Mooney, John. "Sports Mirror." *The Salt Lake Tribune*, December 19, 1964.
"Mom: Rodriguez family suffers threats and insults." Associated Press, January 8, 2008.
Moran, Duke. "Kern's Swan Song Ends in 17-2 Victory for West Virginia." Associated Press, November 30, 1947.
Morrison, Dave. "Panthers enter bowl atmosphere." *The Register-Herald* (Beckley, W.Va.), November 26, 1997.
——. "Pittsburgh defensive back truly dislikes West Virginia." *The Register-Herald* (Beckley, W.Va.), November 28, 1997.
"Mountaineers' Harris to skip senior year, go pro." United Press International, February 7, 1989.
"Mountaineers Host Pitt – Exciting Game Visualized." United Press International, November 7, 1979.
"Mountaineers Leave For Pittsburgh Today, 2 Regulars Injured; Pitt Heavy Favorite." United Press, October 24, 1952.
"Mountaineers Make Pitt Fight To Gain Hard-Earned Victory." Associated Press, October 9, 1949.
"Nehlen: OT procedure needs a little rethinking." *The Dominion Post*, November 29, 1997.
"Nehlen Takes Stab At WVU-Pitt Buttons." United Press International, September 29, 1983.
Nichols, Cliff. "Pitt frustrates WVU in 34-3 win." *Times West Virginian* (Fairmont, W.Va.), September 1, 1991.
——. "Voice Of The Mountaineers Jack Fleming: 'My Enthusiasm for WVU athletics is sort of built-in.'" *The Better Times*, May 13, 1981.
O'Brien, Jim. "Warning: Sophomore Sports Editors Can Be Dangerous." University of Pittsburgh Official Game Program, 1984.
"Our Kids Knew They Were Going To Win." *Charleston Daily Mail*, October 3, 1983.
Pane, Jim. "Marino A Hero In 24-17 Panther Win." *The Indiana Gazette*, November 12, 1979.
"Panthers Await Strong Bid By Mountaineers." United Press International, October 11, 1961.
"Pitt Alumni Urges Changes In Athletics." United Press, February 2, 1939.
"Pitt Arrives Just Like In '95 – When It Lost." Associated Press, October 19, 1963.
"Pitt Coach Tabs WVU 11 Biggest." Associated Press, November 9, 1955.
"Pitt Drubbing Like Terp Tilt." United Press, November 14, 1955.
"Pitt Football Receipts Also De-Emphasized." United Press, December 22, 1940.
"Pitt's Michelosen Takes 'Hike' After Loss to Mounties." Associated Press, October 16, 1961.
"Pitt Overcomes 35-8 Deficit and Stuns WVU 36-35." Associated Press, October 18, 1970.

"Pitt pushes West Virginia out of national title picture." Associated Press, December 2, 2007.
"Pittsburgh University Adopts Athletic Policy of West Conference." United Press, February 1, 1939.
"Pitt, WVU Revving Up For 'Backyard Brawl.'" United Press International, September 29, 1982.
"Police Arrest 36 WVU Celebrants After Game." Associated Press, November 10, 1975.
"Printed Quote By Pitt End Enraged The Mountaineers." *Charleston Daily Mail*, October 16, 1961.
"QB Harris To Enter NFL Draft." Associated Press, February 16, 1990.
Rahme, Dave. "Frozen Moments." *The Post-Standard* (Syracuse, N.Y.), October 8, 2004.
"Rejuvenated WVU Preps for Syracuse." United Press International, October 19, 1959.
"'Revenge 54' Emblazoned on Panthers' Practice Field." United Press, November 11, 1955.
Robinson, Alan. "Hostile crowd worries Pitt's Hackett." Associated Press, August 21, 1991.
——. "Pitt officially fires Gottfried." Associated Press, December 19, 1989.
——. "Pitt vs. WVU: not a marquee matchup." Associated Press, October 11, 1994.
——. "Pitt's changes just not enough." Associated Press, October 17, 1994.
——. "QB Loyalties Switched for This 'Backyard Brawl.'" Associated Press, September 27, 1989.
"Rodriguez testifies he felt pressured to sign contract." Associated Press, May 11, 2008.
Sampsell, Steve. "Pitt keeps bowl hopes alive with triple OT victory." *Pittsburgh Tribune-Review*, November 29, 1997.
Scala, Nick. "Big Chance Came Too Soon for Gray." *Parkersburg Sentinel*, September 3, 1991.
"SC Votes To Ease Present Bowl Ban." United Press, November 17, 1953.
Sell, Jack. "Pitt's Application Remains on File of Big Ten." *Pittsburgh Post-Gazette*, December 5, 1951.
Schwerin, Bo. "A Season to Remember." *Pitt Magazine*, Fall 2006.
Smith, Bill. "Bowden Has Worries Other Than 'Fans.'" *Charleston Daily Mail*, October 19, 1970.
——. "Dream game becomes nightmare." *Charleston Daily Mail*, October 2, 1989.
——. "Panthers have Sharp Claws." *Charleston Daily Mail*, November 12, 1976.
——. "Pitt's Dorsett Shows It All – Including Lack Of Class." *Charleston Daily Mail*, November 15, 1976.
——. "Win in Trenches." *Charleston Daily Mail*, October 3, 1983.
Smith, Chester L. "Pitt Hunts Successor to 'Shag.'" *The Pittsburgh Press*, February 5, 1946.
——. "Pitt Regrets Losing Art Lewis As Foe It Long Respected." *The Pittsburgh Press*, April 19, 1960.
Smith, Ned. "It Was a State of Mind." *West Virginia University Alumni Magazine*, Fall 1947.
Smizik, Bob. "Backyard Brawl finally no bore." *Pittsburgh Post-Gazette*, November 27, 1997.
——. "Pitt Should Take Eastern Bull By The Horns." *The Pittsburgh Press*, July 6, 1981.
——. "Pitt's Football Biggest Loss is Jackie Sherrill." *Pittsburgh Post-Gazette*, January 21, 2007.
——. "The Record Tells the Story of Cas Myslinski." *The Pittsburgh Press*, May 2, 1982.
Springer, George. "Fantastic, Grand, Unbelievable; Also Incredible, Great." *Beckley Post-Herald*, October 4, 1965.
——. "Greatest Mountaineer Grid Win Ever." *Beckley Post-Herald*, October 4, 1965.
Starkey, Joe. "Game tape proves Pitt's dominance." *Pittsburgh Tribune-Review*, December 5, 2007.
"State Unity Essential, Cignetti Says." Associated Press, January 21, 1976.
"Straying Panthers Fed Up With Pitt." Associated Press, October 30, 1954.
"Strong Pitt Attack Averages 416 Yards." *Charleston Daily Mail*, October 17, 1963.
Talbot, Gayle. "Bowl Bid May Hinge On Pitt Tilt." Associated Press, October 26, 1954.
Talkington, Greg. "Who's in Charge?" *The Exponent Telegram* (Clarksburg, W.Va.), August 14, 2002.
Taylor, Phil. "Happy Feet." *Sports Illustrated*, October 2, 2008.
"Tony Dorsett: 'I did what any man would.'" Associated Press, November 15, 1976.
Underwood, John. "Football's Week." *Sports Illustrated*, October 18, 1965.
" 'U' TD Favorite Over Pitt; Odd-Makers 'Mixed up.'" United Press, November 6, 1957.

Vingle, Mitch. "An ugly end to an era." *The Charleston Gazette*, December 17, 2007.
——. "Credit Pastilong for smooth hire." *The Charleston Gazette*, November 29, 2000.
Vingle, Mitch. "Pittsburgh celebrates the return of Backyard Brawl." *The Charleston Gazette*, November 29, 1997.
——. "Rodriguez situation has no upside for WVU." *The Charleston Gazette*, December 16, 2007.
Wiley, Ralph. "Up From The Hill." *Sports Illustrated*, December 19, 1988.
"Wintersville's Alford To Start For WVU's Frosh." *Weirton Daily Times*, September 24, 1963.
"WVU Battles Pitt Today." *Dominion-News*, October 17, 1970.
"WVU Coach Awaiting Word On His Future." United Press International, November 19, 1979.
"WVU Gives Pitt Record Book Beating in Wildest Scoring 'Game' of Series." United Press International, October 4, 1965.
"WVU Upsets Pitt." Associated Press, October 26, 1952.
Zeise, Paul. "One that got away." *Pittsburgh Post-Gazette*, December 1, 2002.
Ziegler, Jack. "Jock Sutherland: Forgotten Coaching Great." *The Coffin Corner* 13, No. 4 (1991).

Books

Bowden, Bobby, with Bill Smith. *More Than Just a Game: My Life on and off the Sidelines*. Nashville, TN: Thomas Nelson, Inc. Publishers, 1994.
Bowden, Bobby, with Mark Schlabach. *Called to Coach: Reflections on Life, Faith and Football*. New York: Howard Books, 2010.
Bowden, Steve. *The Bowden Way*. Atlanta: Longsteet Press, Inc., 2001.
Boyles, Bob, and Paul Guido. *Fifty Years of College Football: A Modern History of America's Most Colorful Sport*. Wilmington, Del: Sideline Communications, Inc., 2005.
Constantine, Tony. *Mountaineer Football 1891–1969*. Morgantown, W.Va.: West Virginia University Department of Intercollegiate Athletics, 1969.
Doherty, William T. Jr., and Festus P. Summers. *West Virginia University: Symbol of Unity in a Sectionalized State*. Morgantown, W.Va.: West Virginia University Press, 1982.
Dunnavant, Keith. *The Fifty-Year Seduction: How Television Manipulated College Football, from the Birth of the Modern NCAA to the Creation of the BCS*. New York: St. Martin's Press, 2004.
Freeman, Mike. *Bowden: How Bobby Bowden Forged a Football Dynasty*. New York: HarperCollins, 2009.
Fulton, Bob. *Never Lost a Game (Time Just Ran Out)*. Apollo, Pa.: Closson Press, 1997.
Furfari, Mickey. *Mickey's Mountaineer Memories*. Beckley, W.Va.: Beckley Newspapers, Inc., 2008.
Holtz, Lou. *Wins, Losses and Lessons*. New York: HarperCollins, 2006.
Hostetler, Jeff, with Ed Fitzgerald. *One Giant Leap*. New York: G.P. Putnam's Sons, 1991.
Keys, Kevin, and Shelly Poe. *Bring on the Mountaineers*. Morgantown, W.Va.: West Virginia University Department of Intercollegiate Athletics, 1991.
MacCambridge, Michael. *ESPN College Football Encyclopedia: The Complete History of the Game*. New York: ESPN Books, 2005.
Mule, Marty. *Sugar Bowl Classic: A History*. Clearwater, Fla.: Mainstream Media International, 2008.
Nehlen, Don, with Bill Smith. *Perfect! ... The Season*. Parsons, W.Va.: McClain Printing Company, 1989.
Nehlen, Don, with Shelly Poe. *Tales from the West Virginia Sideline*. Champaign, IL.: Sports Publishing, LLC, 2006.
O'Brien, Jim. *Hail To Pitt: A Sports History of the University of Pittsburgh*. Pittsburgh, Pa.: Wolfson Publishing, Co., 1982.

Sciullo, Sam. *Pitt Football Vault*. Atlanta: Whitman Publishing, Co., 2008.
——. *Pitt Stadium Memories: 1925-1999*. University of Pittsburgh, 2000.
——. *Tales from the Pitt Panthers*. Champaign, Ill.: Sports Publishing, LLC, 2004.

Interviews by Author and Oral Histories

Abraham, Zach. Telephone interview. Tape recording. March 8, 2011.
Antion, Bob. Email correspondence. August 4, 2009.
Barrett, Eddie. Oral History. Tape recordings. September 2001;
——. Telephone Interview. Tape Recordings. April 3, 2004, March 2, 2005, June 22, 2005, October 6, 2006, January 20, 2006, November 7, 2008 and February 20, 2012.
Beasley, Aaron. Telephone interview. Tape recording. May 20, 2009.
Boczek, Joe. Telephone interview. Tape recording. April 10, 2012.
Bowden, Bobby. Press Conferences. Tape recordings. December 14, 2004 and December 21, 2009.
Bowden, Tom. Telephone interview. Tape recording. November 7, 2010.
Brooks, Dana. Telephone interview. Tape recording. January 17, 2011.
Byrd, Leland. Telephone interview. Tape recording. September 25, 2009.
Caridi, Tony. Telephone interview. Tape recording. February 25, 2012.
Carlen, Jim. Telephone interview. Tape recording. December 22, 2009.
Casteel, Jeff. Telephone interview. Tape recording. February 26, 2012.
Cignetti, Frank. Telephone interviews. Tape recordings. December 23, 2009, September 28, 2010 and September 29, 2010.
Cook, Beano. Telephone interview. Tape recording. February 20, 2012.
Corum, Gene. Telephone interview. Tape recording. August 9, 2002.
Dawson, Mike. Telephone interview. Tape recording. November 10, 2009.
Dunlap, Steve. Tape recording. November 7, 2010.
Dunlevy, Bob. Telephone interview. Tape recording. February 20, 2011.
Farley, Dale. Telephone interview. Tape recording. August 9, 2004.
Fazio, Foge. Telephone interview. Tape recording. November 18, 2005.
Ford, Garrett. Tape recording. July 24, 2006, June 13, 2007 and July 7, 2011.
Furfari, Mickey. Tape recordings. August 9, 2004, October 28, 2010 and October 3, 2011.
Galiffa, Bernie. Telephone interview. Tape recording. July 28, 2009.
Graham, Todd. Press conference transcription. November 25, 2011.
Harris, Major. Telephone interview. Tape recording. August 11, 2006, April 30, 2009 and December 10, 2011.
Havern, Dave. Telephone interview. Tape recording. August 9, 2004.
Herock, Ken. Telephone interview. Tape recording. April 18, 2012.
Holgorsen, Dana. Press conference transcriptions. June 17, 2011, November 21, 2011 and January 4, 2012.
Hostetler, Jeff. Telephone interview. April 11, 2012.
Howley, Chuck. Telephone interview. Tape recording. July 8, 2007.
Hudson, Dick. Telephone interview. Tape recording. February 21, 2011.
Huff, Sam. Telephone interview. Tape recording. November 19, 2008.
Johnston, Chad. Telephone interview. Tape recording. March 7, 2011.
Jozwiak, Brian. Telephone interview. Tape recording. July 10, 2007.
Juskowich, Ken. Telephone interview. Tape recording. July 13, 2011.

Kendra, Dan. Telephone interview. Tape recording. October 18, 2010.
Kercheval, Hoppy. Telephone interview. Tape recording. February 22, 2012
Kirelawich, Bill. Telephone interview. Tape recording. April 9, 2012.
Klausing, Chuck. Telephone interviews. Tape recordings. August 25, 2005 and December 23, 2009
Kramer, Alex. Telephone interview. Tape recording. October 3, 2011.
Johnson, Dave. Tape recording. November 10, 2009.
Lamb, Eleanor. Tape recording. June 22, 2005.
Luck, Oliver. Telephone and personal interviews. Tape recordings. August 11, 2006, June 12, 2007, November 10, 2009, May 17, 2011 and January 17, 2012.
McKenzie, Bill. Telephone interview. Tape recording. November 28, 2007.
Maisel, Ivan. Email correspondence. July 14, 2010.
Mallory, John. Telephone interview. Tape recording. July 10, 2007.
Marshall, Rasheed. Telephone interview. Tape recording. May 24, 2011.
Martin, Dick. Telephone interview. Tape recording. August 11, 2006.
Nehlen, Don. Telephone interview. Tape recordings. November 18, 2005, August 11, 2006, April 30, 2009, April 14, 2011 and December 10, 2011.
Newberry, Steve. Telephone interview. Tape recording. May 22, 2011.
Oblak, Dave. Telephone interview. Tape recording. November 10, 2009.
Owens, Artie. Telephone interview. Tape recording. November 7, 2010.
Pastilong, Ed. Tape recording. January 3, 2011.
Patrick, Mike. Email correspondence. July 14, 2010.
Patterson, Keith. Tape recording. April 6, 2012.
Peters, Andy. Telephone interview. Tape recording. November 7, 2010.
Polen, Dick. Telephone interview. Tape recording. August 9, 2004.
Pushkin, Martin. Tape recording. April 21, 2001.
Schaus, Fred. Telephone interview. Tape recording. April 13, 2003.
Sherwood, Mike. Telephone interviews. Tape recording. August 9, 2004 and June 3, 2007.
Slater, Mike. Telephone interview. Tape recording. August 9, 2004.
Smith, Chuck. Telephone interview. Tape recording. September 27, 2010.
Stevens, Gary. Telephone interview. Tape recording. June 10, 2010.
Stewart, Bill. Mountaineer Sports Network Television interview. August 29, 2008;
——. Postgame press conference. Tape recording. November 27, 2009.
Swinson, Randy. Telephone interview. Tape recording. November 7, 2010.
Talley, Darryl. Telephone interviews. Tape recordings. November 18, 2005, July 10, 2007, November 10, 2009 and May 16, 2011.
Van Halanger, Dave. Telephone interview. Tape recording. November 7, 2010.
Wannstedt, Dave. Press conference. Transcription. November 23, 2009. Pittsburgh, Pa.;
——. Postgame press conference. Tape recording. November 27, 2009.
White, Kevin. Telephone interview. Tape recording. September 28, 2011.
Williams, Eddie. Telephone interview. Tape recording. August 9, 2004.
Woodeshick, Tom. Telephone interview. Tape recording. June 20, 2007.
Woodside, Paul. Telephone interview. Tape recording. June 20, 2007.
Wyant, Fred. Telephone interview. Tape recording. October 28, 2010 and October 3, 2011.
Young, Donnie. Tape recording. June 22, 2005 and August 25, 2005.

Media Guides

University of Pittsburgh Football Media Guides: 2008, 2009, 2010 and 2011.

West Virginia University Football Media Guides: 1952, 1953, 1954, 1955, 1956, 1957, 1958, 1959, 1960, 1961, 1962, 1963, 1964, 1965, 1966, 1967, 1968, 1969, 1970, 1971, 1973, 1974, 1975, 1976, 1977, 1979, 1980, 1982, 1983, 1985, 1989, 1991, 1994, 2000, 2002, 2007, 2008, 2009, 2010, 2011.

Online Sources

Crouthamel, Jake. "A BIG EAST History & Retrospective (Part I)" *SU Athletics.com*. Last modified December 8, 2000. http://www.suathletics.com/sports/gen/2001/history.asp

Forde, Pat. "Stewart's resume topped with Fiesta Bowl win." *ESPN.com*. Last modified January 2, 2008. http://sports.espn.go.com/espn/columns/story?columnist=forde_pat&id=3178487&sportCat=ncf

"In Stewart, WVU's successor to Rodriguez right under their nose." *ESPN.com*. Last modified January 3, 2008. http://sports.espn.go.com/ncf/news/story?id=3178538

Lapchick, Richard. "Jerry Gaines paved the way at Virginia Tech." *ESPN.com*. Last modified February 26, 2007. http://sports.espn.go.com/espn/blackhistory2007/columns/story?columnist=lapchick_richard&id=2780228

Long, Tony. "Dec. 1, 1942: Mandatory Gas Rationing, Lots of Whining." *Wired.com*. Last modified November 30, 2009. http://www.wired.com/thisdayintech/2009/11/12011world-war-2-gasonline-rationing/

"New: Former Rose AD and football coach, MVC commissioner Dick Martin dies." *TribStar.com*. Last modified March 10, 2008. http://tribstar.com/collegesports/x1155740808/NEW-Former-Rose-AD-and-football-coach-MVC-commissioner-Dick-Martin-dies

"Rodriguez denies 'Bama, will return to Morgantown." *ESPN.com News Services*. Last modified December 8, 2006. http://sports.espn.go.com/ncf/news/story?id=2691319

"Rich Rodriguez discusses West Virginia regrets, 'Shawshank Redemption' parallel." *Freep.com*. Last modified February 9, 2011. http://www.freep.com/article/20110209/SPORTS06/110209099/Rich-Rodriguez-discusses-West-Virginia-regrets-Shawshank-Redemption-parallel

"Rodriguez ponders 'Bama, Morgantown." *ESPN.com News Services*. Last modified December 7, 2006. http://sports.espn.go.com/ncf/news/story?id=2690016

Ruibal, Sal. "West Virginia still feeling spurned after Rodriguez's departure." USA Today.com. Last modified January 23, 2008. http://www.usatoday.com/sports/college/football/bigeast/2008-01-23-wvu-disgruntled-fans_N.htm

Shrum, Rick. "Memories of Pitt's 1970 October Surprise Linger." *Pittsburgh Post-Gazette*. Last modified November 23, 2000. http://www.post-gazette.com/sports/pitt/20001123rally7.asp

"Source: Attorneys to contest ex-coach having to pay $4M to WVU." *ESPN.com News Services*. Last modified December 18, 2007. http://sports.espn.go.com/ncf/news/story?id=3159677

"Starkey: The miracle of 13-9." *PittsburghLive.com*. Last modified November 24, 2011. http://www.pittsburghlive.com/x/pittsburghtrib/sports/columnists/starkey/s_768927.html

"World War II Rationing on the U.S. Homefront." *American Historical Society.org*. http://www.americanhistoricalsociety.org/exhibits/events/rationing.htm

ABOUT THE AUTHOR

John Antonik joined the WVU athletic staff in 1991 after working as a graduate assistant for one year and a student assistant for two years in the Sports Communications Office. From 1991–98, Antonik served as associate sports information director, coordinating the publicity efforts of West Virginia University's 19 varsity sports as well as working with the Mountaineer football and basketball programs. Antonik earned several CoSIDA writing citations during his tenure as associate sports information director, including a "Best in the Nation" award for his work on the 1992 women's basketball media guide. In addition to his publicity duties, he also directed WVU's community relations program.

In 1999, Antonik, a past member of CoSIDA, the West Virginia Sports Writers and the National Collegiate Baseball Writers associations, assumed his current role as director of new media in charge of promoting West Virginia University's 17 intercollegiate sports through the World Wide Web. Antonik is responsible for all facets of the department's web services program, including editorial oversight, site design and content development.

During his 20-year WVU tenure, Mountaineer football has made 16 bowl appearances, including trips to the 1994 and 2006 Sugar, 2008 Fiesta and 2012 Orange bowls; men's basketball has made nine NCAA tournament appearances, including three Sweet 16 trips, an Elite Eight appearance in 2005 and a Final Four appearance in 2010, while the women's basketball program has made seven NCAA tournament appearances.

A native of New Martinsville, W.Va., Antonik received a bachelor's degree in journalism from WVU in 1990 and a master's degree in sport management from WVU in 1992. He received "The Lifetime Achievement Award" from Magnolia High School in August, 2008, and in 2010 was the recipient of the Paul B. "Buck" Martin Award, presented by the WVU Alumni Association to an individual who has helped to preserve and maintain West Virginia University's traditions.

Antonik has previously authored two books on Mountaineer athletics: *West Virginia University Football Vault: The History of the Mountaineers* and *Roll Out the Carpet: 101 Seasons of West Virginia University Basketball.*

INDEX OF NAMES